Environmental Change, Forced Displacement and International Law

This book explores the increasing concern over the extent to which those suffering from forced cross-border displacement as a result of environmental change are protected under international human rights law. Formally, they are not entitled to admission or to stay in a third-state country, a situation that has been identified as an international "legal protection gap".

The book seeks to provide answers to two basic questions: whether and to what extent existing international law protects cross-border environmental displacement, and whether and how existing formalised regional complementary protection standards can interpretively conceptualise and solidify and protection for cross-border environmental displacement. The discussion outlines that the protection of the human person is not only an *ex post facto* obligation of states but must increasingly be seen as an *ex ante* one. The analysis further suggests that the regionally orientated protection regime of the European Union can help states to consolidate an evolving protection paradigm of proactive and reactive measures being erected at the international level. It can also narrow the identified legal protection gaps. In so doing, it can help states to reconceptualise protection as a holistic and dynamic enterprise.

This book will be of great interest to academics in law, political science, and human rights as well as to policymakers and civil society organisations at both the national and international level.

Isabel M. Borges is an Adjunct Associate Professor at BI, Department of Law and Governance, the Norwegian Business School and Guest Researcher at the Faculty of Law, Department of Public and International Law, University of Oslo, Norway.

Law and Migration
Series Editor
Satvinder S. Juss
King's College London, UK

Migration and its subsets of refugee and asylum policy are rising up the policy agenda at the national and international level. Current controversies underline the need for rational and informed debate of this widely misrepresented and little understood area.

Law and Migration contributes to this debate by establishing a monograph series to encourage discussion and help inform policy in this area. The series provides a forum for leading new research principally from the Law and Legal Studies area but also from related social sciences. The series is broad in scope, covering a wide range of subjects and perspectives.

Other titles in this series

Gender and Migration in Italy
A Multilayered Perspective
Edited by Elisa Olivito

Bureaucracy, Law and Dystopia in the United Kingdom's Asylum System
John R. Campbell

Children's Rights and Refugee Law
Conceptualising Children within the Refugee Convention
Samantha Arnold

Law and Asylum
Space, Subject, Resistance
Simon Behrman

Ethical, Legal and Social Aspects of Healthcare for Migrants
Perspectives from the UK and Germany
Edited by Katja Kuehlmeyer, Corinna Klingler and Richard Huxtable

Conflict Displacement and Legal Protection
Understanding Asylum, Human Rights and Refugee Law
Charlotte Lülf

For more information about this series, please visit: www.routledge.com/Law-and-Migration/book-series/LAWANDMIG

Environmental Change, Forced Displacement and International Law

From Legal Protection Gaps to Protection Solutions

Isabel M. Borges

Routledge
Taylor & Francis Group
LONDON AND NEW YORK

First published 2019
by Routledge

2 Park Square, Milton Park, Abingdon, Oxfordshire OX14 4RN
52 Vanderbilt Avenue, New York, NY 10017

Routledge is an imprint of the Taylor & Francis Group, an informa business

First issued in paperback 2020

British Library Cataloguing-in-Publication Data
A catalogue record for this book is available from the British Library

Library of Congress Cataloging-in-Publication Data
Names: Borges, Isabel M., author.
Title: Environmental change, forced displacement and international law: from legal protection gaps to protection solutions/Isabel M. Borges.
Description: New York, NY: Routledge, 2019. | Series: Law and migration | Includes bibliographical references and index.
Identifiers: LCCN 2018040749 | ISBN 9781138560130 (hardback)
Subjects: LCSH: Forced migration. | Environmental refugees. | Refugees – Civil rights. | Climatic changes – Social aspects. | Human rights.
Classification: LCC KZ6530 .B67 2019 | DDC 341.4/86 – dc23
LC record available at https://lccn.loc.gov/2018040749

ISBN: 978-1-138-56013-0 (hbk)
ISBN: 978-0-367-53415-8 (pbk)

Typeset in Galliard
by Apex CoVantage, LLC

To Jørgen, Patrick and Nina

Contents

Table of cases and other materials

Cases before international, regional, and domestic bodies

International Court of Justice (ICJ)

Case concerning military and paramilitary activities in and against Nicaragua, *Nicaragua v The United States of America*, ICJ Reports (27 June 1986)
Case concerning the North Sea Continental Shelf Cases (*Federal Republic of Germany v Denmark*; *Federal Republic of Germany v Netherlands*, ICJ Reports (20 February 1969)
Case concerning asylum, *Colombia v Perú*, ICJ Reports (20 November 1950)

European Court of Human Rights (ECtHR)

ECtHR, *Ahmed v Austria*, Application No. 25964/94 (17 December 1996)
ECtHR, *Airey v Ireland*, Application No.6289/73 (9 October 1979)
ECtHR, *Artico v Italy*, Application No. 6694/74 (13 May 1980)
ECtHR, *Budayeva and Others v Russia*, Application Nos. 15339/02, 21166/02, 20058/02, 11673/02, and 15343/02 (20 March 2008)
ECtHR, *Chahal v United Kingdom*, Application No. 22414/93 (15 November 1996)
ECtHR, *Chapman v United Kingdom*, Application No. 27238/95 (18 January 2001)
ECtHR, *Cruz Varas and Others v Sweden*, Application No. 15576/89 (20 March 1991)
ECtHR, *Fadeyeva v Russia*, Application No. 55723/00 (30 November 2005)
ECtHR, *Guerra and Others v Italy*, Application No. 14967/89 (19 February 1998)
ECtHR, *H.L.R. v France*, Application No. 24573/94 (29 April 1997)
ECtHR, *Hatton and Others v United Kingdom*, Application No. 36022/97 (08 July 2003)
ECtHR, *Hilal v UK*, Application No. 45276/99 (06 March 2001)
ECtHR, *Ireland v United Kingdom*, Application No. 5310/71 (18 January 1978)

ECtHR, *Kolyadenko v Russia*, Application Nos. 17423/05, 20534/05, 20678/05, 23263/05, 24283/05, and 35673/05 (09 July 2012)
ECtHR, *Loizidou v Turkey*, Application No. 15318/89 (23 March 1995)
ECtHR, *Lopez Ostra v Spain*, Application No. 16798/90 (09 December 1994)
ECtHR, *McGinley and Egan v United Kingdom*, Application Nos.21825/93 and 23414/94 (08 June 1998)
ECtHR, *N. v United Kingdom*, Application No. 26565/05 (27 May 2008)
ECtHR, *NA v United Kingdom*, Application No.25904/07 (17 July 2008)
ECtHR, *Okyay v Turkey*, Application No. 36220/97 (12 July 2005)
ECtHR, *Öneryildiz v Turkey*, Application No. 48939/99 (30 November 2004)
ECtHR, *Pretty v United Kingdom*, Application No. 2346/02 (29 April 2002)
ECtHR, *Salah Sheek v The Netherlands*, Application No. 1948/04 (11 January 2007)
ECtHR, *Soering v United Kingdom*, Application No. 14038/88 (07 July 1989)
ECtHR, *Sufi and Elmi v United Kingdom*, Application Nos. 8319/07 and 1149/07 (28 June 2011)
ECtHR, *Taskin v Turkey*, Application No. 46117/99 (30 March 2005)
ECtHR, *Tatar v Romania*, Application No. 67021/01 (27 January 2009)
ECtHR, *Tyrer v United Kingdom*, Application No. 5856/72 (23 April 1978)
ECtHR, *Vilness and Others v Norway,* Application No. 52806/9 (05 December 2013)
ECtHR, *Vilvarajah v United Kingdom,* Application Nos. 13163/87, 13164/87, 13165/87, 13447/87, and 13448/87 (30 October 1991)

Inter-American Commission /Court on Human Rights (IACtHR)

IACtHR, *Yanomami Community v Brazil,* Case No. 7615 (5 March 1985)
IACtHR, *Claude Reyes et al. v Chile*, Series C No. 151 (19 September 2006)
IACtHR, *Mapiripán Massacre v Colombia*, Series C No. 134 (15 September 2005)
IACtHR, *Sawhoyamaxa Indigenous Community v Paraguay*, Series C No.146 (29 March 2006)
IACtHR, *Velasquez Rodriguez v Honduras*, Series C No.4 (29 July 1988)

African Commission on Human and People's Rights (ACmHPR)

ACmHPR, *Malawi Association and Others v Mauritannia*, Comm. Nos. 54/91, 61/91, 98/93, 164/97 à 196/97, and 210/98 (11 May 2000)

ACmHPR, *Social and Economic Rights Action Centre (SERAC) and Centre for Economic and Social Rights (CESR) v Nigeria*, Comm. No. 155/96 (27 October 2002)

Court of Justice of the European Union (CJEU)

CJEU, *Adidas-Salomon AG and Adidas Benelux BV v Fitnessworld Trading Ltd.*, Case C- 223/98 (14 October 1999)

CJEU, *Commission of the European Communities v United Kingdom of Great Britain and Northern Ireland*, Case C-180/96 (07 September 2006)

CJEU, *Dieter Krombach v André Bamberski*, Case C-7/98 (28 March 2000)

CJEU, *Elgafagi v Staatssecretaris van Justitie*, Case C-465/07 (17 February 2009)

CJEU, *Federal Republic of Germany v European Commission*, Case T-576/08 (13 April 2011)

CJEU, *Germany v Y. and Z.*, Joined Cases CJEU C-71/11 and C-99/11 (5 September 2012)

CJEU, *Hoechst v Commission*, Joined Cases 46/87 and 227/88 (21 September 1989)

CJEU, *International Transport Workers' Federation and the Finnish Seamen's Union v Viking Line*, Case C-438/05 (11 December 2007)

CJEU, *Kadi and Al Barakaat International Foundation v Council and Commission*, Joined Cases C-402/05 P and 415/05 (03 September 2008)

CJEU, *Laval v Svenska Byggnadarbetareföbundet*, Case C-341/05 (18 December 2007)

CJEU, *M.M. v Minister for Justice, Equality and Law Reform, Ireland, Attorney General*, Case C-277/11 (22 November 2012)

CJEU, *Merck v Hauptzollamt Hamburg-Jonas*, Case 292/82 (17 November 1983)

CJEU, *Mostafa Abed El Karem El Kott, Chadi Amin A Radi, Hazem Kamel Ismail v Bevandorlasi es Allampolgarsagi Hivatal (BAH)*, Case C-364/11 (19 December 2012)

CJEU, *Omega Spielhallen-und Automatenaufstellungs Gmbh v Oberbürgermeisterin der Bundesstadt Bonn*, Case C-36/02 (14 October 2004)

CJEU, *Orkem v Commission*, Case 374/87 (18 October 1989)

CJEU, *P. Baustahlgewerbe v Commission*, Case C-185/95 (17 December 1998)

CJEU, *P. v S. and Cornwall County Council*, Case C-13/94 (30 April 1996)

CJEU, *Sayn-Wittgenstein v Von Wien*, Case C-208/09 (22 December 2011)

CJEU, *Schmidberger v Austria*, Case C-112/00 (12 June 2003)

CJEU, *Society for the Protection of Unborn Children Ireland Ltd. v Grogan*, Case C-159/90 ECR 4685 (04 October 1991)

CJEU, *St.Nikolaus Brennerei und Likörfabrik, Gustav Kniepf-Melde GmbH v Hauptzollamt Krefeld*, Case 337/82 (21 February 1984)
CJEU, *Stander v Ulm*, Case 26/69 (12 November 1969)
CJEU, *The Queen v Ministry of Agriculture, Fisheries and Food and Commissioners of Customs & Excise, ex parte National Farmers' Union and Others*, Case C-157/96 (05 May 1998)
CJEU, *Vereniging voor Energie, Milieu en Water and Others v Directeur van de Dienst uitvoering en toezicht energie*, Case C-17/03 (07 June 2005)
CJEU, *Wauchaf v Germany*, Case 5/88 (13 July 1989)

New Zealand

New Zealand High Court (NZHC), *Teitiota v The Chief Executive of the Ministry of Business and Employment*, NZHC 3125 (26 November 2013)
New Zealand Immigration and Protection Tribunal (NZIPT), *AD (Tuvalu) v New Zealand Immigration and Protection Tribunal*, NZIPT 501370–371 (04 June 2014)
New Zealand Supreme Court (NZSC), *Teitiota v The Chief Executive of the Ministry of Business and Employment*, NZSC 107 (20 July 2015)

Table of international and regional treaties and other instruments

Additional Protocol to the American Convention on Human Rights in the Area of Economic, Social, and Cultural Rights, adopted on 17 November 1988, into force since 16 November 1999, OAS Treaty Series No.69, 28 ILM 161

African Charter on Human and People's Rights (ACHPR), adopted 27 June 1981, into force since 21 October 1986, 21 ILM 58

Agenda 21, action plan adopted at the U.N. Conference on Environment and Development (UNCED), Rio de Janeiro, 3–14 June 1992

American Convention on Human Rights (ACHR), adopted on 22 November 1969, into force since 18 July 1978, 1144 UNTS 123

Arab Charter on Human Rights (ArCHR), adopted by the Council of the League of Arab States in 2004, into force since 2008

Arab Convention on Regulating Status of Refugees (Arab States Refugee Convention) in the Arab Countries, adopted 1994 by the League of Arab States, not in force

Basel Convention on the Control of Transboundary Movements of Hazardous Wastes and their Disposal, adopted 22 March 1989, into force since 5 May 1992, 1673 UNTS 57

Cartagena Declaration on Refugees (CDR), adopted on 19–22 November 1984

Charter of Fundamental Rights of the European Union, adopted on 18 December 2000, into force since 1 December 2009, OJ 2000/C 364/01

Charter of the Organization of American States (OAS Charter), adopted on 30 April 1948, in force since 13 December 1951, 119 UNTS 3, amended by the Protocols of Buenos Aires (1967, into force 1970), Cartagena de Indias (1985, into force 1988), Managua (1993, into force 1996), and Washington (1992, into force 1997)

Charter of the United Nations (UN Charter), adopted on 26 June 1945, into force since 24 October 1945, 1 UNTS XVI

Consolidated version of the Treaty on the Functioning of the European Union (TFEU), into force since 26 October 2012, OJ L. 326/47–326/390

Convention Against Torture and Other Cruel, Inhuman or Degrading Treatment or Punishment (Convention Against Torture, CAT), adopted on 10 December 1984, into force since 26 June 1987, 1465 UNTS 85

Convention concerning Migration for Employment N° 97 (Revised), adopted 01 July 1949, into force 22 January 1952, C97

Convention concerning Migrations in Abusive Conditions and the Promotion of Equality of Opportunity and Treatment of Migrant Workers N° 143, adopted 24 June 1975, into force 09 December 1978, C143

Convention concerning the Protection of the World Cultural and Natural Heritage, adopted on 16 November 1972, in force since 17 December 1975, 1037 UNTS 151

Convention for the Protection and Assistance of Internally Displaced Persons in Africa (Kampala Convention), adopted on 23 October 2009, into force since 6 December 2012, 52 ILM 397

Convention No. 169 (ILO) concerning Indigenous and Tribal Peoples in Independent Countries, adopted 27 June 1989, into force since 5 September 1991, 28 ILM 1383

Convention on Access to Information, Public Participation in Decision-making and Access to Justice in Environmental Matters (Aarhus Convention), adopted on 25 June 1998, into force since 30 October 2001, 2161 UNTS 447

Convention on Biological Diversity, adopted 5 June 1992, into force since 29 December 1993, 1760 UNTS 79

Convention on Long-Range Transboundary Air Pollution, adopted 13 November 1979, into force since 16 March 1983, 1302 UNTS 217

Convention on the Elimination of All Forms of Discrimination Against Women (CEDAW), adopted on 18 December 1979, into force since 3 September 1981, 1249 UNTS 14

Convention on the Elimination of All Forms of Racial Discrimination (CERD), adopted on 21 December 1965, into force since 4 January 1969, 660 UNTS 195

Convention on the Prevention and Punishment of the Crime of Genocide, adopted on 9 December 1948, into force since 12 January 1951, 78 UNTS 277

Convention on the Protection of All Migrant Workers and Members of Their Families (Migrant Workers Convention), adopted on 18 December 1990, into force since 1 July 2003, 2220 UNTS 3

Convention on the Rights of Persons with Disabilities (CRPD), adopted on 13 December 2006, into force since 3 May 2008, 2515 UNTA 3

Convention on the Rights of the Child (CRC), adopted on 20 November 1989, into force since 2 September 1990, 1577 UNTS 3

Convention Related to the Status of Refugees (CRSR or Refugee Convention), adopted on 28 July 1951, into force since 22 April 1954, 189

UNTS 137, amended by the Protocol relating to the Status of Refugees, adopted on
31 January 1967, in force since 4 October 1967, 606 UNTS 267

Convention Relating to the Status of Stateless Persons, adopted on 28 September 1954, into force since 6 June 1960, 360 UNTS 117

Convention to Combat Desertification in Those Countries Experiencing Serious Drought and/or Desertification, Particularly in Africa (UNCCD), adopted on 17 June 1994, into force since 26 December 1996, 1954 UNTS 3

Council of the European Union Directive 2001/55/EC of 20 July 2001 on minimum standards for giving temporary protection in event of a mass influx of displaced persons and on measures promoting a balance of efforts between Member States in Receiving such persons and bearing the consequences thereof (EU Temporary Protection Directive)

Council of the European Union Directive 2004/83/EC of 29 April 2004 on minimum standards for the qualification and status of third country nationals or stateless persons as refugees or as persons who otherwise need international protection and the content of protection granted and European Parliament and Council of the European Union Directive 2011/95/EU of 13 December 2011 on standards for the qualification of third country nationals or stateless persons as beneficiaries of international protection, for a uniform status for refugees or for persons eligible for subsidiary protection, and for the content of the protection granted (Recast) (EU Qualification Directive)

Covention governing the Specific Aspects of Refugee Problems in Africa (African Refugee Convention), adopted on 10 September 1969, into force since 20 June 1974, 1001 UNTS 45

Declaration of the U.N. Rio Conference on Environment and Development, adopted 14 June 1992, U.N. Doc. A/Conf.151/5Rev 1, 31 ILM 874

Declaration of the U.N. Stockholm Conference on the Human Environment, adopted on 16 June 1972, U.N. Doc. A/Conf.48/14/Rev 1, 31 ILM 874

Declaration on the Rights of Indigenous People, adopted on 13 September 2007, U.N. Doc. A/RES/61/295

Draft Declaration of Principles on Human Rights and the Environment, Annex 1 to the Final Report of the U.N. Special Rapporteur on human rights and the environment, presented to the U.N. Sub-Commission on Prevention of Discrimination and Protection of Minorities, U.N. Doc. E/CN.4/sub.2.1994/9, 6 July 1994

European Commission Staff Working Document SEC (2009) 1240 final of 18 September 2009 Mobility Partnerships as a Tool of the Global Approach to Migration (Mobility Partnerships)

European Convention on Human Rights (ECHR), adopted on 4 November 1950, into force since 3 September 1953, 213 UNTS 222

European Convention on the Legal Status of Migrant Workers, adopted on 24 November 1997, into force since 1 May 1983, CETS No.093

European Parliament and of the Council Directive 2003/4/EC of 28 January 2003 on public access to environmental information

European Parliament and the Council of the European Union Directive 2014/36/EU of 26 February 2014 on the conditions of entry and stay of third-country nationals for the purpose of employment as seasonal workers (Seasonal Workers Directive)

European Social Charter (ESC), adopted on 18 October 1961, in force since 26 February 1965, 529 UNTS 89, revised 1996

First Optional Protocol to the ICCPR, adopted on 16 December 1966, into force since 23 March 1976, 999 UNTS 302

Geneva Convention relative to the Protection of Civilian Persons in Time of War (Fourth Geneva Convention) adopted 12 August 1949, into force since
21 October 1950, 75 UNTS 287

Guiding Principles on Internal Displacement (GPID), U.N. Doc. E/CN.4/1998/53/Add.2

Hyogo Framework for Action 2005–2015 Building the Resilience of Nations and Communities to Disasters, adopted on 16 March 2005, U.N. Doc. A/CONF.206/6

International Covenant on Civil and Political Rights (ICCPR), adopted on 16 December 1966, into force since 23 March 1976, 999 UNTS 171

International Covenant on Economic, Social and Cultural Rights (ICESCR), adopted on 16 December 1966, into force since 3 January 1967, 993 UNTS 3

Kyoto Protocol to the United Nations Framework Convention on Climate Change (1997), adopted on 11 December 1997, into force since 16 February 2005, 2303 UNTS 148

Peninsula Principles on Climate Displacement within States, adopted 19 August 2013

Protocol Additional to the Geneva Conventions of 12 August 1949, and relating to the Protection of Victims of International Armed Conflicts (Protocol I), adopted 08 June 1977, into force since 07 December 1978, 1125 UNTS 3

Protocol Additional to the Geneva Conventions of 12 August 1949, and relating to the Protection of Victims of Non-International Armed Conflicts (Protocol II), adopted 08 June 1977, into force since 07 December 1978, 1125 UNTS 609

Protocol on the Protection and Assistance to Internally Displaced Persons to the Pact on Security, Stability and Development in the Great Lakes Region, adopted on 14–15 December 2006 by the Member States of the International Conference on the Great Lakes Region, into force since June 2008

Protocol to the African Charter on Human and People's Rights on the Rights of Women in Africa, adopted 11 July 2003, into force since 25 November 2005

Protocol to the African Charter on Human and People's Rights, adopted 10 June 1998, into force since 25 January 2004

Protocol to the African Charter on Human and Peoples' Rights on the Establishment of an African Court on Human and Peoples' Rights, adopted on 10 June 1998, into force since 25 January 2004

Rotterdam Convention on the Prior Informed Consent Procedure for Certain Hazardous Chemicals and Pesticides in International Trade, adopted 10 September 1998, into force since 24 February 2004 (revised 2013), 2244 UNTS 337

Sendai Framework for Disaster Risk Reduction 2015–2030, adopted 14–18 March 2015, U.N. Doc. A/CONF.224/L.2

Statute of the International Criminal Court (ICC Statute), adopted on 17 July 1998, into force since 1 July 2002, 2187 UNTS 90

Treaty of Lisbon Amending the Treaty on European Union and the Treaty Establishing the European Community, adopted on 13 December 2007, into force since on 1 December 2009, OJ 2007/C 306/01

United Nations Framework Convention on Climate Change (UNFCCC), adopted on 09 May 1992, into force since 21 March 1994, 1771 UNTS 107

Universal Declaration of Human Rights (UDHR), adopted on 10 December 1948, U.N. Doc. A/810 at 71, UNGA Res. 217 A (III)

Vienna Convention on the Law of Treaties (VCLT), adopted on 23 May 1969, into force since 27 January 1980, 1155 UNTS 331

World Charter for Nature, adopted U.N. General Assembly 28 October 1982, U.N. Doc. A/RES/37/7

Frequently used abbreviations

ACHPR or Banjul Charter	African Charter on Human and People's Rights
ACHR	American Convention on Human Rights
ACmHPR	African Commission on Human and People's Rights
African Refugee Convention	Convention Governing the Specific Aspects of Refugee Problems in Africa
Arab States Refugee Convention	Arab Convention on Regulating Status of Refugees
ArCHR	Arab Charter on Human Rights
ASIL	American Society of International Law
CAT	Convention against Torture and Other Cruel, Inhuman or Degrading Treatment or Punishment
CDR	Cartagena Declaration on Refugees
CEDAW	Convention on the Elimination of All Forms of Discrimination against Women
CESCR	Committee on Economic, Social and Cultural Rights
CETS	Council of Europe Treaty Series
CRC	Convention on the Rights of the Child
CRSR or Refugee Convention	United Nations Convention Relating to the Status of Refugees
DRR	Disaster Risk Reduction
EC	European Commission
ECHR	European Convention on Human Rights
ECSR	European Committee of Social Rights
EDPs	Environmentally Displaced Persons
EJF	Environmental Justice Foundation
ESC	European Social Charter
EU	European Union
EU Mobility Partnerships	European Commission Staff Working Document SEC (2009) 1240 final of 18 September 2009 Mobility Partnerships as a Tool of the Global Approach to Migration

EU Qualification Directive	Council of the European Union Directive 2004/83/EC of 29 April 2004 on minimum standards for the qualification and status of third-country nationals or stateless persons as refugees or as persons who otherwise need international protection and the content of protection granted European Parliament and Council of the European Union Directive 2011/95/EU of 13 December 2011 on standards for the qualification of third-country nationals or stateless persons as beneficiaries of international protection, for a uniform status for refugees or for persons eligible for subsidiary protection, and for the content of the protection granted (Recast)
EU Seasonal Workers Directive	European Parliament and the Council of the European Union Directive 2014/36/EU of 26 February 2014 on the conditions of entry and stay of third-country nationals for the purpose of employment as seasonal workers
EU Temporary Protection Directive	Council of the European Union Directive 2001/55/EC of 20 July 2001 on minimum standards for giving temporary protection in the event of a mass influx of displaced persons and on measures promoting a balance of efforts between member states in receiving such persons and bearing the consequences thereof
GAMM	Global Approach to Migration and Mobility
GPID	Guiding Principles on Internal Displacement
HRC	Human Rights Committee
IACmHR	Inter-American Commission on Human Rights
IACtHR	Inter-American Court of Human Rights
ICC	Statute Statute of the International Criminal Court
ICCPR	International Covenant on Civil and Political Rights
ICESCR	International Covenant on Economic, Social and Cultural Rights
ICJ	International Court of Justice
ICRC	International Committee of the Red Cross
IDMC	Internal Displacement Monitoring Centre
IDP Protocol to the Great Lakes Pact	Protocol to the Pact on Security, Stability and Development in the Great Lakes Region on the Protection and Assistance to Internally Displaced Persons
IDPs	Internally Displaced Persons
ILC	International Law Commission
ILO	International Labour Organisation
IOM	International Organization for Migration

IPCC	Intergovernmental Panel on Climate Change
Kampala Convention	Convention for the Protection and Assistance of Internally Displaced Persons in Africa
LDCs	Least Developed Countries
Migrant Workers Convention	Convention on the Protection of All Migrant Workers and Members of Their Families
NGOs	Non-Governmental Organisations
OAS	Organization of American States
OCHA	U.N. Office for the Coordination of Humanitarian Affairs
OHCHR	U.N. Office of the High Commissioner for Human Rights
SIDS	Small Island Developing States
TEU	Treaty of the European Union or Lisbon Treaty
TFEU	Treaty on the Functioning of the European Union
UDHR	Universal Declaration of Human Rights
UNDP	United Nations Development Programme
UNEP	United Nations Environment Programme
UNFCCC	United Nations Framework Convention on Climate Change
UNGA	United Nations General Assembly
UNHCR	United Nations High Commissioner for Refugees
UNSC	United Nations Security Council
UNTS	United Nations Treaty Series
VCLT	Vienna Convention on the Law of Treaties

Preface

As we see images of increasing numbers of displaced people around the world entering Europe's borders and elsewhere, it seems that this work is appearing at an opportune time. While the causes of people's displacement may be manifold and complex, the time has urgently come for states and the international community at large to gather and (re)consider the protection of the human person to be a holistic endeavour in all phases of displacement (before, during, and after displacement occurs). This book offers the reader a fulcrum upon which an analysis of existing human rights protection standards, in the short term, might lead the way in the wake of new displacement challenges, such as those posed by a changing environment. More importantly, as the fields of human rights law and the environment expand and intertwine, and the jurisprudential glow continues to enlighten our path, so does the transformative capacity of the law. The conscious interpretation of the law made in the context of this work aims at offering constructive and effective solutions and serves as a critical function for the advancement of the law of the protection of the human person. The book aims at obliging the reader to think of the subject under discussion as a common concern, to erase the individualistic side, and to unpretentiously accept this research path as just one of many others.

While it is always difficult to separate feelings of activism from objective academic research when humanity is at stake, the protection of the human person should remain anything but a utopian pursuit. Writing this book has been a very enriching learning experience, both academically and personally. If it succeeds in reaching a befitting mind it will have achieved an even more rewarding undertaking.

Acknowledgements

This work is the outcome of my doctoral thesis, written at the Norwegian Centre for Human Rights at the Faculty of Law, University of Oslo. I am thankful for the invaluable feedback, generosity, trust, and support of my supervisors, Mads Andenæs, University of Oslo and Yutaka Arai, University of Kent, throughout the writing process and beyond. A special thank you note to all the academic and administrative staff at the Faculty of Law who have offered me, over the years, an intellectually stimulating setting to conduct my research. I express my greatest gratitude for their kind words and insightful critique on my work to Malcolm Langford, University of Oslo, Patrick Thornberry, University of Keele, and Hélène Tigroudja, Aix-Marseille University, who acted as the committee for my defence.

I was fortunate to be accepted as a Visiting Researcher at Georgetown University Law, Washington DC in 2014. This time was essential for the structure of this work. I greatly benefited from discussions with distinguished scholars: Edith Brown Weiss, who encouraged me to keep on writing down my "interdisciplinary thinking", and Andrew I. Schoenholtz, who encouraged me to keep on grasping "new legal protection" terrains. I am also grateful to Susan Martin for involving me in the Symposium on Environmental Change and Migration organised under the auspices of the Global Knowledge Partnership on Migration and Development and Dilip Ratha and his staff for welcoming me at the World Bank. At the Brookings Institution, Elizabeth Ferris was graceful in welcoming me and allowing me to discuss my research. I am very thankful for being a beneficiary of the Ryoichi Sasakawa Young Leaders Fellowships Fund (SYLFF) of the Tokyo Foundation without which this cross-Atlantic journey would not have been possible.

Whilst a thank you list can only be indicative, there are people whom I must particularly mention since they helped me burst and shape my intellectual thinking, offered their support, and contributed in many ways to this work: Inger-Johanne Sand, Anne Hellum, Beate Sjåfjell, Jan Helgesen, Harm Schepel, Alexandra Aragão, Desmond McNeill, Jane McAdam, Walter Kälin, Ilan Kelman, and Karen O´Brien. At the institutional level, a special thanks to Agata Sobiech and Markus Sperl from the European Commission and the Office of Jean

Lambert, Member of the European Parliament. Thanks also to the staff of Routledge for their patience and help.

I cannot thank enough the motivating and encouraging words and deeds of my extended family, friends, and colleagues (those near and those spread throughout the world) during the writing of this book. There are simply too many to mention individually, but I wish to particular thank my parents, Maria and Manuel Borges, my sister Lourdes Mota, my friends and colleagues Cathrine Kullgreen, Marta Herkenhoff, Joanna Nicholson, Anna Andersson, Nertila Kuraj, Eléonore Maitre, and Sofie Høgestøl. Above all, my greatest gratitude goes to my loving husband and soulmate Jørgen and my two wonderful children Patrick and Nina. You have made me appreciate more and more the simple things in life. Thank you for your support and unconditional love in good times and in vulnerable times. I love you.

1 Introduction

Every year, millions of people are forced to leave their homes and become displaced. They are cut off from their roots, communities, social ties, and support networks. In 2012, an estimated 32.4 million people were displaced by sudden-onset natural disasters.[1] Another 42 million people were affected by drought in the same year.[2] Climate change and natural hazard-related disasters are understood to play a crucial part in some of these events.[3] While the causes of displacement are manifold and complex,[4] this book deals particularly with the impacts of environmental change on cross border human displacement. The effects of environmental change have been described as the "defining human development issue of our generation"[5] and probably "the biggest humanitarian

1 *See* Internal Displacement Monitoring Centre (IDMC) (2013) "Global Estimates 2012: People Displaced by Disasters" p. 6 and (2014) "Global Estimates 2014: People Displaced by Disasters" p. 15 IDMC and Norwegian Refugee Council (NRC). In 2013, nearly 22 million people were displaced by disasters in at least 119 countries, almost three times as many as were newly displaced by conflict and violence.

2 EM-DAT: The OFDA/CRED International Disaster Database (2012) "Université Catholique de Louvain, Belgium" ***available from:*** www.emdat.be [accessed 17 August 2018]. The word "affected" is defined in the EM-DAT database as "people requiring immediate assistance during a period of emergency; it can also include displaced or evacuated people".

3 Intergovernmental Panel on Climate Change (IPCC) (2012) "Managing the Risks of Extreme Events and Disasters to Advance Climate Change Adaptation" ***available from:*** www.ipcc.ch/pdf/special-reports/srex/SREX_Full_Report.pdf [accessed 17 August 2018].

4 Morel, M. (2014) "The Right Not to Be Displaced in International Law" (Intersentia) p. 17. The causes of displacement can broadly be framed into five categories: conflict-related displacement, development-related displacement, displacement related to systemic human rights violations (such as violations committed by non-state actors including ethnic cleansing, crimes against humanity, discrimination), environmental-related displacement (natural and/or human-induced disasters), and displacement related to other circumstances (e.g. real estate and land disputes; property and housing market forces; government decisions to remove or reduce housing subsidies for low-income groups, among others).

5 United Nations Development Programme (UNDP) (2007) "Human Development Report 2007/2008: Fighting Climate Change: Human Solidarity in a Divided World" (UNDP) p. 1.

and economic challenge that the developing world will face in the coming decades".[6] It is now widely recognised that large-scale cross-border environmental degeneracy impacts on human beings and their surroundings and are largely due to anthropogenic greenhouse gas emissions (which are primarily credited to developed countries). Its noticeable effects are found in extreme droughts and heat waves, floods and hurricanes, sea level rise and the submersing of low-lying coastal areas, and other recurrently extreme weather conditions. Although the effects of environmental change may impact us indiscriminately, they will be felt more acutely in some parts of the world than others.[7]

By 1990, the First Assessment Report of the Intergovernmental Panel on Climate Change (IPCC) foresaw that the largest single impact of environmental change could be on forced human displacement. Today, experts estimate that by 2050 the number of environmentally displaced persons will be between 50 and 200 million,[8] either within their own countries or across their borders, on a permanent or temporary basis.[9] Though scientific uncertainty surrounds these numbers, in general, there will always be uncertainty surrounding the impacts of environmental issues.[10] The forced displacement of millions of people in the drought-stricken Horn of Africa is yet more clear evidence of the causal link between environmental change and forced human displacement.[11] With weather-related natural disasters projected to increase both in frequency and intensity in several parts of the world as global average temperatures continue to rise over the next decades,[12] environmental change-related displacement is becoming

6 Rajan, S. (2008) "Climate Migrants in South Asia: Estimates and Solutions" (Greenpeace India Society) p. 1.

7 *See* Chapter 2.

8 *See* Meyers, N. & Kent, J. (1995) "Environmental Exodus: An Emergent Crisis in the Global Arena" (Climate Institute) pp. 15–16; Stern, N. (2007) "The Economics of Climate Change: The Stern Review" (Cambridge University Press) pp. 128–130. Brown, L. R. (2009) "Plan B 2.0: Rescuing a Planet under Stress and a Civilization in Trouble" Earth Policy Institute (W.W. Norton & Company); Environmental Justice Foundation (2009) "No Place Like Home: Where Next for Climate Refugees" (Environmental Justice Foundation) p. 4.

9 United Nations High Commissioner on Refugees (UNHCR) (2009) "Forced Migration in the Context of on Long-Term Cooperative Action under the Convention" (AWG-LCA 6) from 1 until 12 June in Bonn (19 May) p. 1 *available from:* http://unfccc.int/resource/docs/2009/smsn/igo/049.pdf [accessed 17 August 2018].

10 Glantz, M. (1994a) "Creeping Environmental: Are Societies Equipped to Deal with Them?" Workshop on Creeping Environmental Phenomena and Societal Responses to Them National Center for Atmospheric Research, Boulder, Colorado USA (7–8 February) pp. 1–10, p. 6.

11 U.N. Secretary General (2013) "Voices Concern over Drought in Sahel, Horn of Africa at Event on Building Resilience to Climate, Disasters" Press Release (3 June) *available from:* www.un.org/News/Press/docs/2013/sgsm15071.doc.htm [accessed 17 August 2018].

12 World Bank (2013) "Turn Down the Heat: Climate Extremes, Regional Impacts and the Case for Resilience" Potsdam Institute for Climate Impact Research and Climate Analytics pp. 7–18 *available from:* http://www-wds.worldbank.org/external/default/WDSContent

part of what U.N. Secretary General Ban Ki-moon has depicted as "the new normal".[13]

Ever since El-Hinnawi used the term "environmental refugee" in a 1985 UNEP report to refer to those affected by devastating impacts of the mismanagement of resources, pollution, biodiversity, and livelihood loss, scholars have failed to build a consensual analytical definition for those displaced by environmental factors, and a proliferation of labels coexist in the literature including "climate refugee", "environmental migrant", "environmental displacee", and "climate migrant", among others. This is mainly due to the divergent views on environmental factors as a root cause of forced displacement.[14] Consequently, methodologies and estimates of persons potentially displaced by environmental factors tend to vary. In addition, this field of research has been fuelled by populist assertions from the media of "sinking island states" and bundled, too, into the international security discourse, which highlights the threat of environmental "refugee floodgates".

Having the protection of the human person in all circumstances as its main driver, the objective of this book is first to explore the role of international law, in particular human rights law and correlated states obligations, in the protection of people suffering from cross-border forced displacement as a result of environmental change, here defined as environmentally displaced persons or EDPs. The plight of the environmentally displaced warrants a human approach to their vulnerability, conveying human rights as an integral part of their protection and recognising that EDPs are plainly entitled to enjoy a wide range of civil, political, economic, and social rights set out in international and regional human rights treaties and customary international law whilst at the same time highlighting the corresponding (home and host) states' obligations. Particularly, the objective is not solely to explore the rights of EDPs as such but rather the

---

Server/WDSP/IB/2013/06/14/000445729_20130614145941/Rendered/PDF/784240WP0Full00D0CONF0to0June19090L.pdf [accessed 17 August 2018].

13 Lewis, B. & Doyle, A. (2012) "Extreme Weather Is New Normal U.N.'s Ban Tells Climate Talks" Reuters (4 December) ***available from:*** www.reuters.com/article/2012/12/04/us-climate-talks-idUSBRE8B217F20121204 [accessed 17 August 2018].

14 *See, e.g.*, Castles, S. (2002) "Environmental Change and Forced Migration: Making Sense of the Debate" New Issues in Refugee Research Working Paper No. 70 (United Nations High Commissioner for Refugees) pp. 4–5. The author emphasises that environmental factors are only one of many interrelated causes of forced displacement; Black, R. (2001) "Environmental Refugees: Myth or Reality?" New Issues in Refugee Research Working Paper No. 34 (United Nations High Commissioner for Refugees). The author rejects environmental degradation as a root cause of displacement; Hugo, G. (1996) "Environmental Concerns and International Migration" 30 International Migration Review 1, Special Issue: Ethics, Migration, and Global Stewardship p. 118, pp. 105–131. The author argues that environmental stressors could trigger movement only when caused by other disruptions; *See generally*, Bates, D. (2002) "Environmental Refugees? Classifying Human Migrations Caused by Environmental Change" 23 Population and Environment 5 pp. 465–477 for a classification of different causes of environmental migration.

obligations of states in securing their protection under the existing international legal regime of protection of forced displacement.

Second, and following from the above, this research attempts to devise and consolidate protection for people in those situations by relying on the European Union's (EU's) regionally orientated protection regime. In order to attempt this, the research path starts by analysing existing or envisaged international legal regimes that can provide effective protection for EDPs. This comprises an analysis of the capability of those norms to produce the desired effects (through reinterpretation or revision) and also their effectiveness in light of current state practice. Presently, there is no formal legal protection framework that can provide any material or legal support to people who cross borders due to environmental degradation or because of the effects of environmental change. Formally, they are not entitled to admission or to stay in a third-state country. This has been identified as an international "legal protection gap" that displaces people and impacts upon their human rights.[15] This creates a situation where people's predicaments do not receive adequate government intervention.

1.1 Basic premises of this book

This book is based on two premises. First, as will be clarified, it takes a holistic approach to protection. In this context, it urges the reader to look upon the displacement challenges before, during, and after displacement occurs. It invites the reader to pragmatically rethink protection as a dynamic guiding concept of not only *reactive* but also *proactive* protection measures. In light of increasing forced displacement and the severe suffering that usually accompanies those situations, the international community in general, and states in particular, should strive to take action to prevent and avoid environmental cross-border displacement. Indeed, prevention is better than the cure. There is much scope to use labour migration (e.g. the Seasonal Workers Directive,[16] Mobility Partnerships)[17] as a consolidating preventative protection measure for people to

15 United Nations High Commissioner for Refugees (2010) "High Commissioner's Dialogue on Protection Challenges: Breakout Session 1: Gaps in the International Protection Framework and Its Implementation: Report by the Co-Chairs" (8–9 December) p. 3; United Nations High Commissioner for Refugees (2011) "Statement by António Guterres United Nations High Commissioner for Refugees Nansen Conference on Climate Change and Displacement in the 21st Century" (Oslo, 6 June) *available from:* www.unhcr.org/4def7ffb9.html [accessed 12 June 2012); "Chairpersons Summary Nansen Conference on Climate Change and Displacement in the 21st Century" (Oslo, 6–07 June) para. 23 *available from:* www.regjeringen.no/globalassets/upload/ud/vedlegg/hum/nansen_summary.pdf [accessed 17 August 2018].

16 European Parliament and the Council of the European Union Directive (2014) "On the Conditions of Entry and Stay of Third-Country Nationals for the Purpose of Employment as Seasonal Workers" (Seasonal Worker´s Directive) 2014/36/EU (26 February).

17 European Commission Staff Working Document (2009) "Mobility Partnerships as a Tool of the Global Approach to Migration" (Mobility Partnerships) SEC (2009) 1240 final (18 September).

adapt to environmentally changing conditions and avoid displacement. In addition, where cross-border displacement occurs, the formalised system of complementary protection (e.g. the Qualification Directive,[18] the Temporary Protection Directive[19]) may offer important pragmatic solutions to protect those who are forced to move on a permanent or quasi-permanent basis where the prospects of return to their country of origin may be slim.

The second basic premise of this thesis is that a human rights approach is the essential cornerstone to the protection of EDPs. The specificity of a human rights approach is that it strengthens the existing (explicit and implicit) states' obligations to protect EDPs' rights under international and regional treaties and interrelated operational frameworks. This recognition, also judicial, is being continuously consolidated through dynamic and contextual interpretation of the conventional obligations of international protection of the human person. Together, this ensures that pragmatic solutions are sought to avoid and to remedy situations of forced cross-displacement by environmental factors while at the same time safeguarding "the continuity of the process of expansion of the *law of protection*".[20] It further highlights that every human being is a person and a rights holder, which empowers him or her to claim their rights against the duty-bearers.

1.2 Guiding threads, concepts, and caveats

To ensure coherence in such a complex theme, there are some guiding threads that underlie this work. Below an outline list of concepts and caveats are deployed and a more detailed account of which will be given throughout this book.

First, this study uses the concept of "environmental change" to explain the dynamic process whereby all environmental factors, whether natural (storms,

18 Council of the European Union Directive (2004) "On Minimum Standards for the Qualification and Status of Third Country Nationals or Stateless Persons as Refugees or as Persons Who Otherwise Need International Protection and the Content of Protection Granted" 2004/83/EC (29 April). This Directive has been recast by the European Parliament and Council of the European Union Directive (2011) "On Standards for the Qualification of Third-Country Nationals or Stateless Persons as Beneficiaries of International Protection, for a Uniform Status for Refugees or for Persons Eligible for Subsidiary Protection, and for the Content of the Protection Granted" Recast (Qualification Directive) 2011/95/EU (13 December).

19 Council of the European Union Directive (2001) "On Minimum Standards for Giving Temporary Protection in the Event of a Mass Influx of Displaced Persons and on Measures Promoting a Balance of Efforts between Member States in Receiving Such Persons and Bearing the Consequences Thereof" (Temporary Protection Directive) 2001/55/EC (20 July).

20 Cançado Trindade, A. (2010) "International Law of Humankind, towards a New *Jus Gentium*" (Martinus Nijhoff Publishers) p. 525.

tornados, volcanic eruptions, earthquakes) or man-made (environmental degradation, climate change, development, disasters), are interconnected and interdependent. This holistic view enables us to understand that modern societies are gradually becoming "risky societies", a product of human agency whereby the term *natural disaster* has become an increasingly anachronic misnomer. For the purposes of convenience however, the terms "environmental change" and "climate change" are used interchangeably, as well as the wording "natural" and "human-made disasters", mirroring their use in several international legal instruments.

Second, as previously mentioned, we use the term *Environmental Displaced Persons* or EDPs to encompass:

> *those individuals of a country who for compelling reasons of sudden disasters (in particular cyclones, storms surges and floods) or progressive environmental degradation (in particular drought, desertification, deforestation, soil erosion, water shortages and other climate change related conditions), natural and/or human-made, impacting in their lives or livelihoods are obliged to leave their country of origin temporarily or permanently to a third State.*

This is not meant to be a legal definition but a descriptive one which can be tested and serve as a benchmark for further development. While recognising the multicausality of displacement within the context of social, political, economic, and environmental conditions, the definition depicts the forced movement of people ("no option") across a border (temporary or permanently), where the negative impact of environmental change over a period of time is more enhanced for the environmental driver. The definition also looks upon the vulnerability of the individual when their livelihood or life is affected and impacts their human rights core (civil, political, economic, cultural, and social). The usage of the vulnerability token as a reflective concept enables us to expose the most vulnerable areas of the world affected by environmental change ("hot spots"), where people's human rights are violated and/or at risk and in need of legal protection contemplation. In this context, the term *vulnerability layers* is used in order to clarify that while all of us are generally vulnerable to the effects of environmental change there are additional layers that render the individual or collective entity vulnerable, which may also be a result of the characteristics of a person, age, sex, or group and the overall capacity to resist or adapt to environmental hazards.

Finally, the study works with the underlying assumption that it needs to cope with what we call the "protection paradox". This states that some of the dangers of environmental change are intangible and that its impact on human displacement are to some extent (in)visible in this day and age. In this context, it challenges international law to work within the known and unknown displacement estimates and requests the need to act and not to wait for forced displacement of populations to become more visible and acute. Large numbers of people routinely being displaced by environmental factors is increasingly becoming a reality while, for the time being, there is no way to get rid of the existing greenhouse gases in the atmosphere. Therefore, while the following chapters take a compartmentalised approach towards the application of international legal regimes of protection of forced displacement and states' obligations towards the human person affected by environmental conditions, it remains necessary to highlight that environmental or climate change impacts are borderless. It is continuously relevant to challenge international law as a basis for international solidarity and responsibility in a more general way.[21] The establishment of cooperation among the global polity of states on these matters must imperatively recognise the establishment of an objective responsibility based on a collective action or shared responsibility.[22] Therefore, there is a need to envisage solidarity as "a communion of responsibilities and interest between individuals, groups and States, connected by the ideal of fraternity and the notion of cooperation. The relationship between international solidarity and international cooperation is an integral one, with international cooperation as a core vehicle by which collective goals and the union of interests are achieved".[23] The preservation of the environment and the challenges of environmental change, including human displacement,[24] should benefit from a balanced system of cooperation founded on principles of equity and social justice.

1.3 The academic and societal contribution of this book

Ideally, any academic research aims to contribute to both academic science largely defined and to society and policy. This thesis aims to offers such a twofold contribution. At an academic level, it contributes to the general knowledge gap regarding EDPs and their lack of protection and legal status *in abstracto* and

21 *See* Wellens, K. (2005) "Solidarity as a Constitutional Principle: Its Expanding Role and Inherent Limitations" in R. St. J. Macdonald & D. M. Johnston (eds.) "Towards World Constitutionalism: Issues in the Legal Ordering of the World Community" (Martinus Nijhoff) pp. 775–807; Wellens, K. (2010) "Revisiting Solidarity as a (Re-) Emerging Constitutional Principle: Some Further Reflections" in R. Wolfrum & C. Kojima (eds.) "Solidarity: A Structural Principle of International Law" (Springer) pp. 3–54; U.N. Human Rights Council (2014) "Report of the Independent Expert on Human Rights and International Solidarity, Virginia Dandan" U.N. Doc. A/HRC/26/34, annex (1 April).

22 *See* Harris, P. (2008) "Climate Change and Global Citizenship" 30 Law Policy 4 pp. 481–501, p. 487. Stating that the preservation of the environment and the challenge to combat climate change is dependent upon solidarity between states and even more when states have a certain capacity to control pollution. *See* also U.N. Human Rights Council (2015) "Report of the Independent Expert on Human Rights and International Solidarity, Virginia Dandan" U.N. Doc. A/HRC/29/35 (2 April) para. 28.

23 U.N. Human Rights Council (2008) "Human Rights and International Solidarity Note by the United Nations High Commissioner for Human Rights" U.N. Doc. A/HRC/9/10 (15 August) para.6.

24 *See* on ethical responsibilities Penz, P. (2010) "International Ethical Responsibilities to 'Climate Change Refugees'" in J. McAdam (ed.) "Climate Change and Displacement: Multidisciplinary Perspectives" (Oxford University Press) pp. 151–173.

how to narrow that gap *in concretu*. The study explains and systemises the legal obligations of states, which are valid in the international legal sphere on the international protection of persons facing threats from the environment. It examines the existing international protection paradigms and corresponding (home and host) states' obligations under human rights law in general and the 1951 Refugee Convention and the 1967 Protocol on the Status of Refugees in particular, with a view not only to seeking legal status but also to constructing a much-needed holistic protection framework for EDPs. More specifically, it offers pragmatic protection solutions that can be consolidated by exploring existing EU regional protection standards for those arriving at EU borders and that could have a "ripple effect" beyond the EU.

The protection of EDPs is far from being only one of those issue areas maintaining a "grip on the imagination of the research community;"[25] the aim is also to gain stronger international recognition of their plight. Displacement affects millions of people every year, severely compromising and disrupting their livelihoods. With environmental change exacerbating these trends, it is the search for the legal mechanisms and their dynamic interpretation to consolidate, prevent, and/or mitigate forced displacement as a result of environmental change that, therefore, underlies the societal value and contribution of this thesis.

1.4 The contribution of this book to existing literature

The research focus on environmental change, the related movement, legal status and rights of EDPs has expanded over recent years. At a scholarly level, international law researchers have attempted to narrow the legal protection gap for those who could potentially cross an international border due to changing environmental conditions. Proposals have varied in content and imagination, with authors balancing their normative proposals between hard and soft law approaches. In this context, scholarship-coordinated efforts have abounded, with many proposing the treaty model approach.[26] However, environmental scholars

25 Nicholson, C. (2012) "The Place of Epistemological Due Diligence in Relation to the Social and Political Science of Climate Change: The Case of Environmental Migration" Paper presentation ClimMig Conference on 'Human Rights, Environmental Change, Migration and Displacement' Ludwig Boltzmann Institute Human Rights; IDDRI, SciencesPo. Vienna, Austria, (20–21 September) p. 2, pp. 1–20.

26 *See, e.g.*, Hodgkinson *et al.* (2008) "Towards a Convention for Persons Displaced by Climate Change: Key Issues and Preliminary Responses" Issue 8 (September) *available from:* www.ias.uwa.edu.au/new-critic/eight [accessed 17 August 2018]. This convention was initially presented at the University of Copenhagen during a conference on Climate Change: Global Risks, Challenges and Decisions, 10–12 March 2009. Other convention proposals include: Docherty, B. & Giannini, T. (2009) "Confronting a Rising Tide: A Proposal for a Convention on Climate Change Refugees" 33 Harvard Environmental Law Review pp. 349–403; Magniny, V. (1999) "Les Réfugiés de L'Environnement Hypothèse Juridique à Propos d'une Menace Écologique" Doctoral Dissertation Paris, Department of Law (University Paris I Panthéon-Sorbonne); McCue, G. S. (1993–1994)

in France have developed the most complete publication to date, a Draft Convention on the International Status of Environmentally Displaced Persons.[27] Less ambitious, but relying on existing mechanisms and treaties, some scholars have suggested a *sui generis* protection that would consist of adding a Protocol to the 1992 United Nations Framework Convention on Climate Change (UNFCCC)[28] or adding a Protocol to the European Convention Human Rights (ECHR) concerning the right to a healthy and safe environment as a means of "enhancing the human rights protection mechanisms vis-à-vis the challenges of climate change and environmental degradation processes".[29] Additional proposals have consisted of extended legal protection or of adding an amendment or additional Protocol to the CRSR.[30] Professor Jane McAdam, who has written extensively on the topic, has favoured a better implementation of the Guiding Principles of Internal Displacement (GPID) that could usefully inform a framework relating to cross-border environmental-related movement.[31] Some authors also favour strengthening "soft law" as an interim measure before there is a global consensus on a binding document for the protection of EDPs.[32] The building of a gradual consensus to address the challenges of cross-border displacement in the context of disasters and climate change has been the cornerstone

"Environmental Refugees: Applying International Environmental Law to Involuntary Migration" 6 Georgetown International Environmental Law Review pp. 151–190.

27 Prieur, M. *et al.* (2008) "Projet de Convention Relative au Statut International des Déplacés Environnementaux University of Limoges (CRIDEAU-CRDP-OMIJ-CIDCE)" 4 Revue européenne de Droit de L'Environnement pp. 391–406.This draft treaty model approach relies on three strands: protection, assistance, and responsibility by including principles of environmental assistance, proximity, proportionality effectiveness, and non-discrimination. It further creates a legal apparatus to grant a status to environmentally displaced persons to be managed by each state through a national commission and to develop cooperation efforts with various international and regional organisations.

28 Bierman, F. & Boas, I. (2011) "Protecting Climate Refugees: The Case for a Global Protocol" 50 Science and Policy for Sustainable Development, 6 pp. 8–17.

29 Council of Europe (CoE) (2008) "Council of Europe Parliamentary Assembly, Committee on Migration, Refugees and Populations, Environmentally Induced Migration and Displacement: A 21st Century Challenge" CoE Doc 11785 (23 December) paras 6.3, 121.

30 Christiansen, S. M. (2010) "Environmental Refugees, a Legal Perspective" (Wolf Legal Publishers); Renaud, F. *et al.* (2007) "Control Adapt or Flee, How to Face Environmental Migration?" Interdisciplinary Security Connection No. 5 (United Nations University Institute for Environment and Human Security); Coinsbee, M. & Simms, A. (2003) "Environmental Refugees: The Case for Recognition" (New Economics Foundation); Cooper, J. (1998) "Environmental Refugees: Meeting the Requirements of the Refugee Definition" 6 New York University Environmental Law Journal pp. 480–488.

31 McAdam, J. (2011a) "Climate Change and International Law: Complementary Protection Standards" (United Nations High Commissioner for Refugees Legal and Protection Policy Series) *available from:* www.unhcr.org/4dff16e99.html [accessed 20 May 2012] *See also* McAdam, J.(2012) "Climate Change, Forced Migration, and International Law" (Oxford University Press) p. 256.

32 Fatima, R., Wadud, A. & Coelho, S. (2014) "Human Rights, Climate Change, Environmental Degradation and Migration: A New Paradigm" Issue No. 8 (International Organization for Migration & Migration Policy Institute) p. 8, pp. 1–11.

of the so-called Nansen Initiative.[33] Whilst all of them are worthy and merit recognition, among other things because they draw attention and offer insightful solutions into enhanced legal protection options surrounding environmental cross-border displacement, none of them address the matter all-inclusively from a normative and pragmatic point of view.

This research aims to contribute to filling this scholarly gap, first by taking a holistic approach to protection in all phases of displacement – before, during, and after displacement – for environmentally displaced persons. This is particularly necessary, given that the solutions that can be envisaged for those who cross an international border due to environmental factors have to be conceptualised and combined with measures to avoid displacement or to adapt to the conditions of a changing environment. While this study concentrates on only two phases of displacement due to time and space reasons (status and protection from cross-border displacement and status and protection after cross-border displacement), it aims at highlighting the needs and rights of EDPs and corresponding home and host states' obligations. This approach is taken from a human rights-based perspective by analysing existing or envisaged international legal regimes (hard and soft law) and their evolution informed by the interpretative dynamics of jurisprudential review. All of these legal forces contribute overall to the ***cumulative effects*** in providing effective protection for EDPs. No overview and analysis of these legal protection instruments and the corresponding states' obligations by analogy towards EDPs currently exists to our knowledge.

Second, the research examines the issue of the legal protection of EDPs in a more detailed manner. This is particularly true as regards the obligations of the country of origin and the analogy of the underlying duty of states to take preventative and adaptive measures for the protection EDPs, which derives from (quasi) jurisdictional decisions and international and regional instruments that consolidate the emerging customary character of such an obligation. This is also done as regards the obligations of the host state deriving from existing international instruments such as the CRSR and the extent to which those duties are transferrable in particular to protect EDPs. It asserts that the ***non-refoulement*** obligation is not confined to the CRSR and that human rights law, through constant judicial review, has increasingly driven the evolution of the law of the protection of the human person – and by analogy to EDPs.

Third, this analysis aims at narrowing the "legal protection gap" by consolidating protection for EDPs in a more pragmatic matter, which has not been done in previous studies. To achieve this, and in order to (re)conceptualise protection for EDPs, it relies on the European Union regional protection regime

33 The Nansen Initiative is an intergovernmental process that was launched in 2012 by Switzerland and Norway to address the challenges of cross-border displacement in the context of disasters and climate change. Its "Protection Agenda" builds upon consultative processes carried out in various regions of the world ***available from:*** http://www2.nanseninitiative.org [accessed 17 August 2018].

as a model for testing and devising both *proactive* and *reactive* protection solutions – and as a way of reflecting states' human rights obligations – with potential replication. In other words, the research intends to look upon the protection of those environmentally displaced within the walls of the academic debate (at the doctrinal level) but also offers pragmatic solutions for states that are already available and that can ultimately open doors beyond the academic walls towards a more formalised system of protection for EDPs (at the level of international law and policymaking).

In sum, this study looks backwards in order to move forwards. It addresses the existing legal framework of protection and underlying principles of forced displacement, which is relevant *in context* (*de lege lata*) and in how it can be utilised, interpreted, and consolidated, to protect EDPs now and in the near future (*de lege ferenda*).[34]

1.5 Research scope and limitations

The subject under investigation has intrinsic methodological difficulties, as the nature of the inquiry is highly complex and prospective. The methodological path chosen may be the subject of criticism. The book chooses the most suitable methodological path to offer "cosmos" in a naturally "chaotic" theme. Displacement due to environmental factors can be conceived from multilayered and interactive approaches from human rights to environmental perspectives or security, migration, and humanitarian perspectives.

The book can be further criticised because it does not take into account all those disciplines or that it takes only one particular path. However, due to time limitations and permitted textual space, tackling such approaches would be an impossible task. Limiting it to the human rights framework was the ultimate choice, given the subject matter – protection of the human person affected by environmental change – and the theoretical and practical points of view. The final focus on EU regional protection strategies embedded in a wider human rights framework as a test case was selected, as it offers formalised statuses and consequently a potential model of legal protection (*proactive* and *reactive*) for those (potentially) displaced by environmental factors.

It should also be noted that the focus of this study lies on a narrowing of the legal protection gap by focusing on the obligations of states to protect environmentally displaced persons in whose territory or whose jurisdiction people are (or potentially will be) displaced. It is essentially a study primarily focused on the applicability of substantive norms under human rights treaties and related

34 *See* Higgins, R. (1994) "Problems and Process: International Law and How We Use It" (Oxford University Press) pp. 5, 10. The author states that the distinction between *lex lata* and *lex ferenda* is in reality a "false dichotomy". This is because both normative considerations and policy factors should be dealt with "systematically and openly" by the authorised decision-maker.

instruments and does not deal with questions regarding the responsibility of states in relation to one another or the international community in general to protect people in other countries from environmental displacement. Inevitably, however, some assertions on this are made. It neither addresses issues of the responsibility of states through the rules governing the responsibility of states for international wrongful acts[35] or the responsibility of United Nations organs per se[36] or through the draft articles on the responsibility of international organisations or the potential implication of the application of the "responsibility to protect" concept.[37]

Therefore, a second issue beyond the scope of this work is the question of the human rights obligations of non-state actors (e.g. UNHCR, corporations, among others) under international law in the environmental displacement context. With regard to non-state actors, it should be noted, however, that the states of origin have a general obligation to take all the necessary measures to protect the human rights of people from potential displacement by non-state actors or in any other circumstances that could potentially lead to displacement. It is from this perspective that non-state actors (in particular, in the case law discussions) are present in this study.

As previously mentioned, this book takes a holistic approach to protection, which imposes obligations on states during all phases of displacement: before, during, and after. The focus is not only on remedial and reactive perspectives but also on a preventative approach to the protection of cross-border environmental-induced displacement and *inter alia* host and home states' obligations under current international protection instruments. The issue of immediate assistance during the time they are displaced, as well as the issues of compensation, redress, and reparation for victims of displacement or the issue of statelessness due to environmental factors, are briefly addressed or, where necessary, referred to, but they do not constitute the heart of this book.

Finally, even if this piece of research constitutes a legal black-letter analysis in a hybrid fashion, it may be appropriate to acknowledge another limitation – or advantage – that may derive from the professional background of the author. Having worked in the Brussels milieu for over a decade as an advocate and legal advisor, policy considerations are (perhaps sometimes naively) inferred. While you can take a girl out of politics, you cannot easily take the politics out of the girl! Let's remember, however, that the issue of protection of the human person (fortunately or unfortunately) is anything but an apolitical subject.

35 *See* Epiney, A. (2011) "'Environmental Refugees': Aspects of International State Responsibility" in E. Piguet, A. Pecoud & P. Guchteneire (eds.) "Migration and Climate Change" (Cambridge University Press) pp. 388–427.

36 *See* Bierman & Boas (2008) *Op. Cit.*

37 According to this concept, in the case of serious or apparent human rights violations within a state, the international community, the UN Security Council, and third states should intervene to protect the people who have been affected by resorting, if necessary, to the use of force.

1.6 Book outline

The structure of this book takes a rather legal compartmentalised approach for two reasons. First, for presentation reasons, it departs from the application and interpretative dynamics of the existing international human rights framework and related instruments, coupled with the states' (home and host) obligations, in order to narrow the identified "legal protection gap" for cross-border environmental displacement. Second, for comprehension reasons, it enables the reader to depict the evolution of the law of protection of the human person and the transformative capacity of the law in order to (re)conceptualise protection for EDPs.

The book begins by exploring the emergence of the environmental human displacement problem and its legal challenges, including the necessary premises and guiding threads that the reader should take into account. Chapter 2 investigates the environmental, legal, and politico-economic factors that influence the discussion. It identifies some vulnerable geographical areas where the effects of environmental change are/will be most acute and where movement is/will be particularly felt and other environmental displacement scenarios. It discusses the concept of environmental change and then explains in more detail the meaning(s) of vulnerability and how this concept – because in human rights law it is intimately related to protection – can be used as a starting point in identifying vulnerable areas in need of legal protection contemplation. The chapter explains why the study of protection of environmental displacement needs to be approached from a human rights-based perspective and the entrenched relevance of a holistic approach to protection – in pre-in-post displacement phases.

The book discusses to what extent people facing threats from the environment are currently protected under international human rights law and related instruments and the corresponding home and host states' obligations. It does so by relying on the interpretative dynamics deriving from the analysis of relevant treaties and (quasi)judicial decisions of international and regional human rights bodies. While Chapter 4 gives the reader an analysis, as a point of comparison, of the status and protection of environmental displacement under CRSR and its Additional Protocol, outlining host states' obligations (which are predicted on the lack of national state protection), Chapter 3 obliges us to take a necessary step back in order to analyse the protection obligations of the country of origin or home state. This is because the home state has the primary duty for the protection of persons and their human rights (respect, protect, fulfil) in its territory or subject to its jurisdiction or control, affected during a disaster or potentially affected before a disaster occurs. This dual-axis approach provides the basis for understanding the holistic approach to protection claimed for environmental displacement in particular, from and after cross-border displacement, which gains an arguable pragmatic ground in Chapter 5.

After a survey of illustrative examples with regards to states' obligations under international human rights law, Chapter 3 makes a further analogy of the protection obligations of states with regards to environmental displacement. It builds on one of the principal tenets of states' obligations: the underlying duty to prevent human rights violations by preventing and reducing environmental risk and – by extension – protecting people from cross-border displacement. It identifies the minimum scope of protection that should be afforded by states, which is not totally dependent on states' financial resources. The manifestation of a preventative dimension in the role of the law is further sustained by surveying a number of interconnected normative texts and operational frameworks that – explicitly or implicitly – place obligations on states to prevent cross-border environmental displacement and the violation of people's human rights. By contrast, and as previously mentioned, Chapter 4 gives not only an account of host states' obligations under refugee law but further enlightens the realities and limits of states' obligations under this framework. It highlights the evolution of the law of protection of the human person that stems from regional instruments, which can arguably be interpreted to encompass situations of environmental distress and *inter alia* enhanced protection obligations of the host state. The extension of protection obligations may also derive from other obligations based upon human rights law that states may have. The principle of *non-refoulement*, as one of the strongest limitations to states' sovereignty, forbids the return of individuals to an area where she or he will face persecution, torture, or serious ill treatment and constitutes a fundamental principle in international law. Despite its potential, the principle does not confer a right of residence or any specific legal status in a foreign country, and this gives considerable discretion to states in how they treat foreigners in their countries. Therefore, the scope of additional complementary regimes – like the EU – are considered.

Against this background, Chapter 5 attempts to devise pragmatic protection strategies and narrow the legal protection gap for EDPs by testing the EU's regionally orientated protection regime. The objective is to highlight protection – as a way of reflecting human rights obligations of states – by way of a process of consolidation of existing proactive and reactive protection measures. In this context, the chapter first seeks the interpretative added protection value of the Seasonal Workers Directive and Mobility Partnerships to deal with the predicted effects of environmental change (protection from cross-border displacement), and it second seeks the interpretative added protection value of temporary protection and subsidiary protection of the Temporary and Qualification Directive respectively (protection after cross-border displacement). It offers an analysis of existing pragmatic solutions to (re)conceptualise protection for environmental displacement within the EU and even beyond its borders and helps the global polity of states to consider protection as a dynamic guiding concept in the wake of new protection challenges. Finally, Chapter 6 draws some overarching conclusions.

2 From environmental change to human displacement

One of the largest and most persistent characteristics of humanity is migration. Movement is also critical in our daily lives. Indeed, changes in the environment have been a key catalyst for forced human migration. It has influenced the global spread and impact of *Homo sapiens.*[1]

However, human mobility, which is forced and exacerbated by environmental factors, blurs the traditional distinctions between refugees, internally displaced people, and international immigrants. At the same time it opens what scholars have called a "legal protection gap" in the international protection regime, which was not specifically built to cater to the needs of those who will cross a border due to environmental factors. There is a general and legal scholarly argument that international law is currently ill-equipped to provide protection to displaced people stemming from environmental factors. Nevertheless, in order to develop more law and more effective law – if necessary – it is essential to focus on the question of how much law exists. This discussion warrants first and foremost the clarification of the concept of environmental change and the impact of environmental change on human displacement in particular in the regions of the world that are/will be most affected through highlighting their *vulnerability layers*. This chapter discusses the displacement estimates and realities, the driving forces behind environmental displacement and the protection paradox that are relevant to conceptualise the notion of EDP. The focus on the human person protection needs as opposed to the reason which led people to leave their homes is of paramount importance. Environmental displacement needs to be approached from a human rights-based perspective. This focus guides the much-needed holistic approach to protection – before, during, and after displacement occurs – which is seen as an essential cornerstone for the protection of the human person in the wake of new displacement challenges, such as those posed by a changing environment.

1 *See* Stringer, C. & Mckie, R. (1996) "African Exodus: The Origins of Modern Humanity" (Henry Holt and Company).

2.1 People on the move

While the decision to migrate may be a result of interconnected factors, the sobering implications of human transformation of one's surroundings or environment are provoking challenges to the long-held assumption about unlimited economic growth, the unavoidability of amplified inequities, and the inviolability of territorial borders. All these factors are intertwined with movement in complex ways. Globalisation and the expansion of global capitalism are prompting many people to leave their homes in search of better lives. Environmental change will further exacerbate such trends. The transformation of or impact on the earth by humans may have generated what some are calling – "the 'Anthropocene' – a stage in human history marked by such profound human impact on Earth's ecosystems and climate as to be considered a new geological age. Migration [particularly forced human displacement] is one of the foundations of this age".[2]

As early as 1990, the Intergovernmental Panel on Climate Change (IPCC)[3] observed that the largest single impact of environmental change could be on human "migration and resettlement outside the national boundaries",[4] with millions of people being forcibly dislocated by coastal flooding, agricultural disruption, and shoreline erosion.[5]

Figures and scenario building vary depending on particular parameters,[6] assumptions,[7] and social values. Depending on favourable or unfavourable

2 Ho, C. & Loucky, J. (2012) "Humane Migration, Establishing Legitimacy and Rights for Displaced People" (Kumarian Press) p. 2.

3 The Intergovernmental Panel on Climate Change (IPCC) is the leading scientific international body for the assessment of climate change under the auspices of the United Nations. It was established in 1988 by the United Nations Environment Programme (UNEP) and the World Meteorological Organisation (WMO) to provide the world and governments with a clear scientific view on the current state of knowledge in climate change and its potential environmental and socio-economic impacts. It reviews and assesses the most recent scientific, technical, and socio-economic information produced worldwide relevant to the understanding of climate change *available from:* www.ipcc.ch/ [accessed 17 August 2018].

4 Watson, R. *et al.* (eds.) (1997) "IPCC Special Report: The Regional Impacts of Climate Change: An Assessment of Vulnerability: Summary for Policymakers" (IPCC November) part 6.8.

5 IPCC (1990) "Climate Change: The IPCC Scientific Assessment Final Report of Working Group I" (Cambridge University Press).

6 The importance of climate-change effects on human displacement seems to depend on a number of parameters such as economic, geographic and other uncertainties about trends in human systems over the next century. IPPC (2007) "Fourth Assessment Report: Climate Change 2007: Impacts, Adaptation and Vulnerability. Contributions of Working Group to the Fourth Assessment Report of the Intergovernmental Panel on Climate Change" p. 365.

7 The above scenario building is based on the most conservative predictions of environmental changes, especially of global warming in the level of 2 degrees, but other authors have examined scenarios taking into account higher levels. *See* for e.g. Gemenne, F. (2011)

conditions, even high estimates might be considered too low.[8] The absence of conceptualisation by the international community of an accurate definition of what constitutes a person displaced by environmental factors has resulted in the incapacity of exactly measuring the number of existing and potential displacement flows. Estimates that have become an accepted figure in relevant publications range from 150 million to 200 million environmental displacees or migrants as a result of environmental change alone by 2050.[9]

These "guesstimates" are hindered by the fact that one cannot clearly demonstrate at present the immediate connection between environmental change and displacement. Indeed it can be conceptually problematic and empirically flawed to link a particular climate event to movement.[10] Scholars have emphasised that the causes of displacement are so complex and compound that they cannot be solely attributed to environmental reasons.[11] Others have asserted that perhaps the key problem is not environmental change itself but the ability of different parts of the world and communities to cope with it. This, in turn, may be closely related to the problems of underdevelopment and North and South relations.[12] The issue of causality of displacement or migration has been much debated because the decision to migrate is often classified as a *subjective* one induced by a cluster of economic, social, political, demographic, and environmental factors.[13]

Despite the different levels of interpretation, the reality is that figures over the years show that there are more people displaced by environmental-related disasters than by armed conflicts.[14] In this context, it is relevant to acknowledge

"Migrations et déplacements de populations dans un monde à + 4°C" 414 Etudes pp. 723–738.

8 *See generally*, Brown, O. (2008) "Migration and Climate Change" International Organization for Migration 31 Migration Research Studies (International Organization for Migration). For an opposing vision see Black, R. (2001) "Environmental Refugees: Myth or Reality?" New Issues in Refugee Research Working Paper No. 34 (United Nations High Commissioner for Refugees) pp. 2–3.

9 Aufenvenne, P. & Felgentreff, C. (2013) "Umweltmigranten und Klimaflüchtlinge – zweifelhafte Kategorien in der aktuellen Debatte". IMIS-Beiträge p. 44 pp. 9–44; Oltmer, J. (2013) "Which Effects Do Global Environmental Change Have for Migration?" Bundeszentrale fur Politische Bildung (10 September) *available from*: www.bpb.de/gesellschaft/migration/kurzdossiers/168682/environmental-changes [accessed 17 August 2018].

10 McAdam, J. (2012) "Climate Change, Forced Migration, and International Law" (Oxford University Press) p. 24.

11 Black (2001) *Op. Cit.* p. 2.

12 Castles, S. (2002) "Environmental Change and Forced Migration: Making Sense of the Debate" New Issues in Refugee Research Working Paper No. 70 (United Nations High Commissioner for Refugees) p. 3.

13 *See* Mayer, B. (2013) "Climate Change and International Law on the Grim Days" 24 The European Journal of International Law 3 p. 963, pp. 947–970.

14 *See* IDMC (2012) "Global Estimates 2011 People Displaced by Natural Hazard-Induced Disasters" (IDMC and NRC June) p. 5; "Estimates show that in 2010 alone 42 million people displaced by sudden-onset natural disasters and that 90 per cent of them were climate related such as floods and storms" IDMC (2014); "Global Estimates 2014 People

the words of Norman Myers: “Although it is difficult to calculate the exact number of people for whom environmental degradation is a primary cause of forced migration, it assuredly is a factor for the majority of non-traditional refugee-seekers”.[15]

In this day and age, nine out of every ten natural disasters are linked to environmental change; over the last 20 years, the number of disasters has doubled (from ca. 200 to over 400 per year).[16] In 2009, the former Global Humanitarian Forum noted that 300,000 people die per year of climate change-related reasons, foreseeing the deaths of half a million people by 2030.[17] In the last six years, for example, eight countries in South Asia (Afghanistan, Bangladesh, Bhutan, India, the Maldives, Nepal, Pakistan, and Sri Lanka) have accounted for 36% (342,000,000) of the total number of people reported to have been displaced by disasters (616,000,000). This reflects the vulnerability of the people exposed to hazards in this region.[18] The impacts of environmental change are now not only predictions; they are realities already happening today.

While not all movements are due to environmental factors alone,[19] it is important to consider the environment as a threat multiplier: an objective and autonomous factor that leads to population displacement. For this reason, it is

---

Displaced by Disasters” (IDMC and NRC September) p. 15. In 2013, nearly 22 million people were displaced in at least 119 countries by natural disasters, almost 3 times as many as were displaced by conflict and violence and IDMC (2015) “Global Estimates 2015: People Displaced by Disasters” (IDMC and NRC July) p. 20. Latest figures from IDMC in 2015 estimate that more than 19.3 million people were forced to flee their homes by disasters in 100 countries in 2014 whilst hundreds of thousands more are still displaced following disasters in previous years.

15 Myers, N. (1997) *Op. Cit.* p. 167.

16 UNHCR (2008) “Climate Change, Natural Disasters and Human Displacement: A UNHCR Perspective” (23 October) p. 2 refers to Holmes J., Under Secretary-General for Humanitarian Affairs and Emergency Relief Coordination, Opening Remarks at the Dubai International Humanitarian Aid and Development Conference and Exhibition “DIHAD 2008 Conference”.

17 Global Humanitarian Forum (2009) “Human Impact Report Climate Change, the Anatomy of a Silent Crisis” p. 1 *available from:* www.ghf-ge.org/human-impact-report.pdf [accessed 17 August 2018].

18 Ginneti, J. & Lavell, C. (2015) “The Risk of Disaster-Induced Displacement in South Asia” Technical Paper IDMC (April) p. 18; Burke, J. & McCurry, J. (2015) “Nepal’s PM Says Earthquake Death Toll Could Reach 10,000” The Guardian (28 April) *available from:* www.theguardian.com/world/2015/apr/28/nepal-earthquake-anger-among-survivors-as-food-and-water-in-short-supply [accessed 17 August 2018] The earthquake on 25 April, which struck an area in central Nepal between Kathmandu and the city of Pokhara, has had a far-reaching impact, highlighting the vulnerability of this area. More than 10,000 people may have lost their lives, along with victims in Bangladesh, India, and Tibet.

19 This includes those displaced due to persecution, armed conflict, generalised violence (communal, ethnic, political, and criminal violence) or human rights violations. Forced displacement also includes those who are displaced by environmental stressors (natural or environmental disasters, human-made chemical or nuclear disasters, famine, and/or development projects).

important to distinguish between those who voluntarily move and for whom relocation does not mean the manifestation of a hazard or deteriorating living conditions (environmental migrants) and those people who are forced to leave their homes due to the presence of a serious environmental threat to their lives or normal functioning (EDPs). The scope of this book relates to the latter, and key factors signalled here will be further developed. This forced movement implies the disenfranchising of the person from his or her community, family, and livelihood and implies a great level of powerlessness where moving is not a choice, either to stay or to go – it becomes the "no choice option".

2.1.1 On the concept of environmental change

The term environment generally means one's surroundings, but the concept is relatively new in many languages. While it can be traced back to the twelfth century in France from the verb *environner*, in other languages new words were formulated during the 1960s (e.g. *umwelt* in German, *milieu* in Dutch, *meio ambiente* in Portuguese, *medio ambiente* in Spanish, *Al.biah* in Arabic, *kankyo* in Japanese).[20] The term is also process-driven in that it includes water, air, and land and their interrelationships as well as relationships between them and human beings. The latter relates to the impact of human activity on the environment in a particular time and space. The United Nations Declaration on the Human Environment, adopted in Stockholm in 1972, states precisely that: "Man is both creature and moulder of his environment, which gives him physical substance and affords him the opportunity for intellectual, moral, social and spiritual growth".[21]

The processes of environmental change, while giving opportunities to mankind to develop abilities that might be regarded as transformative or developmental, has also increasingly produced negative effects in the form of environmental detriment. Glantz classifies these problems as "creeping environmental problems" such as air pollution, acid rain, global warming, ozone depletion, deforestation, droughts, famines, and the accumulation of nuclear and solid waste that all are the result of "low-grade, long-term, and cumulative processes".[22] Such problems are interconnected, cross-disciplinary, and cross-boundary. Indeed, there are many reasons for the deterioration of the environment. Some are the result of natural causes (storms, tornados, volcanic eruptions, earthquakes), while others are human-induced (environmental pollution, the construction of river dams, the logging of

20 Chandrappa, R. *et al.* (2011) "Coping with Climate Change" (Springer) p. 45.

21 U.N. General Assembly (1972) "United Nations Conference on the Human Environment" (Stockholm 15 December) U.N. Doc. A/RES/2994 (1972) para. 1.

22 *See* Glantz, M. H. (1994b) "Creeping Environmental Problems, Natural Science Essay" The World and I pp. 218–225. The author explains that while the destruction of a small part of a mangrove forest in Southeast Asia to create a shrimp pond might be seen as transformation and will not destroy the forest ecosystem, the proliferation of ponds and many human interventions can become a problem after a threshold is crossed over a certain period of time, leading to degradation.

tropical forests, chemical warfare). However, as observed by former U.N. Secretary General Kofi Annan, "the term 'natural disaster' has become an increasingly anachronistic misnomer. In reality, human behaviour transforms natural disasters into what should really called unnatural disasters".[23] Historical accounts have provided ample evidence of how human beings have always been at risk from changing environmental conditions.[24] However, modern risks are different because they are "manufactured risks", a product of human agency.[25] Environmental change clearly illustrates this idea of modernisation of risk.

There is a fine line between what is natural or human-induced because very often a disaster can be a blend of both factors (e.g. floods or droughts can be attributable to extreme weather, climate events, global warming, or development issues). This dichotomy of natural/human influence on the environmental conditions over time has been clearly pinpointed by the United Nations Convention on Climate Change (UNFCCC)[26] under Article 2, when it refers to climate change as "a change of climate which is attributed *directly or indirectly to human activity* that alters the composition of the global atmosphere and which is in addition to natural climate variability observed over comparable time periods" (emphasis added).

Climate change is expected to increase, and the amount and intensity of disasters (in particular floods, storms, and heat waves) will exacerbate these trends. In the Fourth Assessment Report the IPCC tabled scientific evidence of the clear relationship between human activity and temperature rise[27] and noted that global warming is *unequivocal* and is *very likely* due to *man-made* (anthropogenic) greenhouse gas emissions.[28] The expression *very likely* means that global warming is caused (between 90% and 99%) by human activity. Because there will always be some degree of scientific uncertainty surrounding many environmental issues,[29] one has to operate, in the context of this book, against the "backdrop of uncertainty" – coping with risk and how to manage it. "A

23 U.N. Secretary General (1999) "Report of the Secretary General to the United Nations General Assembly on the Work of the Organisation U.N." Doc. No. A/54/1 (1999) para.11.

24 *See* Khondker, H. (2010) "Globalisation, Disasters and Disaster Purpose" in B. Turner (ed.) "The Routledge International Handbook of Globalisation Studies" (Routledge) p. 231.

25 *See* Beck, U. (1992) "Risk Society" (Sage) p. 21; Giddens, A. (1999) "Risk and Responsibility" 62 Modern Law Review 1 pp. 1–10.

26 United Nations Convention on Climate Change (UNFCC) adopted on 09 May 1992, in force since 21 Match 1994, 1771 UNTS.

27 *See generally*, IPCC (2007) "Summary for Policymakers" in M. L. Parry *et al.* (eds.) "Climate Change 2007: Impacts, Adaptation and Vulnerability. Contribution of Working Group II to the Fourth Assessment Report of the Intergovernmental Panel on Climate Change" (Cambridge University Press) pp. 7–22.

28 *See* IPCC (2007) "Climate Change. Synthesis Report" *Op. Cit.* p. 72 *available from:* www.ipcc.ch/publications_and_data/ar4/syr/en/mains6-1.html [accessed 17 August 2018] and www.ipcc.ch/pdf/assessment-report/ar4/syr/ar4_syr.pdf [accessed 17 August 2018].

29 *See* Glantz (1994b) *Op. Cit.* p. 223.

probability risk management framework is the most appropriate one for analysing, the link between climate change and extreme weather events, since it enables policymakers to better understand how risk is changing so that prevention and adaptation strategies can be prioritised".[30]

Understanding the environmental change dynamic process is realising that all environmental factors, whether natural and/or man-made (climate change, disasters, development, and environmental degradation), are interconnected and interdependent. This holistic view of environmental change is essential in the context of this book. For purposes of convenience, one uses the term environmental change and climate change interchangeably. The terms natural disaster and man-made disaster will also be used to the extent that they are enshrined in international instruments, even though one recognises they are misnomers.

2.2 The vulnerability token of environmental change

Environmental change impacts are unevenly distributed in the world. While the developed world is in a better position to cope with environmental changing conditions, least developed countries (LDCs)[31] are on the whole at risk and the most likely to be affected. Today, LDCs are and probably will continue in the future to engage in activities that are highly prone to environmental variations (agriculture and fishing). LDCs also suffer from economic dependency, high poverty rates, low education levels, and meagre financial resources and lack the corresponding institutional, human, and technical resources. Therefore, the challenges of environmental adaptation are higher for LDCs than for developed countries with adequate human capital and financial resources.

There are some geographical areas where the effects of environmental change are most acute, and it is here that the movement of people is/will be particularly felt: the Arctic, as predictions of global warming are high on ecosystems and human communities; Africa, because of the low level of adaptation capacity and high risk of predicted environmental impacts; and small islands,[32] because of the high exposure of population and infrastructure stemming from environmental factors, particularly in the Asian and African mega deltas, where populations are most at risk from sea level rise, flooding, and storms.[33]

30 *See* McAdam, J. (2012) "Climate Change, Forced Migration, and International Law" (Oxford University Press) p. 24.

31 LDCs are a group of 48 countries. This list is ***available from:*** http://unctad.org/en/Pages/ALDC/Least%20Developed%20Countries/UN-list-of-Least-Developed-Countries.aspx [accessed 21 July 2018].

32 The location of Small Island Developing States (SIDS) are namely, the Caribbean, the Pacific and the Atlantic, Indian Ocean, Mediterranean and South China ***available from:*** http://unohrlls.org/about-sids/ [accessed 21 July 2018].

33 *See* IPCC (2007) *Op. Cit.* Synthesis Report ***available from:*** www.ipcc.ch/publications_and_data/ar4/syr/en/mains6-2.html [accessed 12 June 2012] emphasising what systems and regions that are most at risk from the impacts of climate change; *See* U.N. Human Rights Council (UNHRC) (2008) "Resolution 7/23 Human Rights and Climate Change"

One can generally affirm that environmental change makes some areas of the globe geographically vulnerable.[34] Looking at the affected or most vulnerable areas can be useful, as it can provide a reference point as to the number of people who currently are affected or are likely to face displacement[35] stemming from environmental factors.

Attempts to define vulnerability abound, and there is no one definition of the term. Within legal scholarship, the concept has been defined as confusing,[36] complex,[37] vague,[38] and ambiguous.[39] The relationship between vulnerability and human rights is contested terrain.[40] However, the concept of vulnerability is important in the context of environmental change and human displacement. The concept of vulnerability can have a reflective use as a "starting point" in framing vulnerable areas where individuals are in need of legal protection.

(Preamble 28 March) *available from:* http://ap.ohchr.org/documents/E/HRC/resolutions/A_HRC_RES_7_23.pdf [accessed 12 June 2012]; Robinson, M. (2006) "Barbara Ward Lecture" Chatham House (London, 11 December): All human beings are born free and equal in dignity and rights. However [. . .] it is poor communities who are suffering most from the effects of climate change, and it is rich countries that are contributing to the problem [. . .] *available from:* http://pubs.iied.org/pdfs/G00101.pdf [accessed 17 August 2018]; McInerney-Lankford, S., Darrow, M. & Rajamani, L. (2011) "Human Rights and Climate Change: A Review of the International Legal Dimensions" (World Bank) p. 11.

34 *See* U.N. International Strategy for Disaster Risk Reduction (2004) "Living with Risk: A Global Review of Disaster Risk Reduction Initiatives" (United Nations) p. 36. Human vulnerability is now widely recognised as a major element of what turns a natural hazard (e.g. rainstorm) into a disaster with enormous consequences (such as a flood-related displacement situation). The UN's International Strategy for Disaster Risk Reduction expresses the concept of human vulnerability as a formula: "Risk = Hazard × Vulnerability", noting that "[t]he negative impact – the disaster – will depend on the characteristics, probability and intensity of the hazard, as well as the susceptibility of the exposed elements based on physical, social, economic and environmental conditions".

35 The term *displacement* in this context encompasses people who move involuntary and not from their own free will.

36 Solbakk, J. H. (2011) "Vulnerability: A Futile or Useful Principle in Healthcare Ethics?" in R. Chadwick, H. ten Have & E. M. Meslin (eds.) The Sage Handbook of Health Care Ethics: core and emerging issues (Sage Publications) p. 228, pp. 228–239.

37 *Ibid.*

38 Ruof, M. C. (2004) "Vulnerability, Vulnerable Populations, and Policy" 14 Kennedy Institute of Ethics Journal p. 411, pp. 411–425.

39 Fineman, M. (2008) "The Vulnerable Subject: Anchoring Equality in the Human Condition" 20 Yale Journal of Law and Feminism pp. 1–23.

40 The scholarly debate has progressively increased. See e.g. Bergoffen, D. (2011) "Contesting the Politics of Genocidal Rape: Affirming the Dignity of the Vulnerable Body" (Routledge); Chapman, A. R. & Carbonetti, B. (2011) "Human Rights Protections for Vulnerable and Disadvantages Groups: The Contributions of the U.N. Committee on Economic, Social and Cultural Rights" 33 Human Rights Quarterly pp. 682–732; Grear, A. (2010) "Redirecting Human Rights: Facing the Challenge of Corporate Legal Humanity" (Palgrave Macmillan); Turner, B. S. (2006) "Vulnerability and Human Rights" (Essays on Human Rights).

2.2.1 *Meaning(s) of vulnerability*

There is a central paradox attached to the concept of vulnerability because it relates both to the universal and the particular.[41] These features arise as a result of our embodiment.[42] In other words, as human beings, we are all vulnerable, but we experience this vulnerability in a unique, corporal way. The term's etymology derives from the Latin *vulnus*, which means "wound".[43] Unsurprisingly, harm and suffering are central features in most interpretations of vulnerability.[44] Neal gracefully summarises the literature:

> [V]ulnerability speaks to our universal capacity for suffering, in two ways. First, I am vulnerable because I depend upon the co-operation of others (including, importantly, the State) (. . .) Second, I am vulnerable because I am penetrable; I am permanently open and exposed to hurts and harms of various kinds.[45]

Essentially, vulnerability is a "relational" concept because people are manifestly dependent on the cooperation of others. This relational approach places "attention to the individual subject by placing him/her in social context".[46] This contextual approach to vulnerability is important in the analysis from both an environmental change and a human rights perspective.

(i) Vulnerability and environmental change

A primary meaning of vulnerability can often imply that human society is in a particularly endangered situation, is susceptible to being harmed, or is unable to cope with adverse factors of environmental change. In a secondary meaning, the concept relates to the sensitivity and the capacity of a system or society to adapt to environmental changing conditions. Both meanings do not exclude one another but are interactive and complementary.

41 Peroni, L. & Timmer A. (2013) "Vulnerable Groups: The Promise of an Emerging Concept in European Human Rights Convention Law" 11 International Journal of Constitutional Law 4 p. 1058, pp. 1056–1085.

42 Fineman (2008) *Op. Cit.* p. 9.

43 Turner (2006) *Op. Cit.*

44 Fineman, M. (2012) "Elderly as Vulnerable: Rethinking the Nature of Individual and Societal Responsibility" 20 The Elder Law Journal 1 pp. 71–112, p. 101. Recently, however, we can see a move towards a more positive understanding of vulnerability. Fineman describes the capacity of vulnerability as "it presents opportunities for innovation and growth, creativity, and fulfilment. It makes us reach out to others, form relationships, and build institutions".

45 Neal, M. (2012) "'Not Gods But Animals:' Human Dignity and Vulnerable Subjecthood" 33 Liverpool Law Review pp. 177–200, pp. 186–187.

46 Fineman (2008) *Op. Cit.* p. 13.

O'Brien *et al.* have attempted to conceptualise the meaning of vulnerability to environmental changing conditions.[47] One of the key outcomes from their studies is that vulnerability is asymmetrically distributed across and within countries, and some individuals or groups (children, older people, disabled people, and women, among others) are likely to be disproportionally affected by environmental change. In addition, they have found that vulnerability is also influenced by a complex intermix of social, economic, political, and environmental factors that operate at different levels and influence vulnerability.

The 2011 IPCC Third Assessment Report defines vulnerability as

> the degree to which a system is susceptible to, or unable to cope with, adverse effects of climate change, including climate variability and extremes. Vulnerability is a function of the character, magnitude and rate of climate change, and the degree to which a system is exposed, along with its sensitivity and adaptive capacity.[48]

Vulnerability can generally be conceptualised as a juggling result of levels of exposure, sensitivity, and the adaptive capacity of a system/society to environmental change. Adger reviews the development of diverse conventional approaches of vulnerability to environmental change and frames these elements as "the state of susceptibility of harm from exposure to stresses associated with environmental and social change and from the absence of capacity to adapt".[49] In other words, vulnerability is a result of ***exposure*** – the extent to which a system/society experiences environmental or socio-political stress (their intensity, duration, rate of recurrence, and geographical scope of the hazard); ***sensitivity*** – the degree to which it is modified or affected by those impacts; and ***adaptive capacity***[50] – its coping capacity or capacity to respond[51]

47 *See* O'Brien, K. *et al.* (2008) "Disaster Risk Reduction, Climate Change Adaptation and Human Security: A Commissioned Report for the Norwegian Ministry of Foreign Affairs" (University of Oslo).

48 IPCC (2001) "Third Assessment Report: Climate Change 2001: Impacts, Adaptation and Vulnerability" ***available from:*** www.preventionweb.net/files/8387_wg2TARfrontmatter1.pdf [accessed 17 August 2018].

49 Adger, W. N. (2006) "Vulnerability" 16 Global Environmental Change p. 268, pp. 268–281.

50 IPCC (2007) "Fourth Assessment Report Climate Change 2007: Working Group II: Impacts, Adaptation and Vulnerability" ***available from:*** www.ipcc.ch/publications_and_data/ar4/wg2/en/contents.html [accessed 17 August 2018]. The IPCC defines adaptive capacity as "the ability of a system to adjust to climate change (including climate variability and extremes), to moderate potential damages, to take advantages of opportunities or to cope with the consequences". ; Adger (2006) *Op. Cit.* defines adaptive capacity as "the ability of a system to evolve in order to accommodate environmental hazards or policy change and to expand the range of variability with which it can cope".

51 Capacity to respond means the institutional framework and measures such as urban and environmental planning, human capacity, and the expertise of local authorities. Other

to environmental change (accommodation of human and physical infrastructures and policy change).[52]

The adaptive capacity is not only dependent on development levels but also on other important determinants, such as social cohesion and governance.[53] For example, "[i]n some situations, the ability to migrate will be part of the adaptive capacity, and migration itself will be an adaptation strategy. In other cases, arguably more frequent, migration will be the result of an adaptive capacity unable to cope with climate impacts in situ".[54] This is why it is important to refer to vulnerability from a relational or contextual perspective. Contextual vulnerability means looking holistically at all the vulnerability elements in a context-specific manner; i.e. that variations exist across (those geographical areas most at risk to the impacts of environmental change), between (LDCs, SIDS, and African states) and within (particularly vulnerable communities and groups, including women, children, and older people who need special attention) regions and countries from community to community and over time. While there will certainly be broad social, economic, political, and environmental conditions that will impact systems or societies (exposure, sensitivity, and adaptive capacity), these elements are/will be exhibited at the individual and community level in different ways.

Vulnerability is not easily measured, and it is not the intention to do it here, as it is something beyond the scope of this book. But generally, "[a] vulnerability assessment identifies who and what is exposed and sensitive to change. A vulnerability assessment starts by considering the factors that make people susceptible to harm, i.e. access to natural and financial resources; ability to self-protect; support networks and so on".[55] Reducing vulnerability to a quantifiable metric does diminish its impact and hides its complexity. The World Bank indicates the "hotspot countries"; i.e. it lists in a map countries that have significant levels of vulnerability to two or more natural hazards. Vulnerability is expressed as "high" (when 50% GDP or more is at risk) or

measures can include socio-political ones such as public awareness, information and participation, and education.

52 Smit, B. & Wandel, J. (2006) "Adaptation, Adaptive Capacity and Vulnerability" 16 Global Environmental Change p. 286, pp. 282–292. These authors do not distinguish between exposure and sensitivity. They argue that "exposure and sensitivity are almost inseparable properties of a system (or community) and are dependent on the interaction between the characteristics of the system and on the attributes of the climate stimulus".

53 *See generally*, Tubiana, L., Gemenne, F. & Magnan, A. (2010) "Anticiper Pour s'Adapter. Le Nouvel Enjeu du Changement Climatique" (Pearson).

54 Asian Development Bank (2012) "Addressing Climate Change and Migration in Asia and the Pacific" (Asian Development Bank) p. 12.

55 Tompkins, E. *et al.* (2005) "Surviving Climate Change in Small Islands: A Guidebook" (Tyndall Centre for Climate Change Research) p. 101.

"medium" (when 30% to 50% GDP is at risk).[56] Because the map uses metrics it tells us little about contextual vulnerability. When one look at these metrics, one needs to apply a contextual vulnerability lens. In other words, within the context of environmental change, some of the vulnerability determinants are known, but some will not be completely known *a priori*. Vulnerability applied to environmental change needs to deal with this dichotomy of known and unknown determinants. This view allows us to frame vulnerable areas where people are/can be potentially displaced by environmental stressors that need legal protection contemplation.

(ii) Vulnerability and human rights

Within the legal sphere, in particular within human rights law, scholars have challenged the concept of vulnerability.[57] Peroni and Timmer noted the tension that exists between group-based and universality-based deployment of vulnerability. This seems due to the puzzling nature of the concept. The authors acknowledge that while the courts[58] have generally used the term to analyse specific populations (capturing the particular), other scholars have proposed to use vulnerability as a "universal, inevitable, enduring aspect of the human condition"[59] (capturing the universal) and suggest that the adequate role of the state is to be actively responsive to this. They argue:

> there is no inherent impediment reconciling these two approaches on a conceptual level – on the contrary that would fit the concept's paradoxical nature as well. When we asked a Strasbourg judge about the Court's reasoning, he replied: "All applicants are vulnerable, but some are more vulnerable than others." The judge neatly merged the universal approach with the group-based approach.[60]

56 Dilley, M. *et al.* (2005) "Natural Disasters Hotspots, a Global Risk Analysis" Disasters Management Series (Vol. 5 World Bank) *available from:* http://documents.worldbank.org/curated/en/621711468175150317/Natural-disaster-hotspots-A-global-risk-analysis [accessed 17 August 2018].

57 Despite the human rights commitment to protecting fundamental rights of vulnerable and disadvantaged individuals or groups, human rights lacks a central theory or framework for doing so. There are no general criteria established for identifying vulnerable or disadvantaged populations, nor is there an agreed definition of vulnerability or a standard list of such groups.

58 Peroni & Timmer (2013) *Op. Cit.* The authors focus their analysis on the case law of the European Court of Human Rights.

59 Fineman (2008) *Op. Cit.* p. 8.

60 Peroni & Timmer (2013) *Op. Cit.* p. 1060.

Vulnerability in human rights law is intimately related to protection.[61] Ever since the *Chapman v United Kingdom*[62] judgement, the Strasbourg court, for example, broadened and refined the content and scope of group vulnerability. This is of particular importance for those forcibly displaced by environmental factors. Based on a close reading of the case law on the concept of group vulnerability as used by the ECtHR, Peroni and Timmer located three main characteristics: *relational*, *particular*, and *harm-based.*

First, group vulnerability is *relational.* In other words, the court tends to locate vulnerability not in the individual alone but rather in the "wider social circumstances".[63] Vulnerability is context-specific and shaped by certain social, historical, and institutional forces, including political and environmental forces. The IPCC has been conclusive in establishing which areas of the world will be most affected by the impacts of environmental change. The U.N. General Assembly has also emphasised the need for the international community to maintain its focus beyond emergency relief and to support medium- and long-term rehabilitation, reconstruction and risk reduction, and stresses the importance of implementing and adapting long-term programmes related to the eradication of poverty, sustainable development and disaster risk reduction management in the most vulnerable regions, particularly in developing countries prone to natural disasters.[64] People living in these areas are particularly vulnerable to environmental stresses and are more and more recognisable in society as in need of protection. The inherent, common, immutable characteristic is one that unites them in a particular territory and in a particular society, making them predominantly

61 Within the human rights framework, the commitment to the protection of fundamental rights of the most vulnerable and disadvantage populations has been translated in various forms in the United Nations system. For example, specialised human rights instruments have been established, including the Convention on the Rights of Persons with Disabilities (CRPD), adopted on 13 December 2006, in force since 3 May 2008, 2515 UNTA 3; Convention on the Elimination of All Forms of Racial Discrimination (CERD), adopted on 21 December 1965, in force since 4 January 1969, 660 UNTS 195; Convention on the Elimination of all forms of Discrimination Against Women (CEDAW), adopted on 18 December 1979, in force since 3 September 1981, 1249 UNTS 14; Convention on the Rights of the Child (CRC), adopted on 20 November 1989, in force since 2 September 1990, 1577 UNTS 3; Convention on the Protection of All Migrant Workers and Members of Their Families (Migrant Workers Convention), adopted on 18 December 1990, in force since 1 July 2003, 2220 UNTS 3. Other mechanisms include the appointment of special rapporteurs and independent experts on topics such as child prostitution, child pornography, violence against women, torture and other inhuman and degrading punishment, contemporary forms of slavery, trafficking in persons, human rights of migrants, human rights and extreme poverty, among others.

62 ECtHR, *Chapman v United Kingdom*, Application No. 27238/95 (18 January 2001) paras. 73, 93, 96.

63 This will also be discussed in Chapter 5.

64 U.N. General Assembly (2005) "Strengthening of the coordination of humanitarian and disaster relief assistance of the United Nations, including special economic assistance" U.N. Doc. A/RES/59/279 (28 January 2005).

vulnerable to external environmental impacts. It is not a single event that affects a certain part of society more strongly and that creates a need of protection but the shared past, current circumstances, and even predictions of ongoing environmental experiences that unite them and make them vulnerable.

Second, both authors acknowledge that that vulnerability may be *particular*. This understanding does not contradict the above-mentioned universal account of vulnerability. It is claimed that there are particular groups such as women, children, older people, disabled people, and indigenous populations including "the poor", who, because they are marginalised by society, will suffer the most from the impacts of environmental change. "In fact, the court tends to talk of 'particular social groups' rather than just 'vulnerable groups'. The inclusion of the word 'particularly' underlines the idea that people belonging to these groups are simply more vulnerable than others".[65] The World Disasters Report 2007, which focused on discrimination in emergency disaster situations, makes it clear that there are groups (minorities such as Roma, older people, disabled people, and women) who are mostly at risk not only because of already-embedded discrimination by society but also by governments as well as by aid agencies, even if this can be unintentional.[66] Figures from the Pakistan flooding in 2010 also noted that more than seven million people were affected, especially in rural areas. The province of Sindh was the hardest hit; 49% of displaced persons were women. Reports state that women in remote areas experienced many challenges, including a lack of access to food, health services, and clean water.[67]

Finally, as previously highlighted, vulnerability has centred its gravity on *harm*. This has been confirmed by the court's formulation of vulnerability in particular of vulnerable groups.[68] Most recently, the understanding of the nature of harm has been linked to social disadvantage and material deprivation in the context of Articles 3 and 8 of the ECHR. Foster has argued that being poor makes one vulnerable to persecutory types of harm.[69] Being poor can be an immutable state if governments do not take action or if they deliberately bar individuals from rising above their poverty. States must enable change and offer alternatives, and these must be available not only at a theoretical level. The Committee on Economic Social and Cultural Rights (CESCR) has noted that women and girls unequally bear the burden of poverty, and children raised in poverty are

65 Peroni & Timmer (2013) *Op. Cit.* p. 1064.

66 International Federation of the Red Cross and Red Crescent Societies (2007) "World Disasters Report: Focus on Discrimination" (International Federation of Red Cross and Red Crescent Societies) p. 12; *See also* International Federation of the Red Cross and Red Crescent Societies (2012) "World Disasters Report: Focus on Forced Migration and Displacement" (International Federation of Red Cross and Red Crescent Societies).

67 Internal Displacement Monitoring Centre (IDMC) (2011) "Briefing Paper on Flood-Displaced Women in Sindh Province, Pakistan" Norwegian Refugee Council p. 6.

68 Peroni & Timmer (2013) *Op. Cit.* pp. 1064–1065.

69 Foster, M. (2007) "International Refugee Law and Socio-Economic Rights Refuge from Deprivation" (Cambridge Studies in International and Comparative Law) pp. 308–310.

frequently permanently deprived.[70] A number of jurisdictions have also acknowledged that the poor may constitute a particularly vulnerable group,[71] even though one could argue that being poor is neither innate nor unchangeable.

Environmental disasters and climate change do, however, not only create new situations of poverty but exacerbate the endemic structural poverty problem in developing countries.[72] The combination of different factors, such as age or gender, together with being poor and the human exposures adjacent to environmental change, can put an individual in a particularly vulnerable situation at a "disproportionate risk of harm". Thus, vulnerability is an especially dynamic concept that encompasses this inherent "universal, inevitable, enduring aspect of the human condition"[73] and also transcends it.

(iii) Vulnerability layers

This book does not aim to use vulnerability as a victimising or stigmatising (negative) or even paternalistic (imposing protection and denying agency) label. The approach is rather to take into account the different "vulnerability layers".[74] The focus is on the various circumstances that render those displaced by environmental factors vulnerable. In other words, the usage of vulnerability as a reflective concept enables us to expose those vulnerable areas affected by environmental change, where people's human rights are at risk and, therefore, in need of legal protection contemplation. Whereas all of us are generally vulnerable to the effects of environmental change (first vulnerability layer), there are *localised vulnerabilities* of collective entities that are obvious (second vulnerability layer). Moreover, that vulnerability may also be a result of the characteristics of a person including age, sex or group (third vulnerability layer), the circumstances or the context, and their capacity to resist and/or recover from environmental hazards

70 CESCR (2001) "Substantive Issues Arising in the Implementation of the International Covenant on Economic Social and Cultural Rights" ESC Res E/C. 12/2001/10, UN ESCOR, 25th session, Agenda Item 5, para. 4 and 5, U.N. Doc. E/C. 12/2001/10 (2001).

71 In Canada, for example, in *Sinora v Minister of Employment and Immigration* [1993] FCJ No. 725, the Federal Court of Appeal stated that the applicant, a national from Haiti, was claiming refugee status on the basis of a particular social group: "the poor". Other decisions have acknowledged the "poor campesinos" of El Savador WBT (Re), No V98-00787, [1997] CRDD No 119, 4 June 1999 and poor young women from the former Soviet Union recruited for the purposes of the international sex trade YCK (Re), No. V95-02904, [1997] CRDD No 26, 26 November 1997 as members of a particular social group.

72 U.N. Human Rights Commission (2011) "Report of the Expert Seminar on Human Rights and Extreme Poverty" U.N. Doc. E/CN.4/2001/54Add.1 (7–10 February) para. 20.

73 Fineman (2008) *Op. Cit.* p. 8.

74 Luna, F. (2009) "Elucidating the Concept of Vulnerability: Layers Not Labels" 2 The International Journal of Feminist Approaches to Bioethics 1 pp. 121–139. The concept is taken from the author.

(*fourth vulnerability layer*). The more layers of vulnerability one has, the more vulnerable one will be to environmental changing conditions and (potential) forced displacement.

To better understand vulnerability in general and environmental displacement in particular, it is relevant to explore the drivers of displacement. The work carried out by Black and his colleagues under the Foresight study[75] offers a conceptual framework to comprehend human mobility in the context of displacement. They outline five main factors that influence human mobility: economic, social, political, demographic, and environmental. Labour market imbalances and financial and economic crises allied with labour market opportunities may lead to population movement. At the same time, the existence of family ties in a particular geographical area and the urge to pursue and obtain a better education may also constitute an incentive to migrate. Other interrelated factors, such as age, sex, education, wealth, marital status, ethnicity, religion, and language, may interfere with people-related mobility. The urge to move can also be a consequence of direct discrimination or persecution, governance factors, conflict and security situations, direct coercion, or even policy incentives. With regard to environmental factors, they acknowledge that exposure to hazards such as floods and earthquakes may also lead to pronounced displacement situations. This is because ecosystem services, such as land productivity, habitability, and food, energy, and water security, may be compromised as a result of environmental stressors. In some areas of the globe, there are particular geographical areas and groups of the population that have a special attachment to their land, sea, and forest and thus are vulnerable to variations that occur in these.

Indeed, ecosystems provide a number of services to society from products (e.g. food, fuel, wood, and fibre) and legislation (e.g. climate change, flood regulation) to cultural (e.g. aesthetic, education, recreation) advantages.[76] The United Nations Millennium Ecosystems Assessment outlines direct "push factors" (climate change, overexploitation of natural resources, land transformation that leads to livelihood change, pollution, disease outspread and plague species) and indirect "pull factors" (economic inequalities, socio-political instability, and religious, cultural, technological, and demographic differential factors) that intermingle with each other, establishing the types of services they are able to provide.[77] When ecosystems are curtailed, the provision of services becomes

75 The Government Office for Science (2011) "Foresight: Migration and Global Environmental Change (2011) Final Project Report" (The Government Office for Science, United Kingdom) *available from:* www.gov.uk/government/publications/migration-and-global-environmental-change-future-challenges-and-opportunities [accessed 17 August 2018]. *See also* for a summary Black, R. *et al.* (2011) "The Effect of Environmental Change on Human Migration" 21 Global Environmental Change pp. S3–S11.

76 Millennium Ecosystem Assessment (2005) "Ecosystems and Human Well-Being: Current State and Trends" (Vol. 1 Island Press) p. 28.

77 *Ibid.* The gap between the North and South of the world is becoming larger in income levels and life expectancy. Whereas the life expectancy in the developed world is 78 years, in the developing world it is 48.

compromised, which can serve as a (push and pull) *trigger* for forced displacement.

There are a number of displacement settings or scenarios that can be devised, depending on the types and degrees of environmental change that are likely to trigger human movement: internally (within one's country) or externally (across the border). These movements can be of an immediate or of a mediate nature and can involve only a few individuals or large crowds. These are people who would not have moved if the environment was not damaged or destroyed by gradual environmental degradation (due to climate change and the overexploitation of natural resources), sudden environmental disruption (together with natural and technological disasters), and calculated damage of the environment.[78] Many other scenario framings are feasible.

The terms *push* and *pull* do not undermine or underestimate the role of agency. While acknowledging the multicausality of displacement, the distinction serves two purposes. First, it serves to acknowledge that environmental stressors over a period of time will be more exacerbated for the environmental driver and, second, that environmental factors may constitute an autonomous force of displacement where people are forced to leave by leaving them with a "no choice option".

2.3 Environmental displacement as a human rights issue

The above analysis shows that the actual and potential impacts of environmental change makes visible a wide range of human rights-related challenges, forced human displacement[79] being the most notable, as a reactive measure.[80] The lack of "adaptive capacity" or "vulnerability" of the least developed countries

78 Typologies are adapted from De Moor, N. & Cliquet, A. (2009) "Environmental Displacement: A New Challenge for European Migration Policy" Proceedings of Protecting People in Conflict and Crisis: Responding to the Challenges of a Changing World p. 3 *available from:* https://biblio.ugent.be/input/download?func=downloadFile&recordOId=761954&fileOId=784741 [accessed 20 April 2013]; Kälin, W. (2008) "The Climate Change-Displacement Nexus Representative of the Secretary General on the Human Rights of Internally Displaced Persons, Panel on Disaster Risk Reduction and Preparedness: Addressing the Humanitarian Consequences of Natural Disasters" ECOSOC Humanitarian Affairs Segment (16 July) *available from:* www.brookings.edu/speeches/2008/0716_climate_change_kalin.aspx [accessed 20 April 2013].

79 *See generally*, International Council on Human Rights Policy (ICHRP) (2008) "Climate Change and Human Rights: A Rough Guide" (ICHRP).

80 Office of the High Representative for the Least Developed Countries, Landlocked Developing Countries and Small Island Developing States (UN-OHRLLS) (2009) "The Impact of Climate Change on the Development Prospect of Least Developed Countries and Small Islands Developing States" *available from:* www.unohrlls.org/UserFiles/File/LDC%20Documents/The%20impact%20of%20CC%20on%20LDCs%20and%20SIDS%20for%20web.pdf p. 5 [accessed 17 August 2018]. According to the UN-OHRLLS, around 860 million people in the developing world and SIDS will be afflicted by environmental change and many will become "environmental refugees".

(especially of particular groups such as women, children, disabled people, indigenous populations, and older people) will contribute to the snowball effects of actual and predictive trends of human displacement. In this context, the causality argument has to be revisited.

Rather than focusing on causality (what drives displacement), the focus should rather be on the rights of the environmentally displaced and *inter alia* the protection obligations of states, exploring the (re)interpretation or revision of current international protection structures to that effect in a proactive and reactive manner. The emphasis on the causality of movement has blurred the essential core of forced environmental displacement, i.e. people's human rights. Focusing too much on causality can be a barrier to research, but most importantly it can be seen as an impediment to helping, to devising legal protection mechanisms, or to outlining policy strategies to protect those who are facing displacement situations as a result of environmental factors. From this perspective, environmental displacement needs to be approached as a human rights issue.

To situate environmental displacement within the human rights realm, it is important to highlight that it is only after the 1980s that human displacement *per se* began to be recognised as a human rights issues by scholars, the United Nations, and non-governmental organisations. Until then, the forced movement of people was largely treated in a reactive manner, focusing on humanitarian aid and technical assistance for those displaced.[81] The shift from a charity approach to a human rights-based approach was gradually implemented during the 1980s and 1990s. Scholars and the international community at large, including non-governmental organisations, started to focus on addressing the "root causes" of displacement and to embrace a more human rights-based approach, increasingly integrating both proactive and reactive views to assistance and protection in their discourses.[82]

It is true, however, that issues of legal protection of those displaced have remained focused on specific types or forms of displacement (e.g. displacement of indigenous populations, development-induced displacement, internal displacement, forced relocation, mass expulsion, and population transfer, among others), and this can lead to situations of a "potential waste of resources and a serious danger of conflicting standards being developed".[83] Nevertheless, focusing on a type of displacement from environmental change can be particularly useful in this context, paving the way to understanding the complexity of environmental

81 *See* Morel, M. (2014) "The Right Not to Be Displaced under International Law" (Intersentia) p. 22.

82 *See* Stavropoulou, M. (1994) "The Right Not to Be Displaced" 9 The American University Journal of International Law and Policy 3 pp. 706–717, pp. 689–749. The author highlights various reports, studies, and statements by the U.N. bodies as well as scholarly articles addressing the "root causes" of displacement and the increasing emphasis on a human rights-based perspective.

83 Stavropoulou, M. (1998) "Displacement and Human Rights: Reflections on UN Practice" 20 Human Rights Quarterly 3 p. 520, pp. 515–554.

displacement per se and to developing an adequate legal protection framework, including the search for durable solutions.

2.3.1 A rights-based approach to environmental displacement

What might be gained from focusing on a human rights framework in the context of environmental displacement? Perhaps one of the most logical but sometimes overlooked features of human rights standards is that it allows us to speak of people as humans – i.e. as individuals, as members of a community, or as families – not as numbers, units, or percentages. This "is far more likely to produce sensible responses to vexing yet unavoidable dilemmas, such as those relating to social well-being, family reunification, and the best interest of future generations".[84] Departing from this perspective permits governments and the international community to advance common agendas prioritising "common sense" and "common interests".

Furthermore, rights-based approaches assert the idea that the human person is also a rights holder (this includes a more holistic perspective of human beings in terms of their civil, political, social, economic, and cultural roles) who is empowered to claim rights against the duty-bearers. In other words, it considers that individuals are entitled to – and not merely morally – assistance and protection when required. "Human rights thus go beyond the notion of physical needs by triggering obligations and responsibilities, identifying duty-bearers and ensuring accountability".[85] Human rights-based approaches look at the whole picture, not only addressing the immediate causes of displacement but also addressing them in a more structural manner, focusing on people's needs, problems, and potentials.[86]

From this perspective, a rights-based approach in the context of displacement is characterised by a relationship between the state and the individual. This relationship is always a power-imbalanced one because the state will always be a strong party against a weak individual who is in need of protection. A rights-based approach in the context of environmental displacement seems to be the most useful approach for a number of reasons.

Overall, the focus on international human rights law may fill a gap where protection standards are currently missing because it can be a reference point for new laws and even help with the harmonisation of regional and national standards. International human rights law outlines "minimum standards of treatment" that must be afforded to every human being. The substantive content of this "minimum core" is constantly being elaborated, in particular by the

84 Ho & Loucky (2012) *Op. Cit.* p. 10.
85 Morel (2014) *Op. Cit.* p. 23.
86 Boesen, J. & Martin, T. (2007) "Applying a Rights-Based Approach: An Inspirational Guide for Civil Society" (Danish Institute for Human Rights) p. 10.

(quasi) judicial decisions of regional human rights courts and under the CESCR in a way that is adapted to national conditions and resource constraints.[87]

The international human rights legal framework displays a permanent concern for discrimination and the vulnerability of individuals whose rights are most at risk. While there is no specific human rights instrument concerning environmental displacement per se, the international human rights regime includes numerous treaties protecting the rights of individuals and groups who may be vulnerable to the adverse impacts of environmental change, including women, children, indigenous peoples, older people, and disabled people, among others. International human rights legal standards help establish normative foundations and essential guarantees for active and meaningful participation processes, including ensuring that those rights affected or potentially affected by environmental change play a role in setting national and international mitigation targets and policies and claim ownership of the design and implementation of adaptation initiatives.[88]

International human rights law also enables the creation of a universal legal framework with legally binding obligations for states and enforceable rights for individuals, thus offering clear guidelines for all stakeholders involved in displacement in general and environmental displacement in particular. Furthermore, it allows the creation of common conceptual criteria or frameworks, both to measure states' obligations and, when they do not respect their obligations, to allow individuals to hold them accountable (redress and reparation) before official institutions. The universality of human rights means that even if there are changes with a state's political landscape, human rights remain intact and apply to everyone and everyone should enjoy their protection. Importantly, a human rights-based approach helps "foster an inclusive, unifying model"[89] based on common human rights values and sometimes found on international standards

87 CESCR (1990) General Comment No. 3: The Nature of State Parties Obligations U.N. Doc. E/C.3/1991/3 (14 December). Under the ICESCR, there is an immediate obligation to "take steps" (concrete, deliberate, and targeted) that is not dependent upon available resources to meet the obligations enshrined in the covenant. The "minimum core" has been defined by the CESCR as immediate obligations at a minimum level to meet people's survival needs ("essential minimum levels"). Beyond this threshold, the rights in the ICESCR are to be realised progressively according to national resources and tailored standards. For illustrations on the "minimum core content" *see* CESCR (1999) "General Comment No. 12: The Right to Adequate Food U. N." Doc. E/C.12/1999/5 (12 May); CESCR (2000) "General Comment No. 14: The Right to the Highest Attainable Standard of Health U.N." Doc. E/C.12/2000/4 (11 August).

88 McInerney, Darrow & Rajamni (2011) *Op. Cit.* p. 30.

89 *See* Morel (2014) *Op. Cit.* pp. 24–25; Centre for Housing Rights and Evictions & The National Law Centre on Homelessness and Poverty (2007) "Housing Rights for All: Promoting and Defending Housing Rights in the United States" (The National Law Centre on Homelessness and Poverty) pp. 15, 16, 18; Centre for Housing Rights and Evictions (2007) "Fair Play for Housing Rights: Mega Events, Olympic Games and Housing Rights" (Centre for Housing Rights and Evictions) p. 30.

or other regional or national protection standards (which may have potential international replication).

Notwithstanding the argumentation in favour of a human rights-based approach to environmental displacement, there may be some inherent challenges, in particular from an implementation point of view. First, states may not have incorporated international human rights standards into their national legislation or may even lack an operative judicial system. In such cases individuals may not be aware of their rights and entitlements under international legal standards; this can be due to a lack of information per se but also a lack of financial means to approach judicial institutions at the international or even regional levels. Furthermore, the international system for supervising and implementing human rights is intrinsically restricted by national sovereignty. Therefore, some authors assert the weakness of legal approaches in general and rights-based approaches in particular: "[t]he utilisation of legal approaches to address fundamental disparities of political and economic power within and between states, let alone redressing these, represent a frustrating, often futile and in many countries a dangerous undertaking".[90] Employing a broader argument, Posner[91] contends that human rights in general are too ambitious, utopian, and vague, arguing in favour of a replacement of the unenforceable human rights treaty model to a charity-driven foreign aid model for poverty reduction and with quantifiable indicators. While all outlined perspectives may be seen as valid, it seems that there is a fundamental misunderstanding in that a rights-based approach should ideally not be disenfranchised from other political and social approaches. In this context, protection for the environmentally displaced should be seen through a "lens of combined forces". This study highlights the value of one of those forces – the human rights perspective – without necessarily disregarding the other political, social, and even moral forces. While the law, in particular international human rights law, may be weak or insufficient to tackle the issue of environmental displacement, the reasoned value of human rights previously highlighted is of unequivocal importance.

The issue of environmental displacement is not merely a charity or humanitarian problem and needs, therefore, to be discussed within this wider human rights context. Consequently, an analysis of the current mechanisms of protection or what they can offer (either through interpretation or revision) for the environmentally displaced must be seen from this human rights prism. The International Law Commission (ILC)[92] synthesises this idea by vividly saying:

90 Leckie, S. (1995) "When Push Comes to Shove: Forced Evictions and Human Rights" (Habitat International Coalition) pp. 35–36.

91 Posner, E. A. (2014) "The Twilight of Human Rights Law" (Oxford University Press).

92 The International Law Commission (ILC) is a body of experts established by the United Nations General Assembly in 1948 for the promotion of the progressive development of international law and its codification *available from:* http://legal.un.org/ilc/ilcintro.htm [accessed 17 August 2018].

> a rights-based approach deals with situations ***not simply in terms of human needs***, but in terms of ***society's obligations to respond*** to the inalienable rights of individuals, empowers them to demand justice as a right, not as a charity, and gives communities a moral basis from which to claim international assistance when needed.[93]
>
> (emphasis added)

2.4 A holistic approach to protection: pre-in-post displacement phases

When supporting a rights-based approach to the protection of environmentally displaced persons, the concept of protection gains centre stage. The Oxford Dictionaries online defines protection as "The action of protecting someone or something; the fact or condition of being protected; shelter, defence, or preservation from harm, danger, damage, etc.; guardianship, care; patronage".[94] Interestingly, the term embodies a holistic meaning, encompassing not only the provision of physical security to an individual and his or her environment but also the prevention from harm. The term is not defined in any international or regional refugee or human rights instrument. Protection itself is a concept that has various subjacent meanings from active to passive protection, to legal protection, physical protection, and so on.[95]

For this reason, some argue that it is a word of art.[96] When it comes to the protection of persons displaced by environmental factors, this may lead to developing another type of "specialized conceptualization of protection".[97]

Part of the problem of dealing with environmental displacement is the conceptualisation of protection. Generally, within the legal realm, protection is a recognised responsibility of states towards their citizens. Governments are responsible for the human rights of their citizens as part of the essence of statehood.[98] When states are unwilling or unable to provide protection, international responsibility arises to protect vulnerable individuals. This responsibility is codified in international law (in particular international humanitarian law, international

93 ILC (2008) "Preliminary Report on the Protection of Persons in the Event of Disasters by Mr Eduardo Valencia-Ospina, Special Rapporteur" 60th Session, UN Doc A/CN.4/598 (5 May) para. 174.

94 Oxford English Dictionaries Online (2013) *available from:* www.oxforddictionaries.com/definition/english/protection?q=protection [accessed 17 August 2018].

95 Phuong, V. (2004) "International Protection of Internally Displaced Persons" (Cambridge University Press) p. 11.

96 Goodwin-Gill, G. S. (1989) "The Language of Protection" 1 International Journal of Refugee Law 1 p. 6, pp. 6–19.

97 International Law Commission (2007) "Protection of Persons in the Event of Disasters" ILC U.N. Doc. A/CN.4/590 (11 December) p. 149.

98 However, protection can also be provided by other non-state actors including international organisations controlling the state or a substantial part of its territory or even private enterprises operating in a territory with the state's consent.

human rights law, and refugee law). From an institutional level, for example, no international body currently exists with a specific mandate to protect the environmentally displaced. The two main international organisations dealing with (forced) displacement/migration, the UNHCR[99] and the IOM,[100] in theory have different functions and focuses, but in practice both organisations have raised the issue of environmental displacement, contributing to their recognition in wider international fora. Organisations like the UNHCR have been crucial, for example, in providing humanitarian assistance in cases of displacement caused by environmental disasters.

Paradoxically, although international law makes reference to protection, the contours of its definition are not clear. For this reason, it is interesting to look at Article 8 of the UNHCR statute[101] and Principle 1 of the Guiding Principles on Internal Displacement (GPID).[102]

The first lists what activities should be carried out to promote protection. While the UNHCR has claimed that people displaced by environmental factors are not within the remit of their mandate, it has been at the forefront of promoting protection for them and highlighting a much-needed government intervention. In comparison, the second articulates what protection potentially entails: full equality, the same rights and freedoms under international and domestic law, and non-discrimination in the enjoyment of any rights and freedoms as do other persons in their country. In reality, this principle does not clarify what protection is, but it seeks holistically to enunciate standards of protection for each stage of displacement.[103] While the GPID are laid down in a non-legal (soft law) instrument, they reflect and are consistent with existing human rights and humanitarian law instruments (and by analogy refugee law), which are binding.[104]

The GPID cover situations of those who are forcibly displaced but have not crossed international borders. However, there is no impediment to re-articulating

99 *See* Loescher, G., Betts, A. & Milner, J. (2008) "The Politics and Practice of Refugee Protection in the Twenty-First Century" (Routledge). The main functions of the UNHCR are the protection of the rights of refugees, the provision of material assistance, and the search for durable solutions.

100 The International Organisation for Migration is an intergovernmental organisation to promote worldwide humane and orderly migration by providing services and advice to governments and migrants ***available from:*** www.iom.int [accessed 17 August 2018].

101 *See* U.N. General Assembly (1950) "Statute of the Office of the United Nations High Commissioner for Refugees" U.N. Doc. A/RES/428(V) (14 December) Article 8.

102 Guiding Principles on Internal Displacement (GPID) (1998) U.N. Doc. E/CN.4/1998/53/Add.2 (22 July) "Principle 1".

103 Phuong (2004) *Op. Cit.* p. 119.

104 *See* Kälin, W. (2000) "Guiding Principles on Internal Displacement: Annotations" Studies in Transnational Legal Policy No. 38 (ASIL & The Brookings Institution). A detailed legal analysis of the principles finds that many have been modelled on the text of human rights and humanitarian law provisions and then tailored to the specific needs of the internally displaced (examples include GPID, Principles 12, 14, 17, 20).

this logical framework to the cross-border environmental displacement context. This is because the GPID look at displacement as a process, taking a holistic stock to what protection entails before, during, and after displacement.

In the pre-displacement phase, the GPID look at protection as prevention from displacement, ensuring that:

> All authorities and international actors *shall* respect for their obligations under international law, including human rights and humanitarian law, in all circumstances, so as to *prevent and avoid conditions* that might lead to the displacement of persons.
>
> (Principle 5 GPID; emphasis added)

The GPID go on to affirm that states' duties entail the respect for the right not to be displaced by avoiding carrying out arbitrary displacement as well as the duty to protect people from particular circumstances, such as natural or human-made disasters (Principle 6 (1) (2 d)). In this context, states might consider the development of new protection statuses. This may include, for example, fostering labour migration as a legitimate strategy to prevent environmental displacement. The GPID do foresee that, in some cases, displacement of the population (e.g. through evacuation) might be permissible, but this must be seen as a last resort measure when all alternatives have been explored to avoid displacement altogether (Principle 7 (1)). Evacuation must be seen as a temporary solution and adhere to adequate procedural standards; it is never to be carried out in a way that violates the rights to life, dignity, liberty, and security of those affected (Principle 6 (3); Principle 7 (2) (3); Principle 8). This is a critical phase in the protection process of environmental displacement, as it requires considerable political will and resources to protect individuals and the environment.

In the subsequent stages of displacement, the GPID look at protection after displacement occurs, whether internally or by extension cross-border environmentally displaced. In the context of this study, protection relates to the individual's status and stay in the host country but also to their rights and entitlements. For those who cross an international border due to environmental stressors, the role of international refugee law is put into the equation. Emphasis may be further placed on existing regional complementary protection standards and the protection of human rights (not only civil and political but also economic and social rights).[105]

Interestingly, the framework also highlights that humanitarian assistance in case of environmental stressors must be carried out in accordance with the principles of humanity and impartiality and without discrimination.[106] This

105 Examples include: GPID, Principle 10 right to life; Principle 11 right to dignity and physical, mental, and moral integrity; Principle 12 right to liberty and security; Principle 14 right to freedom of movement; Principle 17 right to respect of his or her family life; Principle 18 right to an adequate standard of living; Principle 21 right to property.

106 GPID, Principles 24 et seq.

embraces the notion that assistance and protection are inextricably linked and complementary to each other. However, it may be reasonable to keep both concepts separate so that they are not confused. Distributing humanitarian goods and services does reinforce the protection of the persons assisted and is instrumental to the enjoyment of human rights but is not per se a protection activity: "They become so insofar as they specifically aim at preventing future, stopping on-going and redressing past violations of such rights".[107] This operational meaning of the protection of human rights is enshrined in the Inter-Agency Standing Committee's revised version of the Operational Guidelines on the Protection of Persons in Situations of Natural Disasters.[108]

Ultimately, of great importance for the environmentally displaced is the fact that, once they have crossed an international border, durable protection solutions are sought upon voluntary return to their country of origin[109] and that resettlement and reintegration mechanisms are adequately carried out in the host country. All these means of protection must be underpinned by enabling conditions and funding by all "competent authorities" (states and other international actors) and guided by the principles of dignity, participation, access, and compensation.[110]

Sensu stricto, we borrow the notion that protection encompasses "all activities aimed at obtaining full respect for the rights of the individual in accordance with the letter and spirit of the relevant bodies of law (i.e. human rights law, international humanitarian law and refugee law)",[111] but we cannot neglect its *sensu lato* meaning. Protection must be seen as a holistic concept – action-oriented and a dynamic balancing exercise intimately linked to social and environmental conditions. "It is something oriented to results and involves a whole spectrum of complementary activities embracing both policy and operational concerns and carried out in co-operation with States and other partners, with the goal of enhancing respect for the rights of (. . .)[environmentally displaced] and resolving their [potential] problems".[112] It embraces a holistic approach to

107 IASC Operational Guidelines on the Protection of Persons in Situations of Natural Disasters (2011) "Brookings-Bern Project on Internal Displacement" ***available from:*** www.brookings.edu/~/media/research/files/reports/2011/1/06-operational-guidelines-nd/0106_operational_guidelines_nd.pdf [accessed 17 August 2018] p. 6 (originally issued as IASC Operational Guidelines on Human Rights and Natural Disasters (2006) Brookings. Bern Project on Internal Displacement).

108 U.N. Inter-Agency Standing Committee (2011) "Revised Version of the Operational Guidelines on the Protection of Persons in Situations of Natural Disasters" (January).

109 This can be inferred from Principle 28 of the GPID.

110 GPID, Principles 28 and 29.

111 Inter-Agency Standing Committee (1999) "Protection of Internally Displaced Persons, Inter-Agency Standing Committee Policy Paper" (December) p. 4. The definition was originally adopted by the International Committee of the Red Cross in a 1999 workshop on protection.

112 Deschamp, B., Azorbo, M. & Lohse, S. (2010) "Earth, Wind and Fire: A Review of UNHCR's Role in Recent Natural Disasters" (United Nations High Commissioner for

environmental displacement where rights and needs enter the equation, complementing each other where appropriate.

The relevance of a holistic approach to protection of environmental-induced displacement means absorbing this dynamic notion of protection from the application of "a subjective criterion of qualification of the individuals, according to the reasons which have led them to abandon their homes, to an objective criterion centred rather on the needs of protection".[113]

2.5 Environmentally displaced persons: the objective trump

Considering the previously debated aspects, in this book the term **environmentally displaced persons** is adopted when discussing issues of legal protection and obligations of states under international human rights law for people forced to move due to environmentally triggered conditions.

The scope of the term encompasses:

> *Environmentally displaced persons are those individuals of a country who for compelling reasons of sudden disasters (in particular cyclones, storms surges and floods) or progressive environmental degradation (in particular drought, desertification, deforestation, soil erosion, water shortages and other climate change related conditions), natural and/or human-made, impacting in their lives or livelihoods are obliged to leave their country of origin temporarily or permanently to a third State.*[114]

The definition is not intended to be a legal definition that binds states but rather a descriptive one. It has an instrumental purpose because it can be tested and serve as a benchmark for further development. Essentially, it builds on the need to take a holistic view to environmental displacement. Only a holistic approach to what constitutes an environmentally displaced person can really capture the current dynamics of human mobility resulting from environmental conditions. However, while some conceptualisations include internally and externally displaced people in their definition, the term *environmentally displaced person* within the context of this book refers to those people who cross the border especially due to environmental-change variables. The cross-border

---

Refugees June) pp. 26–27 *available from:* www.unhcr.org/4c1228e19.html [accessed 17 august 2018]. See, for example, where the operational meaning of human rights in delivering assistance during disasters by humanitarian agencies participating in the IASC is highlighted. This meaning is visible in the recently revised version of the Operational Guidelines on the Protection of Persons in Situations of Natural Disasters.

113 Cançado Trindade (2010) *Op. Cit.* p. 512.

114 The definition is drafted by the author and includes some of the items that have been put forward by Myers and Kent (1995) *Op. Cit.* pp. 18–19.

element helps states and the wider international community recognise displacement and protection as a dynamic process.

The definition also excludes – for limitation reasons and textual space – stateless persons with habitual residence (e.g. cases of submerging island states). However, both internally displaced persons and stateless people will be used as illustrative examples whenever necessary. The wording *in particular* implies that the listing within the definition is not exhaustive but merely indicative. Other displacement dynamics (including conflict and/or development-related displacement) can be further included within the scope of the definition. It is a flexible concept embedded in the bedrock of moral and empirical discourses. It is of a moral nature because it suggests the existence of rights and obligations between the individual(s) and his/her country of origin, which are at risk or even broken when they cross the border to a third state due to environmental conditions. Furthermore, it also bolsters some sort of ethical claim to protection and assistance from third states. It is of an empirical nature because the environment is one of the key drivers that over time will have enhanced and recognised impact on human displacement, seriously threatening people's lives.

The definition includes many of the previously debated issues. The definition aims to fulfil the criteria previously put forward: 1) it is easily understandable, simply written, and provides examples; 2) it focuses not on forced internal displacement but on cross-border forced movement on a temporary or permanent basis where wide levels of consensus exist with regard to a legal gap in protection, and its emphasis is on forced movement ("no option") rather than on a voluntarily made decision, and 3) it is – to some extent – measurable and easily documented since it provides a non-exhaustive list that can be applied by government agencies so that discretion can be minimised. New and similar examples of environmental stresses can be added. By avoiding the characterisation of cross-border displaced persons as refugees or migrants, we try to draw clear lines to assert the protection of environmentally displaced persons by existing international human right guarantees and the obligation of third states for providing an adequate level of protection. The cause for displacement is, therefore, an objective one; i.e. outside an individual's choice. This goes in line with the basic nature of international human rights, which obliges states to respect objective standards of human dignity as defined in universal terms.[115] The definition builds on this objective trump throughout this book.

2.5.1 Root cause of displacement

The definition of the term includes people who are forced to move across the border due to threatening situations to their lives or livelihoods or who have

115 Saario, V. & Cass, R. H. (1977) "United Nations and the International Protection of Human Rights: A Legal Analysis and Interpretation" 7 California Western International Law Journal p. 597, pp. 591–614.

experienced serious harm directly due to climate-induced change, environmental degradation, or disasters.

The definition aims to look upon the vulnerability of the individual when his or her livelihood or life is affected as well as the impacts on the individual's human rights core (civil and political, as well as economic and social). From the perspective of those displaced by environmental stressors, there is no forceful reason to differentiate between climate-related and other disaster-related causes. As previously mentioned, the concept of environmental change is – in reality – a holistic one. The definition aims to highlight the fact that from a purely humane perspective, a distinction should perhaps not even be drawn between sudden or gradual displacement because, from the perspective of the individual, the requirement for relocation, assistance, and protection arises in all circumstances (even if different protection solutions can be foreseen). What really matters is the severity of the threat to life and to the person's livelihood or the seriousness of the harm to life or livelihood that actually occurred. Gradual or sudden environmental deterioration may lead to different human flows – some will be immediate and massive while others will be fewer and over time – but in both instances represent a serious threat or harm to people's lives and livelihoods and a need of legal protection contemplation.

2.5.2 Type of displacement

The definition refers to involuntary displacement as opposed to voluntary displacement typical of migratory movements. Migration scholarship describes the process of migration as a continuum from individuals with no control over their relocation (involuntary) to individuals with absolute control (voluntary).[116] In this book, we essentially refer to forced movement as comprising a process taking place over time in a space within the context of social, political, economic, and environmental conditions but where the impact of environmental change over the continuum of time is more enhanced for the environmental driver and where large groups of people become a critical mass and begin to flow across national boundaries into territories of adjoining or other states.

2.5.3 Consequences of displacement

The returnability criterion is an essential element to take into account to examine to what extent an environmentally displaced person can be protected against forced return in a third state when the conditions in his or her country of origin are destroyed. Displacement will be therefore temporary or permanent if the environmental conditions in the country of origin of the individual affected can (or cannot) be restored.

116 *See e.g.* Bates, D. (2002) "Environmental Refugees? Classifying Human Migrations Caused by Environmental Change" 23 Population and Environment 5 pp. 465–477.

2.6 The environmental displacement protection paradox

There will always be doubts about the impact of environmental change and human displacement. As shown, currently there is no certainty about the numbers of human displacement due to environmental factors or even what constitutes an EDP. This can primarily be explained by two factors: a lack of current mechanisms and research that can account for this reality[117] on the one hand and the overall lack of certainty of the impact of environmental change (especially climate change). The protection of EDPs has to cope with what we call the *protection paradox* – a theme that appears throughout this book. It states that some of the dangers of environmental change are intangible and that its impact on human displacement is to some extent (in)visible in this day and age. Yet, there is a need to act and not to wait for the forced displacement of populations to become more visible and acute. From what we know, the fear of people becoming displaced by environmental factors has become a reality and there is no way for the time being to get rid of the current greenhouse gases in the atmosphere. Furthermore, with the increased rate of environmental disasters, it is necessary to deal with those who are increasingly displaced not only within but also beyond borders. This is why the protection of those displaced by environmental factors needs to be seen not as a back-of-the-mind issue but rather a front-of-the-mind one.

Concomitantly, the environmental displacement *protection paradox* invites us to look backwards in order to move forwards. Given the lack of a formalised framework for the environmentally displaced per se the following chapters address the existing legal protection frameworks and underlying principles of forced displacement, which are relevant *in context* (*de lege lata*) and how they can be utilised, (re)interpreted, revised, and consolidated to protect EDPs now and in the near future (*de lege ferenda*).

2.7 Conclusion

This chapter sets the scene on how the changing environment affects human displacement. It particularly highlights that, while people have been on the move for years, the transformation of or the impacts by humans on the environment are leading us to a new geological age, "the Anthropocene", where forced human displacement is one of the foundations.

The chapter also aims to clarify the understanding of environmental change as a holistic and dynamic process of natural and/or human-made factors that include climate change, disasters, development, and environmental degradation, which are all interdependent and interrelated. This view also helps us understand

117 Gradually being overcome by the Platform for Disaster Displacement *available from:* https://disasterdisplacement.org/ [accessed 17 August 2018] – including this one – in particular.

today's "risky society", which is mostly a product of manufactured human risks and the need to cope and manage them, including displacement.

Importantly, it notes that while all of us all are vulnerable to the effects of environmental change, the geography of the impact of environmental change is unevenly distributed. LDCs, because they are highly prone to environmental variations, also suffer from economy dependency, low education levels, and high poverty rates. Therefore, as illustrated by the various authoritative figures, one can easily identify "environmental hotspots", and looking at these affected or most vulnerable areas is a useful reference point to the number of people who are currently displaced or likely to face displacement. In this context, it suggests that the usage of "vulnerability layers" as a reflective concept enables us to expose those vulnerable areas which are affected by environmental change and where people's human rights are at risk and in need of legal protection contemplation. It asserts that whereas all of us are generally vulnerable to environmental change, vulnerability layers are added depending on location; the characteristics of a person including age, sex, or group; and the capacity to resist and/or recover from environmental stressors.

While recognising the multicausality of human mobility (stemming from economic, social, political, demographic, and environmental factors), in the context of displacement the chapter asserted that the environmental displacement debate has generally underestimated the binary "voluntary" and "forced". In other words, while not all flows are generally due to environmental factors alone, it is important to consider the environment as an autonomous factor that leads to displacement. This is because, first, environmental stressors over a period of time will be more exacerbated for the environmental driver, and second, those people will be forcibly displaced (where moving is not an option and is a "no choice option").

In this context, this study situates the environmental displacement debate beyond the causes of human mobility and concentrates on the protection of the human person. The human rights-based approach concentrates on the rights of the environmentally displaced and the protection obligations of states, exploring the application, (re)interpretation, or revision of current international protection standards to that effect. As protection gains centre stage, the study departs from a holistic understanding of protection increasingly codified in international law, which is based on the needs of the individual in all stages of displacement (before, during, and after displacement occurs).

3 Protection obligations of states under international human rights law and related instruments

Traditionally, international protection is predicated on the lack of national state protection, so first it is necessary to analyse the protection obligations of both the home and host states.

In this book, the protection obligations of the home and host states are discussed separately but are not conflicting. Instead, this dual-axis approach provides the basis for a comprehensive understanding of protection of EDPs upon cross-border displacement.

The country of origin has the primary responsibility to *respect* (negative duty of non-violation), to *protect* (positive duty to prevent violation, including of private and international actors), and to *fulfil* (positive duty to take actions for improvement) the human rights of EDPs. Home states have an underlying duty to prevent human rights violations and, to first and foremost protect EDPs from displacement. This duty is further consolidated in a number of other interconnected normative texts that place obligations on states (explicitly and implicitly) to prevent environmental displacement as well to ensure the protection of human rights.

3.1 Determining home state obligations: a survey of illustrative examples

The OHCHR message on disaster risk reduction neatly summarises and provides context to the discussion of the protection of EDPs and states' corresponding obligations:

> All states have positive human rights obligations to protect human rights. Natural hazards are not disasters, in and of themselves. They become disasters depending on the elements of exposure, vulnerability and resilience, all factors that can be addressed by human (including state) action. A failure (by governments and others) to take reasonable and preventative action to reduce exposure and vulnerability and to enhance resilience, as well as to provide effective mitigation, is therefore a human rights question.[1]

1 OHCHR "Organisation Profile: Policies and Programmes in DRR" *available from:* www.preventionweb.net/english/professional/contacts/profile.php?id=1370 [accessed 17 August 2018].

Eduardo Valencia-Ospina, Special Rapporteur "on the protection of persons in the event of disasters" for The International Law Commission, declared that: "[s]tates are under a permanent and universal obligation to provide protection to those on their territory under the various international human rights instruments and customary international human rights law".[2]

Certainly, the extension of the human rights regime to the environmental displacement context is entrenched in the application of the universality of the human rights regime, together with the legally binding obligations owed, especially by the state of origin, to ***respect***, ***protect***, and to ***fulfil***. Asbjørn Eide, the UN's Special Rapporteur for Food, introduced these tripartite obligations of states in the early 1980s. Later, Godefridus Van Hoff replaced the obligation to fulfil with two more nuanced obligations, to ***ensure*** and to ***promote***. These obligations are "programmatic", meaning that they require a positive action by the state and have a progressive (temporal) element.[3] In the words of Craig Scott: "while the obligation to respect is the classic negative obligation of non-interference, forbidding a state to directly encroach upon a right. The other three require varying degrees of positive action or state policy".[4]

Indeed, states' obligations are confirmed in many treaties and have been elaborated on in both regional and international jurisprudence.[5] The whole arena of human rights is affected by environmental change.[6]

3.1.1 Right to life

The right to life is well established in major international and regional frameworks, such as the Universal Declaration of Human Rights[7] (UDHR), the

2 ILC (2008) "Preliminary Report on the Protection of Persons in the Event of Disasters by Mr. Eduardo Valencia-Ospina, Special Rapporteur" 60th Session, UN Doc A/CN.4/598 (5 May) para. 25.

3 Van Hoof, G. J. H. (1984) "The Legal Nature of Economic, Social and Cultural Rights: A Rebuttal of Some Traditional Views" in P. Alston & K. Tomasevski (eds.) "The Right to Food" (Martinus Nijhoff) p. 106.

4 Scott, C. (1989) Interdependence and Permeability of Human Rights Norms: Towards a Partial Fusion of the International Covenants on Human Rights" 27 Osgoode Hall Law Journal 3 p. 834; pp. 769-878.

5 The (quasi-) judicial decisions discussed below are from the UN Human Rights Committee (UNHRC) or Committee on Civil and Political Rights (CCPR); the Committee on Economic, Cultural and Social Rights (CESCR); the European Court of Human Rights (ECtHR); the Inter-American Commission on Human Rights (IACmHR); the Inter-American Court of Human Rights (IACtHR); and the African Commission on Human and People's Rights (ACmHRP).

6 *See* Maldives Submission under Resolution Human Rights Council 7/23 (2008) "Human Rights and Climate Change" (25 September) ***available from:*** www.ohchr.org/Documents/Issues/ClimateChange/Submissions/Maldives_Submission.pdf [accessed 17 August 2018].

7 Art. 3 of UDHR (1948).

International Covenant on Civil and Political Rights[8] (ICCPR), the African Charter on Human and People's Rights[9] (Banjul Charter), the American Convention on Human Rights[10] (ACHR), and the European Convention on Human Rights[11] (ECHR). It has been referred to as the "first right of man"[12] and the most fundamental of all rights[13] from which no derogation is permitted, even in the case of a public emergency.[14] In its General Comment 6[15] of the ICCPR on the scope and content of the right to life, the United Nations Human Rights Committee (HRC) stressed the right to life as "supreme" and one that should not be interpreted in a restrictive way. The committee highlighted that states' failure to prevent, mitigate, or remedy life-threatening harms from environmental degradation or change (within national borders or effective control) could theoretically constitute a violation of the right to life. The *jus cogens* essence of the right to life emphasises that the state of origin bears the duty, not only in cases of inadequate action but also in cases of failure to prevent its violation.[16] It proposes that governments cannot simply rely on non-interference but instead must take positive action to ensure that traditional civil and political rights are guaranteed.

The HRC has reinforced this idea in its General Comment No.31, acknowledging that states have both positive and negative obligations.[17] States are required to take positive actions in order to protect human life; reduce child mortality; increase life expectancy; and eradicate hunger, malnutrition, and the proliferation of diseases.[18] The committee has "opened the door for the right to life to stretch beyond the traditional threat coming from public authorities to include environmental threats affecting the welfare and livelihoods of millions of people around the world".[19] Environmental stresses act as a threat multiplier in already-fragile regions, aggravating the conditions that lead to failed states, challenging global peace and stability, and risking people's lives.[20]

8 Art. 3 of the ICCPR (1966).
9 Article 4 Banjul Charter (1981) (notably distinguishable from most international human rights instruments by its lack of a derogation clause allowing limitation of enumerated rights during emergencies or other special circumstances).
10 Article 4 ACHR (1978).
11 Article 2 ECHR (1950).
12 Newman, F. & Vasak, K. (1982) "Civil and Political Rights" in K. Vasak (ed.) "The International Dimensions of Human Rights" 2 (UNESCO) p. 144.
13 HRC (2004) "General Comment No. 31, Nature of the General Legal Obligation on States Parties to the Covenant" U.N. Doc. CCPR/C/21/Rev.1/Add.13 (29 March).
14 HRC (1982) CCPR "General Comment No. 6: Article 6 (Right to Life)" (30 April).
15 *Ibid.* para. 1.
16 Leib, H. L. (2011) "Human Rights and the Environment Philosophical, Theoretical and Legal Perspectives" (Brill) p. 72.
17 HRC (2004) CCPR General Comment No. 31 *Op. Cit.* para. 6.
18 HRC (1982) CCPR General Comment No. 6 *Op. Cit.* para. 5.
19 Leib (2011) *Op. Cit.* p. 73.
20 *See* (2008) "The National Security Strategy of the United Kingdom: Security in an interdependent world"; German Advisory Council on Global Change (2008) "World in

Particular communities are especially at risk, including those in the Arctic and coastal regions. These communities already suffer the impacts of environmental change on their right to life. In 2005, the Inuit petition to the Inter-American Commission on Human Rights (IACmHR) explained the adverse effects of climate change on the right to life of the Inuit, stating: "[c]hanges in ice and snow jeopardize individual Inuit lives, critical food sources are threatened, and unpredictable weather makes travel more dangerous at all times of the year".[21] The petition argued that the US government was responsible due to its failure to take appropriate action to address climate change. Despite its rejection of the Inuit petition, the Commission has nevertheless, on other occasions, stated that the "realisation of the right to life, and to physical security and integrity is necessarily related to and in some ways dependent upon one's physical environment".[22] Thus, the IACmHR did not limit its interpretation of the right to life to Article 4 of the American Convention on Human Rights (ACHR) as protection solely against arbitrary killing but expanded its approach.

The IACtHR emphasised the connection between the right to life and health and the role of the state to protect these rights, first in *Yanomami Community v Brazil*[23] and, later, in Sawhoyamaxa *Indigenous Community v Paraguay.*[24] Each

---

Transition: Climate Change as a Security Risk". *See also* 2007 Norwegian Nobel Committee comment *available from:* www.nobelprize.org/nobel_prizes/peace/laureates/2007/presentation-speech.html [accessed 17 August 2018] ("[t]he chief threats may be direct violence, but deaths may also have less direct sources in starvation, disease or natural disasters. A goal in our modern world must be to maintain 'human security' in the broadest sense").

21 IACmHR, *Petition to the Inter-American Commission on Human Rights Seeking Relief from Violations Resulting from Global Warming Caused by Acts and Omissions of the United States* ("Inuit petition") (7 December 2005) pp. 90–91 *available from:* http://climatecasechart.com/non-us-case/petition-to-the-inter-american-commission-on-human-rights-seeking-relief-from-violations-resulting-from-global-warming-caused-by-acts-and-omissions-of-the-united-states/ [accessed 17 August 2018] (claiming that US climate change policy violated rights of Inuit). Although unsuccessful, the petition argued Inuit lives are at jeopardy from the effects of climate change: the sea ice on which the Inuit travel and hunt freezes, thaws earlier, and is thinner; food supplies are threatened, making harvesting more difficult; increases of unforeseen weather events and decreases in snow prevents the Inuit from building emergency shelters, increasing casualties among hunters; and the decrease in summer ice makes travelling more dangerous due to rougher seas and more dangerous storms.

22 IACmHR, *The Report on Human Rights Situation in Ecuador*, OAS/Se.L/V/II.96, Doc.10 rev.1 (24 April 1997) Chap. VIII.

23 IACmHR, *Yanomami Community v Brazil* Case No. 7615 (5 March 1985) paras. 175, 176, 177 (where Brazilian government allowed construction of trans-Amazonian highway in Yanomami territory and exploitation of surrounding mineral resources led to influx of non-indigenous populations who spread diseases which decimated lives, court found state failed to take appropriate, timely, and effective measures to protect integrity Yanomami rights to life, liberty, and personal security, guaranteed by Article 1 of the American Declaration).

24 IACtHR, *Sawhoyamaxa Indigenous Community v Paraguay*, Series C no. 146 (29 March 2006).

addressed the well-being of indigenous populations. In the latter, the court acknowledged Paraguay's failure to protect the Sawhoyamaxas' right to life by failing to protect their lands and displacing them to peripheral roadside areas, resulting in the loss of their traditional means of subsistence.[25] As a consequence, many members of the community, including seniors and children, died from malnourishment and lack of medical attention. The court held that "[s]tates have the duty to guarantee the creation of the conditions that may be necessary in order to prevent violations of such inalienable right"[26] and "must adopt any measures that may be necessary to create an adequate statutory framework to discourage any threat to the right to life".[27] The right to life is warranted by states' positive obligations. The Inter-American System indirectly promotes the protection of the environment for present and future generations, maintaining that states should take necessary legal measures to prevent violation of the right to life.

Numerous cases decided by the ECtHR have asserted violation of Article 2 of the ECHR. Two such cases warrant discussion. *Budayeva v Russia*[28] addressed the failure of the state to prevent a mudslide that destroyed a dam (killing eight), and *Öneryildiz v Turkey*[29] concerned the explosion of methane at a waste plant (killing 26 and injuring 11). In both cases, the court concluded that because the states failed to have adequate frameworks to prevent the threats to the right to life, they breached their obligation to take proactive measures to protect the lives of those within their borders.

The decision in *Öneryildiz* relied on a finding that the risks were "immediate and known", as they were documented in a report to Turkish authorities nearly two years earlier.[30] The state knew of the potential and actual harm of industrial and other "dangerous activities" and had a duty to act. The court confirmed that the right to life "does not solely concern deaths resulting from the use of force by an agent of the State but also [. . .] lays down a positive obligation on States to take appropriate steps to safeguard the lives of those within their jurisdiction".[31] It further stressed "this positive obligation entails above all a primary duty on the State to put into place a legislative and administrative framework designed to provide effective deterrence against threats to the right to life".[32] In reality, what the court acknowledges is that the threshold of harm

25 *Ibid.* Article 1 (2) ICCPR.
26 *Ibid.* para. 151.
27 *Ibid.* para. 153.
28 ECtHR, *Budayeva and Others v Russia*, Application Nos. 15339/02, 21166/02, 20058/02, 11673/02 and 15343/02 (20 March 2008) para. 132.
29 ECtHR, *Öneryildiz v Turkey* Application No. 48939/99 (30 November 2004) paras. 89–90.
30 *Ibid.* para. 101. The explosion occurred in 23 April 1993 and reporting evidence next to the government authorities was made available on 27 May 1991.
31 *Ibid.* paras. 128–129.
32 *Ibid.*

relates to inaction by the state not to harm the environment alone but also the duty to protect right-holders from environmental harm.

Similarly, in *Budayeva* the court highlighted the obligation of the Russian government to protect people's basic human rights before, during, and after a disaster. The court concluded:

> In the sphere of emergency relief, where the State is directly involved in the protection of human lives through the mitigation of natural hazards, these considerations should apply in so far as the circumstances of a particular case point to the imminence of a natural hazard that has been clearly identifiable, and especially where it concerned a recurring calamity affecting a distinct area developed for human habitation or use [. . .] The scope of positive obligations imputable to the State in the particular circumstances would depend on the origin of the threat and the extent to which one or the other risk is susceptible to mitigation.[33]

The court found that Russia did not have in place an early-warning system to facilitate evacuation in time, ignored the early warnings that a mudslide might happen, disregarded the protection and repair of dams,[34] and did not investigate the causes of the mudslide.[35] The court held that positive and procedural duties to protect the right to life arise when a natural hazard is clearly identifiable and the state has the effective means to mitigate the risk. In *Kolyadenko v Russia*,[36] the court also found a breach of Article 2 where the government failed to impose planning controls in an area at risk of flooding.

In the context of environmental displacement, an important idea can be derived from these decisions: the need to have adequate frameworks to protect the right to life to both prevent and reduce the risk of its violation. Considering the loss of life that has occurred in many climate change related events – hurricanes, storms, and heat waves – over the years, one can foresee claims (for example in European Courts) against states for their failure to address the

33 *Ibid.* para. 137.

34 ECtHR, *Budayeva and Others v Russia Op. Cit.* paras. 147–158.

35 *Ibid.* paras. 159–160.

36 ECtHR, *Kolyadenko v Russia*, Application Nos. 17423/05, 20534/05, 20678/05, 23263/05, 24283/05 and 35673/05 (9 July 2012) (finding that although national authorities in tune with local needs have a "margin of appreciation" since they are best placed to make regulatory decisions, the measures taken by Russian authorities were inadequate to discharge Russia's Article 2 positive obligation to safeguard the right to life of those within its jurisdiction.) The court found that even though exceptional weather conditions required the release of water from a reservoir, the authorities knew release may be necessary and should have foreseen the potential consequences, yet they failed to implement adequate measures to reduce the risk. Paras. 163–165, 169–173. This case as well as those discussed previously suggest that the "margin of appreciation" of states is narrow (or does not apply) where the government failed to take preventative measures or that such measures were wholly inadequate.

problem of environmental change proactively or for not complying with mandatory greenhouse gas emission reduction. The same reasoning could be applied to issues such as pollution and general environmental degradation. As Judge Jambrek states in his concurring opinion in *Guerra and Others v Italy*:[37]

> It may therefore be time for the Court's case law on Article 2 (right to life) to start evolving, to develop the respective implied rights, articulate situations of real and serious risk to life, or different aspects of the right to life. Article 2 also appears relevant and applicable to the facts of the instant case, in that 150 people were taken to hospital with severe arsenic poisoning. Through the release of harmful substances into the atmosphere, the activity carried on at the factory thus constituted a "major accident hazard dangerous to the environment".

The law is evolving to better address violations of human rights caused by environmental-related damage and displacement. In 2008, the government of the Maldives submitted to the OHCHR a preliminary study on climate change and human rights. Its report described how climate change (sea level rise, warming water, and melting ice) endangers its citizens' right to life (increased floods, storms surges, and erosion).[38] The report also cited predictions that by 2025 an increase of 0.5 metres of water would inundate 15% of the most populated island of the Maldives (Male') and by 2100 inundate half of it.[39] Furthermore, because about 42% of the population lives within 100 m of the shoreline, even a moderate increase in water level over time is "likely to result in drowning, injury, and loss of life".[40]

3.1.2 Right to private and family life

The right to privacy, as a civil and political right, is also relevant to environmental displacement, as it imposes on the state the obligation to protect one's private and family life. Article 17 of the ICCPR states that "[n]o one shall be subjected to arbitrary or unlawful interference with his privacy, family, home or correspondence (. . .) Everyone has the right to protection of the law against such interference or attacks". Similar provisions can be found under the American Convention on Human Rights[41] and the European Convention on Human

37 ECtHR, *Guerra and Others v Italy*, Application No. 14967/89 (19 February 1998), Jambrek, J. concurring.
38 OHCHR (2008) "Submission of the Maldives to the Office of the UN High Commissioner for Human Rights" (25 September) *available from:* www.ohchr.org/Documents/Issues/ClimateChange/Submissions/Maldives_Submission.pdf [accessed 17 August 2018].
39 *Ibid.* pp. 19–20.
40 *Ibid.* p. 21.
41 Article 11 (2) and 21 ACHR.

Rights.[42] Many cases brought before the ECtHR have alleged, pursuant to Article 8, that environmental degradation impacts the individual's right to privacy.

In *Lopez Ostra v Spain*,[43] the applicant argued that the state breached its positive duty to protect her rights under Article 8 by failing to stop a leather processing waste-treatment plant near her home from emitting toxic fumes and smells that "immediately caused health problems and nuisance".[44] The ECtHR did not affirm the duty of the state to prevent pollution but implied it by finding that the government did not strike "a fair balance between the interest of the town's economic well-being – having a waste-treatment plant – and the applicant's effective enjoyment of her right of respect for her home and her private and family life".[45] The court thus indirectly acknowledged the state's duty to balance the prevention of pollution with the applicant's right to privacy, even when the individual's health was not acutely endangered.[46] The court found a breach of Article 8 and ordered compensation.

In *Guerra and Others v Italy*,[47] the ECtHR reinforced its view of the relationship between environmental pollution and the state's violation of Article 8 in the failure of the state to act and to provide information about risks and emergency procedures. Similarly, in *Fadeyeva v Russia*,[48] the ECtHR found a violation of Article 8 based on the state's unwillingness to provide applicants effective solutions for moving from a polluted area[49] and failure to take positive measures to regulate the emission levels[50] near Russia's largest iron smelting plant. It held that, "despite the wide margin of appreciation left on the respondent state, it has failed to strike a fair balance between the interests of the community and the applicant's effective enjoyment of her right to respect for her home and her private life. There has accordingly been a violation of Article 8".[51] The court held that it was not necessary for the adverse polluting effects to reach a "certain minimum level" because that determination depends on "all the circumstances of the case".[52]

42 Article 8 (1) ECHR.
43 ECtHR, *Lopez Ostra v Spain*, Application No. 16798/90 (9 December 1994).
44 *Ibid.* para. 8.
45 *Ibid.* para. 56.
46 ECtHR, *Lopez Ostra v Spain Op. Cit.* para. 51 (finding sufficient that the pollution impact "individuals' well-being and prevent them from enjoying their homes in such a way as to affect their private and family life adversely").
47 ECtHR, *Guerra and Others v Italy Op. Cit.* paras. 58, 60.
48 ECtHR, *Fadeyeva v Russia*, Application No. 55723/00 (30 November 2005).
49 *Ibid.* para. 88.
50 *Ibid.* para. 133.
51 *Ibid.* para. 134 The court ordered the Russian government to pay the applicant non-pecuniary damages (equalling 6,000 Euro) plus case-related costs and expenses. *Ibid.* para. 152.
52 *Ibid.* para. 69 ("[t]he assessment of that minimum is relative and depends on all circumstances of the case, such as the intensity and duration of the nuisance, its physical or mental effects [and] (. . .) [t]he general environmental context (. . .)".

The European jurisprudence is relevant for EDPs as it emphasises the obligations of home states to act to protect them against environmental harm caused both by pollution or the state's failure to protect against environmental hazards and private actors.[53] The ECtHR has used the "fair balance" approach to adjudicate the rights of the individual versus the interests of the wider community, whether environmental harm is caused directly by the state or by a private actor.[54] In balancing interests, they defer to states on how to reach the acceptable environmental threshold. And while states may undertake or allow environmental degradation that impacts the enjoyment of human rights, they must act preventatively to ensure that such degradation does not pose undue risk.[55]

3.1.3 Right to adequate standard of living

Article 25(1) of the UDHR states that "[e]veryone has the right to a standard of living adequate for the health and well-being of himself and of his family". The strong link between an individual and his surrounding natural environment means that a healthy environment is a prerequisite for a person's health and well-being. State parties to the ICESCR also acknowledge that the right to have an adequate standard of living (Article 11) is overarching. The article bundles the right to adequate food, clothing, and housing, access to safe and potable water, continuous progress of living conditions,[56] and the right to be free from hunger (adequate food and nutrition).[57] The World Health Organisation has determined that these basic health determinants will be most at risk by changing environmental conditions.[58]

(i) Right to food

Many international human rights instruments protect the right to adequate food.[59] In 2001, the right to food was defined as "[A] human right, inherent

53 *Ibid.*
54 ECtHR, *Hatton and Others v United Kingdom*, Application No. 36022/97 (8 July 2003) para. 98; ECtHR, *Fadeyeva v Russia Op. Cit.* para. 105; ECtHR, Lopez *Ostra v Spain Op. Cit.* para. 51 and ECtHR, *Taskin v Turkey*, Application No. 46117/99 (30 March 2005) para. 116.
55 McInerney-Lankford, S., Darrow, M. & Rajamani, L. (2011) "Human Rights and Climate Change: A Review of the International Legal Dimensions" (World Bank) pp. 32–33.
56 Article 11 (1) ICESCR.
57 Article 11 (2) ICESCR.
58 World Health Organization (2008) "Protecting Health from Climate Change: World Health Day 2008" (World Health Organization), p. 6 *available from:* www.who.int/world-health-day/toolkit/report_web.pdf?ua=1 [accessed17 August 2018].
59 Article 11 (1) of the ICESCR recognises "the right of everyone to an adequate standard of living for himself and his family, including adequate food, clothing and housing and to the continuous improvement of living conditions". Article 11 (2) recognises that urgent steps may be necessary to ensure "the fundamental right to freedom from hunger and

in all people, to have regular, permanent and unrestricted access, either directly or by means of financial purchases, to quantitatively and qualitatively adequate and sufficient food to the cultural traditions of people to which it belongs, and which ensures a physical and mental, individual and collective fulfilling and dignified life free of fear".[60] The right requires that states meet a minimum standard: "States have a core obligation to take the necessary action to mitigate and alleviate hunger as provided for in paragraph 2 of article 11, even in times of natural or other disasters".[61]

Environmental instruments have also emphasised the importance of the right to food and of climate mitigation measures to "ensure that food production is not threatened".[62] The CESCR considers the right to food an inherent part of the dignity of the human person and essential for the fulfilment of other human rights mirrored in the International Bill of Human Rights.[63] The committee noted that the availability and accessibility to food provisions are major components of the right to food and the interdependency between the environment and the right to food (indicating the need to take "appropriate economic, environmental and social policies").[64] The CESCR has also linked environmental conditions to the right to food, stating that "even where the State faces severe resources constraints, whether caused by a process of economic adjustment, economic recession, climate conditions or other factors, measures should be undertaken to ensure that the right to adequate food is especially fulfilled for vulnerable population groups and individuals".[65]

There is strong evidence that changing environmental conditions significantly impact the right to food (both availability and accessibility).[66] In 2008, Olivier de Schutter, the Special Rapporteur on the right to food, argued for increased reliance on technology for agricultural production to cope with population

malnutrition". The right to food is recognised in Article 25 of UDHR; Article 12(2) CEDAW; Articles 24 (2) (c) and 27; and in many national constitutions such as those of Bangladesh, Brazil, Colombia, India, Iran, Pakistan, South Africa, and Sri Lanka.

60 "Report by the Special Rapporteur Jean Ziegler on the Right to Food to the Commission on Human Rights 57th Session" U.N. Doc. E/CN.4/2001/53 (7 February 2001) p. 8 para14.

61 Committee on Economic, Social and Cultural Rights (CESCR) (1999) "General Comment No. 12: Right to adequate food (Article 11 of the Covenant)" (12 May) para.6.

62 Article 2 UNFCCC.

63 *Ibid.* para. 4.

64 *Ibid.*

65 *Ibid.* para. 28.

66 Von Doussa, J., Corkery, A. & Chartres, R. (2008) "Human Rights and Climate Change" (Australian Human Rights and Equal Opportunity Commission, Background Paper) p. 5; *See generally*, Bals, C. *et al.* (2008) "Climate Change, Food Security and the Right to Adequate Food" (Diakonisches Werk derEKD and German Watch e.V.); Söllner, S. (2007) "The Breakthrough of the Right to Food" 11 Max Planck Yearbook of UN Law pp. 391–415.

growth and climate change.[67] He further noted the negative effects of the development of agrofuel as a means to replace fossil fuels in order to mitigate climate change.[68] His report has prompted states in the international community to develop policies that encourage sustainable and diverse resilient agricultural practices to address environmental change disruptions.[69]

(ii) Right to water

Human existence is dependent on water. Despite this, the right to water has gained international recognition only over the past decade, particularly in several international human rights instruments.[70] General Comment No. 15 of the U.N. Committee on Economic, Social and Cultural Rights (CESCR) noted the rise of the right to water and its inextricable relation to the other enumerated human rights: "The human right to water is indispensable for leading a life in human dignity. It is a prerequisite for the realization of other human rights".[71] The U.N. General Assembly, in its Resolution 64/292, has also acknowledged "clean drinking water and sanitation as a human right that is essential for the full enjoyment of life and all human rights".[72]

State protection for EDPs thus also includes the protection of water resources, entailing that water resources must be made available to all and physically and economically accessible without discrimination.[73] Forecasts predict that the

67 Schutter (2008) "Report of the Special Rapporteur on the Right to Food: Building Resilience: A Human Rights Framework on World Food and Nutrition Security" U.N. Doc. A/HRC/9/23 *available from*: www.unhcr.org/refworld/docid/48cf71dd2.html [accessed 17 August 2018].

68 *Ibid.* para. 25–34.

69 UNGA (2009) "Statement prepared by Special Rapporteur Olivier de Schutter on the Right to Food, Interactive Thematic Dialogue of the U.N. General Assembly on the Global Food Crisis and the Right to Food" (6 April 2009) *available from*: www.un.org/ga/president/63/letters/conceptfoodcrisis.pdf [accessed 17 August 2018]; "United Nations Special Rapporteur on the Right to Food Olivier de Schutter, Contribution to the U.N. Commission on Sustainable Development at Its 17th Session" (4–15 May 2009) *available from*: www.srfood.org/images/stories/pdf/otherdocuments/19-srrtfsubmissioncsd-01-05-09-1.pdf [accessed 17 August 2018].

70 *See, e.g.*, CEDAW, Article 14, paragraph 2 (stating that parties shall ensure women the right to "enjoy adequate living conditions, particularly in relation to [. . .] water supply"); CRC, Article 24, paragraph 2 (requiring states to combat disease and malnutrition "through the provision of adequate nutritious foods and clean drinking water").

71 CESCR (2003) "General Comment No. 15: The Right to Water (Arts. 11 and 12 of the Covenant)" U.N. Doc. E/C.12/2002/11 (20 January) para. 1.

72 UNGA (2010) "The Human Right to Water and Sanitation" U.N. Doc. RES/64/292 (28 July) para.1. The 2003 version of the UNGA, "International Decade for Action, 'Water for Life', 2005–2015" U.N. Doc. RES/58/217 (23 December 2003) Para.1 ("water is critical for sustainable development, including environmental integrity and the eradication of poverty and hunger, and is indispensable for human health and well-being").

73 CESCR (2003) "General Comment No. 15: The Right to Water" *Op. Cit.* para. 12.

increase of global temperature will threaten water availability for 50 million people and will be further exacerbated by weather extremes such as drought and flooding. For example, in 2011 the island of Tuvalu declared a state of emergency due to lack of potable drinking water.[74] Today, it is estimated that 1.1 billion people are denied access to safe drinking water, constituting a major cause of illness and morbidity.[75] This, too, can be linked to other major natural disasters where the destruction of water and sanitation systems directly curtailed access to potable water, causing the outbreak of disease. The 2000 Mozambique and 2004 Bangladesh floods, as well as the 2004 Asian tsunami and 2005 Pakistan earthquakes, serve as examples.[76]

(iii) Right to adequate housing

The right to housing is not only a right to refuge but also "the right to live somewhere in security, peace and dignity".[77] This right is found under Article 11 of the ICESCR and in an array of other conventional instruments,[78] international declarations, and general comments.[79] In the context of climate change, the Office of the High Commission for Human Rights has precisely highlighted the guarantees of the right to housing:

> (a) adequate protection of housing from weather hazards (habitability of housing); (b) access to housing away from hazardous zones; (c) access to shelter and disaster preparedness in cases of displacement caused by extreme weather events; (d) protection of communities that are relocated away from hazardous zones, including protection against forced evictions without

74 BBC News (2011) "Tuvalu Declares Emergency over Water Shortage" (3 October) *available from*: www.bbc.com/news/world-asia-pacific-15147043 [accessed 17 August 2018].

75 U.N. Human Rights Council (2009) U.N. Doc. A/HRC/10/61 (15 January) *Op. Cit.* para. 29.

76 *See* Watson, J., Michelle, G. & Connolly, M. (2007) "Epidemics after Natural Disasters" 13 Emerging 1 pp. 1–5 and International Federation of the Red Cross and Red Crescent Societies (2009) "Tsunami Five-Year Progress Report 2004–2009" (International Federation of the Red Cross and Red Crescent Societies) p. 14.

77 CESCR (1999) "General Comment No. 12: Right to Adequate Food" *Op. Cit.* para. 6.

78 The right to adequate housing is also found under Article 5 (e) of the Convention on the Elimination of All Forms of Racial Discrimination (CERD); Article 14 of the CEDAW; Article 27 of the CRC; and Article 43 of the International Convention on the Protection of the Rights of All Migrant Workers (IMWC).

79 *See, e.g.*, "Principle 4 of the Declaration on the Rights of the Child" UNGA Res 1386 (XIV) (29 November 1959); "Article 10 (f) of the Declaration of Social Progress and Development" UNGA Res 2542 (XXIV) (11 December 1969); Se. III (8), Chap. II(A.3) of the Vancouver Declaration on Human Settlements, adopted by the U.N. Conference on Human Settlements in 1976; "Article 8.1 of the Declaration of the Right to Development" UNGA Res 41/128 (4 December 1986); and CESCR General Comment No. 4 (1991) Article 11 (1) (right to adequate housing).

appropriate forms of legal or other protection, including adequate consultation with affected persons.[80]

This right thus imposes on states an overarching obligation to prevent – and protect individuals from – the impacts of climate change, including ensuring access to housing away from recognised hazardous areas as well as providing shelter when a disaster causes displacement. The Special Rapporteur on the right to housing, Raquel Rolnik, stated that "[s]tates have clear obligations under international human rights law to respect, protect and fulfil the right to adequate housing and to pursue, through international cooperation, global solutions to the global problem of climate change and its impact on housing".[81]

The preventative approach to protection of the right to housing also imposes on states a duty to relocate communities away from hazardous zones and take precautionary measures to avoid forced evictions. Based on UNDP and IPCCC reports, the OHCHR observed that "[s]ea level rise and storm surges will have a direct impact on many coastal settlements. In the Arctic Region and in low-lying island States such impacts have already led to the relocation of peoples and communities. Settlements in the low-lying mega-deltas are also particularly at risk, as evidenced by millions of people and homes affected by flooding in recent years".[82]

Notably, though, the right to housing can be a doubled-edged sword for EDPs. While states must proactively relocate at-risk populations to safer areas, they must also inform people of their choice to return whenever possible. The Special Rapporteur on the right to adequate housing suggests that policymakers heed lessons learned from post-tsunami reconstruction processes, where some countries relocated those most affected but never gave them the opportunity to return to their homes (in essence, a form of indirect forced evictions).[83]

80 U.N. Human Rights Council (2009) "Report on the Relationship between Climate Change and Human Rights" U.N. Doc. A/HRC/10/61 (15 January) para. 38.

81 UNGA (2009) "The Right to Adequate Housing Report Submitted by the Special Rapporteur on Adequate Housing as a Component of the Right to an Adequate Standard of Living, and on the Right to Non-Discrimination in This Context, Raquel Rolnik, Submitted Pursuant to Human Rights Council Resolution 6/27" U.N. Doc. A/64/255 (6 August) p. 14, para. 36.

82 *Ibid.* para. 36.

83 *Ibid.* Indirect forced evictions of EDPs take place when environmental degradation or catastrophe is the major cause of "eviction". According to the Special Rapporteur on Housing, Raquel Rolnik, while the government enacted a temporary protection measure by providing housing elsewhere, the EDPs never had the option to return to their property because the state decided to confer their land to commercial interests. The CESCR defines a forced eviction as "the permanent or temporary removal against their will of individuals, families and/or communities from the homes and/or land which they occupy, without the provision of and access to, appropriate forms of legal or other protection". *See CESCR*, General Comment No. 7 (1997) "General Comment No. 7 The Right to Adequate Housing (Art. 11.1): Forced Evictions" U.N. Doc. E/1998/22 (20 May).

Instead the abandoned regions became tourist and commercial areas.[84] The safety and security of the population becomes a camouflaged priority of states over other governmental and commercial interests. The realisation of the right to housing requires, therefore, that states take adequate "resource allocations and policy initiatives", including developing processes that provide those relocated with adequate consultation[85] and the development of effective "international cooperation" strategies.[86]

3.1.4 Right to health

The ICESCR recognises the right to "the enjoyment of the highest standard of physical and mental health" (Article 12(1)). General Comment 14 explains that the right to health is intrinsically reliant on environmental circumstances and other rights.[87]

The right to health is also discussed in articles in the CRC,[88] CEDAW,[89] and regional instruments, such as the European Social Charter,[90] the EU Charter

84 U.N. News Centre (2009) "Climate Change Talks Must Include Focus on Adequate Housing, Says UN" Expert (23 October 2009) *available from:* www.un.org/apps/news/story.asp?NewsID=32695[accessed 17 August 2018]. *See* the joint Statement by Special Rapporteur on Housing, Raquel Rolnik, and United Nations Special Rapporteur for Internationally Displaced Persons, Ms. Chaloka Beyani, during World Habitat Day Celebrations (3 October 2011) *available from:* http://mirror.unhabitat.org/content.asp?cid=10482&catid=7&typeid=8&AllContent=1 [accessed 17 August 2018].

85 U.N. Human Rights Council (2009) UN Doc A/HRC/10/61 *Op. Cit.* p. 15.

86 CESCR (1991) General Comment No. 4: Right to adequate housing *Op. Cit.* paras. 10 and 15.

87 The CESCR (2000) "General Comment No. 14 (2000): Right to the highest attainable standard of health" (Art. 12) U.N. Doc. E/C.12/2000/4 (11 August) para. 11 ("*an inclusive right extending* not only to timely and appropriate health care but also to the underlying determinants of health, such as access to safe and potable water and adequate sanitation, an adequate supply of safe food, nutrition and housing, healthy occupational and environmental conditions, and access to health-related education and information, including on sexual and reproductive health. A further important aspect is the participation of the population in all health-related decision-making at the community, national and international level") (emphasis added).

88 Article 24 (1) CRC ("States Parties recognize the right of the child to the enjoyment of the *highest attainable standard of health and to facilities for the treatment of illnesses and rehabilitation of health.* States parties *shall* strive to ensure that no child in deprived of his or her right of access to such health care services") (emphasis added).

89 Article 12 CEDAW ("1. States Parties *shall* take all appropriate measures to eliminate discrimination against women in the field of health care in order to ensure, on a basis of equality of men and women, access to health care services, including those related to family planning. 2. Notwithstanding the provisions of paragraph I of this article, States Parties *shall* ensure to women appropriate services in connection with pregnancy, confinement and the post-natal period, granting free services where necessary, as well as adequate nutrition during pregnancy and lactation") (emphasis added).

90 Article 11 European Social Charter (ESC) adopted on 18 October 1961, in force since 26 February 1965, 529 UNTS 89, revised 1996 ("[t]he right to protection of health

of Fundamental Rights,[91] the Protocol of San Salvador,[92] and the Banjul Charter.[93] These articles suggest that states are obligated to implement processes that ensure full realisation of the right to health and to promote *international cooperation* with the same. The obligation entails a system of protection that enables access to preventative care, medical treatment, and conditions that guarantee the right without discrimination.

As reflected in the Draft Declaration of Principles on Human Rights and the Environment[94] and under other environmental instruments, such as the Stockholm Declaration[95] and the Rio Declaration,[96] Agenda 21,[97] the UNFCCC,[98]

---

with a view to ensuring the effective exercise of the right to protection of health, the Contracting Parties undertake, either directly or *in co-operation with public or private organisations*, to take appropriate measures designed *inter alia:* 1. *to remove* as far as possible the causes of ill-health; 2. to provide advisory and *educational facilities for the promotion of* health and the encouragement of individual responsibility in matters of health; 3. *to prevent* as far as possible epidemic, endemic and other diseases") (emphasis added).

91 Article 35 Charter of Fundamental Rights of the European Union, adopted 18 December 2000, legally binding since the Treaty of Lisbon entered into force on 1 December 2009, 2000/C 364/01 18 ("[e]veryone has the right of access to *preventive health care and the right to benefit from medical treatment* under the conditions established by national laws and practices. A high level of human health protection shall be ensured in the definition and implementation of all Union policies and activities") (emphasis added).

92 Article 10 Protocol of San Salvador.

93 Article 16 Banjul Charter.

94 The Draft Declaration of Principles on Human Rights and the Environment Annex I (1994), Principle 7 ("[a]ll persons have the right to the highest attainable standard of health free from environmental harm").

95 The Stockholm Declaration (1972), Principle 1 ("Man has the fundamental right to freedom, equality and adequate conditions of life, in an environment of a quality that permits a life of dignity and well-being, and he bears a solemn responsibility to protect and improve the environment for present and future generations. In this respect, policies promoting or perpetuating apartheid, racial segregation, discrimination, colonial and other forms of oppression and foreign domination stand condemned and must be eliminated").

96 The Rio Declaration (1992), Principle 1 ("[h]uman beings are at the centre of concerns for sustainable development. They are entitled to a healthy and productive life in harmony with nature"); Principle 14 ("States should effectively cooperate to discourage or prevent the relocation and transfer to other States of any activities and substances that cause severe environmental degradation or are found to be harmful to human health").

97 Agenda 21, an action plan adopted at the U.N. Conference on Environment and Development (UNCED), Rio de Janeiro, 3–14 June 1992 is a comprehensive global, national, and local plan of action for organisations of the United Nations system, governments, and major groups in every area in which humans impact the environment.

98 The UNFCCC (1992), Articles 1 (1) and 4 (1) (f) (referring to adverse effects of climate change including "significant deleterious impacts on human health and welfare" and urging state parties to take *inter alia* health impacts into account in the relevant social, economic, and environmental policies).

and many other multi-environmental agreements,[99] the right to health is not confined to medical assistance. It includes all aspects of environmental improvements and protection from hazards (air, water, food pollution).[100] Notably, though, the right to an adequate standard of living and the right to health is a "duty of [not only the state of origin/residence but of] all Governments;" it is a "shared responsibility". A WHO report shows that more than 160,000 deaths from malaria and malnutrition may be due to an increase in world temperatures, and that number is predicted to double in the next decade.[101] Paul Hunt, the Special Rapporteur on the right to health, explained that health is a broad concept which entails more specific elements, such as the right to healthy workplaces and natural environments.[102] He documented how, in Peru, pollution, a lack of clean drinking water, and poor sanitation affected the most marginalised parts of the population, including children, indigenous people, and the poor.[103]

The health inequalities between countries all over the world will widen with changing environmental conditions. State action at the national and international levels to protect EDPs and humankind is not only timely, but necessary. As the Alma-Ata Declaration acknowledged, "the gross inequality in the health status of the people, particularly between developed and developing countries, as well within countries, is politically, socially and economically unacceptable and is, therefore, of common concern of all countries".[104]

99 Convention on Long-Range Tranboundary Air Pollution, adopted 13 November 1979, in force since 16 March 1983, 1302 UNTS 217 (Article 2); Basel Convention on the Control of Transboundary Movements of Hazardous Wastes and their Disposal, adopted 22 March 1989 1673 UNTS 57 Chapter XXVII-3 (Article 2 (8) (9)); and the Rotterdam Convention on the Prior Informed Consent Procedure for Certain Hazardous Chemicals and Pesticides in International Trade, adopted 10 September 1998, in force since 24 February 2004 (revised 2013) 224 UNTS 337 Chapter XXVII (Article 1).

100 Thorme, M. (1991) "Establishing Environment as a Human Right" 19 Denver Journal of International Law and Policy p. 322, pp. 301–342.

101 Bhattacharya, S. (2003), "Global Warming Kills 160,000 a Year" New Scientist (1 October) *available from:* www.newscientist.com/article/dn4223-global-warming-kills-160000-a-year.html [accessed 17 August 2018].

102 U.N. Commission on Human Rights (now U.N. Human Rights Council) (2005), "Report of the Special Rapporteur on the Right of Everyone to the Enjoyment of the Highest Attainable Standard of Physical and Mental Health, Paul Hunt, Mission to Peru" UN Doc. E/CN.4/2005/51/Add.3 (4 February) para. 52.

103 In Belen, the contamination of the River Nanay with mercury from mining companies led to increases in infant mortality due to diarrhoea and other water-related diseases. In Callao, more than half of children possess high levels of lead in their blood due to the export and storage of lead ore. In San Mateo de Huanchor, toxic mining affected local residences and, in particular, indigenous populations.

104 "Declaration of Alma-Ata International Conference on Primary Health Care, Alma-Ata" USSR (6–12 September 1978), Article II *available from:* www.who.int/publications/almaata_declaration_en.pdf [accessed 17 August 2018]. It was the first declaration requiring urgent action by all states and international actors to promote and protect health equality for all people.

Regional and national courts have also cited the right to health and its inextricable dependency on the environment with regards to air and water pollution, environmental protection, and food scarcity.[105] In *Social Economic Rights Action Centre v Nigeria*,[106] the African Commission on Human and People's Rights (ACmHPR) found that the Nigerian government violated the right to health, the right to dispose of wealth and natural resources, the right to a clean environment, and family rights, among others, when it condoned and facilitated the operations of oil corporations in Ogoniland.[107] The Commission urged the government of Nigeria "to ensure protection of the environment health and livelihood of the people of Ogoniland",[108] thereby finding governmental duties of protection in the present and in the future. The Commission highlighted that Nigeria should guarantee "adequate compensation to the victims of human rights violations, including relief and undertaking resettlement assistance to victims of government sponsored raids and a comprehensive clean-up of lands and rivers damaged by oil operations".[109] The Commission ordered the government to take positive measures to stop and reverse the environmental degradation. It also recommended that, prior to any further oil extraction developments, the government obtain environmental and social impact assessments prepared by independent bodies and provide at-risk communities clear information on how to access regulatory and decision-making bodies.[110]

Similarly, in the 1997 report on human rights in Ecuador,[111] the IACmHR acknowledged that the government's failure to control the adverse effects of pollution (including contaminations and deaths in the local community) caused by oil and mining exploitation in the Orient region constituted a violation of the right to life and health of the affected communities. Like the African Commission, it held that the state is obligated "to take reasonable measures to

105 For example, in the aforementioned *Yanomami* case, where the government of Brazil forced indigenous populations from their territory without compensation to build a highway, the IACmHR acknowledged the impact on the right to life but also on the right to health and well-being. The petitioners also claimed violation of other rights, including free movement, residence, liberty, and security. While the court did not grant a remedy, it nevertheless recommended that the state take action to protect the Yanomami Indians.

106 ACmHPR, *Social and Economic Rights Action Centre (SERAC) and Centre for Economic and Social Rights (CESR) v Nigeria*, Comm. No. 155/96 (27 October 2002).

107 *Ibid.* p. 12 ("[D]espite its obligation to protect persons against interferences in the enjoyment of their rights, *the Government of Nigeria facilitated the destruction* of the Ogoniland. Contrary to its Charter obligations and despite such internationally established principles, the Nigerian Government has given green light to private actors, and oil companies in particular, to *devastatingly affect the well-being* of the Ogonis. By any measure of standards, its practice falls short of the minimum conduct expected of governments, and therefore, is in violation of Article 21 of the African Charter") (emphasis added).

108 *Ibid.* p. 15.

109 *Ibid.* p. 14.

110 *Ibid.* p. 15.

111 IACmHR (1997) Report on the Situation of Human Rights in Ecuador *Op. Cit.*

prevent such risk, or the necessary measures to respond when persons have suffered injury".[112] It, thus, endorsed a preventative approach coupled with the obligation to "respond with appropriate measures of investigation and redress"[113] in order to protect the right to life and health.

In the context of EDPs, these cases are crucial, as they reinforce the protection obligations of states of origin. They highlight the responsibility of the governments for their past failures and urge them to take steps now to reverse the damage (by allocating compensation and resettlement mechanisms to the victims). They also set forth future obligations, including guaranteeing substantive and procedural processes to prevent the undermining of human rights.

3.1.5 *Other human rights*

Environmental change may impact an array of other human rights, as well. The effects of environmental change have been characterised as a "profound denier of freedom of action and source of disempowerment".[114] Extreme weather patterns, increased floods and droughts, and related crop impacts will further hamper the realisation of the rights to property,[115] means of subsistence,[116] culture, freedom of residence, and movement.[117]

For indigenous groups, environmental changes are likely to disrupt the strong relationship that they have with their land,[118] their natural resources, and their

112 *Ibid.* Chapter VIII.
113 *Ibid.*
114 United Nations Development Programme (2007/2008) "Human Development Report 2007/2008 Fighting Climate Change: Human Solidarity in a Divided World" p. 31 *available from:* http://hdr.undp.org/sites/default/files/reports/268/hdr_20072008_en_complete.pdf [accessed 17 August 2018].
115 Article 17 UDHR; Article XXIII American Declaration; Article 21 American Convention. *See* Ardilez-Martinez D. *et al.* (2008) "Human Rights and Climate Change Study" p. 14 *available from:* www.ohchr.org/Documents/Issues/ClimateChange/Submissions/NSW_Young_Lawyers_HR_ClimateChange.pdf [Accessed 20 December 2014] (noting that the effects of climate change may result in deprivation of property without compensation, particularly regarding rising sea levels in coastal areas and the use and enjoyment of property where temperature changes affect weather patterns (including more droughts or more tropical storms) and consequently possible land uses).
116 Article 1 (2) ICCPR.
117 Article 13 UDHR.
118 Some national jurisdictions have highlighted the strong relationship between certain communities and their land. In 1993, the U.N. Sub-Commission on Prevention of Discrimination and Protection of Minorities issued a second report of its Special Rapporteur on Human Rights and the Environment (Fatma Zohra Ksentini). It emphasised the Colombian case *Organización Indigena de Antioquia v Codechoco et Madarien*, which concerned environmental damages caused by forestry exploitation, highlighting that the court not only recognised the existence of material damages but also that the devastation of the forest alters the relationships of indigenous populations with their environment and puts in danger not only their lives but also their cultural and ethnic existence. U.N. Commission on Human Rights (now U.N. Human Rights Council) (1993), Second

way of life, affecting a further set of protected rights and interests.[119] This was highlighted in the 2005 Sub-Commission on the Promotion and Protection of Human Rights on the prevention of discrimination and protection of indigenous peoples[120] and again in 2008 during the seventh session of the Permanent Forum on Indigenous Issues.[121] The U.N. Declaration on the Rights of Indigenous People[122] recognises that indigenous populations have rights to the conservation and protection of their environment[123] and the productive capacity of their lands.[124] They also have the right to redress (which can include restitution or, when this is not possible, just, fair, and equitable compensation) for their lands or resources that have been damaged without their free, prior, and informed consent.[125] For these and other communities whose existence is threatened and displacement is imminent, such as those living in SIDS, environmental change further endangers their right to self-determination,[126] as well as the right to the benefits of their culture.[127] The government of Tuvalu eloquently affirmed within the international fora the need for states to take action at both the national and international levels to prevent displacement of their population: "While Tuvalu faces an uncertain future because of climate change, it is our view that Tuvaluans will remain in Tuvalu. We will fight to keep our country, our culture and our

---

Report prepared by Mrs Fatma Zohra, Special Rapporteur (U.N. Doc. E/CN.4/Sub.2/1993/7) 23 July 1993 p. 17 para. 31.

119 *See* the Indigenous People's Global summit on Climate Change, The Anchorage Declaration, 24 April 2009 para.2; Combined reading of Article 3 UNFCCC and U.N. Committee on Social and Cultural Rights General Comment No. 14: The Right to the Highest Attainable Standard of Health (Art. 12 of the Covenant) Doc. E/C.12/2000/4, 11 August 2000 para. 27 ("[i]n this respect, the Committee considers that development-related activities that lead to the displacement of indigenous peoples against their will from their traditional territories and environment, denying them their sources of nutrition and breaking their symbiotic relationship with their lands, has a deleterious effect on their health").

120 *See* U.N. Commission on Human Rights (now U.N. Human Rights Council) (2005) "Prevention of Discrimination and Protection Indigenous People's" Expanded working paper by Françoise Hampson on the human rights situation of indigenous peoples in States and other territories threatened with extinction for environmental reasons U.N. Doc. E/CN.4/Sub.22005/28 16 June 2005 paras. 6, 7, 8.

121 United Nations Permanent Forum on Indigenous Issues (2008) "Special Theme: Climate Change, Bio-Cultural Diversity and Livelihoods: The Stewardship Role of Indigenous Peoples and New Challenges Seventh Session" (New York, 21 April–2 May) paras. 5, 6.

122 U.N. Declaration on the Rights of Indigenous People, adopted 13 September 2007 U.N. Doc. A/RES/61/295 (2 October 2007).

123 *Ibid.* Article 29.

124 *Ibid.* Article 26 (1).

125 *Ibid.* Article 28 (1).

126 Article 13 UDHR; Article 1 & Article 12 (1) ICCPR; Article 1 ICESCR; *See* HRC (1984) CCPR "General Comment No. 12 the Right to Self-Determination of People's" UN Doc. HRI/GEN/1/Rev.1, (13 March 1984).

127 Article 27 UDHR; Article 15 ICESCR and Article XIII of the American Declaration.

way of living. (. . .) We believe if the right actions are taken to address climate change, Tuvalu will survive".[128]

Another right at risk from environmental change is the fundamental human right of freedom of movement and residence. Freedom of movement, characterised as "the right to leave and return to one's country", is considered "an indispensable condition for the free development of a person".[129] Article 12 of the ICCPR sets forth the three aspects of the right of freedom of movement: 1) the right of every person who is residing lawfully[130] in the state to move freely and to choose his/her place of residence therein; 2) the right to leave a country;[131] and 3) the right to enter one's country. This means that individuals affected by environmental factors have the right to choose to return to their place of origin, to relocate to another part of the country, or to integrate themselves in another region. More importantly, the state is obligated to protect against violations of this right, including all forms of internal[132] (and, by extension, external)[133] displacement and to respect the will of the affected populations (which can only be subject to limitations in the case of national security, public emergency, and public health).[134] Governments should provide communities with sufficient information to enable them to avoid or overcome displacement. In General Comment No. 27, the U.N. Human Rights Committee noted that forced displacement is best prevented by ensuring that freedom of movement and residence is fully protected. In *Malawi Association and Others v Mauritania*, the African Commission on Human Rights decided that Mauritania failed to respect its citizens' freedom of movement and residence by failing to prevent

128 European Parliament (2009) "Climate Change Threatens Tuvalu's Survival, Says Prime Minister Apisai Ielemia" Press Release Development and Cooperation Commission 10 December 2009 *available from:* www.europarl.europa.eu/sides/getDoc.do?pubRef=-//EP//TEXT+IM-PRESS+20091207IPR66100+0+DOC+XML+V0//EN [Accessed 17 August 2018].

129 HRC (1999) CCPR General Comment No. 27 Freedom of Movement (Art. 12) UN Doc. CCPR/C/21/Rev.1/Add.9 (18 October 1999) para. 1. *See* Beyani, C. (2000) "Human Rights Standards and the Movement of People Within States" (Oxford University Press) p. 3 (noting that the deprivation of freedom of movement may bar other human rights such as the freedom of assembly and association, right to property, and the right to employment).

130 The access and criteria of a lawful resident in the territory of a state is a matter of domestic law. *See* HRC (1999) *Op. Cit.* General Comment No. 27 para.4.

131 Importantly, there is no corresponding general right to enter another state. *See generally*, Harvey, C. & Barnidge, R. (2005) "The Right to Leaves One's Own Country under International Law" paper prepared for the Policy Analysis and Research Programme of the Global Commission on International Migration (September) pp. 16–17.

132 HRC (1999) *Op. Cit.* General Comment No. 27 para.7 ("[t]he right to reside in a place of one's choice within the territory includes protection from all forms of forced internal displacement. It also precludes preventing the entry or stay of persons in a defined part of the territory").

133 HRC (1999) *Op. Cit.* General Comment 27 paras. 8–9 (citing to protection against external displacement, including expulsion).

134 Article 12 (3) ICCPR.

displacement.[135] The IACtHR, in *Mapiripán Massacre v Colombia*, has also asserted that freedom of movement and residence is the core principle upon which the prevention of displacement depends.[136]

The weakening of the right of freedom of movement and residence is particularly visible with regard to disappearing Islands States, where residents have been unable to return. As noted by Walter Kälin, the former Special Rapporteur on the human rights of internally displaced people, where possible, "[T]he right of return is a key principle; when the original residential areas have proven dangerous, voluntary relocation or resettlement elsewhere are options, provided that the livelihoods and access to basic services are provided".[137]

3.2 Analogy of protection obligations for EDPs: the underlying duty to prevent human rights violations

Regardless of the way states' obligations are viewed (direct and conscious interference,[138] inaction,[139] or a combination of both),[140] the foregoing analysis demonstrates that the quintessence of protection is the prevention of human rights violations. Unequivocally, prevention is the starting point and one of the states' principal positive obligations as emphasised by the section titles of the ECtHR's *Öneryildiz* judgement[141] and made clear by its *Fadeyeva* decision: "the Court's first task is to assess whether the State could reasonably be expected to act so as to prevent or end the alleged infringement of the applicant's rights".[142] The courts, especially the ECtHR, hold that the right to life compels

135 ACmHPR, *Malawi Association and Others v Mauritannia* Comm. No. 54/91 61/91, 98/93, 164/97 à 196/97 and 210/98 (11 May 2000) pp. 21–23 (addressing allegations of institutionalised racial discrimination in Mauritania by ruling Moor community against more populous black community including slavery and analogous practices). Petitioners alleged, amongst other things, that black Mauritanians were enslaved and routinely evicted from their lands, which the government then confiscated along with their livestock. The Commission found that the confiscation and looting of the property of black Mauritanians and the expropriation or destruction of their land and houses before forcing them to go abroad constituted a violation of the right to property (Article 14, ACHPR) as well as of the right to freedom of movement and residence (Article 12(1), ACHPR).

136 IACtHR, *Mapiripán Massacre v Colombia*, Series C No. 134 (15 September 2005).

137 U.N. News Service (2010) "Faute de stratégie adaptée, Haïti est toujours dans la crise humanitaire, selon un expert" 19 October 2010 *available from:* http://reliefweb.int/report/haiti/faute-de-stratégie-adaptée-haïti-est-toujours-dans-la-crise-humanitaire-selon-un-expert (author's own translation) [accessed 25 December 2014] (quoting comments of previous Special Rapporteur on the human rights of internally displaced people, Walter Kälin, regarding the situation in Haiti nine months after the 2010 earthquake).

138 ECtHR, *Hatton and Others v the United Kingdom Op. Cit.*

139 ECtHR, *Guerra and Others v Italy Op. Cit.*; *Öneryildiz v Turkey Op. Cit.*

140 ECtHR, *Öneryildiz v Turkey Op. Cit.*; *Taskin and Others v Turkey Op. Cit.*

141 ECtHR, *Öneryildiz v Turkey Op. Cit.* Point 3 paras. 90, 101, 107.

142 ECtHR, *Fadeyeva v Russia Op. Cit.* para. 89.

states to take all measures to prevent both natural and human-made disasters.[143] While the issue of environmental displacement was touched upon in the Inuit Petition to the IACmHR, it has not been examined in any other national or international jurisdiction. This does not mean, however, that states do not have obligations towards EDPs. On the contrary, states' duties with regards to environmental degradation are, arguably, transferrable in the environmental displacement context. While states' obligations do not warrant the creation of a particular status *per se*, they impose the responsibility to prevent and reduce environmental risks and resulting population displacement, including protection of human rights. Thus, protection not only relates to actual violations of human rights but also consists of an obligation to prevent their occurrence.[144]

The jurisprudence indicates that advanced analysis of human rights infringements is possible; thus, an *ex ante* assessment may be required where there is credible evidence of the potential impact of environmental change on human rights. The increasingly reliable and country-specific data on environmental change and human displacement can, in turn, serve as the basis of states' response measures and arguably impose on states' obligations to implement them.

3.2.1 Minimum scope of protection

International law obligates states to promote the "universal respect for, and observance of, human rights and fundamental freedoms for all without distinction as to race, sex, language, or religion".[145] The obligation to protect civil, political, economic, social, and cultural rights includes communities affected by environmental factors. The protection of vulnerable populations must be a top priority for states. But this obligation is viewed in a holistic way and is owed not only to persons within the states' territory but to all persons ***under their jurisdiction***.[146] As noted, General Comment 15 explains that the enjoyment of Covenant rights must be available to all individuals regardless of nationality or statelessness, including asylum seekers, refugees, or migrants.[147]

The scope of states' positive obligations can be viewed as both *abstract* and *concrete* notions of protection. Abstractly, states have the duty to satisfy the most elementary needs ("minimum core obligation [in abstracto]") of individuals

143 *See, e.g.*, ECtHR, *Öneryildiz v Turkey Op. Cit.*; ECtHR, *Budayeva and Others v Russia Op. Cit. See* Kälin, W. & Dale, C. H. (2008) "Disaster Risk Mitigation: Why Human Rights Matter" 31 Forced Migration Review p. 38.

144 Van Boven, T. (1991) "Prevention of Human Rights Violations" in A. Eide & J. Helgesen (eds.) "The Future of Human Rights Protection in a Changing World: Fifty Years since the Four Freedoms Address. Essays in Honour of Torkel Opsahl" (Norwegian University Press) p. 191.

145 Article 55 (c) U.N. Charter (1945).

146 HRC (2004) "General Comment No. 31 [80] The nature of the general legal obligation imposed on States Parties to the Covenant" *Op. Cit.* para. 10.

147 HRC (2004) "CCPR General Comment No. 15 (1986) The Position of Aliens under the Covenant" U.N. Doc. HRI/GE/1/Rev.7 (12 May) para.1.

that are "deprived of essential foodstuffs, of essential primary health care, of basic shelter and housing, or of the most basic forms of education",[148] even in times of severe resources constraints. States must protect the vulnerable members of society "by the adoption of relatively low-cost targeted programmes".[149] Conversely, the scope of states' positive obligations is related to the concrete content of protection, i.e. the protection that can be effectively secured by states' resources.

In *Budayeva and Others*, for example, the ECtHR reasoned that an "impossible or disproportionate burden must not be imposed on the authorities without consideration being given, in particular, to the operational choices which they must make in terms of priorities and resources; (. . .) this results from the wide margin of appreciation States. This consideration must be afforded even greater weight in the sphere of emergency relief in relation to a meteorological event, which is as such beyond human control, than in the sphere of dangerous activities of a man-made nature".[150] It follows that the protection of human rights will depend on the finances of the state. In reality, though, the content of protection may vary based on whether there is a need to establish, as Dimitris Xenos puts it, "a minimum content of protection in order to deal with positive obligations in a non-theoretical matter".[151] Where only one protection measure is feasible, it does not negate states' positive obligations; it merely implies that "positive obligations can arise and be accordingly imposed in relation to this measure alone, provided that the effectiveness of protection is guaranteed".[152] The right of information, for example, does not impose an impossible burden on state's resources.

The protective function of the state is often reflected in existing laws or constitutional provisions to ensure and to promote the protection of human rights. Consequently, states' responsibilities lie in their enabling and protecting role and not necessarily in existing financial resources. In *Öneryildiz*, discussed previously, which addressed a fatal industrial accident in which 39 people lost their lives, the court discerned abstract and concrete measures of protection in the forms of various administrative steps, stating that

> The positive obligation to take all appropriate steps to safeguard life for the purposes of Article 2 entails above all a primary duty on the State to put in place legislative and administrative framework designed to provide deterrence against threats to the right to life (. . .) and must make it compulsory for all those concerned to take practical measures to ensure effective

148 CESCR (1990) "General Comment No. 3: The Nature of States Parties' Obligations (Art. 2, Para. 1, of the Covenant)" E/1991/23 (14 December 1990) para. 10.

149 *Ibid.* para. 12.

150 ECtHR, *Budayeva and Others v Russia Op. Cit.* para. 135.

151 Xenos, D. (2012) "The Positive Obligations of the State under the European Convention of Human Rights" (Routledge) p. 106.

152 *Ibid.*

> protection of citizens whose lives might be endangered by the inherent risks. Among these preventative measures, particular emphasis should be placed on the public's right to information as established in the case-law of the Convention institutions.[153]

Applied to displacement, this concrete notion of protection requires states to not only respond ad hoc after displacement occurs but to ensure a system of protection is in place prior to displacement. The Strasbourg court highlighted that imposing duties that are commensurate with states' financial resources or priorities does not negate states' obligation to forestall risk and to "do everything within their power to protect [people] from the immediate and known risks to which they were exposed".[154] The content of measures and standards for protection of human rights is addressed to both states and private actors.

3.2.2 Obligations of states and procedural rights

Notably, the link between states' procedural obligations in the environmental domain and the environmental displacement context enables governments to provide complete and effective protection of human rights. Outlined in several international documents, and overtly recognised by regional human rights jurisprudence, the right to information, the right to public participation in decision-making processes, and the right to remedy are all cornerstones to safeguarding the human rights of people menaced by environmental stressors. As Dinah Shelton explains, procedural human rights "[refer] to the reformulation and expansion of existing human rights and duties in the context of environmental protection".[155]

Undoubtedly, information dissemination in the case of disasters (as the nuclear accident in Japan or Hurricane Katrina) spares lives. In other cases, the public's participation in decision-making processes ensures preventative action if evacuation is needed, as in the case of sea level rise. For violations of human rights stemming from environmental factors, the right to remedy must enter the equation. Interestingly, the procedural obligations of states towards EDPs, particularly the right to information, were highlighted by the United Nations Population Fund during the Cancun discussions in December 2010.[156]

153 ECtHR, *Öneryildiz v Turkey Op. Cit.* paras. 71, 89–90.
154 *Ibid.* para. 109.
155 Shelton, D. (1991) "Human Rights, Environmental Rights and the Right to Environment" 28 Stanford Journal of International Law p. 117, pp. 103–138.
156 United Nations Population Fund (UNFPA) (2010) "Displacement and Migration: Examples of Initiatives to Support Resilience and Adaptation" U.N. System Side Event Cancun (30 November 2010) p. 2.

(i) Right to information

In cases of environmental risks, states should ensure that the public is provided the *right to access information* necessary for their protection. States must not only provide people the right to seek information but must disseminate information that will provide the public with a basis for informed decision-making.

The codification of the governmental obligation to provide to the public information about environmental hazards upon request derives from both international and regional instruments including the International Covenant on Civil and Political Rights[157] and the Universal Declaration of Human Rights.[158] It is also made evident under the United Nations Convention on Climate Change[159] and under Principle 10 of the Declaration on Environment and Development adopted by the 1992 Conference of Rio de Janeiro. The latter can be viewed as international recognition of the right to information concerning the environment, including information on hazardous materials and activities. It is the Aarhus Convention,[160] however, where state parties to the U.N. Economic Commission for Europe produced a landmark agreement on 25 June 1998 to promote procedural rights. The landmark Aarhus Convention, though, specifically imposed two procedural obligations on state parties: 1) to make information available to the public on environmental matters; and 2) in case of an imminent threat to human health – whether from human or natural causes – to provide the information necessary to enable those at risk to take measures to prevent or mitigate the consequences. Therefore, states must have in place an information system to inform the public about environmental risks and provide regular updates. In Article 4(4), though, the treaty provides numerous exceptions to the duty to inform, accommodating economic, political, and legal concerns; this could enable states to withhold important information. Nevertheless, all

157 Article 19 (2) ICCPR. *See* HRC (2011) "General Comment No. 34, Article 19, Freedoms of opinion and expression" U.N. Doc. CCPR/C/GC/34 (12 September 2011) (connecting the right of access to information to other rights in the Covenant including Article 2's non-discrimination, Article 17's respect for private life and privacy, and Article 25's political participation).

158 Notably, the right to information in the human rights context derives from the right to freedom of expression and opinion. *See, e.g.*, Article 19 UDHR. Other instruments, however, highlight the relevance of the right to information. *See, e.g.*, Article 27 of the Convention concerning the Protection of the World Cultural and Natural Heritage, adopted on 16 November 1972, in force since 17 December 1975, 1037 UNTS 151; Article 21(a) of the 1982 World Charter for Nature UNGA World Charter for Nature UN Doc. A/RES/37/7 (28 October 1982); European Parliament and of the Council Directive 2003/4/EC of the on public access to environmental information (28 January 2003).

159 Article 6 (a) (ii) UNFCCC (stating that in carrying out its commitments, state parties shall "[p]romote and facilitate at the national and, as appropriate, subregional and regional levels, and in accordance with national laws and regulations, and within their respective capacities: (ii) Public access to information on climate change and its effects").

160 Aarhus Convention *Op. Cit.*

exceptions must be read restrictively, and states may wish to provide broader information rights. In any event, as illustrated in the Strasbourg *Örnerlydiz* case, respecting the right to information is, alone, insufficient to absolve states from their responsibilities.[161]

The right to information is especially important to populations that are particularly vulnerable to the effects of environmental change. By adopting adequate *ex ante* protection measures, states enable people to take preventative action including evacuating to safer areas or even permanent relocation. After displacement, states' *ex post* protection measures ensure that the affected population can make an informed decision about whether to return to their homes.[162]

States' obligations to disseminate environmental risk information is implied in the ECtHR's *Guerra and Others*, which held that the right to information includes not only states' obligation to make environmental information publicly available but also "a positive obligation to collect, process and disseminate such information, which by its nature could not otherwise come to the knowledge of the public".[163] The ECtHR reiterated its holding in *Oneryildiz*, finding that Turkey had violated several provisions of the ECHR (including Article 2's right to life).[164] Similarly, in *McGinley and Egan v U.K.*, which concerned potentially adverse health effects of nuclear testing, the court reasoned that Article 8 (right to respect private life) implicitly obligated the state to implement procedures to provide information on hazardous activities to exposed individuals.[165] Later, in *Tatar v Romania*, the court made clear that the right to respect private and family life also imposed on states the positive obligation to assess the risks to

161 ECtHR, *Öneryildiz v Turkey* (2004) *Op. Cit.* para. 108.

162 UNGA (2009) "Report of the Representative of the Secretary-General on the Human Rights of Internally Displaced Persons" U.N. Doc. A/64/214 (3 August 2009) para. 30 (highlighting certain universal principles with regards to persons displaced or at risk of displacement from environmental change who wish to freely return to their homes, including: 1) information on the process, consultation with and participation of the affected communities; 2) safety; 3) recovery of land and property upon return, including through settlement of property and land disputes; 4) physical needs and livelihoods).

163 ECtHR, *Guerra and Others v Italy Op. Cit.* para. 52 (finding violation of Article 8 (right to respect private life) and reasoning that that right implied a right to information if pertinent to the enjoyment of that right). Notably, the ECtHR did not follow the interpretation of the former European Commission on Human Rights (EcmmHR), which held that Italy violated its obligations not under Article 8 but rather Article 10 (right to freedom of expression), by withholding risk information from residents living close to a chemical plant. The EcmmHR found that Article 10 placed positive obligations on states to make information available and actively publish where the protection of the public's well-being and health, or the environment, is at stake. ECommHR, *Guerra and Others v Italy*, Application No. 14967/89 (29 June 1996).

164 ECtHR, *Oneryildiz v Turkey* (2004) *Op. Cit.* para. 60.

165 ECtHR, *McGinley and Egan v U.K.*, Application Nos. 21825/93 and 23414/94 (8 June 1998).

which populations are exposed.[166] In *Vilness and Others v Norway*, the ECtHR took a further step by acknowledging that, in certain situations, states' obligations to provide access to information and to assess health risks encompass not only the non-refusal to provide but also a duty to actively provide information regarding the scope and extent of the risks, regardless of scientific uncertainty.[167]

These cases help ensure that, with regards to (pre-)displaced populations, the right to information extends not only to classic environmental matters but also, by analogy, to other situations, including those stemming from environmental change factors.[168] As noted, this is also seen in (quasi) judicial decisions in both the African and American regions, which have acknowledged the right to information and the parallel obligation of states to take preventative measures to protect human rights.[169]

(ii) Right to public participation in decision-making

The right to public participation in decision-making is intrinsically linked with the right to information. The public plays a major role in decision-making, especially concerning environmental and, by extension, human rights impacts. The right to participation is found in various human rights and environmental law

166 ECtHR, *Tatar v Romania*, Application No. 67021/01 (27 January 2009) paras. 88, 113, 118, 122, 124, 128 (unanimously holding that the Roman authorities violated ECHR's Article 8 (right to respect for private and family life) when they failed to protect the right of the applicants, who lived near a gold mine, to enjoy a healthy and protected environment.

167 ECtHR, *Vilness and Others v Norway*, Application No. 52806/9 (5 December 2013) para. 244.

168 Importantly, while other human rights treaties seem to recognise the right to information as a discrete or implied right deriving from the right to freedom of expression and opinion, the ECHR does not recognise that right under Article 10 Freedom of Expression. The ECtHR has yet to sustain the interpretation that Article 10 (right to information) gives rise to a positive obligation requiring a state to disclose relevant information but has, nevertheless, recognised the right to information in relation to other substantive rights (Article 2 right to life and Article 8 right to privacy). *See* Donders, Y. (2015) "International Covenant on Economic, Social and Cultural Rights: Accessibility and the Right to Information" in T. MacGonagle & Y. Donders (eds.) "The United Nations and Freedom of Expression and information critical perspectives" (Oxford University Press) p. 98, pp. 89–120 ("the Court (ECtHR) is ready to accept far-reaching positive obligations concerning the dissemination of information under Art. 8 (and 2), in particular when it concerns potential health risks, whereas it has not (yet) been ready to accept such obligations under Article 10").

169 *See, e.g.*, IACtHR, *Claude Reyes et al. v Chile* Series C No. 151 (19 September 2006) paras. 73, 151(acknowledging violation of the right to information but also reaffirming states' parallel obligation to take preventative measures, where company engaged in deforestation of a Chilean region).

instruments,[170] most notably under Article 21 of the Universal Declaration of Human Rights and Article 25 of the International Covenant on Civil and Political Rights. The right to public participation is especially relevant in the context of climate change. Under the UNFCCC, states are responsible for facilitating "[P]ublic participation in addressing climate change and its effects and developing adequate responses".[171] Thus, the right to public participation comprises not only the right to be heard but also the right to affect decisions. This dual component can also be found under the United Nations Convention to Combat Desertification, which calls for an integrated commitment of national governments, local populations and authorities, non-governmental organisations, the scientific community, and international (bilateral and multilateral) partners.[172]

Participation is largely a matter of legitimacy in which the public plays an active role (through representation, deliberation, or other forms of action) in decision-making processes, including the ways in which proposed rules become norms and then law. Indeed, in the words of Alexandre Kiss, "public participation is based on the right of those who may be affected, including foreign citizens and residents, to have a say in the determination of their environmental future".[173] But, most importantly, the right includes the public having say as to the protection of their human rights. In *Hatton and Others v United Kingdom*, the European Court explained that states' public authorities in decision-making processes affecting environmental issues must "ensure that due weight has been accorded to the interests of the individual".[174]

This rights-based approach to public participation is intimately related to environmental displacement and has been particularly highlighted by Raquel Rolnik, the Special Rapporteur on adequate housing:

> A rights-based approach would also ensure that, while affected communities are able to relocate away from hazardous zones (e.g. sinking cities), all efforts are made to ensure adequate and genuine consultation with the communities before any relocation decision is taken. In no circumstances should individuals be subject to forced evictions. A rights-based approach

170 Article 14 (1) (a) Convention on Biological Diversity adopted 5 June 1992, in force since 29 December 1993, 30619 UNTS Chapter XXVII.

171 Article 6 (a) (iii) UNFCCC.

172 Article 3 United Nations Convention to Combat Desertification in Those Countries Experiencing Serious Drought and/or Desertification, Particularly in Africa (UNCCD) adopted 14 October 1994, in force since 26 December 1996, 954 UNTS 3/ [2000] ATS 18/ 33 ILM 1328.

173 Kiss, A. (2003) "The Right to the Conservation of the Environment" in R. Picolotti & J. D. Taillant (eds.) "Linking Human Rights and the Environment" (The University of Arizona Press) p. 36.

174 ECtHR, *Hatton and Others v United Kingdom* (2003) Application No. 36022/97 (8 July 2003) para. 99 (holding that the public decision-making process under Article 8 implies realisation of studies and investigations to ensure fair balance between competing interests of individuals affected by increased night time airport noise and community as a whole).

accordingly brings a focus on participation in planning and decision-making and on access to information, as well as accountability.[175]

A rights-based approach to public participation is linked to principles of equality and non-discrimination, requiring that governments pay special attention to vulnerabilities and inequities not only before but also after displacement to better protect the most vulnerable. Generally, women, children, disabled people, older people, and indigenous groups are disproportionately affected by environmental disasters, including many who live in unstable conditions and in vulnerable areas exposed to strong winds, flooding, and landslides. Examples include Honduras in the wake of Hurricane Mitch in 1998 (indigenous populations and women),[176] the Colombia floods throughout 2010 and 2011 (indigenous and Afro-Colombians),[177] or even Hurricane Katrina in the United States in 2005 (poor African Americans).[178]

States should take special measures to protect the human rights of disadvantaged groups. Post-displacement, this may mean ensuring adequate access to information and public participation in decision-making and, especially, supporting those displaced in returning or finding alternative living arrangements. Governments should take the most adequate participative approach.[179] The Indian government made a comprehensive and generally successful rehabilitation effort in Gujarat after the 2001 earthquake, which included the reconstruction of the affected villages three kilometres from the original location. Though the local population agreed to the plan, six years after the earthquake the new villages were empty. The villagers had rebuilt their original village, alleging either a special attachment with their land or few local integrating infrastructures.[180]

Thus, while it is true that governments should ensure the rights to participation and information in the context of displacement by environmental factors,

175 UNGA (2008) "Report of the Special Rapporteur on Adequate Housing as a Component of the Right to an Adequate Standard of Living, and on the Right to Non-Discrimination in This Context" U.N. Doc. A/63/275 (13 August 2008) para. 38.

176 UNGA (2010) "Report of the Special Rapporteur on Adequate Housing as a Component of the Right to an Adequate Standard of Living, and on the Right to Non-Discrimination in This Context, Raquel Rolnik" U.N. Doc. A/HRC/16/42 (20 December 2010) paras. 31, 32.

177 Ferris, E. & Petz, D. (2011) "A Year of Living Dangerously: A Review of Natural Disasters in 2010" (London, The Brookings Institution–London School of Economics) p. 19.

178 The Brookings Institution (2005) "New Orleans after the Storm: Lessons from the Past, a Plan for the Future" (October 2005) p. 6 *available from:* www.brookings.edu/~/media/research/files/reports/2005/10/metropolitanpolicy/20051012_neworleans.pdf [accessed 17 August 2018].

179 *See generally*, International Red Cross and Red Crescent Societies (2010) "A Practical Guide to Gender-Sensitive Approaches for Disaster Management" *available from*: www.ifrc.org/PageFiles/96532/A%20Guide%20for%20Gender-sensitive%20approach%20to%20DM.pdf [accessed 17 August 2018].

180 UNGA (2010) A/HRC/16/42 (20 December 2010) *Op. Cit.* paras. 42, 43.

they must be collaborative. There is an increasing need of available remedy mechanisms to reinforce and protect the human rights of EDPs.

(iii) Right to access to justice

The International Covenant on Civil and Political Rights[181] and other international instruments[182] extensively discuss the right to access to justice. Authors like Frédéric Sudre state that the right to access to justice is complementary[183] to other proscribed international rights. Though arguable, that position understates the relevance of the right in itself, the power of which derives from both the possibility of an effective remedy and also the eligibility for reparations. In the displacement context, such remedies should involve, for example, full investigation and disclosure of the cause as well as the prosecution for criminal acts.[184] Victims of displacement should also be eligible for reparations, which can include compensation for the loss of family, property damage, and loss of revenue.[185] Both avenues may or may not involve the judicial system but should always be addressed expeditiously.

Generally speaking, states cannot be responsible for disasters,[186] but as demonstrated, the right to life and other human rights impose on states positive obligations to safeguard against disaster risks for those who are within their jurisdictions.[187] In this context, the right to access to justice seems justified,

181 Article 2 (3) (a) ICCPR ("[e]ach State Party to the present Covenant undertakes: To ensure that any person whose rights or freedoms as herein recognized are violated shall have an effective remedy, notwithstanding that the violation has been committed by persons acting in an official capacity)".

182 *See*, *e.g.*, Article 6 (1) and Article 13 ECHR; Article 25 ACHR; Principle 10 of the Rio Declaration ("effective access to judicial and administrative proceedings, including redress and remedy, shall be provided"); Agenda 21 (calling on governments to establish judicial and administrative procedures for legal redress and remedy of actions that affect the environment or infringe the human rights of those concerned); Article 9 (3) Aarhus Convention.

183 Sudre, F. (2005) "Droit Européen et International des Droits de l'Homme" (Presses Universitaires de France, 7éme éd.) p. 387.

184 Brookings Institution & University of Bern (2005) "Protecting Internally Displaced Persons: Manual for Law and Policy Makers" (Brookings Institution October 2008) p. 58.

185 *Ibid.*

186 The Parliamentary Assembly of the Council of Europe, in its Recommendation 1862 (2009), "Environmentally Induced Migration and Displacement: A 21st-Century Challenge" (30 January) para. 5 (highlighting the concern that Europeans have no specific legal remedy against human activity-caused environmental degradation and climate change that affects their health and safety).

187 *See* ECtHR, *Okyay v Turkey*, Application No. 36220/97 (12 July 2005) paras. 67–69 (finding violation of Article 6 (1)'s right to fair trial where Turkish government decided that three thermal power stations should continue to operate in defiance of administrative courts' orders to suspend their activities, where government's conduct was unlawful under Turkish constitutional provision entitling applicants to live in healthy and balanced

particularly when a state is unable or unwilling to take precautionary measures to protect from a foreseen disaster (e.g. temporary evacuation, relocation to safer areas) prohibiting return to unsafe locations.

The IACtHR explicitly obligated states to take reasonable steps to prevent human rights violations:

> The duty to prevent includes all those means of a legal, political, administrative and cultural nature that promote the protection of human rights and ensure that any violations are considered and treated as illegal acts, which, as such may lead to the punishment of those responsible and the obligation to indemnify the victims for damages. It is not possible to make a detailed list of all such measures, since they vary with the law and the conditions of each State Party.[188]

The human rights agenda includes the environment and government actions concerning the environment and can be challenged through international tribunals. Because the environment and human rights are common denominators for EDPs, the right to access to justice might motivate governments to enact measures to minimise or avoid the effects of environmental displacement. Effective protection of human rights to avoid irreparable harm to the person is "a *law of protection* of the human being, [where] provisional measures reach effectively their plenitude, being endowed with a character, more than precautionary, truly *tutelary*" (emphasis added).[189]

3.3 Explicit recognition of the duty of states to protect from displacement

In his book *International Law for Humankind: Towards a New Jus Gentium*, Cançado Trindade highlights the preventative dimension of protection of the human person. He acknowledges that previous rules of international law were crystallised in a static outlook of the international legal order. Globally, the world was safer. He argues that today's outlook is different:

> In our days, amidst an acute consciousness of vulnerability, one begins to rethink those rules bearing in mind the temporal dimension, the incidence – perhaps less tangible, but real – and influence of which on juridical solutions

environment). *See also Taskin and Others v Turkey Op. Cit.* para. 132 (holding that exploitation of a gold mine constitutes a genuine and serious threat to the right to live in a healthy and balanced environment guaranteed under Article 56 of the Turkish Constitution).

188 IACtHR, *Velasquez Rodriguez v Honduras*, Series C No.4 (29 July 1988), paras. 174–175.

189 Cançado Trindade, A. (2010) "International Law of Humankind towards a New *Jus Gentium*" (Martinus Nijhoff Publishers) p. 43.

> begins to be felt with increasing intensity, as a feature of our times. There is, in this connection, a much greater awareness of the relevance of the preventative dimension in the role of law. [. . .] In recent developments concerning in particular environmental protection and human rights protection, the preventative dimension becomes manifest.[190]

The preventative dimension concept (the state's underlying duty to prevent the violation of human rights) is evident in a number of relevant interconnected normative texts and operational frameworks that, explicitly or implicitly, place obligations on states to prevent environmental displacement and violation of human rights.

3.3.1 *Guiding principles on internal displacement*

The Guiding Principles on Internal Displacement (GPID) were developed in 1998 by the former United Nations Secretary General Representative on internally displaced persons, Francis M. Deng. They offer to states pre- and post-displacement guidance. Their holistic perspective plays a key role in the conceptualisation of protection for EDPs contained herein. The GPID have served as a basis for states' national laws and policies on IDPs. They have also been acknowledged by the (former) U.N. Commission on Human Rights and the U.N. General Assembly[191] and have been well received by the Inter-Agency Standing Committee (IASC), composed of heads of key international humanitarian relief and development agencies. The Principles have been widely disseminated by both international and regional bodies (such as the Organisation of American States, the African Union, and the Organisation for Security and Cooperation in Europe) and grass-roots organisations.[192] The GPID are considered primarily soft law since they address the international community as a whole[193] and seek to reassert previously documented human rights and humanitarian norms, whilst being innovative within the context of internal displacement.

Though the GPID articulate displacement prevention in a subsidiary way, they are germane to certain issues of human vulnerability and state obligations. The Principles, in paragraph 2, include both human-caused and natural disasters

190 *Ibid.* pp. 39–40.

191 U.N. Commission on Human Rights (now U.N. Human Rights Council) (1998) "Res. 1998/50, Internally Displaced Persons" (17 April); UNGA (1999) "Res. 54/167, Protection of and Assistance to Internally Displaced Persons" (17 December).

192 *See* Kälin, W. (2008) "Guiding Principles on Internal Displacement: Annotations" Studies in Transnational Legal Policy No. 38 (Washington DC, ASIL, The Brookings Institution Project on Internal Displacement). The Annotations are the most authoritative for interpreting the GPID.

193 *See* Shelton, D. (2000) "Commentary and Conclusions" in D. Shelton (ed.) "Commitment and Compliance" (Oxford University Press) pp. 449–450.

within the scope of displacement. Principle 3 also articulates that national authorities bear the primary duty for ensuring protection and assistance.[194]

The GPID offer three relevant provisions: Principles 5, 6, and 9. Principle 5 requires states to abide by their obligations under international law to prevent the conditions that may lead to displacement. Principle 6 recognises that individuals have the right to protection from "arbitrary displacement", which it does not define but does illustrate with a list of examples of displacement caused by (unfounded) human intervention. States cannot forcibly evacuate (displace) people unless vital for their safety and health in the context of disasters.[195] Displacement in the case of disasters would hardly be justifiable in any other circumstance.[196] Michèle Morel explains that, though much of the GPID is binding upon states that are party to the relevant instruments (or customary law), this is not the case with the definition of an internally displaced person or with Principle 6.[197] These provisions are not binding but are only "soft law" because they have not been officially adopted by states by means of a treaty or a convention.[198]

However, the purpose of Principle 6's express statement of a right to not be arbitrarily displaced was to "defin[e] explicitly what is now only implicit in international law 'specifically' a general rule according to which forced displacement may be undertaken only exceptionally and, even then may not be effected in a discriminatory matter nor arbitrarily imposed".[199] Whereas the implicit displacement prohibition derives from provisions such as freedom of movement and residence, the right to freedom from arbitrary interference within one's home, and the right to housing, the explicit prohibition of arbitrary displacement derives from humanitarian law and the law related to indigenous peoples.[200]

194 This general principle is repeated several times throughout the text (e.g. Principle 25 – provision of assistance; Principle 28 – establishment of conditions and provisions of means to voluntarily return; Principle 29 – assistance in recovery or compensation for property and lost possessions GPID).

195 Principle 6 (2) (d), GPID.

196 Kälin (2008) *Op. Cit.* p. 18.

197 Morel, M. (2014) "The Right Not to Be Displaced in International Law" (Intersentia) p. 84.

198 *Ibid.*

199 Kälin (2008) *Op. Cit.* p. 14; Stavropoulou, M. (1994) "The Right Not to Be Displaced" 9 The American University Journal of International Law and Policy 3 p. 738, pp. 689–749 (opining that the notion of "arbitrary" displacement refers to the classical approach under which a lawful restriction of human rights may be pursued as long as it is legal, legitimate, necessary, and proportionate).

200 *See* Kälin (2008) *Op. Cit.* p. 14; Article 12 UDHR; Articles 12 (1) and 17 ICCPR; Articles 11 and 21 (1) ACHR; Article 8 ECHR and Article 2(1) Protocol No.4 to the ECHR; Article 12(1) ACHRP; Articles 49 and 147 Geneva Convention relative to the Protection of Civilian Persons in Time of War (Fourth Geneva Convention) adopted 12 August 1949, in force since 21 October 1950, 75 UNTS 287; Articles 51(7), 78(1) and 85 (4) of Protocol Additional to the Geneva Conventions of 12 August 1949, and relating to the Protection of Victims of International Armed Conflicts (Protocol I) adopted 08 June 1977, in force since 07 December 1978, 1125 UNTS 3; Articles 4(3)(e) and

"Taken together, these rights and guarantees constitute a sound legal basis for restating, in general terms, a general prohibition against arbitrary displacement".[201]

Though Principle 6 focuses on evacuation rather than the effects of disasters, the latitude of the definition of internally displaced persons (covering both human and natural disasters) and the combined reading of Principles 5 and 6 suggest that displacement could be "arbitrary" if imputable to government authorities. Indeed, displacement can be a result of an active state policy – if the government acts unreasonably in exposing people to disaster risks – or passive state policy – if it fails to mitigate disaster risks under human rights law.[202] Furthermore, Principle 9 provides that "states are under a particular obligation to protect against the displacement of indigenous peoples, minorities, peasants, pastoralists and other groups with a special dependency on and attachment to their lands".[203] A GPID-based study on the law relating to the protection against arbitrary displacement stated that "forced displacement" includes "policies that have the purpose or the effect of compelling people to leave their home and place of habitual residence, including in some cases relocating them to another area of the country, against their will".[204] It emphasised the role of the state:

> In many cases the State will be responsible for and actively involved in carrying out displacement policies. In other cases the State may condone, tolerate or acquiesce to such policies and its role may be more difficult to discern. However, even in cases where the precise role of the State is unclear, the effect of such policies and their consequences for the enjoyment of

17 of Protocol Additional to the Geneva Conventions of 12 August 1949, and relating to the Protection of Victims of Non-International Armed Conflicts (Protocol II) adopted 08 June 1977, in force since 07 December 1978, 1125 UNTS 609; and Article 16 of Convention No. 169 (ILO) concerning Indigenous and Tribal Peoples in Independent Countries, adopted 27 June 1989, in force since 5 September 1991, 28 ILM 1383 ("[t]he peoples concerned *shall not* be removed from the lands which they occupy" (emphasis added).

201 Kälin (2008) *Op. Cit.* p. 14.

202 Fisher, D. (2010) "Legal Implementation of Human Rights Obligations to Prevent Displacement Due to Natural Disasters" in K. Koser & A. Solomon (eds.) "Incorporating the Guiding Principles on Internal Displacement into Domestic Law: Issues and Challenges" pp. 551–590, p. 553.

203 ILO Convention no 169 of 1989 *Op. Cit.* Article 13 (1) ("governments shall respect the special importance for the cultures and spiritual values of their relationship with their lands or territories, or both as applicable, which they can occupy or otherwise use, and in particular the collective aspects of this relationship"); The U.N. Declaration of the Rights of Indigenous Peoples (2007) ("States shall provide effective mechanisms for prevention of, and redress for (. . .) [a]ny action which has the aim or effect of dispossessing [indigenous peoples and individuals] of their lands, territories or resources"); UNGA Res. 61/1295, UN Doc. No A/RES/61/1295 (13 September 2007). Arguably, these broadly written provisions can include cases where states fail to adequately protect the rights of indigenous populations from loss of their homes due to environmental stressors.

204 Compilation and Analysis of Legal Norms (1998), Part II, Introduction para.3.

> human rights will be sufficient to determine the legality or illegality of forced movement and the obligations of the State concerned vis-à-vis the persons so moved (displaced). Where it is determined that the forced removal of people is a result of (active or passive) State policy and is illegal questions of State responsibility arise.[205]

It follows that the GPID provide a basis for a state obligation (positive and negative) to refrain from arbitrarily displacing people, as well as a duty to prohibit and prevent displacement by both human-made and natural disasters. Practically, a state may violate its duty by a general lack of policy (such as disaster preparedness or even climate adaptation policies) or by failure to protect its people when a disaster occurs. Authors like Maria Stavropoulou have argued that this preventative approach, or even the consolidation of the right not to be displaced, "would provide governments of developed countries weary of refugees with a pretext for increased efforts to contain them in their country of origin".[206] In reality, Principle 2(2) of the GPID clearly articulates that they "shall not be interpreted as restricting or modifying or impairing the provisions of any international human rights or international humanitarian law instrument or rights granted to persons under domestic law. In particular, these Principles are without prejudice to the right to seek and enjoy asylum in other countries".

Protection from displacement is thus complementary to the right to seek and enjoy asylum in other countries.[207] More importantly, protection from, during, and after displacement fully interact with each other, highlighting the much-needed holistic and integrative approach to protecting EDPs. The domino effect of a preventative approach implies an extension of the scope to externally displaced persons (even if established in the context of GPID) because, in the context of environmental change, any legal or policy framework that prevents internal displacement can implicitly obligate the avoidance of cross-border displacement. Because the GPID do not merely reproduce existing norms, they do not formally bind states, thereby limiting their innovative impact. But, the fact that the GPID have been incorporated into the national legislation and policies of approximately 20 states solidifies an explicit preventative approach to protection and a certain degree of recognition of this obligation by national states.

3.3.2 Internal displacement protocol to the Great Lakes Pact

The GPID and its normative foundations have influenced many regional and subregional processes, such as the adoption of the Kampala Convention (see next section) and the Protocol on the Protection and Assistance to Internally

205 *Ibid.* Introduction para. 5.

206 Stavropoulou, M. (2010) "The Kampala Convention and Protection from Arbitrary Displacement" 36 Forced Migration Review pp. 62–63.

207 Morel (2014) *Op. Cit.* p. 87.

Displaced Persons added to the Pact on Security, Stability, and Development in the Great Lakes Region (IDP Protocol).[208]

With the objective of ending the region's endemic conflicts and the consequences thereof, the IDP Protocol is the first multilateral instrument legally obliging states to enact national legislation implementing the GPID. Article 3(1) directs states to enact necessary legislative frameworks to prevent arbitrary displacement and to eliminate root causes of displacement.[209]

Like the GPID, the IDP Protocol thus imposes both positive and negative obligations upon states to protect people from displacement by both natural and human-made disasters. Specifically, Article 3(2) obliges states, to the extent possible, to mitigate the consequences of displacement caused by natural disasters.[210] By emphasising the obligation of states to not only prevent arbitrary displacement but also eliminate its root causes, the IDP Protocol establishes, in a way, a legal framework that explicitly obligates state parties to prevent displacement. It further articulates this obligation by prescribing the use of the Annotations of the Guiding Principles for their interpretation and annexing the GPID to the IDP Protocol.

As to EDPs, this obligation involves both preventative and proactive approaches to mitigate and/or adapt to the effects of environmental change and thus avoid displacement. Examples include measures to reduce greenhouse emissions, national adaptation plans, and cooperation between organs of government to develop adequate regional circular migration schemes to adapt to environmental stressors and ensure cooperation with international partners, as well as effective participation of those displaced (or potentially) in the policy-making process.[211] By signing the IDP Protocol, the states committed to adopting

208 In December 2006, at the International Conference on the Great Lakes Region, eleven states (Angola, Burundi, Central African Republic, Chad, Democratic Republic of Congo, Republic of Congo, Rwanda, Sudan, Tanzania, Uganda and Zambia) adopted the Pact on Security, Stability and Development in the Great Lakes Region (Great Lakes Pact), which became effective in June 2008. The IDP Protocol is one of ten Protocols to the Great Lakes Pact; the Great Lakes Pact and its Protocols were ratified by all participating states.

209 Article 3(1) IDP Protocol ("Member States undertake to prevent arbitrary displacement and to eliminate the root causes of displacement").

210 Article 3(2) IDP Protocol ("Member States shall, to the extent possible, mitigate the consequences of displacement caused by natural disasters and natural causes").

211 Many of these ideas are (can be) domesticated in Article 6 of the IDP Protocol ("[a]doption and Implementation of the Guiding Principles 1. Member States undertake to adopt and implement the Guiding Principles as a *regional framework for providing protection and assistance to internally displaced persons* in the Great Lakes Region; 2. Member States accept to use the *'Annotations of the Guiding Principles on Internal Displacement' as an authoritative source for interpreting the application of the Guiding Principles*; 3. Member States shall enact national legislation to domesticate the Guiding Principles fully and to provide a legal framework for their implementation within national legal systems; 4. Member States undertake to ensure that such legislation shall: a. *Define internally displaced persons according to Article 1(4)(5)* of this Protocol; b. Prescribe the

and implementing the GPID. The IDP Protocol also endeavours to adapt the GPID to the characteristics of internal displacement within the region (particularly, by defining the scope of the states' duties and establishing a regional mechanism for monitoring protection of those displaced).

3.3.3 Kampala Convention

The 2009 African Union Convention for the Protection and Assistance of Internally Displaced Persons in Africa (Kampala Convention) is the first human rights pan-regional document adopted by the African Union acknowledging the duty of prevention. Its legal framework requires states to fully honour international law obligations to prevent and avoid conditions that might lead to displacement.[212] No other international or regional human rights instruments (ICCPR, ICESCR, ECHR, ACHR, or ACHPR) offer such recognition. By setting the normative and legal framework for the governance of internal displacement, the Kampala Convention aims to promote and strengthen regional and national measures to "prevent or mitigate, prohibit and eliminate root causes of internal displacement as well as provide for durable solutions".[213]

The latitude of the Convention's provisions is commendable, especially with regards to Article 4's non-exhaustive causes and consequences of internal displacement.[214] Like the GPID, the Kampala Convention provides a set of rights of internally displaced persons and the corresponding pre- and post-displacement duties of states. Internationally accepted, the Kampala Convention ensures that states bear an extensive catalogue of obligations. It goes further than the GPID, though, as it also specifies the obligations of non-state actors.[215] Mehari Maru

---

procedures for undertaking development induced displacement; c. *Specify the organs of government responsible for providing protection and assistance to internally displaced persons, disaster preparedness and the implementation of the legislation incorporating the Guiding Principles*; d. *Provide for the channels of engagement and cooperation* between the organs of government, organs of the United Nations, the African Union, and civil society; e. *Enable the holistic incorporation* of the Guiding Principles. 5. Member States shall ensure the *effective participation of internally displaced persons in the preparation and design of the said legislation*") (emphasis added).

212 Article 4 (1) Kampala Convention.

213 Article 2 (a) Kampala Convention.

214 *See* Kampala Convention, Article 4 (4) (h)(enumerating non-exclusive prohibited categories of arbitrary displacement, including "Displacement caused by any act, event, factor, or phenomenon of comparable gravity to all of the above and which is not justified under international law, including human rights and international humanitarian law").

215 The Kampala Convention imposes obligations on non-state actors, such as armed groups; NGOs; civil society organisations; international aid agencies; businesses, including private military and security companies; and other global governance multilateral bodies such as the African Union. *See* Articles 3 (1) (g) (h) (i), 4 (3), 5 (11), 6, 7, 8, 13, 14 of the Kampala Convention. Importantly, the Kampala Convention establishes criminal responsibility for individuals involved in arbitrary displacement. *See* Article 3 (1) (g) of the Kampala Convention.

explains that "[b]y proscribing all kinds of action that may cause arbitrary displacement and imposing duties on [states and non-state] actors who may come in contact with IDPs, the Kampala Convention aspires towards effective prevention of displacement as its main aim".[216]

Indeed, the Kampala Convention exerts prevention, mitigation, and, perhaps, avoidance of displacement caused by conflict, natural and man-made disasters, and development. Disasters, though, provide limited options, and people might have to retreat from affected areas to adapt to or mitigate the impacts of environmental change. Overall, the Convention offers protection against all kinds of displacement.

The Kampala Convention's innovative approach to natural and man-made disasters is relevant in the context of this work as it formalises for the first time, in a legally binding document, states' duties towards those displaced by environmental change who are not protected under traditional international law.[217] It does so in a holistic and inclusive manner, thereby narrowing the protection gap of over 20 million people in Africa alone[218] and the increasing number of EDPs.[219] Like Principles 5 and 6 of the GPID, the Kampala Convention imposes both negative and positive duties on states to refrain from, prohibit, and prevent arbitrary displacement.[220] It explicitly references avoiding forced evictions (or arbitrary displacement) during disasters (Article 4(4)(f)). It further imposes the duty to "devise early warning systems, in the context of the continental early-warning systems, in areas of potential displacement, establish and implement

216 Maru, M. T. (2011) "The Kampala Convention and Its Contribution in Filling the Protection Gap in International Law" 1 Journal of Internal Displacement 1 pp. 91–130, p. 98. *See* Article 2 (a); Article 3 (1) of the Kampala Convention.

217 *See* Articles 1(k), 4 (4) (f), 5 (4), and 12 (3) Kampla Convention.

218 *See* IDMC and UN OCHA (2009) "Monitoring Disaster Displacement in the Context of Climate Change: Finding of a Study by the United Nations Office for the Coordination of Humanitarian Affairs and Internal Displacement Monitoring Centre" (Norwegian Refugee Council) pp. 11–12.

219 *See* Pachauri, R. & Reisinger, A. (eds.) (2007) "IPCC Climate Change 2007: Synthesis Report, Summary for Policymakers" contribution of Working Groups I, II, and II to the Fourth Assessment Report, IPCC, p. 104.

220 *See* Article 3 (1) (a) Kampala Convention. *See also* Article 4 (1) Kampala Convention (similar to Principle 5 of GPID). Mehari Maru neatly summarises states' duty to respect, protect and fulfil: "[i]n the Kampala Convention, prevention mainly means the prohibition, effective deterrence, and avoidance of arbitrary population displacements. In other words, it refers to the freedom from arbitrary displacement and the obligations of states and the international community to eliminate when possible and reduce the causes of displacement, and mitigate their negative impact when they occur. As the old wisdom dictates 'prevention is better than the cure', thus addressing the root causes of displacement constitutes the most effective measure to prevent displacement from occurring". Maru (2011) *Op. Cit.* p. 109.

disaster risk reduction strategies, emergency and disaster preparedness and management measures".[221]

The Convention unequivocally imposes obligations to protect people internally displaced "as a result of or in order to avoid the effects of (. . .) natural or manmade disasters" (Article 1(k)) – including disasters associated with climate change (Article 5(4))[222] – and the need to seek durable protection solutions. It also requires states "to protect communities with special attachment to, and dependency on, land due to their culture and spiritual values from being displaced from such lands, except for compelling and overriding public interests".[223]

The document solidifies binding legal provisions that were previously only found in soft law, i.e. the GPID. It provides comprehensive solutions by addressing the legitimate concerns of EDPs while narrowing the prior regional legal protection gap.[224] Through this holistic optic, one must agree with Maria Stravoupoulou that the Kampala Convention inadvertently (or not) includes both internal and external displacement, thus exceeding the scope of its title.[225] Thus, the Convention extends obligations of protection to EDPs, ensuring that they are protected through all phases of displacement as any other internally displaced person. Corroboration is found in the general openness of its provisions, especially Article 4(4)'s definition of protection from displacement (not limited to internal displacement)[226] and where prevention of internal displacement, and timely response, can significantly reduce the number of refugees and asylum seekers (notwithstanding the complementary character of the right to seek asylum in other countries derived from the GPID and incorporated into the Kampala Convention).[227]

221 Article 4 (2) Kampala Convention. As noted, similar provisions exist regarding the duties of states parties with regards to disaster-induced displacement in Articles 3 (2) and (5) of the Great Lakes Pact.

222 *See* Articles 5 (4), 9, and 11 Kampala Convention.

223 Article 4 (5) Kampala Convention.

224 *See* African Union Explanatory note to the Kampala Convention p. 2 ("[t]he absence of a specific and binding international legal regime specific to IDPs represented a serious gap creating numerous challenges for their protection, assistance and finding durable solutions for their problems. It is to address this gap in Africa, a continent disproportionally affected by internal displacement that the African Union embarked on the development of a binding legal framework)". *See also* Maru *Op. Cit.* p. 94.

225 Stravropoulou, M. (2010) "The Kampala Convention and Protection from Arbitrary Displacement" 36 Forced Migration Review pp. 62–63, p. 62 (suggesting that the Kampala Convention complements the 1951 Convention on the Status of Refugees). *See* Morel (2014) *Op. Cit.* p. 93 (expressing the opposite view that protection from displacement under the Kampala Convention was established specifically for the protection and assistance of IDPs and not for those across the international border, even if Article 4 (4) speaks about displacement generally).

226 *See* Article 4 (4) of the Kampala Convention.

227 *See* Preamble para. 11 of the Kampala Convention ("[r]ecognising the inherent rights of internally displaced persons as provided for and protected in international human rights and humanitarian law and as set out in the 1997 United Nations Guiding Principles on

One of the most crucial issues of the Kampala Convention is the enforcement of its provisions, including the duty of states to protect from displacement. As remarked unequivocally by Mukirya Nyanduga, the Special Rapporteur on Refugees, Asylum Seekers, and Internally Displaced Persons in Africa,: "[u]nless African states address the gap between the assumption of international legal obligations, their implementation and domestication, adoption of additional instruments, including those related to IDPs, will not alleviate human rights violations".[228] The Convention's monitoring mechanisms are not particularly strong and are limited to periodic meetings of the Conference of State Parties and the submission of reports to the African Commission on Human and People's Rights. The African Union is given a prominent role in coordinating states' efforts and protecting and assisting IDPs in extreme cases. States' questions regarding interpretation and application of the Kampala Convention can be referred to the African Court of Justice and Human Rights once operational. Importantly, individuals' access to justice in the future Court (on a violation of rights guaranteed in any human rights instrument ratified by the state parties) is limited and is only permitted if the state party expresses and accepts the competence of the court. Ultimately, the best option for redress of a human rights violation, including under the Convention, is the African Commission on Human and People´s Rights. Yet, its decisions are not legally binding upon the states.

3.3.4 *Peninsula Principles*

The Peninsula Principles on climate displacement within states[229] resulted from a five-year process of consultations with communities in affected countries. They took into account the views of governments, civil society organisations, U.N. agencies, and affected populations. They gained momentum in August 2013 when a team of international legal and climate experts gathered in the Red Hill on the Mornington Peninsula near the Victorian capital Melbourne (the place that also inspired the Principles' name) under the headship of Displacement Solutions.[230]

Internal Displacement, which are recognized as an important international framework for the protection of internally displaced persons").

228 Nyanduga, T. B. (2006) "The Role of the African Commission on Human and People's Rights in Addressing Internal Displacement" Coalition for an Effective African Committee on Human and Peoples Rights (26 April 2006) p. 12 *available from*: http://africancourtcoalition.org/index.php?option=com_content&view=category&layout=blog&id=20&Itemid=29&lang=en [accessed 17 August 2018].

229 Peninsula Principles on Climate Displacement within States (19 August 2013) *available from:* http://displacementsolutions.org/peninsula-principles/ [accessed 17 August 2018].

230 Displacement Solutions is a non-governmental organisation that works with displaced populations, communities, governments, and the U.N. to find rights-based land solutions to climate displacement. More information is *available from*: http://displacementsolutions.org/about-ds/ [accessed 17 August 2018].

The Peninsula Principles seek to minimise the impact of climate change displacement on individuals within their own countries. The definition of a climate-displaced person is limited to "individuals, households or communities who are facing or experiencing climate displacement",[231] which is "the movement of people within a State due to the effects of climate change including sudden and slow-onset environmental events and processes, occurring alone or in combination with other factors".[232] The preamble of the Principles demonstrates their overarching humanitarian purpose and their international sources. Like the GPID, the Principles are not crafted in a legal vacuum, as they "build on and contextualize the [GPID] to climate displacement within states"[233] and acknowledge and incorporate provisions of the United Nations Principles on Housing and Property Restitution for Refugees and Displaced Persons (Pinheiro Principles).

Interestingly, the Principles recognise that "climate displacement can involve both internal and cross-border displacement" but limit their scope to internal displacement, finding that "most climate displacement will likely occur within State borders".[234] This assumption may be naïve. First, by excluding other persons in need of protection (those who cross the border due to environmental factors), they worsen an already-identified protection gap. Second, they fail to see protection of EDPs as a holistic enterprise. More generally, Elizabeth Ferris criticised the Principles because they "do not tackle the difficult issue of determining when climate change forces people to leave or how to differentiate those who are displaced by the effects of climate change and other environmental/ economic reasons".[235] The question therefore arises as to whether another set of principles is really necessary and their overall added value.

The Principles' focus on the needs of EDPs rather than the interests of the states is praise-worthy. They emphasise that focus in the beginning of the document by articulating "the right of climate displaced persons to remain in their homes and retain connections to the land on which they live for as long as possible" and the corresponding home state's obligations "to prioritise appropriate mitigation, adaptation and other preventative measures to give effect to that

231 Principle 2 (c) Peninsula Principles.
232 Principle 2 (b) Peninsula Principles.
233 Preamble para. 3 Peninsula Principles.
234 Preamble para.6 Peninsula Principles.
235 Ferris, E. (2014) "Planned Relocations in the Context of climate Change: The Time to Get Ready Is Now" (Brookings 18 June 2014) *available from:* www.brookings.edu/blogs/planetpolicy/posts/2014/06/18-relocations-climate-change-ferris [accessed 17 August 2018]. Such criticism can be refuted, as the Peninsula Principles seem to build on the same assumption of this work: that forced displacement can occur both by "sudden and slow-onset environmental events and processes, occurring alone or in combination with other factors" (Principle 2 (b)). As mentioned, while not all movements are due to environmental factors alone, in this context it is important to consider the environment as an *objective* and *autonomous* factor that leads to displacement (threat multiplier).

right".[236] Indeed, "[s]tates should, in all circumstances, comply in full with their obligations under international law so as to prevent and avoid conditions that might lead to displacement",[237] particularly taking preventative and remedial measures at local, state, and national levels and "prioritising the prevention of displacement".[238] This pre-emptive approach is also reflected in a rights-based and participatory relocation process, highlighting the value of the victims' involvement in choices affecting their future.[239] The added value of the Principles is that the home states' have a duty to maximise prevention of environmental displacement.

Even if not targeted at cross-border environmental displacement, the Principles take a preventative approach that also applies in that situation. Any preventative action taken by home states to avoid internal displacement also helps avoid external displacement. The Principles, for example, focus on the responsibilities of the country of origin while also recognising obligations of international cooperation and assistance and adding that "climate displacement is [also] a matter of global responsibility".[240] They recognise that affected states have the right to seek and demand, from other states and/or international agencies, cooperation in providing adaption and assistance, as well as protection of those displaced (shared responsibility).[241] Recognition of the role of third parties is a step forward for also recognising their responsibility in protecting both internal and – even if not intentionally – cross-border displacement.

3.3.5 International Law Commission Draft Articles on Protection of Persons in the Event of Disasters

Since 2007, the ILC has worked on the Draft Articles on the Protection of Persons in the Event of Disasters. It aptly noted that while the primary duty of the disaster-affected state is to provide protection,[242] it also has an "obligation to prevent harm to its own population, property, and the environment generally".[243] The ILC's Special Rapporteur, Eduardo Valencia-Ospina, in his

236 Preamble para. 7 Peninsula Principles.
237 *See* Principle 5 "Prevention and Avoidance" of the Peninsula Principles.
238 *See* Principle 7 (a), (b), and (c) "National implementation measures" and Principle 9 "Climate Change and Risk Management" of the Peninsula Principles.
239 Principle 7 (d) "National implementation measures" and Principle 10 "Participation and consent" Peninsula Principles.
240 Principle 8 (a) "International cooperation and assistance" Peninsula Principles.
241 *See* Principle 8 (b), (c), and (d) and Principle 13 ("[i]nstitutional frameworks to support and facilitate the provision of assistance and protection") of the Peninsula Principles.
242 ILC (2007) "Protection of Persons in the Event of Disasters-Memorandum by the Secretariat" U.N. Doc A/CN.4/590 (11 December 2007) para. 23 ("A further corollary of the principle of territorial sovereignty is the recognition that the receiving State has the primary responsibility for the protection of persons on its territory or subject to its jurisdiction or control during a disaster").
243 *Ibid.* Para. 24.

sixth report on the pre-disaster phase, acknowledges prevention as a principle of international law, which "implies rights and obligations both horizontally (the rights and obligations of States in relation to one another and the international community) and vertically (the rights and obligations of States in relation to persons within a State's territory and control)" and "finds support in human rights law and environmental law".[244] In 2016, the ILC adopted, on second reading, a draft preamble and 18 draft articles including commentaries on the protection of persons in the event of disaster and, based on these, recommended the U.N. General Assembly the development of a convention.[245]

Importantly, the ILC Draft Articles identify international law norms that are useful to fill existing gaps in the law and give precision to general principles, thereby helping craft legal frameworks to avoid environmentally induced cross-border displacement. Thus, the ILC's work reinforces the holistic notion of protection of human rights for those displaced by disasters and extends protection to prevention and mitigation of their effects. Interestingly, the ILC clarifies that these measures apply to the state of origin or home state as well as among and between states and non-state actors. The ILC also reaffirms the duty to cooperate as a relevant principle of international law, not only in the context of disaster relief but also in connection with prevention.[246] The OHCHR's Human Rights Council Resolution 24/16 highlights the role of prevention in the promotion and protection of human rights by encouraging states and other relevant stakeholders to encourage pertinent policies and strategies at the national, regional, and international levels.[247]

244 ILC (2013) "Sixth Report on the Protection of Persons in the Event of Disasters" by Eduardo Valencia-Ospina, Special Rapporteur U.N. Doc. A/CN.4/662 (3 May) para. 36 p. 12; para. 41 sq. p. 14 (emphasising the positive obligations of states to prevent violation of human rights explicitly enshrined in case law and Treaties including Article 2 of the CAT; Articles 2 (2); 3 (a), (b); Article 6 of the ICCPR; Article 3 of the UDHR; Article 11 of the ICESCR; and Article 27(1),(3) of the CRC and general legal obligations of states to prevent, i.e. not to cause, environmental harm and to ensure activities within their jurisdiction do not harm the environment within or without their territories). The report highlights the ICJ and ILC's agreement that the principle of prevention stems from two distinct but interrelated state obligations: due diligence and the precautionary principle.

245 ILC (2016) "Protection of Persons in the Event of Disasters" Chapter IV, U.N. Doc. A/71/10 (12 August).

246 *Ibid.*

247 OHCHR (2014) "Summary Report on the Outcome of the Human Rights Council Panel Discussion on the Role of Prevention in the Promotion and Protection of Human Rights" U.N. Doc. A/HRC/28/30 (10 December) paras. 45, 51, 52, 53 (highlighting that prevention of human rights violations is the primary responsibility of states even if other actors also play an important role ("spirit of cooperation"); that early-warning systems and education are critical; and that other advisable practices include tackling risk factors such as poverty and inequality and providing good governance, including a democratic system and the rule of law and accountability). Interestingly, higher compliance with human rights standards "did not necessarily correlate with countries with high levels of resources".

3.3.6 The Nansen Initiative and the "Protection Agenda"

In 2012, recognising the legal, operational, and institutional challenges of environmental displacement, the governments of Norway and Switzerland launched the Nansen Initiative. The main objective of this initiative was to build consensus among states on how they could respond to the challenge of cross-border displacement in the context of disasters and the effects of climate change. To this end, between 2012 and 2015 seven sub-intergovernmental consultations within five subregions (the Pacific, central America, the Greater Horn of Africa, Southeast Asia, and South Asia) and other stakeholder meetings took place. The Initiative provided an operational stage for a discussion forum to both adequately prepare and respond to the challenge of cross-border environmental displacement. It identified communities' needs and protection and migration measures for disaster-affected people, including highlighting the potential role of present regional agreements to address cross-border displacement and/or to develop temporary protection measures associated with durable solutions.[248]

In 2015, the outcomes of the Initiative culminated in a non-legally binding document endorsed by 109 states – "The Protection Agenda" – which draws on states' practices and outlines recommendations and priority areas for further development.[249] While its normative value is weak, it nonetheless reflects international consensus-building towards the formulation of a global guiding thread on environmental displacement. In order to promote the implementation of the Protection Agenda, the Platform on Disaster Displacement[250] became operational in Geneva in 2016. Through enhanced cooperation, coordination, and action it aims to improve the protection of people displaced by environmental disasters by promoting concerted efforts at national, regional, and international levels and with a wide range of stakeholders including humanitarian, development, human rights, migration, refugee, disaster risk reduction and climate change adaptation. Much of its success, both to prevent and to deal with environmental displacement, will be on their operational, technical, and capacity-building efforts including enhancing policy coherence in the nearest future. Otherwise, it may risk in culminating in yet another tunnelled vision, top down, and weak organisation.

248 *See* Kälin, W. (2015) "The Nansen Initiative: Building Consensus on Displacement in Disaster Contexts" 49 Forced Migration Review pp. 5–7.

249 The Nansen Initiative (2015) Agenda for the Protection of Cross-Border Displaced Persons in the Context of Disasters and Climate Change ('Protection Agenda') Vol. I and Vol. II. *See also* McAdam, J. (2016) "From the Nansen Initiative to the Platform on Disaster Displacement: Shaping International Approaches to Climate Change, Disasters and Displacement" 39 University of New South Wales Law Journal 4 pp. 1518–1546.

250 The Platform on Disaster Displacement *available from*: https://disasterdisplacement.org [accessed 5 July 2018].

3.3.7 Outlook

Beyond the conceptual wrangling of the establishment of a "right not to be displaced in international law",[251] the obligation of states to prevent displacement due to natural and human-made disasters has progressively gained recognition in both hard and soft law at the international, regional, and subregional levels: at the international level in Principles 5 and 6 of the GPID; at the regional level in Article 4 of the Kampala Convention; and at the subregional level through the IDP Protocol to the Great Lakes Pact's obligation to adopt and implement the GPID.

This recognition protects every vulnerable individual by guaranteeing that states take necessary action to prevent and avoid displacement altogether. In this vein, states have both negative and positive obligations to respect, protect, and fulfil the rights of those who are or may be displaced. States must refrain from and prohibit arbitrary displacement while also preventing and, where possible, mitigating displacement caused by nature or third parties. In this context, prevention from displacement does not curtail the right to seek asylum abroad but, rather, reinforces it and provides a complementary means of protection. In this sense, the GPID have had an exponential influence, bearing in mind that they were not drafted by states but by a team of experts.

The majority of the instruments analysed in the previous section focus on internal displacement, thus limiting their scope of application but not their relevance. The Kampala Convention offers some conceptual clarity on various fronts for those displaced across international borders. Legally, it is the most powerful – even if regional – because it is binding and solidifies a general preventative approach to protection found in international instruments. Also, its recognition of a duty to prevent displacement, especially vulnerabilities due to natural and human-made disasters, elevates the recognition of a group in need of protection that is often ignored by international law. It fills at a regional level a previous international legal protection gap. Furthermore, intentionally or not, it enriches and clarifies the legal definition of displacement (both internally and across international borders). Finally, by applying the adage "prevention is better than the cure", the Convention splinters its protection potentials towards EDPs, serves as a model and incentive for other regions, and contributes overall to the much-needed holistic approach to protection.

The Principles and the ILC Draft Articles, meanwhile, represent an apparent legal synthesis of the all of the aforementioned legal sources. They embody interdisciplinary approaches including operative measures necessary to tackle such a complex issue as displacement and serve as a reference point for states. They are a valuable source because they recognise both internal and external environmental displacement and also clearly obligate states to tackle internal displacement and implicitly avoid, by extension, cross-border displacement of

251 *See generally*, Morel (2014) *Op. Cit.*

populations. On a process-driven level, the developments of the Nansen Initiative and its operationalisation via the Platform on Disaster Displacement give the opportunity to states to strengthen their cooperation to promote policy and normative solutions to prevent, reduce, and address cross-border environmental displacement.

3.4 Implicit recognition of the duty of states to protect from displacement

The recent international and regional operational frameworks on disaster risk reduction and adaptation to climate change have influentially contributed to the environmental displacement debate, as increasingly highlighted in the literature. These frameworks do not deal with displacement per se but extensively elaborate on prevention and adaptation, thus highlighting states' obligations to take preventative action, reduce vulnerabilities, and protect the human rights of those affected (or potentially affected) and demonstrating their importance in the context of this book.

Though not an exhaustive analysis, it is worthwhile to reference certain international and regional instruments, in particular the Hyogo Framework on Disaster Risk Reduction (Hyogo Framework) and the supporting obligations of the EU and its member states towards disaster risk reduction in developing countries.

3.4.1 Disaster risk reduction and adaptation to a changing environment

(i) At the international level: Hyogo Framework

The Hyogo Framework (2005–2015)[252] is probably the most well-known international instrument establishing a coordinated system for disaster prevention.

The U.N. paved the way towards such a coordinated system when, in 1972, the General Assembly declared: "the vital importance to lessen the impacts of disasters, of assistance to disaster-prone countries in preventative measures, disaster contingency planning and preparedness".[253] The tragic human, economic, and social impacts of disasters in the subsequent decades raised international consciousness of the need to take cooperative preventative action and to reduce

252 "Hyogo Framework for Action 2005–2015: Building the Resilience of Nations and Communities to Disasters" U.N. Doc. A/CONF.206/6 (16 March 2005).

253 UNGA (1972) Resolution RES/2959 (XXVII) (12 December) para. 4. Prevention of natural or human-made disasters was continuously highlighted in United Nations General Assembly Resolutions, such as UNGA (1987) Resolution A/RES/42/169 (11 December); UNGA (1989) RES/44/236 (22 December) para. 1; UNGA (1991) RES/46/182 (19 December); UNGA (1993) RES/48/188 (21 December) Article 6; and UNGA (1994) RES/49/22 (13 December) paras. 5–6.

the effects of natural and human-made disasters. Most importantly, a recognition of the need to protect vulnerable populations gained ground, predominantly in international fora, as governments gathered to reaffirm their commitments in the Millennium Summit.[254]

Building upon a previous international consensus document (the Yokohama Strategy for a Safer World: Guidelines for Natural Disaster Prevention, Preparedness, and Mitigation and its Plan of Action),[255] the Hyogo Framework, a ten-year strategic plan to make the planet safer and more resilient from natural hazards, was endorsed by the U.N. General Assembly[256] following acknowledgement by 168 states at the 2005 World Disaster Reduction Conference. It set out five priorities for governments and other stakeholders for the period 2005–2015: 1) ensure that disaster risk reduction is a national and local priority with a strong institutional basis for implementation; 2) identify, assess, and monitor disaster risks and enhance early-warning systems; 3) build a culture of safety and resilience at all levels by using knowledge, innovation, and education; 4) reduce underlying risk factors; and 5) strengthen disaster preparedness for effective response at all levels.[257]

The Hyogo Framework applies to both natural disasters and man-made disasters – those generated by environmental and technological risks.[258] Although non-binding, it was complemented by binding human rights obligations, including the duty of states to reduce natural and man-made environmental risks and protect populations by introducing legislation, programmes, and policies aimed at reducing natural threats.[259] Particularly important were, for example, the development of adequate urban planning and construction infrastructures, the establishment of early-warning and information systems to protect vulnerable populations, and the creation of emergency funding in case of a disaster.[260]

254 UNGA (2000) "Millennium Declaration Resolution" RES/55/2 (13 September) paras. 23, 26. The Millennium Declaration was adopted during the Millennium Summit organised in New York from 6 to 8 September 2000. By 2015, the main objectives of the Declaration were the elimination of poverty; the protection of vulnerable groups; and the promotion of peace, security, human rights, and democracy.

255 The Yokohoma Strategy for a Safer World: Guidelines for Natural Disaster Prevention, Preparedness and Mitigation and its Plan of Action (Yokohoma 23–27 May 1994) *available from:* www.ifrc.org/Docs/idrl/I248EN.pdf [accessed 8 October 2014]. This strategy, in turn, built upon the conclusions attained through the "International Decade of Disaster Reduction" that was proclaimed by UNGA (1987) Res. 42/169, UN Doc. No. A/RES/42/169 (11 December 1987).

256 UNGA (2005) "Resolution 60/195 International Strategy for Disaster Reduction" UN Doc. No. A/RES/60/195 (2 March).

257 Hyogo Framework for Action (2005) *Op. Cit.* para. 14.

258 *Ibid.* para. 6.

259 *See Ibid.* paras. 16–19 and Kälin, W. (2010) "Conceptualising Climate-Induced Displacement" in J. MacAdam (ed.) "Climate Change and Displacement: Multidisciplinary Perspectives" (Hart Publishing) p. 93, pp. 81–103.

260 Hyogo Framework for Action (2005) *Op. Cit.* paras. 12–20.

As noted, courts are increasingly recognising states' responsibility to protect human rights against recognised environmental risks.[261] As way of example, the Convention on the Rights of Persons with Disabilities[262] and the African Charter on the Rights and Welfare of the Child,[263] both human rights treaties, articulate the need to protect and assist these vulnerable groups affected by disasters.

As evidence suggests that disasters may increase in scale and frequency due to the effects of climate change, disaster risk reduction structures are an especially important component of climate resilience. The Inter-Agency Standing Committee (IASC), composed of heads of key U.N. and non-U.N. humanitarian international relief and development agencies, highlighted that disaster reduction frameworks give "some of the most practical actions that support the goals of climate change adaptation".[264] Koko Warner explains that the effectiveness of such strategies may determine whether population displacement occurs and, if so, how rapidly the displaced population can return,[265] because the destruction of crops, livelihoods, and assets may encourage (or force) people to move.[266] A study of those displaced in Nepal by the severe flooding in 2008 and 2009 showed that approximately 25% were reluctant to return even though their agricultural land was still viable, because of other inherent vulnerabilities in their households.[267]

On a more operational level it is worthwhile to highlight both the IASC Operational Guidelines on the Protection of Persons in Situations of Natural Disasters[268] and the Red Cross Guidelines for the Domestic Facilitation and Regulation of International Disaster Relief and Initial Recovery Assistance[269] which aim to "ensure that disaster relief and recovery efforts are conducted

261 As discussed previously, the ECHR has highlighted the states' obligations to implement early-warning and evacuation systems to reduce disaster risk and vulnerabilities of populations, as well as to take all appropriate action when a disaster is foreseeable.

262 Convention on the Rights of Persons with Disabilities, UNGA Res 61/106, Annex1 adopted 13 December 2006, entered into force 3 May 2008, Art. 11.

263 African Charter on the Rights and Welfare of the Child, OAU Doc CAB/LEG/24.9/49 adopted 11 July 1990, entered into force 29 November 1999 Articles 23 and 25.

264 IASC Task Force on Climate Change (2010) "Quick Guide to Climate Change Adaptation" p. 1 *available from*: https://interagencystandingcommittee.org/system/files/legacy_files/IASC%20Quick%20Guide%20Adaptation.pdf [accessed 17 August 2018].

265 Warner, K. (2010) "Assessing Institutional and Governance Needs Related to Environmental Change and Human Migration" (Study Team on Climate-Induced Displacement, German Marshall Fund of the United States) p. 3.

266 *Ibid.*

267 United Nations Resident and Humanitarian Coordinator's Office (2011) "Long Term Disaster Displaced: A Forgotten Group" (Field Bulletin Nepal, 11 July 2011) *available from:* http://reliefweb.int/sites/reliefweb.int/files/resources/Full_Report_1759.pdf [accessed 17 August 2018].

268 IASC (2011) Operational Guidelines on the Protection of Persons in Situations of Natural Disasters (2011) "Brookings-Bern Project on Internal Displacement" *available from:* www.brookings.edu/~/media/research/files/reports/2011/1/06-operational-guidelines-nd/0106_operational_guidelines_nd.pdf [accessed 17 August 2018].

269 IFRC (2007) "Guidelines for the Domestic Facilitation and Regulation of International Disaster Relief and Initial Recovery Assistance" (IFRC).

within the framework that protects and furthers human rights of the affected persons".[270] Though not legally binding, several states have included these frameworks in their national disaster plans.[271]

The Hyogo Framework's strategies have enhanced states' abilities to respond to disasters and solidified their human rights obligations while simultaneously significantly impacting the extent of displacement. Many nations have codified these obligations through constitutional provisions[272] or national regulations.[273] As the Hyogo Framework neared its end, the U.N. General Assembly requested that the United Nations Office for Disaster Risk Reduction facilitate development of a post-2015 framework.[274] This process, inspired by the Hyogo Framework (for knowledge, practice, implementation, and the science for DRR), culminated in the adoption of the Sendai Framework for Disaster Risk Reduction 2015–2030 (Sendai Framework)[275] at the Third United Nations World Conference on DRR, which took place in March 2015 in Sendai, Japan. The recognition that "[t]here has to be a broader and a more people-centred preventive approach to disaster risk" reflected the states' commitment to a human rights-based approach to disaster reduction and, by extension, displacement prevention.[276]

270 IASC Operational Guidelines (2011) *Op. Cit.* p. 7.

271 McAdam (2011) *Op. Cit.* p. 243 citing Gemenne, F. (2009) "Environmental Changes and Migration Flows: Normative Frameworks and Policy Responses" (PhD thesis, Institut d'Etudes Politiques de Paris and University of Liège) p. 234.

272 *See, e.g.*, "Article 89 1994 Ethiopian Constitution" *available from:* www.wipo.int/edocs/lexdocs/laws/en/et/et007en.pdf [accessed 25 March 2014] (stating that the government "shall take measures to provide protection against natural and human-made disasters; and in the event of disasters, it shall provide timely assistance to victims").

273 *See, e.g.*, India's 2005 "The Disaster Management Act" *available from*: www.ndma.gov.in/en/disaster.html [accessed 8 October 2014]; Tuvalu's 2008 "National Disaster Management Act" *available from:* www.ifrc.org/docs/idrl/Tuvalu_DMAct_2007.PDF [accessed 8 October 2014]; the Philippines' 2010 "Disaster Risk Reduction and Management Act" *available from*: www.ndrrmc.gov.ph/index.php?option=com_content&view=article&id=45:republic-act-no-10121&catid=24:disaster-risk-reduction-and-management-laws&Itemid=39 [accessed 08 October 2014]; Pakistan's 2010 "National Disaster Management Act" *available from*: www.na.gov.pk/uploads/documents/1302135719_202.pdf [accessed 8 October 2014]; Bangladesh's 2012 "Disaster Management Act" *available from*: www.ddm.gov.bd/pdf/diastermanagementact%202012.pdf [accessed 8 October 2014].

274 UNGA (2011) "Resolution Adopted by the General Assembly [On the Report of the Second Committee (A/66/440/Add.3)] 66/199 International Strategy for Disaster Reduction" 22 December 2011, U.N. Doc. A/RES/66/199 (28 February).

275 UNGA (2015) "Sendai Framework for Disaster Risk Reduction 2015–2030" Third United Nations World Conference on Disaster Risk Reduction Sendai, Japan, 14–18 March 2015, U.N. Doc. A/CONF.224/L.2 (7 April 2015).

276 *Ibid.* para. 7, p. 4 ("There has to be a broader and a more people-centred preventive approach to disaster risk. Disaster risk reduction practices need to be multi-hazard and multisectoral, inclusive and accessible in order to be efficient and effective. While recognizing their leading, regulatory and coordination role, Governments should engage with relevant stakeholders, including women, children and youth, persons with disabilities, poor people, migrants, indigenous peoples, volunteers, the community of practitioners

(ii) At the regional level: European Union strategy for supporting disaster risk reduction in developing states

The 2007 European Consensus on Humanitarian Aid recognised the importance of disaster preparedness. The EU Disaster Preparedness ECHO (DIPECHO) programme targets highly vulnerable communities living in eight disaster-prone regions[277] of the world and reflects how the EU has progressed from simply providing immediate assistance to establishing long-term operational support strategies, such as the integration of protection and DRR.[278] Over the years, financial support has increased for disaster preparedness from an average of €8 million in 1996 to €34.3 million in 2011.

To increase its effectiveness and positively prevent displacement spill-overs, the DIPECHO programme needs to enhance its community-based approach by including other disaster-prone regions. For example, countries within the Africa Sahel region are susceptible to both slow- and fast-onset environmental changes, making them highly vulnerable, and should be included. The 2011 African drought and food crisis motivated the EU to begin development of a more effective and inclusive approach that combined humanitarian aid and development, including tabling two targeted initiatives to strengthen the resilience of vulnerable populations: Supporting the Horn of Africa Resilience (the "SHARE initiative")[279] and the Alliance Globale pour L'Initiative Resilience Sahel (the "AGIR Sahel initiative").[280] They aimed at not only responding immediately to a crisis situation but creating durable solutions for EDPs (e.g. land resource management and improving income opportunities for nomadic populations dependent on livestock, among others).

Aware of the negative impacts of the increasingly changing environment, especially in the developing world, in 2008 the European Council[281] opted for

---

and older persons in the design and implementation of policies, plans and standards. There is a need for the public and private sectors and civil society organizations, as well as academia and scientific and research institutions, to work more closely together and to create opportunities for collaboration, and for businesses to integrate disaster risk into their management practices").

277 *See* EU Disaster Preparedness ECHO (DIPECHO) programme ***available from:*** http://ec.europa.eu/echo/what/humanitarian-aid/risk-reduction_en [accessed 17 August 2018].

278 COM (2010) 722 final 08.12.210 "The mid term review of the European Consensus on Humanitarian Aid Action Plan-implementing effective principles of EU humanitarian action".

279 *See* "SHARE Initiative" ***available from:*** https://reliefweb.int/sites/reliefweb.int/files/resources/EU_building_resilience_en.pdf [accessed 17 August 2018].

280 *See* "AGIR Sahel Initiative" ***available from:*** www.oecd.org/site/rpca/agir/ and European Commission, Humanitarian Aid and Civil Protection (2015) "Building Resilience in the Sahel & West Africa" http://ec.europa.eu/echo/files/aid/countries/factsheets/sahel_agir_en.pdf [accessed 17 August 2018].

281 The European Council became an institution upon the entry into force of the Treaty of Lisbon on 1 December 2009. It defines the general political direction and priorities of

a more proactive approach to DRR in developing countries. Its approach was guided by two emphatic principles: "*national responsibility*, whereby each Member State takes appropriate *preventive and operational* measures for the *protection and safety of people* and *EU solidarity*, which is the basis for the *provision of assistance* rendered on request to (. . .) *third countries and their people, when affected by disaster that exceeds their response capacity*".[282] It invited the European Commission to present a proposal for this effect. (emphasis added)[283]

In 2009, the EU tabled a strategy for supporting DRR in developing countries. It aimed to integrate and systematise the ad hoc and project-based DRR work performed by EU member states and the European Commission in developing countries while simultaneously reinforcing its policy on development cooperation and humanitarian aid in support of the 2005–2015 Hyogo Framework and the Millennium Development Goals. Many felt that although the EU and its member states were addressing the issue, progress was incoherent, limited, lacked a common voice, and needed improvement. The strategy, though, reflects partnership and cooperation with developing countries, in line with the EU's treaty obligations.[284]

While the strategy covers developing countries and overseas countries and territories, it especially focuses on "disaster-prone regions, least developed and highly vulnerable countries and localities and the most vulnerable groups".[285] Importantly, it presents a "multi-hazard approach", encompassing not only natural and man-made disasters but holistically acknowledging that other hazards, such as environmental degradation or flooding, can also impact populations, creating a domino effect. The strategy considers both slow- and fast-onset disasters, as well as large and small-scale recurring events (e.g. landslides, flash floods, fires, storms). It excludes effects of conflict and war, instead emphasising the importance of addressing environmental impacts on vulnerable countries and their populations.

The strategy not only reinforces the EU's disaster response policy but shows the EU's increased efforts to address prevention, preparedness, mitigation, and

---

the European Union and consists of the heads of state or government of the member states, together with its President and the President of the Commission.

282 Council of the European Union (2008) "Council Conclusions on Reinforcing the Union's Disaster Response Capacity: Towards an Integrated Approach to Managing Disasters" 2878th General Affairs Council meeting (16 June 2008) para. 5 *available from:* www.eu2008.si/en/News_and_Documents/Council_Conclusions/June/0616_GAERC-Disaster_Response.pdf [accessed 17 August 2018].

283 Council of the European Union (2008) "Presidency Conclusions" Doc 10128/08 (29 May 2008) paras. 5, 6. *available from:* www.consilium.europa.eu/ueDocs/cms_Data/docs/pressData/en/ec/101346.pdf [accessed 17 August 2018].

284 *See* Articles 208; 209, 210 and 211 of the TEU.

285 Communication from the Commission to the Council and the European Parliament of 23 February 2009–EU strategy for supporting disaster risk reduction in developing countries COM (2009) 84 final (23 February 2009) p. 6.

development, something the Hyogo Framework is currently lacking.[286] By building on preventative disaster solutions and creating synergies between environmental, development, and humanitarian initiatives, it aims to benefit socio-economic development, create more resilient communities, and ultimately avoid the displacement of populations in vulnerable areas. Arguably, it has the unintended effect of building a preventative protection framework for environmentally induced displacement.

Consequently, it links the supporting obligations of the EU and its member states towards developing countries with the overall objective "to contribute to sustainable development and poverty eradication by reducing the burden of disasters on the poor and the most vulnerable countries and population groups [and by extension EDPs], by means of improved Disaster Risk Reduction".[287]

3.4.2 Adaptation to a changing environment

Over the years, the international community has implemented strategies to reduce greenhouse gas emissions to avoid the impacts of climate change and, incidentally, displacement of populations. The IPCC describes this process, called "mitigation", as "an anthropogenic intervention to reduce the anthropogenic forcing of the climate system; it includes strategies to reduce greenhouse gas sources and emissions and enhancing greenhouse gas sinks".[288] The adoption of the UNFCCC in 1992[289] and Kyoto Protocol[290] in 1997 crystallised these mitigation efforts at the international level. The international community soon realised, however, that climate change impacts are not entirely preventable, so attention turned to adaptation (or "adjustment in natural or human systems in response to actual or expected climatic stimuli or their effects, which moderates harm or exploits beneficial opportunities").[291]

286 U.N. General Assembly Resolution 60/195 (2005) *Op. Cit.* para. 4. In fairness, the Hyogo Framework for Action does recognise the mutually supportive objectives of sustainable development, poverty reduction, and good governance. Its Annex also highlights multilateral developments relevant to wider sustainable development objectives (e.g. third Action Programme for Least Developed Countries; the Millennium Declaration). Overall, it does link prevention, preparedness, mitigation, and development in an effective way.

287 COM (2009) 84 final *Op. Cit.* p. 5

288 IPCC (2007) "Fourth Assessment Report" Working Group II, Glossary of Terms p. 878.

289 The UNFCCC is the primary international instrument addressing climate change. Per Article 2, the main goal of the Convention is "[s]tabilisation of greenhouse emissions in the atmosphere at a level that would prevent dangerous anthropogenic interference with the climate system. Such level should be achieved within a time-frame sufficient to allow ecosystems to adapt naturally to climate change, to ensure that food production is not threatened and to enable economic development to proceed in a sustainable manner".

290 Kyoto Protocol to the United Nations Framework Convention on Climate Change (1997) adopted on 11 December 1997, in force since 16 February 2005, 2303 UNTS 148.

291 IPCC (2007) "Fourth Assessment Report" Working Group II, Glossary of Terms p. 869.

This became noteworthy during the climate negotiations in 2007 with the thirteenth conference of the parties (COP 13). While environmental change and human displacement was not directly referenced during the negotiations, the potential impact of environmental change on vulnerable populations and regions received attention. Consequently, the Bali Road Map was adopted as a negotiating strategy for climate change, including adaptation, resulting in the creation of the Bali Action Plan,[292] which led to the development of the Ad Hoc Work Group on Long-Term Cooperative Action (AWG-LCA). The Bali Action Plan emphasised risk-reduction approaches to helping vulnerable communities adapt to climate change.

As noted, environmental change and human displacement, in particular cross-border movement, were referenced by December 2010 in Cancun (COP 16) as part of the negotiations on enhanced action on adaptation (as part of the Bali Action Plan under the AWG-LCA). Paragraph 14(f) of the Cancun Adaptation Framework:[293]

> 14. Invites all Parties to enhance action on adaptation under the Cancun Adaptation Framework, taking into account their common but differentiated responsibilities and respective capabilities, and specific national and regional development priorities, objectives and circumstances, by undertaking, inter alia, the following:
>
> > (f) Measures to enhance understanding, coordination and cooperation with regard to *climate change induced displacement, migration and planned relocation, where appropriate, at the national, regional and international levels.*
>
> (emphasis added)

It portrays the protection of cross-border displaced persons as a triangulation of efforts at the international, regional, and national levels and planned relocation as part of protection and assistance measures. But, more importantly, as Walter Kälin rightly affirms: "it *recognises migration as a form of adaptation*, and this

292 UNFCCC (2007) Climate Negotiations "Report of the Conference of the Parties on Its Thirteenth Session, Held in Bali from 3 to 15 December 2007" (Bali Action Plan) UN. Doc. FCCC/CP/2007/6/Add.1 (14 March 2008).

293 UNFCCC (2010) Climate Negotiations "Report of the Conference of the Parties on Its Sixteenth Session, Held in Cancun from 29 November to 10 December 2010" (Cancun Adaptation Framework) U.N. Doc. FCCC/CP/2010/7/Add.1 (15 March 2011) *available from:* http://unfccc.int/adaptation/items/5852.php (accessed 25 November 2014) ("The objective of the Cancun Adaptation Framework (paras 11–35) is to enhance action on adaptation, including through international cooperation and coherent consideration of matters relating to adaptation under the Convention. Ultimately enhanced action on adaptation seeks to reduce vulnerability and build resilience in developing country Parties, taking into account the urgent and immediate needs of those developing countries that are particularly vulnerable").

means that international adaptation funding may be directed towards *preventing displacement and developing relocation and migration schemes*"[294] (emphasis added). Arguably, it urges states to consider measures to protect against environmentally induced displacement as part of their overall prevention strategy, in accordance with their common but differentiated responsibilities.[295]

Although environmental-induced displacement has entered the UNFCCC agenda, whether the UNFCCC can make an effective protection framework or basis for states' protection responsibilities is unclear.[296] Neither the UNFCCC nor the Kyoto Protocol treaties specifically provide for protection against environmentally induced displacement.[297] Nevertheless, the treaties' language specifically obliges states to assist least developed countries with climate adaptation frameworks, including the National Adaptation Programme of Action (NAPAs),[298]

294 McAdam (2012) *Op. Cit.* p. 232.

295 UNFCCC (1992) *Op. Cit.* Articles 3 (1), (2), and (3); 4 (1) (b), (3), and (4). *See* Cancun Adaptation Framework (2010) *Op. Cit.* The Conference of the Parties (COP 16) also formed an Adaptation Committee and Subsidiary Body for Implementation work programme on loss and damage, focusing on longer-term foreseeable impacts such as sea level rise and desertification and their wider implications for society, and established the new Green Climate Fund. More recently, with the creation of the "Warsaw International Mechanism for Loss and Damage" (under the UNFCCC) to address, in a comprehensive, integrated, and coherent manner, damage associated with climate change impacts in particularly vulnerable developing countries, creates the opportunity to address the issue of environmental displacement. More information on this is *available from:* https://unfccc.int/topics/adaptation-and-resilience/workstreams/loss-and-damage-ld/warsaw-international-mechanism-for-loss-and-damage [accessed 23 July 2018].

296 As world leaders met in Paris to negotiate what would be a final version of a new climate agreement in December 2015, they removed a paragraph that previously (July 2015) comprised provisions to establish a climate change and displacement coordination facility: to provide support for emergency relief, to assist in providing organised migration, and to plan relocation and undertake compensation measures. Despite the openness to the idea by the governments of the United States, United Kingdom, and France, states such as Australia did not approve of such a coordination facility for displacement as it did not see it as the most effective way to progress meaningful international action to address climate change. *See* "Scenario Note on the Tenth Part of the Second Session of the Ad Hoc Working Group on the Durban Platform for Enhanced Action" Point 26, ADP.2015.4.Informal Note (24 July 2015) *available from*: http://unfccc.int/resource/docs/2015/adp2/eng/4infnot.pdf [accessed 28 July 2018] and "Draft Agreement" Ad Hoc Working Group on the Durban Platform for Enhanced Action ADP.2015.8.Informal Note (5 October 2015) *available from*: http://unfccc.int/resource/docs/2015/adp2/eng/8infnot.pdf [accessed 28 October 2015] as well as "UN Drops Plan to Help Move Climate Change Affected People" The Guardian (7 October 2015) *available from*: www.theguardian.com/environment/2015/oct/07/un-drops-plan-to-create-group-to-relocate-climate-change-affected-people [accessed 28 October 2015].

297 *See* IASC (2008) "Climate Change, Migration and Displacement: Who Will Be Affected?" IASC, Working Paper (31 October 2008) *available from:* http://unfccc.int/resource/docs/2008/smsn/igo/022.pdf [accessed 17 July 2018].

298 National Adaptation Programme of Action (NAPAs) *available from:* https://unfccc.int/topics/resilience/workstreams/national-adaptation-programmes-of-action/introduction [accessed 17 August 2018]. The National Adaptation Programmes of Action (NAPAs)

a programme aimed at providing least developed countries[299] with adaptation program funding and assistance. The main work on human mobility in the context of climate change under the UNFCCC is now conducted by the so-called task force on displacement. This task force is the result of negotiations on the Paris Agreement in 2015 "to develop recommendations for integrated approaches to avert, minimize and address displacement related to the adverse impacts of climate change".[300]

(i) *Measures of adaptation to avoid the displacement of populations*

One can flesh out developed countries' adaptation measures to reduce vulnerability and prevent displacement. These projects have been put into *in situ* actions in accordance with the needs and priorities of each country. Concrete adaptation measures at international, regional, and local levels can include ameliorating agriculture methods, protecting water supply infrastructure, developing early-warning systems, or constructing dikes to prevent flooding from sea level rise.[301] Austria and Switzerland have made efforts to protect populations from floods and avalanches.[302] The UK has put into place a programme to manage risks

---

use a less flexible, eight-step process resulting in a list of discrete projects, not a holistic plan. The UNFCCC established the NAPAs in 2001 to help the least developed countries address their most urgent and immediate adaptation needs. Completing a NAPA made the least developed countries eligible to apply for NAPA project funding under the Global Environment Facility's Least Developed Countries Fund. The NAPAs have been criticised as small-scale projects not integrated with national development and poverty reduction. However, they were never meant to be a holistic long-term approach, but rather to ascertain urgent priorities.

299 *See* UNFCCC (1992) *Op. Cit.* Article 4, para. 8 (stating that developing countries particularly vulnerable to climate change are: "(a) Small island countries; (b) Countries with low-lying coastal areas; (c) Countries with arid and semi-arid areas, forested areas and areas liable to forest decay; (d) Countries with areas prone to natural disasters; (e) Countries with areas liable to drought and desertification; (f) Countries with areas of high urban atmospheric pollution; (g) Countries with areas with fragile ecosystems, including mountainous ecosystems; (h) Countries whose economies are highly dependent on income generated from the production, processing and export, and/or on consumption of fossil fuels and associated energy-intensive products; and (i) Land-locked and transit countries").

300 U.N. (2015) "Report of the Conference of the Parties on Its Twenty-First Session, Held in Paris from 30 November to 13 December 2015" 1/CP.21 Adoption of the Paris Agreement, para. 49. U.N. Doc. FCCC/CP/2015/10/Add. (29 January 2016). *See* Task Force on Displacement ***available from***: https://unfccc.int/wim-excom/sub-groups/TFD [accessed 25 July 2018].

301 International Strategy for Disaster Reduction (2008) "Climate Change and Disaster Risk Reduction" Briefing Note 1 (September) p. 7.

302 Gagnon-Lebrun, F. & Agrawala, S. (2006) "Progress to Adaptation to Climate Change in Developed Countries" Organization for Economic Co-Operation and Development (OECD) (May), pp. 33–40.

from flooding of the river Thames.[303] Perhaps noteworthy, the Netherlands, part of which is situated below sea level, constructed a network of dikes to both control flooding from sea level rise and protect its population from displacement.[304] The adaptation strategy implemented by the EU in 2013[305] is already a priority of community action, recognising that "the Mediterranean basin, mountain areas, densely populated floodplains, coastal zones, outermost regions and the Arctic are particularly vulnerable".[306]

In developing countries, especially in regions likely to be most affected by climate change, the issue of environmentally induced displacement and/or migration has been increasingly highlighted. Countries like Mozambique and Ethiopia underscored the enormous social cost of drought and desertification, leading to loss of means of subsistence and the migration of the populations.[307] Bangladesh and Mauritania stressed the social consequences of the exodus of populations to the big urban centres, and the African Central Republic warned of the consequences of changing weather patterns leading to migration towards southern regions.[308] Other countries, like Haiti, emphasised that poverty caused by environmental degradation and drought leads to migration.[309]

To promote better climate resilience, some countries, like Nepal, developed early-warning systems (such as raised watchtowers) in flood-risk zones and have reinforced embankments to prevent glacial lakes from bursting their banks.[310] Other relevant examples include Tuvalu, which strengthened community disaster

303 *Ibid.*

304 *Ibid.*

305 Communication from the Commission to the European Parliament, The Council, The European Economic and Social Committee and the Committee of the Regions "An EU Strategy on Adaptation to Climate Change" COM (2013) 216 final (16 April 2013).

306 *Ibid.* p. 2. The European Climate Adaptation Platform (Climate-ADAPT), an initiative of the European Commission, was developed to support Europe's climate change adaptation. It helps users access and share information on expected climate change in Europe, current and future vulnerability of regions, national and transnational adaptation strategies, adaptation case studies and potential adaptation options, and adaptation planning tools *available from:*http://climate-adapt.eea.europa.eu [accessed 17 August 2018].

307 Ministry for the Coordination of Environmental Affairs (MICOA) (2007) "National Adaptation Programme of Action" Maputo, pp. 15–16; The Federal Democratic Republic of Ethiopia (2007) "Climate Change National Adaptation Programme of Action" (June) p. 5.

308 Ministry of Environment and Forest Government of the People's Republic of Bangladesh (2005) "National Adaptation Programme of Action" (November) p. 36; Islamic Republic of Mauritania (2004) "National Adaptation Programme of Action" (November) p. 11.

309 Ministère de L'environnement Programme Changements Climatiques République d'Ha ïti (2006) "Plan D'Action National D'Adaptation" (October) p. 16. *See* more generally, on reducing vulnerability through adaptation World Bank *et al.* (2003) "Poverty and Climate Change: Reducing the Vulnerability of the Poor through Adaptation" (World Bank, January).

310 Government of Nepal Ministry of the Environment (2010) "National Adaptation Programme of Action" (September).

preparedness and created a preventative action plan,[311] and the Maldives' "safe island" programme,[312] a market-driven strategy designed in 1998 providing incentives for voluntary migration to alternative islands with better economic opportunities and better protection against disasters.[313] In reality, most NAPAs have focused on preventing environmental displacement, rather than migration or mobility, in their adaptation planning processes. Nevertheless, as Susan Martin sustains:

> in some cases, the NAPA identifies migration as an adaptation strategy itself. This perspective appears in two contexts. First, some countries see migration as a way to reduce population pressures in places with fragile ecosystems. Second, countries recognise that resettlement of some populations may be inevitable, given the likely trends, and should be accomplished with planning.[314]

The Cancun Adaptation Framework established a process to enable LDCs to formulate and implement National Adaptation Plans (NAPs), building upon the experience of the NAPAs. By providing technical support and project-specific funding, NAPs enable parties to identify medium- and long-term adaptation

311 Tuvalu's Ministry of Natural Resources, Environment, Agriculture and Lands (2007) "Tuvalu's National Adaptation Programme of Action" (May) pp. 51–52.

312 In 2008, the "safe islands" programme was replaced by a more holistic and reinforcing (physical, societal, and economic resilience) programme called "Resilience Communities". *See* Venton, C. *et al.* (2009) "Cost Benefit Study of Disaster Mitigation Measures in three Islands in the Maldives" UNDP Maldives (September) p. 28. In May 2014, U.N. agencies acting in the Maldives and the Maldives government launched the "Low Emission Climate Resilient Development" (LECReD) Programme, a three-year joint programme worth US $9.2 million that responds to the United Nations Development Assistance Framework (UNDAF) Outcome 9: "Enhanced capacities at national and local levels to support low carbon life-styles, Climate Change Adaptation and Disaster Risk Reduction". The programme aims at assisting Laamu Atoll and its islands to realise low-emission and climate-resilient development while attempting to mainstream issues pertaining to LECReD into local development planning and service delivery for greater community-level ownership and sustainability. *Available from:* www.mv.undp.org/content/maldives/en/home/presscenter/articles/2014/05/18/un-agencies-and-government-of-maldives-launch-the-low-emission-climate-resilient-development-programme-lecred-/ [accessed 17 August 2018].

313 Other adaptation priority measures in the Maldives include building capacity for coastal protection, coastal zone management and flood control, integrating climate change adaptation into a national disaster management framework, strengthening tourism institutions to coordinate climate response in the tourism sector, improving building designs to increase resilience and strengthen enforcement of building codes, and acquiring appropriate sewage treatment and disposal technologies to protect water resources. *See* Ministry Environment, Energy and Water of the Republic of Maldives (2008) "National Adaptation Programme of Action" (March) pp. 43–44.

314 Martin, S. (2010) "Climate Change Migration and Adaptation" The German Marshall Fund of the United States. Study Team on Climate Induced-Migration, p. 3 *available from:* https://seors.unfccc.int/seors/attachments/get_attachment?code=X30QEH9FOO3WU37DO4W675SSDX63PNC6 [accessed 17 August 2018].

needs posed by climate change and implement strategies to address those needs.[315] Notably, some countries in South America, such as Bolivia, Peru, Brazil, and Colombia, have begun to include migration as part of their NAPs.[316]

Successful adaptation plans will help reduce forced displacement but still face challenges. First, the economic and human resources required for implementing adaptation programmes are often limited. Second, they require a transformational change in government practices to working in a proactive rather than reactive matter. Finally, adaptation plans must take a dual-axis approach to prevent displacement yet also consider migration as a legitimate adaptation strategy.

(ii) Migration as a legitimate strategy of adaptation

Rather than seeing migration as a failure to adapt[317] to environmental change, new theoretical and empirical studies posit migration as an effective and legitimate strategy.[318] Migration emerges, therefore, as a proactive and appropriate measure to face environmental stressors that, particularly at early stages, can help reduce risks to lives, livelihoods, and ecosystems and boost the overall ability of affected populations to cope with the adverse effects of environmental and climate change.[319] Furthermore, it may be one of the best short-term responses given the costs of mitigation and other forms of adaptation.[320]

315 *See* NAPs *available from:* https://unfccc.int/topics/adaptation-and-resilience/workstreams/national-adaptation-plan-entry-page [accessed 17 August 2018]. The NAPs, a more holistic approach, offer a continuous, progressive, interactive, and flexible process, which follows country-driven, gender-sensitive, fully transparent participation. They are also an opportunity to align with other international initiatives, such as the Millennium Development Goals and the Hyogo Framework for Action and its successor.

316 *See* Warn, E. (2013) "Adaptation, Adaptation, Adaptation; Migration, Climate Change and National Adaptation Plans in South America" (International Organization for Migration) *available from:* http://weblog.iom.int/adaptation-adaptation-adaptation-migration-climate-change-and-national-adaptation-plans-south [accessed 17 August 2018]; *See also* Warner, K. *et al.* (2014) "Integrating Human Mobility Issues within National Adaptation Plans" Policy Brief No.9; United Nations University Institute for Environment and Human Security (June).

317 Brown, O. (2008) "Migration and Climate Change" 31 Migration Research Studies (International Organization for Migration) pp. 34, 38.

318 *See generally*, Davies, S. (1993) "Are Coping Strategies a Cop Out?" 24 Institute for Developing Studies Bulletin 4 pp. 60–72; Adger, W. N. *et al.* (2003) "Adaptation to Climate Change in the Developing World" 3 Progress in Development Studies pp. 179–195; McLeman, R. & Smit, B. (2006) "Migration as an Adaptation to Climate Change" 76 Climate Change pp. 31–53; Tacoli, C. (2009) "Crisis of Adaptation? Migration and Climate Change in a Context of High Mobility" 21 Environment and Urbanization pp. 513–525; Barnett, J. & O'Neil, S. J. (2012) "Islands, Resettlement and Adaptation" 2 Nature Climate Change pp. 8–10.

319 Climate Change, Environment and Migration Alliance (2010) "Climate Change, Environment and Migration: Frequently Asked Questions" (International Organization for Migration M & United Nations University) p. 5.

320 Johnston, J. S. (2008) "A Looming Policy Disaster" Regulation Fall p. 44, pp. 38–44.

Migration, however, may not be suited for all vulnerable populations, such as the poor, old, very young, or disabled, given their physical and financial limitations. But it does enable those who can to improve their livelihood development then transfer remittances, knowledge, and skills upon their return, thereby boosting the overall economic development of the country, particularly working in tandem with other adaptation and development strategies. Thus, migration should be conceived to protect those who leave but also those who stay behind, as they are often the most vulnerable.

Countries at particular risk from environmental changing conditions, like Bangladesh, favour including migration policies within wider adaptation strategies, both at the international and national levels.[321] For others, like Mali, "migration has increasingly become a strategy in view of these new precarious climatic and environmental conditions".[322] In some cases, such as islands like Tuvalu, the Solomons, and the Comoros, migration and relocation are the last chance to adapt.[323]

Governments at the Global Forum on Migration and Development[324] in 2010 highlighted migration as a complementary preventative displacement strategy for those in climate hotspots, through new cooperation agreements between neighbouring countries or by taking stock of existing bilateral and regional migration solutions.[325] They noted that developing international temporary and circular labour migration schemes could build the resilience of environmentally

321 UNFCC, AWG-LCA (2009) "Ideas and Proposals on the Elements Contained in Paragraph 1 of the Bali Action Plan" Doc FCCC/AWGLCA/2009/MISC.4 (Part I) (19 May) Paper 6 Bangladesh, p. 27 ("Develop and implement measures including those related to national and international migration to address those impacts for which it is difficult to build resilience or planned relocation for climate refugees. In extreme circumstances, provision should be made in the immigration policies of Annex I countries to accept climate refugees").

322 Ministry of Environment and Sanitation Republic of Mali (2008) "Elements of a National Policy for Adaptation to Climate Change" (May) p. 41.

323 *See* Tuvalu's Ministry of Natural Resources, Environment, Agriculture and Lands (2007) *Op. Cit.* p. 25; Solomon Islands Ministry of Environment, Conservation and Meteorology (2008) "National Adaptation Programmes of Action" (November) p. 39, 40; Union des Comores, Ministère du Développement Rural, de la Pêche, de l'Artisanat et de l'Environnement (2006) "Programme d'Action National d'Adaptation aux Changements Climatiques" (March) p. 11.

324 The Global Forum on Migration Development is a voluntary, informal, non-binding, and government-led process open to all member states and observers of the United Nations. It aims to advance understanding and cooperation on the relationship between migration and development and to foster practical and action-oriented outcomes. *Available from:* www.gfmd.org/process [accessed 17 August 2018].

325 Global Forum on Migration and Development (2010) "Report of Proceedings, Fourth Meeting of the Global Forum on Migration and Development" Roundtable 3, Policy and institutional coherence to address the relationship between migration and development, assessing the relevance and impact of climate change on migration and development (Mexico, November 8–11 2010) p. 37 *available from:* www.gfmd.org/docs/mexico-2010 [assessed 25 November 2014].

vulnerable communities, particularly through reinvestment of remittances[326] and skill transfer mechanisms. The Asian Development Bank's study on climate-related migration in the Asia-Pacific region also recommended a new migration governance to address the effects of environmental change that often lead to "undocumented migration, [trafficking], lack of protection and exploitation of migrant workers".[327]

International agencies and experts increasingly call for re-examining the strict limitations of migration and considering new possibilities for protecting those forced to migrate in the context of adaptation,[328] particularly looking at existing labour migration models.

326 *See* World Bank (2014) "Migration and Remittances: Recent Developments and Outlook Special Topic: Forced Migration" 23 Migration and Development Brief p. 3 (reporting that officially recorded remittances to developing countries are expected to reach US $435 billion this year, an increase of 5% over 2013; that the growth rate in 2014 is substantially faster than the 3.4 % growth recorded in 2013, driven largely by remittances to Asia and Latin America; and in 2015 the outlook is expected to be a bit more moderate to 4.4 % raising flows of US $454 billion).

327 University of Adelaide, Flinders University and University of Waikato (2009) "Climate Change and Migration in Asia and the Pacific" (Asian Development Bank) pp. 25–27.

328 *See generally*, Barnett, J. & Webber, M. (2009) "Accommodating Migration to Promote Adaptation to Climate Change" (Commission on Climate Change and Development); Tacoli, C. (2009) "Crisis or Adaptation? Migration and Change in the Context of High Mobility" 21 Environment and Urbanization pp. 513–525; The Government Office for Science (2011) "Foresight: Migration and Global Environmental Change (2011) Final Project Report" (The Government Office for Science, United Kingdom) *available from:* www.gov.uk/government/publications/migration-and-global-environmental-change-future-challenges-and-opportunities [accessed 12 July 2015]; Black, *et al.* (2011) "The Effect of Environmental Change on Human Migration 21S" Global Environmental Change pp.S3–S11; Asian Development Bank (2012) "Addressing Climate Change and Migration in Asia and the Pacific" (Asian Development Bank Philippines); Baberjee, S., Black, R. & Kniveton, R. (2012) "Migration as an Effective Model of Adaptation to Climate Change: Policy Paper for the European Commission" (Sussex Centre for Migration Research). *See* more recently, "Human Mobility in the Context of Climate Change Elements for the UNFCC Paris Agreement" (March 2015) *available from:* http://climatemigration.org.uk/wp-content/uploads/2015/05/FINAL-ADVISORY-GROUP-Human-Mobility-in-the-Context-of-Climate-Change_4May2015.pdf [accessed 17 August 2018]. Recommendations from the Advisory Group on Climate Change and Human Mobility, The United Nations' High Commissioner for Refugees (UNHCR), the International Organization for Migration (IOM), the United Nations University Institute for Environment and Human Security (UNU-EHS), the United Nations Development Programme (UNDP), the Norwegian Refugee Council/Internal Displacement Monitoring Centre (NRC/IDMC), Refugees International, the Center for International Relations Studies de Sciences Po (Sciences Po-CERI), and the Arab Network for Environment and Development (RAED) opine how the upcoming climate change negotiations in Paris should address migration and displacement, based on Paragraph 14 (f) of the Cancun Adaptation Platform. They outline the impacts of climate change and their extension to human migration and displacement and mention migration as an adaptation strategy.

Regional models of interest for SIDS include the Kiribati Australia Nursing initiative,[329] which facilitates knowledge and work exchange for those in nursing school, or the Seasonal Employers Programme between New Zealand and insular states in the Pacific. They are similar to guest worker programmes, allowing a person from a designated country to work in a particular sector for a fixed amount of time. Internationally, the Seasonal Agricultural Workers Programme between Canada and the Caribbean[330] or the Temporary and Circular Labour Migration scheme between Spain and Colombia[331] are cited as relevant examples.

Some experts propose the creation of a new protection status through temporary relocation schemes (TRS) (enabling individuals displaced by a sudden disaster to apply for legal temporary status in a host country when they may need to relocate within their country of origin) or temporary protection status (TPS) (for those who cannot return to their country of origin).[332] However, existing normative standards offered under the EU's Global Approach to Migration – such as circular migration proposed in Seasonal Workers Directive and Mobility Partnerships – warrant consideration. They offer EU legal migrant status to people living in environmentally vulnerable areas and may constitute a future model to promote both international and regional migration. For those forced to move on a permanent or quasi-permanent basis with slim prospects of returning to their country of origin, *reactive* complementary protection under the EU Qualification Directive (QD) offers interesting solutions.[333] For those forced to cross an international border due to fast-onset environmental change, other temporary protection measures should be explored. While temporary protection measures vary

329 Leighton, M. (2012) "Population Displacement, Relocation, and Migration" in M. B. Gerrard & K. F. Kuh (eds.) "The Law of Adaptation to Climate Change: U.S. and International Aspects" (American Bar Association) p. 711, pp. 693–729.

330 *See* Henneby, J. & Pribisch, K. (2010) "A Model for Managed Migration? Re-Examining Best Practices in Canada's Seasonal Agricultural Worker Program" (International Organization for Migration) and Basok, T. (2007) "Canada's Temporary Migration Programme: A Model Despite Flaws" Migration Policy (12 November) *available from*: www.migrationpolicy.org/article/canadas-temporary-migration-program-model-despite-flaws [accessed 17 August 2018].

331 De Moor, N. (2011) "Temporary Labour Migration for Victims of Natural Disasters: The Case of Colombia" in M. Leighton, X. Shen & K. Warner (eds.) "Climate Change and Migration: Rethinking Policies for Adaptation and Disaster Risk Reduction" Source No. 15/2001 (United Nations University for Environment and Human Security April 2011) pp. 92–103.

332 Leighton (2012) *Op. Cit.* p. 713.

333 European Council Directive 2004/83/EC of 29 April 2004 "On Minimum Standards for the Qualification and Status of Third Country Nationals or Stateless Persons as Refugees or as Persons Who Otherwise Need International Protection and the Content of Protection Granted" (recast by European Council Directive 2011/95/EU of the European Parliament and of the Council of 13 December 2011 "On Minimum Standards for the Qualification and Status of Third Country Nationals or Stateless Persons as Refugees or as Persons Who Otherwise Need International Protection and the Content of Protection Granted" (Recast)).

worldwide, the EU Temporary Protection Directive provides provisional protection for situations of mass influx that ensures emergency protection from *refoulement* and great manoeuvring to protect EDPs.

3.4.3 Convergence between disaster risk reduction and climate change adaptation

To reiterate, disaster risk reduction is an essential element for adaptation and climate resilience.[334] This convergence is important to increase the resilience of vulnerable communities and tackle displacement. Full complementarity between these two areas that have been working somewhat in isolation is necessary.[335] The disaster risk community is now increasingly attempting to address uncertainty and new long-term risks typical within the climate change agenda.[336] Because the disaster risk reduction agenda is largely based on bottom-up community-level actions allowing the tailoring of local laws and practices to the risk environment, it offers much to the climate change agenda, which is generally top-down global and still in development.[337] Both agendas have analogous and reinforcing objectives: preventing damage, reducing negative impacts, protecting the most vulnerable populations using risk and vulnerability assessment tools, and mainstreaming cross-sector regimes to developing national strategies. Integration and increased cooperation are widely reflected in international and regional disaster risk reduction instruments already analysed as well as in other operational platforms for dialogue and cooperation, such as the Global Climate Change Alliance.[338]

334 *See* COM Staff Working Document SEC (2011) 215 final (16 February 2011) p. 4. This is also reflected in IASC, Task Force on Climate Change *Op. Cit.* (2010) "Quick Guide to Climate Change Adaptation" p. 4.

335 Thomalla, F. *et al.* (2006) "Reducing Hazard Vulnerability: Towards a Common Approach between Disaster Risk Reduction and Climate Adaptation" Disasters, pp. 40–41, pp. 39–48.

336 *Ibid.* p. 42. This has been particularly visible since the 1990 U.N. International Decade for Natural Disaster Reduction (launched by the United Nations, following the adoption of Resolution 44/236 (22 December 1989)). The 1994 Yokohama Strategy and Plan of Action for a Safer World Guidelines for Natural Disaster Prevention, Preparedness and Mitigation launched at the World Conference on Natural Disaster Reduction Yokohama, Japan, 23–27 May 1994 and the World Conference on Disaster Risk Reduction have contributed to a shift in disaster management towards developing a coordinated understanding of the root causes of vulnerability and the development of a long-term strategy for predicting and managing risk.

337 *Ibid.* pp. 40, 42.

338 *See* Global Climate Change Alliance (GCCA) *available from:* www.gcca.eu/ [accessed 17 August 2018].

3.4.4 *Prophylactic nature of the duty to protect deriving from environmental law principles*

As mentioned, international environmental instruments do not explicitly address either environmentally displaced persons or their protection, instead typically referring to specific environmental problems. However, the increasing complexity of environmental issues has led to the development of environmental legal principles, which are creating support or the internationalisation of environmental protection. International law has stepped in to regulate activities traditionally belonging to states' internal affairs.[339] Because of their latitude, common principles of environmental law (as enshrined, for example, in conventions such as UNFCCC, the Kyoto Protocol, and the Convention on Long-Range Transboundary Air Pollution) are crucial for EDPs. They emanate prophylactic obligations for states, given current environmental changing conditions, and are built upon the idea of considerable risks. Three noteworthy principles reflect the states' duty to protect the environment and (even if indirectly) EDPs from displacement: the principle of prevention of harm, the precautionary principle, and the overarching principle of sustainable development.

(i) Principle of prevention of harm

The principle of prevention of harm promotes measures that reduce and control the effects of climate change and environmental degradation. It seeks to avoid environmental harm, irrespective of transboundary impacts.[340] This rationale derives from the interdependency of all environmental segments and the difficulty of remedying environmental damage (e.g. the extinction of species of fauna or flora, erosion, and pollution of the seas).[341]

For example, in the *Gabčíkovo-Nagymaros Project* case, the International Court of Justice highlighted states' duty to prevent harm: "in the field of environmental *protection, vigilance and prevention* are required on account of the often irreversible character of damage to the environment and of the limitations inherent in the very mechanism of reparation of this type of damage" (emphasis added).[342] Similarly, in the *Pulp Mills on the River Uruguay* case, the court found that that the principle of prevention is part of customary international law and that states should use all available means to avoid activities in their territories that cause

339 Atapattu, S. (2006) "Emerging Principles of International Environmental Law" (Transnational Publishers) p. 7.

340 Kiss, A. & Shelton, D. (2007) "International Environmental Law" (Martinus Nijhoff Publishers) p. 91.

341 *Ibid.*

342 ICJ, "Gabčíkovo-Nagymaros Project" *Hungary v Slovakia* (25 September 1997) p. 78, para. 140.

significant environmental damage to another state.[343] The principle, therefore, reflects the obligation of all states to implement measures to reduce even seemingly inevitable environmental risks.[344]

The principle of prevention can be viewed as an overarching aim giving rise to a number of legal mechanisms.[345] Amongst these, action plans are, according to Sands, *conditio sine qua non* to minimise the effects of an eventual disaster.[346] In fact, authors like Kiss and Shelton have acknowledged that "the objective of almost all international environmental instruments is to prevent environmental deterioration, whether the texts concern pollution of the sea, inland waters, the atmosphere, or the protection of living resources".[347] These measures of prevention (protection and conservation) of the environment do not adequately protect for EDPs, though. In reality, environmental degradation and the effects of environmental change may indeed lead to the displacement as well as migration

343 ICJ, "Pulp Mill on the River Uruguay" *Argentina v Uruguay* (20 April 2010) p. 45, para. 101.

344 *See* ICJ. "Nuclear Testing" *New Zealand v France* (22 September 1995), p. 411, para. 87 ("As the law now stands it is a matter of legal duty to first establish before undertaking an activity that the activity does not involve *any unacceptable risk to the environment*") (emphasis added).

345 *See* Kiss & Shelton (2007) *Op. Cit.* pp. 91–92. These can include prior assessment of environmental harm, licensing and authorisation procedures for hazardous activities, conditions of operations, consequences of violations, emission limits, product and process standards, the use of best available techniques, the adoption of overarching strategies and policies, and monitoring notification and exchange of information. *See* ICJ "Gabčíkovo-Nagymaros Project" *Hungary v Slovakia Op. Cit.* p. 78, para. 140 ("Throughout the ages, mankind has, for economic and other reasons, constantly interfered with nature. In the past, this was often done without consideration of the effects upon the environment. Owing to new scientific insights and to a growing awareness of the risks for mankind – for present and future generations – of pursuit of such interventions at an unconsidered and unabated pace, new norms and standards have been developed, set forth in a great number of instruments during the last two decades. Such new norms have to be taken into consideration, and such new standards given proper weight, not only when States contemplate new activities but also when continuing with activities begun in the past").

346 Sands, P. (2003) "Principles of International Environmental Law" (Cambridge University Press) p. 247.

347 Kiss & Shelton (2007) *Op. Cit.* p. 92. (citing as examples Article 2 of the 1992 Convention on the Transboundary Effects of Industrial Accidents; the Preamble of the 1992 Convention on Biological Diversity; Article 5 para.1 of 1986 the Convention for the Protection of the Natural Resources and Environment of the South Pacific Region; Article 2 of the 1992 Convention for the Protection of the Marine Environment; Article 4 para.1 of the 1983 Convention for the Protection and Development of the Marine Environment of the Wider Caribbean Region; Article 145 of the 1982 United Nations Convention on the Law of the Sea; Article 2 para.1 of the 1985 Vienna Convention for the Protection of the Ozone Layer; Article 2 para.1 of the 1992 the Convention on the Protection and Use of Transboundary Watercourses and International Lakes; Article 4 of the 1991 Bamako Convention on the Ban of the Import into Africa and the Control of Transboundary Movement and Management of Hazardous Wastes within Africa; Article 191 para. 2 of the Treaty of the Functioning of the European Union).

of populations. Nevertheless, the general obligation to prevent environmental degradation and the need to evaluate the environmental impacts of human activity allows the necessary manoeuvring for the protection from environmental displacement even if not foreseen in the treaties.[348]

(ii) Precautionary principle

The precautionary principle requires that states take measures to protect the environment where there is evidence of serious environmental damage, even if scientific certainty is lacking. The principle, which gained momentum with the Rio Declaration in 1992,[349] is considered the most developed form of prevention and remains the general basis for environmental law.[350] It is also enshrined under Article 3 para. 3 of the UNFCCC of 1992[351] and in many other international environmental protection instruments.[352]

The precautionary principle is action-oriented because it implies preparation for even uncertain and hypothetical threats, marking a positive step from the traditional approach requiring states to act solely based on scientific knowledge. It recognises that, in certain circumstances, waiting for scientific proof may

348 Indeed, international treaties did not foresee the migration or even displacement of people due to environmental factors. For further discussion *see* Cournil, C. & Mazzega, P. (2007) "Refléctions Prospectives sur une Protection Juridique des Refugies Écologiques" 23 Revue des Migrations Internationales pp. 7–34, pp. 13–14.

349 Rio Declaration (1992) Principle 15 ("in order to protect the environment, the precautionary approach shall be widely applied by states according to their capabilities. Where there are threats of serious or irreversible damage, lack of scientific uncertainty, shall not be used as a reason for postponing cost-effective measures to prevent environmental degradation"). The precautionary principle was initially coined during the First International Conference of the North Sea in 1987.

350 Kiss & Shelton (2007) *Op. Cit.* p. 95.

351 UNFCCC (1992) Article 3, para. 3 ("[t]he Parties should take precautionary measures to anticipate, prevent or minimize the causes of climate change and mitigate its adverse effects. Where there are threats of serious or irreversible damage, lack of full scientific certainty should not be used as a reason for postponing such measures, taking into account that policies and measures to deal with climate change should be cost-effective so as to ensure global benefits at the lowest possible cost. To achieve this, such policies and measures should take into account different socio-economic contexts, be comprehensive, cover all relevant sources, sinks and reservoirs of greenhouse gases and adaptation, and comprise all economic sectors. Efforts to address climate change may be carried out cooperatively by interested Parties").

352 *See* V of the Preamble of the 1992 Convention on Biological Diversity; Preamble of the 1987 Montreal Protocol on Substances that Deplete the Ozone Layer; Article 4 para. 3 (f) of the 1991 Bamako Convention on the Ban of the Import into Africa and the Control of Transboundary Movement and Management of Hazardous Wastes within Africa; Article 2 para. 5 of The Convention on the Protection and Use of Transboundary Watercourses and International Lakes; Article 3 para.2 of the 1992 Convention on the Protection of the Marine Environment of the Baltic Sea Area; Article 3 para. 1 of the 1996 Protocol to the Convention on the Prevention of Marine Pollution by Dumping of Wastes and Other Matter of 1972; Article 191 of the Treaty of the Functioning of the EU.

prevent states from acting.[353] Precaution recognises that the consequences of non-action could be serious or irreversible and assumes the vulnerability of natural systems rather than their invulnerability or resilience.[354] The Court of Justice of the European Union (CJEU) has, on several occasions, considered the precautionary principle,[355] laying its groundwork in EU law, and has also defined the conditions that trigger its invocation.[356]

The principle does not directly apply to EDPs but, if strictly applied, will safeguard an increasingly responsible exposure to environmental harms, including environmental change. Recognising that risks are not always certain, it does not require an absolute knowledge of the risk but only that it is of probable and conjectured nature.[357] The IPCC's reports have many times warned of the consequences of environmental change with increasing proof. In 2013, for example, an IPCC report acknowledged that "[i]t is *extremely likely* that human activities caused more than half of the observed increase in GMST [Global Mean Surface Temperature] from 1951 to 2010. This assessment is supported by robust evidence from multiple studies using different methods".[358] From this increasing proof of the consequences of potential risks derives states' obligations to act. The increasing international recognition of environmental displacement and migration could mean, in reality, as Agnès Michelot-Draft has appropriately noted, the non-application of the precautionary principle.[359]

(iii) Principle of sustainable development

The sustainable development concept is now legally recognised[360] and is generally defined as "development that meets the needs of the present without compromising the ability of future generations to meet their own needs".[361] It

353 Shaw, M. (2003) "International Law" (5th edition Cambridge University Press) p. 776.
354 Atapattu (2006) *Op. Cit.* p. 207.
355 *See* CJEU, Case C-157/96 *The Queen v Ministry of Agriculture, Fisheries and Food and Commissioners of Customs & Excise, ex parte National Farmers' Union and Others* (5 May 1998) and Case C-180/96 *Commission of the European Communities v United Kingdom of Great Britain and Northern Ireland* (7 September 2006).
356 For further discussion, *see* Alemanno, A. (2007) "The Shaping of the Precautionary Principle by European Courts from Scientific Uncertainty to Legal Certainty" in L. Cuocolo & L. Luparia (eds.) "Valori Costituzionale e Nuove Politihe del Diritto, Scritti raccolti in occasione del decennale della rivista" (Cahiers Europèens).
357 De Sadeleer, N. (2002) "Environmental Principles from Slogans to Legal Rules" (Oxford University Press) p. 91.
358 IPCC (2013) "Climate Change 2013, The Physical Science Basis" p. 869.
359 Michelot-Draft, A. (2006) "Enjeux de la Reconnaissance du Statut de Réfugié Ecologique pour la Construction d'une Nouvelle Responsabilité International" 4 Revue Européenne du Droit de l'Environnement pp. 428–445, p. 435.
360 Sands (2003) *Op. Cit.* p. 231.
361 United Nations World Commission on Environment and Development (1987) "Report of the World Commission on Environment and Development: Our Common Future" Chapter 2 para.1 commonly known as the "Brudtland Report".

bundles the concept of present needs and the concept of limitations. In order to meet the needs of future generations, states should prioritise the needs of the most deprived and most vulnerable and be aware of the environmental limitations imposed by the state of technology and social organisations.

The principle is, therefore, overarching and relevant for EDPs in that it refers to the present and the future and to a wide range of economic, environmental, and social factors,[362] including human rights. After all, "[h]uman beings are at the centre of concerns for sustainable development".[363] From this prism, states must create conditions to preserve the environment, favour solidarity, improve living conditions, foster development, and protect human rights (and by large, avoid displacement). The ICJ mentioned, at least twice, that "[t]his need to reconcile economic development with protection of the environment is aptly expressed in the concept of sustainable development",[364] thus recognising that "the environment is not an abstraction but represents the living space, the quality of life and the very health of human beings, including generations unborn".[365] Similarly, the Institute of International Law, in its resolution concerning the "The Environment", affirmed that "the effective realization of the right to live in a healthy environment should be integrated into the objectives of sustainable development".[366]

The environmental vulnerability of developing states (especially small independent islands) – the consequences of environmental changing conditions – creates a critical barrier to their sustainable development.[367] The U.N. General Assembly has cited environmental problems such as transboundary-pollution, climate change, environmental degradation due to pollution or desertification, and drought as dangers to the well-being of states' populations and development.[368] The 2000 Millennium Declaration, aimed at improving living conditions in developing countries, endorses the integration of sustainable development

362 The principle of sustainable development comprises four legal elements enshrined in the various international agreements: preservation of natural resources for the benefit of future generations (principle of intergenerational equity); sustainable exploitation of natural resources (principle of sustainable use); equitable use of natural resources (the principle of sustainable use, or intergenerational equity); and integration of environmental considerations into economic plans and other development programmes (principle of integration). *See* Shaw (2003) *Op. Cit.* p. 779.

363 Principle 1 of the Rio Declaration.

364 ICJ, "Gabčíkovo-Nagymaros Project" *Hungary v Slovakia Op. Cit.* p. 78, para. 140.

365 ICJ (1996), "Legality of the Threat or Use of Nuclear Weapons" Advisory Opinion (8 July), para. 29.

366 Institute of International Law (1997) "Resolution on the Environment Adopted by the Institute of International Law" Strasbourg (4 September) Article 2.

367 UNGA (2010) "Keeping the Promise: United to Achieve the Millennium Development Goals" Doc. A/65/L.1, 17 (September) para. 32, para. 35.

368 UNGA (1989) "United Nations Conference on Environment and Development" RES/44/228, para. 6.

policies to address climate change.[369] Other legal instruments, such as the Desertification Convention, highlight the relationship between sustainable development and desertification and drought, including the social repercussions "arising from migration [and] displacement".[370] In this regard, the UNFCCC urges states to develop open economic systems to guarantee sustainable growth and development for all parties, but particularly developing countries, "thus enabling them to address the problems of climate change".[371]

The principle of sustainable development, in the context of this study, dictates that both developing and developed countries must take legal and operational measures to protect people, first and foremost, from displacement but also after displacement occurs. Such measures may include, for example, policies to prevent human rights violations, action plans to reduce risks, early-warning systems, emergency alerts, and recovery and reconstruction processes, including enactment of legal statuses and reintegration measures where necessary The realisation of sustainable development also highlights the need for cooperation between states to attain these objectives. Particularly, support to developing countries must be guaranteed "to enable them to better deal with the displacement of people as a result of natural disasters (. . .) and put in place rapid response mechanisms".[372]

3.4.5 Outlook

While international and regional operational disaster risk reduction frameworks do not particularly target environmental-induced displacement, they arguably act as a complementary protection strategy, as they seek to avoid displacement. Other international mechanisms reinforce this notion, in particular UNFCCC framework concerning adaptation. Research indicates that states should concentrate on prevention of displacement of populations and, at the same time, consider labour migration as a proactive measure to face environmental change.

The analysis shows that international and regional disaster risk reduction and adaptation structures have splintering effects that seek to reduce the vulnerability of populations and prevent their displacement. In reality, though, disaster risk reduction and climate change agendas work separately; their increasing integration and their analogous and reinforcing convergent objectives are essential for increasing the resilience of vulnerable populations and tackling displacement.

The related elements of the prophylactic nature of the state's duty to protect are further grounded in common principles of environmental law, especially the

369 UNGA (2000) "United Nations Millennium Declaration" RES/55/2 (8 September) paras. 17, 21 & 23.

370 *See* Preamble of the Convention to Combat Desertification in those Countries Experiencing Serious Drought and/or Desertification, Particularly in Africa (UNCCD), adopted on 17 June 1994, in force since 26 December 1996.

371 Article 3 para. 5 UNFCCC; *See also* Article 2 para.1 of the Kyoto Protocol.

372 U.N. (2002) "Report of the World Summit on Sustainable Development" DOC.A/CONF.199/20, 2002 (Johannesburg, South Africa) 26 August–4 September p. 56.

principle of prevention of harm, the precautionary principle, and the overarching principle of sustainable development. However, why are these principles relevant in the context of displacement? Some authors posit that because neither hard law nor soft law has raised those principles to the level of customary status under international law,[373] their relevance to the displacement context may be weak. The categorisation of a principle as customary law[374] enhances its legal power, as it gains strength from universal acceptance and serves as a backup where no treaties exist. Even if certain principles are not widespread or consistently applied, numerous national and international legal instruments, including *opinio juris* and operational frameworks (e.g. DRR and adaptation), progressively strengthen their content, thus refining and developing a substantive collective obligation to exercise precaution. For EDPs, the principles' normative value lay not in the granting of rights, per se, but rather – if strictly applied – in safeguarding an increasingly responsible exposure to environmental harm, preventing a state from directly encroaching upon a right, and avoiding displacement. They further reflect the cross-fertilisation and complementarity between international environmental law and human rights law.

3.5 Conclusion

The analysed legal instruments and normative and operational processes consolidate a degree of awareness – explicitly and implicitly – of the legal obligation of states to prevent displacement where possible. As environmental degradation and change affect the enjoyment of human rights, states have positive and negative obligations (duty to protect, fulfil, ensure, and promote) to protect the bundle of internationally agreed human rights of displaced persons and their environment. The underlying duty to prevent and reduce environmental risks, including displacement risks, is the starting point and one of the principal aspects of states' positive obligations towards EDPs. A healthy environment is therefore a *conditio sine qua non* for the protection of substantive rights. While human rights violations are generally established after the harm has occurred, contemporary judicial review

373 Atapattu (2006) *Op. Cit.* p. 286; Leroy, S. F. (2006) "Can Human Rights Bodies be Used to Produce Interim Measures to Protect Environment-Related Human Rights?" 15 Review of European Comparative & International Environmental Law 1 p. 67, pp. 66–81.

374 Per Article 38 of the statute of the ICJ, a practice or concept is considered part of customary law if it combines two elements: state practice and *opinio juris.* In *Federal Republic of Germany v Denmark* and *Federal Republic of Germany v Netherlands*, 1969 ICJ cases concerning the North Sea Continental Shelf, the court noted that a provision must satisfy several criteria to be considered part of customary law: a) the provision should be of a fundamentally norm-creating character and could be regarded as forming the basis of a general rule of law; b) there should be widespread and representative state practice or participation in the convention, including of those states whose interests were affected; and c) the state practice in question should be extensive and virtually uniform and should be the result of a conviction that such practice is required by law. ICJ Reports (20 February 1969).

and OHCHR acknowledge that the "imminent" impact on a human right may suffice.[375] Thus, the increasingly reliable data on environmental change and human displacement can trigger states' response obligations.

While some relevant international and regional legal standards have limited application because they are particular to the internal displacement context, their relevance is not diminished. First, they offer protection against displacement (internal and external) and imply a general rule of displacement prevention. Second, they provide rights for those displaced and the corresponding state duties in the pre- and post-displacement phases. More importantly, they are part of the *corpus juris* that formalise the plight of EDPs.

Though much of this analysis has focused on the country of origin's duties towards EDPs, the obligations of other actors cannot be discarded, because the risks of environmental change are collective. Even if countries of origin must satisfy a ***minimum content of protection*** towards EDPs, many will need the help of other states and non-state actors. National states may lack the necessary resources or know-how to fulfil their protection obligations, especially as to socio-economic rights, the application of which is not restricted by a jurisdictional clause. Some developing countries have not only imposed environmental change but have also created an environment of violations of human rights.[376] Therefore, extraterritorial duties of third states and the role of international cooperation and assistance are salient as existing parallel and mutually inclusive obligations.[377] In this sense, "[i]nternational human rights law complements the UNFCCC by underlying that international cooperation is not only expedient but also a human rights obligation and that its central objective is the realisation of human rights".[378] This may include the reduction of emissions to safe levels,

375 OHCHR (2009) "Report of the Office of the United Nations High Commissioner for Human Rights on the Relationship between Climate Change and Human Rights" UN Doc. A/HRC/10/61 (15 January) para. 70.

376 Limon, M. (2010) "Human Rights and Climate Change: Constructing a Case for Political Action" 33 Harvard Environmental Law Review p. 572, pp. 439–576 (citing the declaration of Marghoob Saleem Butt, Counselor, Permanent Mission of Pakistan to the United Nations at Geneva, Panel on Human Rights and Climate Change at the eleventh Session of the Human Rights Council (15 June 2009)).

377 While Article 2 (1) of the ICCPR requires states parties "to respect and to ensure to all individuals within its territory and subject to its jurisdiction the rights recognized in the present Covenant", Article 2 (1) of the ICESCR requires each party "to take steps, individually and through international assistance and cooperation, especially economic and technical, to the maximum of its available resources, with a view to achieving progressively the full realization of the rights recognized in the present Covenant by all appropriate means". The extraterritorial duties of third states *per se* is beyond the scope of this work but is relevant in this context. For further discussion *see* Maastricht Principles on Extraterritorial Obligations of States in the area of Economic, Social and Cultural Rights (January 2013) *available from:* www.etoconsortium.org/nc/en/main-navigation/library/maastricht-principles/?tx_drblob_pi1%5BdownloadUid%5D=23 [accessed 17 August 2018].

378 OHCHR (2009) "Report of the Office of the U.N. High Commissioner for Human Rights on the Relationship between Human Rights and Climate Change" *Op. Cit.* para.99.

funding of adaptation mitigation strategies for EDPs in vulnerable areas (including *new status of protection* through labour migration), and appropriate national and international forums where they can participate and be heard.

Viewing prevention as protection helps states find ways to narrow the legal protection gap for those at risk of cross-border displacement. While "prevention is better than the cure", prevention from displacement does not curtail the right to seek asylum abroad. This comprehensive approach to protection obliges us to also address host states' obligations to protect EDPs under human rights law, in particular refugee law.

4 Status and protection obligations of states under international refugee law

Attention now turns to host states' obligations to protect EDPs. There is a lack of international consensus as to the status of EDPs for purposes of protection, so reviewing existing international protection standards is an important starting point. The most relevant international legal framework is refugee law, particularly the 1951 United Nations Convention Relating to the Status of Refugees and its 1967 Additional Protocol (CRSR or Refugee Convention). Refugee law materialises host states' collective responsibilities towards refugees and, in this context, are an important means to explore to what extent those duties are transferrable to EDPs.

The formalistic reading of the international principle of state sovereignty dictates that states have no obligation to admit persons except under treaty obligations. The CRSR imposes such obligations. Traditionally, international protection forms the core of host states' refugee obligations. The need for international protection is predicated on the lack of national state protection, i.e. states' failure to provide basic guarantees normally afforded citizens.[1] Those who cross national borders due to changing environmental conditions also justifiably deserve international protection. The consolidated framework for protection of refugees is instructive in determining host states' protection obligations towards EDPs.

4.1 Determining host states' obligations

The value of the CRSR in this context is that despite being an international agreement, it does not regulate "inter-state" but rather "state-individual" relations. Its main purpose is not to benefit state parties but quite the opposite: "to impose on them a general obligation of effective protection" (. . .) "inter alia, the life and liberty of a particular vulnerable category of individuals".[2] It

1 McAdam, J. (2007) "Complementary Protection in International Refugee Law" (Oxford University Press) pp. 19–20.

2 Sitaropoulos, N. (1999) "Refugee: A Legal Definition in Search of a Principled Interpretation by Domestic Fora" 52 Revue hellénique de droit international p. 161, pp. 151–190.

constitutes a human rights treaty, given that the centre of gravity of its corpus is a consolidated promise of host states aimed at the protection of individuals' interests, not states' interests. Despite being a product of the Cold War, it embraces international society's human rights awareness and sensitivity, epitomised mainly by Western states in World War II's aftermath.[3] It is a core of human rights and a recognition of states' collective responsibility, making it relevant for EDPs.

The first step is to ascertain whether EDPs can fulfil the CRSR's Article 1A(2) refugee criteria, which identifies those who can be admitted and granted refugee status and those who cannot. Refugee status grants persons safe asylum in another territory, enabling the right to work, the right to adequate shelter, and the right to health and social security, among others. When not possible, CRSR provides for other types of assistance, such as health clinics, shelters and food, education facilities, and monetary funding.

Though it is important to determine EDPs' status under international law, ascertaining the evolution of the international protection regime, and *inter alia* host states' obligations, is equally important. The evolution of international protection has enhanced its autonomy and dynamic, as reflected not only by the number of signatories to the CRSR[4] but also through additional regional protection arrangements and the development of principles of customary char acter (such as the principle of *non-refoulement*).

4.1.1 Criteria for determining refugee status vs EDPs

Jane McAdam argues that refugee law protection comprises two features: the qualification threshold (refugee) and the rights attached to it (status). The author proclaims that international protection for an individual is solely based on the scope of threshold qualification (accentuated by the principle of *non-refoulement*),[5] but the rights attached arguably give meaning to the qualification threshold in the first place. Both of these elements crystallise over time to a particular conceptualisation of refugee protection. The term *refugee* entails a specific legal meaning under the CRSR[6] which does not explicitly cover EDPs.

3 For a more historical overview, *see* Grahl-Madsen, A. (1983) "Identifying the World's Refugees" in "Annals of the American Academy of Political and Social Science: The Global Refugee Problem: U. S. and World Response" (Vol. 467) pp. 11–23, p. 13 (Sage Publications); Friedmann, W. (1962) "The Changing Dimensions of International Law" 62 Columbia Law Review 7 pp. 1147–1148, pp. 1147–1165.

4 As of September 2015, there are 145 states that are parties to one or both of the instruments.

5 *Ibid.*

6 The CRSR recognises a collective responsibility of states to protect refugees, a recognition that emerged at the end of the Second World War.

In turn, non-compliance with the conventional classification criteria of refugees bars EDPs from acquiring any status under international refugee law.[7]

Convention Article 1A(2) sets the benchmark for refugee status. It defines a *refugee* as a person who holds a:

> well founded fear of being persecuted for reasons of race, religion, nationality, membership of a particular social group or political opinion, is outside the country of his nationality and is unable or, owing to such fear, is unwilling to avail himself of the protection of that country; or who, not having a nationality and being outside the country of his former habitual residence as a result of such events, is unable or, owing to such fear, is unwilling to return to it.

It has four basic legal requisites: 1) the person must have a well-founded fear of persecution; 2) the person's feared persecution must be based on race, religion, nationality, or membership in a particular social group or political opinion; 3) the person must have fled and crossed the border of the country of origin or place of normal residence; and 4) the person is unable or unwilling to return home.

The 1951 Convention does not define the terms "*well founded*" or "*persecution*". Furthermore, environmental degradation is not listed as a qualifying form of persecution. Persecution may encompass the threat to life or freedom, the infliction of suffering or harm frequently resulting from to torture, substantial economic deprivation, or systemic violations of human rights under government consent.[8] The well-founded fear of an act of persecution may be based on existing, looming, or potential circumstances of uncertainty giving rise to a sentiment of vulnerability to serious harm that a reasonable person in the same situation also would fear and which the government cannot or will not prevent.[9] To help governments and courts determine who qualifies as a refugee, the UNHCR produced the UNHCR Handbook on Procedures and Criteria for Determining Refugee Status (UNHCR Handbook).[10]

7 UNHCR (2009) "Climate Change, Natural Disasters and Human Displacement: A UNHCR Perspective" *available from:* www.unhcr.org/4901e81a4.html [accessed 17 August 2018] p. 9.

8 Hathaway, J. (1991) "The Law of Refugee Status" (Butterworth's) pp. 105, 112.

9 Islam, R. (2013) "Climate Refugees and International Refugee Law" in R. Islam & J. Bhuiyan (eds.) "An Introduction to Refugee Law" (Martinus Nijhoff Publishers) p. 221. UNHCR (1992) Handbook *Op. Cit.* B (2) (a) para. 37 sq.; Alexander, M. (1999) "Refugee Status Determination by UNHCR" 11 International Journal of Refugee Law 2 p. 264, pp. 251–289.

10 UNHCR (1992) "Handbook on Procedures and Criteria for Determining Refugee Status under the 1951 Convention and the 1967 Protocol" (UNHCR Geneva 1979, re-edited) para. 39 (explaining that the expression "owing to well-founded fear of being persecuted" excludes persons as victims of famine or natural disaster, unless they also have a well-founded fear of persecution for one of the reasons stated but that, nevertheless, other

The UNHCR Handbook, the most authoritative interpretation of the CRSR, asserts that "[t]he expression 'owing to a well-founded fear of being persecuted' – for the reasons stated – by indicating a specific motive automatically makes all other reasons for escape irrelevant for the definition. It rules out such persons as victims of famine or *natural disaster*, unless they also have well-founded fear of persecution for one of the reasons stated. *Such other motives may not, however, be altogether irrelevant* to the process of determining refugee status *since all circumstances* need to be taken into account for a proper understanding of the applicant's case" (emphasis added).

The literature forms a triangulation of opinions between "fitters", "expanders", and "deniers". Fitters posit that EDPs already fall within the refugee definition.[11] Expanders assert that the refugee definition should be expanded according to human rights principles to include EDPs.[12] Deniers neither accept that refugee protection standards directly apply to EDPs nor believe there is a need for a new Convention.[13] A subset of deniers deny that the CRSR affords protection but propose development of a new Convention to bridge the protection gap.[14] Although a number of scholars, governments, and NGOs have used the term environmental or climate refugee, there are many barriers to qualifying EDPs as refugees. Refugee law is not irrelevant, though. As an established body of law, the CRSR can, under certain situations, afford protection to some EDPs. Furthermore, the status it envisages for refugees can serve as a standard for future legal protection developments for EDPs.

(i) "Well-founded fear" requirement

An applicant's requirement of "well-founded fear", it is asserted, has a dual component: a subjective one and an objective one. Commentators argue that the element of *fear* requires a state of mind – psychological analysis of the claimant's prospects of return to their country of origin or their "terror of persecution". In addition, the qualifier *well-founded* corresponds to fear that is tangibly "supported by an objective situation"[15] that leads a "reasonable person"

motives may be relevant to determining refugee status, since all circumstances should be taken into account).

11 *See* Cooper, J. B. (1998) "Environmental Refugees: Meeting the Requirements of the Refugee Definition" 6 New York University Environmental Law Journal pp. 480–592.

12 *See* Keane, D. (2004) "The Environmental Causes and Consequences of Migration: A Search for the Meaning of Environmental Refugees" 16 Georgetown International Environmental 2, pp. 209–223; Moberg, K. (2009) "Extending the Refugee Definitions to Cover Environmentally Displaced Persons Displaces Necessary Protection" 94 Iowa Law Review pp. 1107–1136.

13 Black, R. (2001) "Environmental Refugees: Myth or Reality?" UNHCR Working Paper No. 34.

14 Conisbee and Simms 2003 Conisbee, M. & Simms, A. (2003) "Environmental Refugees, the Case for Recognition" (New Economics Foundation) p. 33.

15 UNHCR Handbook *Op. Cit.* para. 38.

to reject his state of origin's protection.[16] It is contested whether EDPs are victims of state persecution and merit protection in another state.

PROSPECTIVE RISK

"While the word *fear* may imply a form of emotional response, it may also be used to signal anticipatory appraisal of risk".[17] James Hathaway points out that, based on the draft history of the Convention, it intended this "forward-looking assessment of risk".[18]

He contends that the receiving country must take an evaluative approach when examining the *prospective risk* of the applicant. Consideration of *well-founded fear* should be an objective assessment in the framework of present and future risk for the applicant. This mindset is relevant to environmental displacement situations, as receiving states must take a holistic approach to assessing the applicant's status based on a humanity yardstick. It is essential that states objectively balance the contextual elements and personal background of the applicant, including inquiring as to: the objective current state of the mind of the applicant, the present and prospective risk of persecution, the conditions and harm that a person would face if he/she returned to her country of origin, and any evidence of acute and prospective environmental harm reasonably likely to pose a severe threat to the individual or his/her community.

Objectively, those who are forced to move due to lack of fertile land, who lose their homes as a result of desertification or natural disaster, and who are unable to feed themselves and their family cannot arguably be returned to a situation that would, inhumanely, amount to starvation. These situations demonstrate that a "reasonable person" would flee, thus rejecting the protection of the state of origin. Such rejection can be justified by the state's incapacity (e.g. lack of socio-economic infrastructures) or unwillingness (e.g. cases of war or

16 *See* UNHCR Handbook *Op. Cit.* para. 42 ("As regards the objective element, it is necessary to evaluate the statements made by the applicant. The competent authorities that are called upon to determine refugee status are not required to pass judgement on conditions in the applicant's country of origin. The applicant's statements cannot, however, *be considered in the abstract*, and must be viewed in the *context of the relevant background situation. A knowledge of conditions in the applicant's country of origin* – while not a primary objective – is an important element in assessing the applicant's credibility. In general, the applicant's fear should be considered well-founded if he can establish, to a reasonable degree, that his continued stay in his country of origin has become intolerable to him for the reasons stated in the definition, or would for the same reasons be intolerable if he returned there") (emphasis added).

17 Hathaway, J. (1991) "The Law of Refugee Status" (Butterworth-Heinemann) p. 66.

18 *Ibid.* pp. 66–67 (reiterating that the predecessor of the contemporary Refugee Convention, the Constitution of the International Refugee Organization, "had competence over persons who *already* suffered persecution in their home state, as well as over persons judged by the administering authorities to face a *prospective risk* of persecution were they to be returned to their own country").

discriminatory practices based on religion, race, nationality, social group, or political opinion) to protect individuals.

(ii) "Persecution" requirement

Though persecution is an essential element of refugee status, the term is not defined under the CRSR. For 60 years, all attempts to devise such a definition have failed,[19] posing a major obstacle to placing EDPs within the refugee law framework. Without a consensus, it is difficult to characterise disasters and other weather-related events as persecution. Carly Marcs asserts that the CRSR's drafters intended to give attention to the circumstances of each case, thus enabling international refugee law to respond to conditions not yet considered at the time of drafting.[20] Hathaway also argues that the drafters viewed persecution as an "inclusive concept".[21] Atle Grahl-Madsen acknowledges that a "flexible concept" would allow its application and adjustment according to states' political and policy developments and great manoeuvrability in the refugee status determination.[22] In practice, it resulted in states interpreting the term more restrictively or liberally according to their own political views.[23]

Hathaway maintains that "persecution is most appropriately defined as the sustained or systemic failure of state protection in relation to one of the core entitlements which has been recognised by the international community"[24] and that

> [a] well founded fear of persecution exits when one reasonably anticipates that remaining in the country of origin may result in a form of serious harm which the government cannot or will not prevent, including either "specific hostile acts or (. . .) an accumulation of adverse circumstances such as discrimination existing in an atmosphere of insecurity and fear".[25]

19 UNHCR Handbook *Op. Cit.* para. 51.

20 Marcs, C. (2008) "Spoiling Movi's River: Towards Recognition of Persecutory Environmental Harm within the Meaning of the Refugee Convention" 24 American University International Law Review p. 53, pp. 31–71.

21 *See* Hathaway (1991) *Op. Cit.* pp. 102–103 ("From the beginning, there was no monolithic or absolute conceptual standard of wrongfulness, the implication being that a variety of measures in disregard to human dignity would constitute persecution. Refugee status was premised on the *risk of serious harm*").

22 Grahl-Madsen, A. (1966) "The Status of Refugees in International Law" (Vol. 1 Sijthoff, Leiden) p. 193.

23 *See* Vevstad, V. (1998) "Refugee Protection A European Challenge" (Tano Aschehoug) p. 63. The granting of refugee status as a "political statement" is illustrated by states' practices over time. For example, the United States traditionally granted refugee status to citizens of Cuba more easily than citizens of Tahiti, and European countries frequently granted refugee status to persons (who may or may not have been victims of persecution) from the former Soviet bloc during the Cold War.

24 Hathaway (1991) *Op. Cit.* p. 112.

25 *Ibid.* p. 105.

He characterises CRSR's refugee status as "surrogate or substitute protection" that activates upon the country of origin's failure to protect.[26] Thus, refugee status due to environmental impairment will depend upon the applicant showing that the cause of harm lies in the (in)actions caused by the government's unwillingness or inability to prevent ongoing persecution. In the context of environmental change, it may be difficult to establish this link.[27] Notably, the UNHCR Handbook states that victims of famine and natural disasters (sea level rise, earthquakes, or flooding) are not intended beneficiaries of refugee status. The documents therefore suggest, at first glance, "that in isolation, the fear of a threat to life prompted by a major environmental disruption, could not create a state of mind that arouses feelings of persecution in an individual".[28]

However, commentators increasingly argue the opposite: that a threat to life or freedom due to race, religion, nationality, political opinion, or membership of a particular social group under Articles 31 and 33 of the CRSR, including other serious violations of human rights norms, may also amount to persecution.[29] Hathaway also notes that "[i]n addition to the Convention's acceptance of deprivation of basic civil and political freedoms as sufficient cause for international concern, serious social and economic consequences were also acknowledged to be within the purview of persecution".[30] This human rights approach to protection focuses on the individual at risk of harm rather than the actions of the state of origin, thus expanding the definition of persecution. Persecution must therefore be identified not only with reference to civil and political rights but also increasingly through the prism of economic, social, and cultural rights.[31] This approach is similarly reflected in Article 9 of the European Union

26 UNHCR Handbook para. 65 reads: "[p]ersecution is normally related to action by the authorities of a country". *See also* Goodwin-Gill, G. S. & McAdam, J. (2007) "The Refugee in International Law" (Oxford University Press) pp. 10–12 ("While the use of the word 'surrogacy' can serve as an introduction to the system of international protection it may be misleading. This is because protection should be driven first and foremost by focusing on the individual at risk of relevant harm (fear of persecution) considered in a social and political context and not so much giving preference to the State of origin and its efforts in providing protection").

27 *See* McAdam, J. & Saul, B. (2009) "An Insecure Climate for Human Security? Climate-Induced Displacement and International Law" University of Sydney, Faculty of Law, Working Paper No. 4, p. 9 *available from:* www.peacepalacelibrary.nl/ebooks/files/357399072.pdf [accessed 20 December 2013] (noting that while sea level rise, earthquakes, persistent flooding and storms may be harmful, they do not comprise persecution within the meaning ascribed both in international and domestic law, because states are generally willing to protect their people in the aftermath of a disaster).

28 Mercure, P. F. (2006) "A la Recherche d'un Statut Juridique pour les Migrants Environnementaux Transfrontaliers: la Problématique de la Notion de Réfugié" 37 Revue de Droit de L'Université de Sherbrooke p. 18, pp. 1–39 (author's own free translation).

29 UNHCR Handbook, para. 51.

30 Hathaway (1991) *Op. Cit.* p. 1033.

31 *See* Juss, S. (2007) "International Migration and Global Justice" (Ashgate Publishing) p. 203.

Qualification Directive, which defines persecution as a "severe violation of basic human rights".[32]

ENVIRONMENTAL HARM AS A FORM OF PERSECUTION?

Though the UNHCR Handbook does not define persecution, it presents no direct barrier to considering environmental harm as persecution. There are a number of examples where environmental harm can be viewed as persecution. Individuals could argue persecution when environmental factors (such as severe pollution), perpetrated by or with consent of their state of origin, constitute a serious threat to life and where harm can be connected to a CRSR ground. Christopher Kozoll argues that "environmental harm is as capable of being a means of persecution as any other form of harm".[33] For example, in *Sarei v Rio Tinto*, residents of the island of Bougainville in Papua, New Guinea (PNG) filed a lawsuit in US federal court against Rio Tinto under the Alien Tort Claims Act.[34] Plaintiffs alleged that Rio Tinto, which operated mines in Panguna, improperly dumped waste rock and tailings, harmed the island's environment and the life and health of its residents, and engaged in racially discriminatory labour practices by paying local black workers lower wages than white workers and by housing black workers in poor conditions. Similarly, in the previously mentioned *Social and Economic Rights Action Centre v Nigeria*,[35] the African Commission on Human and People's Rights acknowledged the negligence and complicity of the Nigerian government in committing "massive [environmental] violations" by facilitating the actions of oil giant Shell in Ogoniland. The Commission found that Nigeria's conduct impacted the Ogoni indigenous people's rights to health, food, and shelter, resulting in "malnutrition and starvation among certain Ogoni communities". In both cases, the complained-of conduct led to the displacement of either poor black people or indigenous populations,

32 Article 9 Directive 2011/95/EU of the European Parliament and of the Council of 13 December 2011 (on standards for the qualification of third-country nationals or stateless persons as beneficiaries of international protection, for a uniform status for refugees or for persons eligible for subsidiary protection, and for the content of the protection granted) (Recast) (EU Qualification Directive).

33 Kozoll C. (2004) "Poisoning the Well: Persecution, the Environment, and Refugee Status" 15 Journal of International Environmental Law and Policy 2 pp. 271–272, pp. 271–307.

34 *Sarei v Rio Tinto PLC*, 9th Cir. Nos. 02-56256, 02-56390 (20 August 2007). In 2002, Rio Tinto sought and was granted dismissal of the case. Rio Tinto argued that the case raised questions that are "nonjusticiable" (not appropriate for resolution by a US court) because they involve acts of state and political questions and because ruling on them would breach standards of international relations. After a lengthy appeals process, the appellate court upheld dismissal of the claims regarding racial discrimination and crimes against humanity but reversed on plaintiffs' claims of genocide and war crimes.

35 ACmHPR, *Social and Economic Rights Action Centre v Nigeria*, Comm. No. 155/96 (27 October 2002).

but the claims were brought as class actions seeking compensation for victims, not refugee status. They are relevant, nevertheless, because they reveal important elements to assess persecution. First, the victims abandoned environments they considered uninhabitable (subjective element of well-founded fear of persecution). Then, the government, or non-state actors with government knowledge, carried out acts deemed persecutory (life threats, including deaths, barriers to access judicial proceedings – objective element of well-founded fear of persecution). Finally, they fled based upon a fear of persecution on the grounds of their membership in a racial group (black) and the social group of the poor or indigenous.[36]

The New Zealand Refugee Status Appeal Authority (RSAA) also suggests that where the right to food can be used as a discriminatory weapon against a certain population (e.g. destruction of crops by the government), resulting in starvation, the right to food, together with the right to life, may meet the persecution standard based on a Convention reason.[37] These examples illustrate that environmental harm, in certain circumstances, can arguably amount to persecution.

Some authors allege that "prejudicial actions or threats" may form the basis of environmental persecution, though the margins of what actions are sufficiently prejudicial remain dependent on evidentiary facts.[38] In addition, when determining refugee status, other factors, even though "not in themselves amounting to persecution [e.g. discrimination in various forms and insecurity in the country of origin] may, if taken together, produce an effect on the mind of the applicant that can reasonably justify a claim to a well-founded fear of persecution on 'cumulative grounds'".[39]

For environmental displacement, the applicant's total circumstances (historical, cultural, and situational, including changing environmental circumstances or "hot spots") must be taken into account to understand and make an informed decision about the applicant's case. However, "to establish that flight based on environmental harm is based on well-founded fear of persecution, an individual will have to show more than generalised environmental degradation".[40] Otherwise, one might qualify, instead, as an economic migrant – one who voluntarily moves for economic reasons.[41] But even in these cases the reason for flight might be "blurred" because "[b]ehind economic measures affecting a person's livelihood there may be racial, religious or political aims or intentions directed

36 *See generally*, Mercure (2006) *Op. Cit.* p. 14 sq.

37 RSAA, Refugee Appeal 74665/03, RSAA (7 July 2004) para. 89. *See* further on this Foster, M. (2007) "International Refugee Law and Socio-Economic Rights-Refugee from Deprivation" (Cambridge Studies in International and Comparative Law).

38 Kozoll (2004) *Op. Cit.* p. 282; UNHCR Handbook para. 52.

39 UNHCR Handbook *Op. Cit.* para. 53.

40 Kozoll (2004) *Op. Cit.* p. 284. *See also* UNHCR Handbook para. 62–64.

41 UNHCR Handbook *Op. Cit.* para. 62.

against a particular group".[42] Thus, the destruction of a person's livelihood or cultural surroundings due to environmental harms may, by analogy, amount to persecution.[43] A study of examples is instructive.

LACK OF EFFECTIVE STATE PROTECTION: INEXISTENCE, COMPLICITY, OMISSION, OR FAILURE

The UNHCR Handbook notes that persons may be unable[44] or unwilling[45] to avail themselves of state protection.[46] The inexistence of state protection beyond an individual's control means that a person may reasonably distrust the government to provide the necessary protection (e.g. cases of war or grave disturbance). In case of "grave disturbance", which may include environmental disruptions, people would logically be unable to avail themselves of state protection when their country cannot extend or ensure effective protection or denies protection. An individual's inability to rely on state protection is highly fact dependent. For example, in the horn of Africa in 2011, a drought considered to be the worst of the last 60 years put at risk more than 12 million people. In Somalia alone, thousands crossed the border to Ethiopia and Kenya in search of relief.[47] The impact of drought, high food prices, and generalised insecurity in Somalia resulted in a situation where individuals clearly could no longer avail themselves

42 *Ibid.* para. 63.
43 Kozoll (2004) *Op. Cit.* p. 284.
44 UNHCR Handbook *Op. Cit.* paras. 98–99. Paragraph 98 states, in full, as follows: "[b]eing *unable* to avail himself of such protection implies circumstances that are beyond the will of the person concerned. There may, for example, be a state of war, civil war or other grave disturbance, which prevents the country of nationality from extending protection or makes such protection ineffective. Protection by the country of nationality may also have been denied to the applicant. Such denial of protection may confirm or strengthen the applicant's fear of persecution, and may indeed be an element of persecution". Paragraph 99 states, in full, as follows: "[w]hat constitutes a refusal of protection must be determined according to the circumstances of the case. If it appears that the applicant has been denied services (e.g. refusal of national passport or extension of its validity, or denial of admittance to the home territory) normally accorded to his co-nationals, this may constitute a refusal of protection within the definition".
45 *Ibid.* para. 100. Paragraph 100 states as follows: "[t]he term *unwilling* refers to refugees who refuse to accept the protection of the Government of the country of their nationality. It is qualified by the phrase 'owing to such fear'. Where a person is willing to avail himself of the protection of his home country, such willingness would normally be incompatible with a claim that he is outside that country 'owing to well-founded fear of persecution'. Wherever the protection of the country of nationality is available, and there is no ground on well-founded fear for refusing it, the person concerned is not in need of international protection and is not a refugee".
46 Of note, however, is that the willingness of an individual to accept protection from his/her own government terminates his/her refugee claim.
47 U.N. News Centre (2011) "UN Ramps Up Aid in Drought-Stricken Horn of Africa as Number in Need Rises" (9 September) *available from:* www.un.org/apps/news/story.asp?NewsID=39495 [accessed 17 August 2018].

of state protection,[48] mainly due to the government's incapacity to cope with the situation, resulting in the violation of social, economic, and other basic rights. When the state is unable to advocate for the protection needs of its own nationals due to the nature of the environmental disaster, one must question this inability.

As previously mentioned, the violation of human rights in general, and persecution in particular, can also arise in cases of a state's complicity, omission, or failure to act.[49] When states do not take reasonable steps to fulfil their duties and their actions disproportionally impact a particular social group (even in times of resource constraint),[50] this conscientious apathy or complicity may amount to persecution.[51] A relevant example is the desertification of the African Sahel region where states allegedly "could have enacted policies and programs to cut population growth, to improve techniques, or to heighten food production".[52] As previously mentioned, a government is also complicit when it consents to private actors' exploitation of natural resources regardless of the environmental and human consequences. This has included perpetrating violations of human rights (e.g. right to life and right to health) and discriminatory practices, usually targeted at sectors of the population (e.g. indigenous peoples). The UNGA explicitly mentions that "contemporary forms of victimization (. . .), may nevertheless also be directed against groups of persons who are targeted

48 The reasoning in *Canada (Attorney General) v Ward*, 2 S.C.R. 689 (30 June 1993), a leading immigration decision by the Supreme Court of Canada, is analogous. There, the court held that when examining the requirement of "well-founded fear of persecution", the persecution need not originate from the state, and mere inability to provide protection is sufficient to establish claim for persecution. It held that "[m]ost states would be willing to attempt to protect when an objective assessment established that they are not able to do this effectively (. . .) [and] it would seem to defeat the purpose of international protection if a claimant would be required to risk his or her life seeking ineffective protection of a state, merely to demonstrate that ineffectiveness".

49 *See* CESCR, General Comment No. 14 *Op. Cit.* at para. 49 ("Violations of the right to health can also occur through the *omission or failure of States to take necessary measures arising from legal obligations.* Violations through *acts of omission* include the failure to take appropriate steps towards the full realization of everyone's right to the enjoyment of the highest attainable standard of physical and mental health, the failure to have a national policy on occupational safety and health as well as occupational health services, and the failure to enforce relevant laws") (emphasis added).

50 *See* CESCR, General Comment No.3 *Op. Cit.* para.12 ("[E]ven in times of severe resources constraints whether caused by a process of adjustment, of economic recession, or by other factors the vulnerable members of society can and indeed must be protected by the adoption of relatively low-cost targeted programmes"). *See also* CESCR General Comment No. 14 at para. 49; CESCR General Comment No. 5 Persons with Disabilities, U.N. Doc. E/C.12/1994/13 (1994).

51 Foster (2007) *Op. Cit.* pp. 201–204.

52 Williams, A. (2008) "Turning the Tide: Recognising Climate Change Refugees in International Law" 30 Law and Policy 4 p. 508, pp. 502–529.

collectively".[53] Similarly, Jessica Cooper acknowledges that environmental persecution can occur "when governments knowingly induce environmental degradation and that degradation harms people by forcing them to migrate".[54] In these cases, an applicant who can show evidence of infliction of environmental harm based on a Convention ground will have a powerful claim for refugee status.

Other noteworthy examples are large-scale development projects[55] that, with government consent, destroy the natural environment and lead to the disappearance of villages and the displacement of millions of people, sometimes without an adequate relocation process.[56] Michael Cernea, who has studied the human dimensions of development projects, concludes that the displacement of populations in these cases has led to deepened poverty that can be materialised in the loss of work, property, or housing; food insecurity; or lack of access to collective resources.[57] Even if, at first glance, it seems difficult to establish an act of persecution in these cases, the lack of available resources that jeopardises the population's survival can, taken together, justify a claim for refugee status on "cumulative grounds".

INTENTION OF THE PERSECUTOR?

Some scholars suggest that, in these cases, an element of intent is required for the state's act to be deemed as persecutory. Aurelie Lopez asserts that "the governmental entity must have been negligent or inactive 'because of' and not merely 'in spite of' its adverse effects upon an identifiable group".[58] However, a government's intent is not a necessary requirement. Furthermore, the source of persecution or risk may be other "non-human" factors, such as the inexistence of adequate economic resources and infrastructures to provide disaster relief.

53 UNGA (2005) "Basic Principles and Guidelines on the Right to a Remedy and Reparation for Victims of Gross Violations of International Human Rights Law and Serious Violations of International Humanitarian Law" U.N. Doc. G.A. Res. 60/147 (16 December) Preamble para.9.

54 Cooper (1998) *Op. Cit.* p. 483.

55 *See* Cernea, M. (1999) "La Dimension Humaine dans Les Projets du Développement: les Variables Sociologiques et Culturelles" (Éditions Karthala) p. 210. According to the author, large-scale development projects include not only dams for electricity production but also road or airport construction, the construction of irrigation channels, urban infrastructures, and factories or industrial areas, as well as the construction of biodiversity-protected areas or national parks.

56 Vlassopoulou, C. (2008) "Les Migrations Environnementales entre Secteurs d'Action Publique" Revue Asylon(s) No. 6 p. 5 *available from*: www.reseau-terra.eu/article848.html [accessed 17 August 2018]. For example, the three Gorges Dams in China.

57 Cernea (1999) *Op. Cit.* p. 218.

58 Lopez, A. (2007) "The Protection of Environmentally-Displaced Persons in International Law" 37 Environmental Law p. 380.

Only when the state is able to remove the applicant's *well-founded fear* is the persecutory criterion not established. "In other words, it is not sufficient that the state is endeavouring to fulfil its obligations pursuant to international human rights law; it must provide sufficient protection to remove the well-founded fear".[59] The availability of state protection has a seemingly implicit duality: *objective action* – must provide at least minimally sufficient protection; and *subjective action* – such protection must remove the well-founded fear from the applicant.

Importantly, the CRSR's drafting history is silent about the intent of the persecutor as a *controlling* factor and both the definition and the refugee status determination procedure.[60] Because *fear* is a key element of the refugee definition ("*owing to well-founded fear of being persecuted*") and the CRSR does not explicitly refer to the persecutor's intent, arguably the focus should be on the applicant's fear. Notably formulated in the passive voice, the test reiterates the subjective element of the "predicament of the applicant rather than on an assessment of the situation from the perspective of the persecutor".[61] This interpretation is also in line with the humanitarian stand of the treaty.

(iii) "For reasons of" requirement

Even if one can show the requisite correlation between environmental consequences and government actions in cases of environmental-induced displacement, other requirements still have to be met.[62] Persecution must have a causal nexus based on one of the specified Convention grounds: "race, religion, nationality, membership in a particular social group or political opinion". It is enough that the Convention ground is an essential factor contributing to persecution; it is not required to be the only or even dominant persecutory factor.[63] Overlaying multiple grounds may be used by the applicant. Furthermore, the individual need not actually fall within the specified grounds as long as the persecutor believes he/she does.[64]

59 Foster (2007) *Op. Cit.* p. 202.
60 Goodwin-Gill & McAdam (2007) *Op. Cit.* pp. 100–101.
61 Foster (2007) *Op. Cit.* p. 273.
62 *See* Aleinikoff, A. (1991) "The Meaning of 'Persecution' in U.S. Asylum Law" in H. Adelman (ed.) "Refugee Policy: Canada and the United States" (Centre for Refugee Studies & Centre for Migration Studies York University) pp. 292, 296.
63 Guidelines on International Protection: The application of Article 1A(2) and/or 1967 Protocol relating to the Status of Refugees to victims of trafficking and persons at risk of being trafficked, UNHCR, U.N. Doc. HCR/GIP/06/07, 7 April 2006, para. 29 *available from:* www.unhcr.org/443b626b2.html [accessed 17 August 2018].
64 *See* Frigo, M. (2011) "Migration and International Human Rights Law" Practitioners Guide No. 6 (International Commission of Jurists) p. 50. *See also* EU qualification Directive Article 10 (2) ("When assessing if an applicant has a well-founded fear of being persecuted it *is immaterial whether the applicant actually possesses* the racial, religious,

When environmental degradation is used as a "weapon" against a particular group, this "environmental cleansing" may constitute persecution, triggering refugee status. "Environmental cleansing" is the "deliberate manipulation and misuse of the environment so as to subordinate groups based on characteristics e.g. race, ethnicity, nationality, religion and so forth".[65] A case from the 1990s addressed the attempt by Saddam Hussein's regime to push Shi'a opposition groups out of southern Iraq and gain political control of the area's people by draining marshes. The environmental effects were profound – the loss of fauna and flora, agricultural land, and people's livelihoods, as well as forced displacement – and cost thousands of human lives. Some characterise the conduct as "genocide",[66] defined as "deliberately inflicting on the group conditions of life calculated to bring about physical destruction in whole or in part".[67]

However, because environmental conditions generally affect individuals indiscriminately, regardless of religion, nationality, social group, or political opinion, establishing the persecution nexus on Convention ground may be difficult, particularly where the state is willing to protect all individuals without discrimination yet unable to do so despite serious harm. In this context, "[d]etailed and accurate research into state responsibility for both the causes and consequences of environmental degradation will therefore be vital to assist in establishing whether the required nexus exists".[68]

While asylum claims likely focus more on non-environmental factors, individuals may indeed suffer environmental persecution based on any ground under the Geneva Convention. Christopher Kozoll argues that victims of environmental change (natural disasters and human-caused degradation) meet the refugee definition under international law on at least two occasions. First, when "a government systematically imposes the risks and burdens of decisions impacting environmental quality on members of a particular race, religion, nationality, social group or political opinion on account of one or more of these protected

---

national, social or political characteristic which attracts the persecution, ***provided that such characteristic is attributed to the applicant by the actor of persecution***") (emphasis added).

65 Drumbl, M. A. (2005) "Symposium: The International Responses to Environmental Impacts of War" 17 "Georgetown International Journal of Environmental Law" pp. 565–643, p. 627.

66 *See* Human Rights Watch (2003) "The Iraqi Government Assault on the Marsh Arabs" (January) ***available from:*** www.hrw.org/legacy/backgrounder/mena/marsharabs1.htm [accessed 17 August 2018]; Tkachenko, A. (2002) "The Economy of the Iraq Marshes in the 1990s" in E. Nicholson & P. Clark (eds.) "The Iraqi Marshlands" (Politco's) pp. 36, 41; Civil Liberty "The War Crimes of Saddam Hussein" ***available from:*** http://civilliberty.about.com/od/internationalhumanrights/p/saddam_hussein.htm [accessed 17 August 2018].

67 *See* Article II (c) Convention on the Prevention and Punishment of the Crime of Genocide, adopted on 9 December 1948, in force since 12 January 1951, 78 UNTS 277.

68 Burson, B. (2010) "Environmentally Induced Displacement and the 1951 Refugee Convention: Pathways to Recognition" in T. Afifi and J. Jäger (eds.) "Environment, Forced Migration and Social Vulnerability" (Springer-Verlag) p. 13.

factors", and second, "where the relevant authority refuses to mitigate or mitigates inadequately environmental disasters, whether of human origin or not, and in so doing 'targets' a group based on one of the listed factors".[69] The second is particularly seen where the government does not implement mitigation or adaptive strategies in a region populated by indigenous people (given available scientific knowledge that displacement is likely to occur there) or where the government is unable to manage a disaster situation either by intended inaction or blocking relief to certain groups. The latter was documented during Cyclone Nargis in 2008[70] where, despite the terrible experience of the 2004 Asian tsunami, Myanmar's government was not only incapable of offering assistance to the victims but also refused aid from humanitarian institutions.[71]

ENVIRONMENTALLY DISPLACED PERSONS: A PARTICULAR SOCIAL GROUP?

The definition of "membership of a particular social group" is important, because many scholars suggest that EDPs should fall within that definition, thus meriting host state protection.[72] Though subject to extensive analysis, a social group essentially encompasses individuals with similar undeniable characteristics, social position, or habits, features considered in the *protected characteristics* approach.[73] A comprehensive understanding of the term "social group" is developing.[74] The group must exist as an independent entity prior to the persecution[75] and need not be of any specific size. Members of the group do not need a certain intentional affiliation with each other, and not all members must be at risk of persecution. That certain members of that social group are at risk is sufficient.[76]

69 Kozoll (2004) *Op. Cit.* pp. 273–274.

70 Tripartite Core Group Report comprised of Representatives of the Government of Myanmar, Association of South Asian Nations and United Nations (2008) "Post-Nargis Assessment" (July) pp. 37–38. According to the report, Cyclone Nargis was one of the worst catastrophes in the history of Myanmar, devastating villages next to coastal areas as well as housing, road, and communication infrastructures and leading to the death and displacement of millions of people.

71 *See* Cohen, R. (2009) "The Burma Cyclone and the Responsibility to Protect" 1 Global Responsibility to Protect 2, pp. 253–257, p. 256.

72 *See generally*, Cooper (1998) *Op. Cit.*

73 UNHCR Handbook *Op. Cit.* para. 77.

74 UNHCR, Guidelines on International Protection: "Membership of a Particular Social Group" within the context of Article 1A (2) of the 1951Convention and/or its Protocol Relating to the Status of Refugees: HCR/GIP/02/02, 7 May 2002 *available from*: www.unhcr.org/3d58de2da.html [accessed 20 December 2011]. These Guidelines define a particular social group as: "a group of persons who share a common characteristic other than their risk of being persecuted, or who are perceived as a group by society (. . .) [and] the characteristic will often be one which is innate, unchangeable, or which is otherwise fundamental to identify, conscience, or exercise of one's human rights".

75 Foster (2007) *Op. Cit.* p. 293.

76 Goodwil-Gill & MacAdam (2007) *Op. Cit.* p. 85.

How the group is externally perceived by society may also be considered[77] and constitutes the *social perception* approach, which "moves beyond protected characteristics by recognising that external factors can [too] be important to a proper social group definition".[78]

Cooper argues that EDPs are victims of environmental injustice and thus bear the disproportionate impact of environmental damage. Under environmental justice theory, these persons belong to a social group since they are politically disenfranchised and powerless to protect their environment.[79] This power imbalance allows states to take persecutory actions against them (e.g. failing to take measures to prevent disasters and displacement, destroying crops and poisoning water, or refusing to receive aid or withholding or obstructing assistance), which may determine the group's visibility in society. However, it can be argued that the power imbalance may result from a number of elements not under governmental control (for e.g. international pressures from non-state actors, the political environment, an established rule of law system or democratic approach). Further, some argue that not all EDPs are politically powerless because environmental change impacts individuals indiscriminately, not in a targeted fashion.[80] Regardless, states are not disenfranchised from affording their population a "minimum content of protection" to promote and protect their human rights in the event of environmental changing conditions or in the aftermath of a disaster (see Chapter 3).

For EDPs, proving that the group "existed prior to the occurrence of persecution" might be difficult to establish, but it is not impossible. The IPCC has conclusively established which areas of the world will be most impacted by environmental change. People living in these areas are particularly vulnerable

77 *See* Council of Europe (2004) Committee of Ministers "Recommendation Rec" (2004) 9 of the Committee of Ministers to Member States on the Concept of "Membership of a Particular Social Group" (MPSG) in the Context of the 1951 Convention Relating to the Status of Refugees, Rec (2004) 9 (30 June) *available from:* www.refworld.org/docid/4278d1524.html [accessed 17 August 2018]. The Committee of Ministers Recommendation considers that "'a particular social group' is a group of persons who have, or are attributed with, a common characteristic other than the risk of being persecuted and who are perceived as a group by society or identified as such by the state of the persecutors. Persecutory action towards a group may however be a relevant factor in determining the visibility of a group in a particular society".

78 Aleinikoff, A. (2003) "Protected Characteristics and Social Perceptions: An Analysis of the Meaning of 'Membership of a Particular Social Group'" in E. Feller, V. Türk & F. Nicholson (eds.) "Refugee Protection in International Law" (Cambridge University Press) p. 297.

79 Cooper (1998) *Op. Cit.*p. 523–526.

80 Falstrom, D. Z. (2001) "Stemming the Flow of Environmental Displacement: Creating a Convention to Protect Persons and Preserve the Environment" 1 Colorado Journal of Environmental Law & Policy pp. 5–6, pp. 5–21; McAdam, J. (2011a) "Climate Change and International Law: Complementary Protection Standards" (UNHCR Legal and Protection Policy Series May 2011) *available from:* www.unhcr.org/4dff16e99.html [accessed 17 August 2018].

to environmental stresses and are increasingly recognisable as needing protection. The inherent common immutable characteristic is their unique vulnerability to external environmental impacts (see Chapter 2's discussion on "vulnerability layers"). Within the category of EDPs, there may be other more vulnerable sub-groups that need special attention (e.g. children, women, and older people, among others). A particular social group is not defined only by the fact that all its members suffer persecution or a common fear of persecution. "[T]here is no rational basis for denying protection to individuals who even divided in lifestyle, culture, interests and politics, may yet be linked across another dimension of affinity".[81] Today, the *protected characteristics* approach might have a new meaning.

In fact, Walter Kälin[82] uses a "vulnerability analysis" to determine when a situation has reached such a point that a person is forced to leave his or her home. This "vulnerability test" derives from the CRSR's Article 1A(2) three-factor refugee definition: 1) being outside of the country of origin; 2) because of persecution on account of specific reasons; 3) being unable or unwilling to avail oneself of the protection of one's country of origin. The author acknowledges that EDPs meet the refugee criteria only in exceptional circumstances but highlights, nevertheless, that EDPs suffer consequences of environmental change (storms, flooding, salinization of groundwater and soils, among others) and its aftermath (limited access to food, drinking water, health services) similar to persecution. This, in turn, may constitute a serious threat to their rights to life and health. Whereas we are all generally vulnerable to the effects of environmental change, certain *localised vulnerabilities* are obvious, given a group's characteristics and capacity to resist and recover from environmental hazards. Accordingly, EDPs could be characterised as a vulnerable social group in need of protection.

(iv) The "cross the border of the country of origin or place of normal residence" requirement

A person must have fled and crossed the border of the country of origin or place of normal residence in order to benefit from international refugee protection. This generally "is a factual issue which is easily determined and, in most cases, uncontroversial".[83] Borders, of course, are important theoretically and practically for the exercise of sovereignty and are at the heart of states' territorial claims and, more importantly, their obligations towards individuals. However, in reality, there is no real conceptual difference between those displaced by

81 Goodwin-Gill & McAdam (2007) *Op. Cit.* p. 85.

82 Kälin, W. (2010) "Conceptualizing Climate-Induced Displacement" in J. McAdam (ed.) "Climate Change and Displacement: Multidisciplinary Perspectives" (Hart Publishing) pp. 81–103.

83 U.N. High Commissioner for Refugees (2001) "Interpreting Article 1 of the 1951 Convention Relating to the Status of Refugees" (April) para. 33, p. 9.

environmental factors internally or externally; both may need imminent protection. Indeed, for an endangered person, the cross-border element may be irrelevant as his or her ultimate goal is safety and, as Andrew Schanove affirms, refugeehood is "exclusively a political relation between citizen and the state, not a territorial relation between countryman and his homeland".[84] More precisely, "the relationship between the state and the citizens may have broken down without a border crossing having taken place, hence the false dichotomy between *refugee* and *internally displaced person* (. . .) [and] the idea of crossing an international border may therefore be both literal and fictitious".[85] Precarious post-disaster conditions may leave people vulnerable, without protection from their government, and physically unable to cross an international border. Yet, international boundaries form the divide between the international and the domestic protection realm and ensure that states protect their citizens, so when the state can no longer guarantee protection, the international community must step in. Importantly, though, protection must be viewed holistically and not only granted once the person has relocated. A pre-emptive approach is necessary to protect those at risk from environmental displacement, and on this point the CRSR reveals its weakness.

(v) Refugee status determination procedure

The Geneva Convention generally assumes that people meeting the outlined criteria automatically qualify for refugee status, meaning that a state's intake of refugees is not a constitutive element. Thus, the domestic Refugee Status Determination (RSD) procedures are essentially declaratory. The system for adjudicating asylum claims leaves each contracting state to establish the most suitable procedures according to its constitutional and administrative structures. The Executive Committee of the High Commissioners Programme (ExCom) suggests the establishment of minimum procedural standards, taking into account each applicant's special situation, to preserve certain essential guarantees.[86] In practice, however, processes vary extensively, leaving states a great deal of discretion and jeopardising protection of the applicant. In certain regions, potential third-country recipients of EDPs have substandard RSD frameworks.[87]

In most countries, the RSD is carried out on a case-by-case basis, leaving the burden on the applicant to prove the *well-founded fear*. However, because the applicant may be unable to support his or her statements with documentary or other evidence, the applicant and host country share the duty to ascertain and evaluate all relevant factual evidence.[88] An EDP would have to demonstrate

84 Schacknove, E. A. (1985) "Who Is a Refugee?" 95 Ethics 2 p. 283, pp. 274–284,.
85 Haddad, E. (2004) "Who Is (Not) a Refugee?" European University Institute, Working Paper No. 2004/6 p. 24, pp. 1–28.
86 UNHCR Handbook *Op. Cit.* para. 192.
87 Burson (2008) *Op. Cit.*
88 UNHCR Handbook (1992) para. 1195–196.

that serious hardship and fear caused by environmental factors forced him/her to move (analogous to a claim based on the refugee criteria). The starting point of this analysis is the applicant's statement, which, if credible, constitutes the subjective assessment of the element of fear. The objective element (the risk that the applicant would face if returned) is established by the RSD decision-making authorities who should have access to relevant informative material (e.g. government, specialist, and NGO reports and impact assessments). Government authorities' analyses would likely benefit from scientific environmental expertise, including, for example, IPCC reports determining areas most likely to be affected by environmental change. An applicant would have to show that "severe environmental harm" threatens his or her life and/or freedom, amounts to serious human rights violations, or is of such level or nature that would "reasonably induce fear".[89] The individual would also have to demonstrate that environmental harm affects him/her as a member of a particular protected group more than other individuals.[90] As mentioned, persecutory intent on the state's part is not necessary, but the well-founded fear of persecution is linked to one of the Convention grounds. If the applicant's statement is trustworthy, the benefit of the doubt standard might work in his or her favour.[91] However, an individual approach may not be the most appropriate in some circumstances, especially sudden environmental disasters and serious drought during which mass displacement can occur.[92] Group determination of refugee status on a *prima facie* basis could offer an alternative.[93]

PRIMA FACIE GROUP REFUGEES

Through a group approach, states can grant refugee status based on objective and urgent factors in the country of origin that led to the large-scale

89 Kozoll (2004) *Op. Cit.* p. 284.

90 *Ibid.*

91 *See* Ammer, M. (2009) "Climate Change and Human Rights: The Status of Climate Refugees in Europe" (Ludwig Boltzmann Institute of Human Rights).

92 In Somalia, for example, thousands of people were displaced by disasters and crossed the border to Kenya and Ethiopia. *See* Kolmannskog, V. & Afifi, T. (2014) "Disaster Related Displacement from the Horn of Africa" Report No.15 United Nations University Institute for Environment and Human Security (UNU-EHS) *available from*: www.nrc.no/resources/reports/disaster-related-displacement-from-the-horn-of-africa/ [accessed 17 August 2018].

93 *See* UNHCR Handbook *Op. Cit.* para. 44 ("While refugee status must normally be determined on an individual basis, situations have also arisen in which *entire groups* have been displaced under circumstances indicating that members of the group could be considered individually as refugees. In such situations the need to provide assistance is often *extremely urgent* and it may not be possible for purely practical reasons to carry out an individual determination of refugee status for each member of the group. Recourse has therefore been had to so-called *'group determination'* of refugee status, whereby each member of the group is regarded prima facie (i.e. in the absence of evidence to the contrary) as a refugee") (emphasis added).

displacement. The main objective is to ensure safe admittance, protection against *refoulement*, and the provision of basic humanitarian treatment. *Prima facie* refugees are individually characterised as refugees under the Refugee Convention unless otherwise excluded. They are afforded all the rights under the Refugee Convention or other relevant human rights instruments. EDPs could, in fact, benefit from a global status determination procedure under which a neutral institution would assess the environmental circumstances that led to displacement. Other circumstances could lead to hybrid solutions, such as a global determination procedure by a neutral entity followed by an individualised national RSD. Prima facie status determination was used for Asian refugees in Vietnam after the fall of Saigon, in Africa, and in Europe for Hungarian refugees fleeing the failed revolution in 1956.

4.2 Realities and limits of states' obligations under the international protection system

The above analysis arguably suggests that, in some situations, the existing refugee criteria may include EDPs. In these cases, host states are obligated to provide international protection in accordance with the CRSR. Authors like Jane McAdam, who is critical of categorising EDPs as refugees, candidly admits that under some circumstances environmental impacts might constitute persecution under the Convention grounds, including when:

- "Victims of natural disasters flee because their government has consciously withheld or obstructed assistance in order to punish or marginalise them on the five Convention grounds;
- Government policies target particular groups reliant on agriculture for survival, in circumstances where climate change is already hampering their subsistence;
- A government induces famine by destroying crops or poisoning water, or contributes to environmental destruction by polluting land or water;
- A government refuses to accept aid from other States when it is in need, such as in the aftermath of a disaster;
- A government does not establish appropriate measures of prevention of disasters".[94]

The refugee concept can be seen as an "entity in movement" able to transform itself and satisfy humanitarian requirements. This expanded interpretative approach to the CRSR might be able to secure – in some situations – effective rights for EDPs.

States and the UNHCR have been reluctant, though, to expand the Refugee Convention definition to include EDPs for fear of opening "refugee floodgates"

94 McAdam (2011) *Op. Cit.* p. 47.

and diluting the conceptual meaning of refugees.[95] In two recent cases, *Teitiota v The Chief Executive of the Ministry of Business and Employment*[96] and *AD (Tuvalu) v New Zealand Immigration and Protection Tribunal*,[97] New Zealand emphasised that refugee law is too strict to apply in this embryonic area. In *Teitiota*,[98] the High Court of New Zealand was sympathetic to the applicant's concern that millions of people suffering from economic deprivation or the "presumptive hardships caused by climate change"[99] must be considered by individual states and the international community. However, the court made clear that it was the states' role, not the court's, to enlarge the scope of protection under CRSR.[100] Interestingly, the court cited a decision in which the Australian Refugee Review Tribunal found no basis to conclude that countries that are high emitters are motivated to impact residents of low-lying countries, such as Kiribati, on the basis of their race, religion, nationality, membership in a particular social group, or political opinion.[101] The court did not decide whether states' use of fossil fuels and *inter alia* emission of high levels of greenhouse gases may constitute discrimination against people belonging to a particular social group.[102] The second case focused on a family from Tuvalu[103] who claimed

95 Hong, J. (2001) "Refugees of the 21st Century: Environmental Injustice" 10 Cornell Journal of Law & Public Policy pp. 323–348.

96 New Zealand High Court (NZHC), *Teitiota v The Chief Executive of the Ministry of Business and Employment*, NZHC 3125 (26 November 2013).

97 New Zealand Immigration and Protection Tribunal (NZIPT), *AD (Tuvalu) v New Zealand Immigration and Protection Tribunal*, NZIPT 501370–371 (4 June 2014).

98 A Kiribati man, Ioane Teitiota, applied for leave to appeal a decision of New Zealand's Immigration and Protection Tribunal, which declined to grant him refugee and/or protected person status. The Republic of Kiribati is an island nation in the central Pacific Ocean comprised of 33 atolls and reef islands and one raised coral island, Banaba. Scientists currently consider the islands as sinking islands due to the impacts of climate change.

99 NZHC, *Teitiota v The Chief Executive of the Ministry of Business and Employment Op. Cit.* para. 44.

100 *Ibid.* paras. 44, 54, 56.

101 *Ibid.* para. 55.

102 Though the court denied the claimant's application, it noted that the ruling did not mean that those affected by climate change would never be recognised as refugees, thereby leaving an open door for future (re)interpretation of the CRSR. Specifically, the court stated that: "[i]n relation to the Refugee Convention, while Kiribati undoubtedly faces challenges, Mr. Teitiota does not, if returned, face 'serious harm' and there is no evidence that the Government of Kiribati is failing to take steps to protect its citizens from the effects of environmental degradation to the extent that it can. (. . .) That said, we note that both the Tribunal and the High Court, emphasised their decisions *did not mean that environmental degradation resulting from climate change or other natural disasters could never create a pathway into the Refugee Convention or protected person jurisdiction. Our decision in this case should not be taken as ruling out that possibility in an appropriate case*". New Zealand Supreme Court (NZSC), *Teitiota v The Chief Executive of the Ministry of Business and Employment*, NZSC 107 (20 July 2015) paras. 12, 13 (emphasis added).

103 Tuvalu is a Polynesian island nation located in the Pacific Ocean comprised of three reef islands and six atolls. Scientists currently consider the islands as sinking islands due to the impacts of climate change.

refugee status because their lives would be endangered if they returned to their country. The court acknowledged that the "exposure to the impacts of natural disasters, can, in general terms, be a humanitarian circumstance"[104] and, in some cases, deporting individuals back to their country of origin, especially young children who are "inherently more vulnerable to natural disasters and the adverse impact of climate change", could be unreasonable or disproportionately harsh.[105] Although the court acknowledged that Tuvalu was particularly at risk from the impacts of environmental change, including "coastal erosion, flooding and inundation, increasing salinity of fresh ground-water supplies, destruction of primary sources of substance, and destruction of personal and community property",[106] it found that these factors were not related to the CRSR criteria but rather an "exceptional circumstance of a humanitarian nature".[107]

At the institutional level, the UNHCR has also discouraged an extensive interpretation of the existing refugee definition, lest it lead to a renegotiation of the CRSR and lower current refugee protection standards under the existing definition.[108] Plus, the U.N. agency's approach to EDPs is morally and legally different from the common refugee: "[w]hereas political and war refugees are victims of home state or regionalised conflict, with no direct responsibility for their plight with the countries that eventually offer refuge, the moral responsibility for climate change is different".[109] While the UNHCR offers no further solutions to the issue,[110] it continues to offer *in situ* protection for those affected by environmental disasters.

Authors like Jessica Cooper[111] and Silke Christiansen[112] controversially suggest changing the Geneva Convention's Article 1 definition to include environmental degraded conditions that imperil the right to life, livelihood, and natural resources, reflecting values and principles enshrined in the wider human rights framework (UDHR, ICCPR, and ICESCR). However, pragmatic difficulties may include host states' lack of human and financial capacity to address the

104 NZIPT, *AD (Tuvalu) v New Zealand Immigration and Protection Tribunal Op. Cit.* para. 27.
105 *Ibid.* para. 25.
106 *Ibid.* para. 29.
107 *Ibid.* para. 30.
108 Parliamentary Assembly Council of Europe (2008) "Environmentally Induced Migration and Displacement: A 21st-Century Challenge" Report Committee on Migration, Refugees and Population Rapporteur: Mrs Tina Acketoft, Sweden, Alliance of Liberals and Democrats for Europe Doc. 11785 (23 December) para. 55 *available from:* www.refworld.org/pdfid/49997bbb0.pdf [accessed 17 August 2018].
109 *Ibid.* para. 56.
110 Gomilova, M. & Jagers, N. (2013) "Climate Change Induced Displacement and International Law" in J. Verscguuren (ed.) "Research Handbook on Climate Change and Adaptation Law" (Edward Elgar Publishing) p. 87.
111 Cooper (1998) *Op. Cit.* pp. 480–488.
112 Christiansen S. (2010) "Environmental Refugees a Legal Perspective" (Wolf Publishers) p. 69.

situation. Overall, "conceptual confusion – about the meaning of refugeehood, its causes, and its management – also contributes to the misery of both refugee and host and to the inflammation of international tension".[113] In reality, states have increasingly seen the entitlement to pertinent rights and benefits under the refugee status "within reasonable limits", making resource scarcity a political rather than a physical element.[114]

The matter is further complicated by inconsistency of terms used within legal, sociological, and anthropological remits.[115] The different labels used in everyday parlance, particularly in the media, (economic migrants, illegal immigrants, asylum seekers, displaced persons, stateless persons, de facto refugees, B-refugees, bogus asylum seekers, political refugees) has created the "image of dependence, helplessness and misery",[116] a stereotype with which most people do not want to be associated. The President of Kiribati's words, as the island-state is faced with possible disappearance due to increased sea level rise, reflects this point of view: "[w]e do not want to lose our dignity. We're sacrificing much by being displaced, in any case. So we don't want to lose that, whatever dignity is left. So the last thing we want to be called is *refugee*".[117] Classifying EDPs as refugees is "putting the stigma on the victims, not the offenders".[118]

The actual notion of refugee is characterised by a "cluster approach" that bundles specific criteria that apply in certain circumstances but *sensu strictu* do not include EDPs. First, EDPs do not lack home state protection, as do most conventional refugees, although the home states may lack the financial and human resource capacity to implement such protection. Second, the state's persecution must be founded in one of the specific grounds, which do not explicitly include environmental changing conditions. The Refugee Convention's protection regime traditionally targets the narrow class of those fleeing political persecution, thereby setting clear boundaries of the treaty's legal application but leaving little room for interpreting the reasons of persecution.[119] Finally, the Convention relies upon an individual status determination procedure, which is

113 Schacknove (1985) *Op. Cit.* P. 276.

114 Martin, D. (1991) "The Refugee Concept: On Definitions, Politics, and Careful Use of Scarce Resource" in H. Aldelman (ed.) "Refugee Policy: Canada and the United States" (York Lanes Press) p. 36.

115 Suhrke, A. (1983) "Global Refugee Movements and Strategies of Response", in M. Kritz (ed.) "U.S. Immigration Policy: Global and Domestic issues" (Lexington Books) pp. 153–173. According to the author, the notion of refugee can be defined in three different ways: juridically (designated by the national laws and the international agreements), politically (interpreted to satisfy the political requirements), and sociologically (reflecting the empirical reality).

116 Harrell-Bond, B. & Voutira, E. (1992) "Anthropology and the Study of Refugees" 8 Anthropology Today 4 pp. 6–10, p. 7. *See also* Balabanova, E. (2015) "The Media and Human Rights: The Cosmopolitan Promise" (Routledge) p. 105.

117 McAdam *Op. Cit.* (2012) p. 41.

118 *Ibid.*

119 *See* Williams (2008) *Op. Cit.* p. 508.

not entirely suitable for EDPs who collectively suffer disaster (in a village, state/province, or region).[120]

In this "definitional cycle", the system of protection finds itself at a crossroads. In the words of Emma Haddad:

> "A wide definition of who falls into the category "refugee" increases the potential burden on the host state, while accepting a greater failure on the part of the state of origin. A narrow definition, on the other hand, runs the risk of denying protection and assistance to individuals in need and thus not fulfilling basic moral and humanitarian obligations. In other words, as with any definition, *contexts are crucial*".[121]
>
> (emphasis added)

This focus on *context* enables the normative evolution and expansion of the refugee concept regionally but, more importantly, it allows the progress of the law to protect people. In other words, regional protection frameworks develop to fill an existing gap in the international protection regime, as many people flee from situations that fall outside the traditional international meaning of political persecution.

4.3 Enhancing the protection of persons at the regional level

4.3.1 Enhancing the protection of persons "in events seriously disturbing public order"

The 1969 Organisation of African Unity Convention governing the specific aspects of refugee problems in Africa (ARC)[122] was adopted to respond to particular needs of the African continent after national liberation struggles and the creation of new states. The ARC reveals an enlarged definition and scope of application *ratione personae* and can, arguably, be interpreted as encompassing situations of environmental distress and *inter alia* enhanced protection obligations of host states.

120 European Parliament (2008) "Climate Migration" Seminar organised by the Green European Free Alliance Brussels, 11 June 2008, Speech by Frank Biermann p. 16: "La Convention de Genève est fondeée sur l'ideée de perseécution personnelle, sur des droits individuels. Dans le cas des réfugiés climatiques, on ne parle pas d'individus, mais de villages, de zones littorales, de villes, voire de provinces, de régions, ou même de nations entières. Ce sont donc des entités collectives qui sont en jeu ici".

121 Haddad (2007) *Op. Cit.* p. 5.

122 Convention governing the Specific Aspects of Refugee Problems in Africa, adopted on 10 September 1969, in force since 20 June 1974, 1001 UNTS 45.

The ARC is complementary to the CRSR[123] as it acknowledges Article 1(1)'s conditions of refugeehood but also includes broader refugee protection under Article 1(2). It states that the term refugee can also apply to every person who:

> owing to external aggression, occupation, foreign domination *or events seriously disturbing public order in either part or the whole of his country of origin or nationality*, is compelled to leave his place of habitual residence in order to seek refuge *in another place outside his country of origin or nationality.*
>
> (emphasis added)

By including people who flee "events seriously disturbing public order", the definition is broader than the CRSR's "well-founded fear" standard. According to Ari Zolberg *et al.,* the ARC reflects the instability and displacement in situations where the interaction between natural and man-made disasters can put at risk the lives of entire communities.[124]

The ARC's innovation is that the *persecution* element is no longer a necessary requirement for a refugee determination. The ARC's extension clauses apply to those in need of protection against acts perpetuated not only by the home state but also by civil wars or in cases of foreign aggression, occupation, domination, or events disrupting public order. This may include the violation of human rights and the displacement of populations occurring in the aftermath of an environmental disaster. For EDPs, whose primary concern is the protection of their lives and the lives of their families, it is apparently irrelevant if the threat comes from a state, a foreign government, or a non-state actor, including an environmental threat. Similarly, Michelle Leighton has considered that the displacement of populations that occurs as a result of sudden-onset disaster (such as a tsunami or earthquake) may demand refugee status in the host state.[125]

Furthermore, the ARC's definition allows the individual to judge the circumstances that have seriously disrupted public order and provoked flight. It also allows an individual to cross the border to seek protection without first seeking protection in another part of the country (commonly known as internal inflight alternative). "In order words, international protection is afforded on the basis

123 *See* Preamble para.9, of the ARC: "[r]ecognising that the United Nations Convention of 28 July 1951, as modified by the Protocol of 31 January 1967, constitutes the basic and universal instrument relating to the status of refugees and reflects the deep concern of States for refugees and their desire to establish common standards for their treatment".

124 Zolberg, R. A., Suhrke, A. & Aguayo, S. (1989) "Escape from Violence: Conflict and the Refugee Crisis in the Developing World" (Oxford University Press) p. 29.

125 Leighton, M. (2010) "Climate Change and Migration: Key Issues for Legal Protection of Migrants and Displaced Persons" in "Syllabus, Protecting Environmental Migrants: Creating New Policy and Institutional Frameworks" (United Nations University Institute for Environment and Human Security) p. 5.

of individual judgement"[126] – a criterion centred on the individual's needs of protection.

By adopting the CRSR's definition and then adapting it to Africa's realities, where mass exoduses are more common, the ARC also represents a significant development in international law, as it introduces the ***group eligibility concept***, or ***prima facie***.[127] This approach may protect a massive displacement of population affected by sudden environmental factors, thus reflecting the ARC's humanitarian character.

In practice, African countries have allowed people who cross the border due to environmental disasters to remain temporarily (e.g. in 2002, the Congolese displacement to Rwanda due to the eruption of Mount Nyiragongo). Alice Edwards argues, however, that the receiving state rarely considers it an obligation arising under the ARC.[128] At most, she adds, this practice contributes to the right to temporary humanitarian protection and is a development of international customary law rather than treaty law.[129] James Hathaway has reached the same conclusion. He argues that the ARC's refugee definition does not obligate states to accept victims of environmental disaster but imposes a more generalised humanitarian obligation to offer temporary protection.[130] Kälin similarly notes that it is "rather unlikely that the States concerned would readily accept such an expansion of the concept beyond its conventional meaning of public disturbances resulting in violence".[131]

Nevertheless, given the recent sudden inflows of thousands of people from Somalia to neighbouring countries such as Kenya, Ethiopia, Djibouti, and Yemen due to drought, the ARC could arguably include victims of environmental stressors since such events affect public order when the home state is unable or unwilling to provide assistance.[132] Regional voices, particularly from the African Commission on Human and People's Rights (ACmHPR), stress that African leaders and the international community must take urgent action to combat environmental change because "families are already being forced to flee their

126 Vevstad (1998) *Op. Cit.* p. 104.

127 *Ibid.*

128 Edwards, A. (2006) "Refugee Status Determination in Africa" 14 African Journal of International & Comparative Law, pp. 204–233, p. 227.

129 *Ibid.*

130 Hathaway, J. (1991) "The Law of Refugee Status" (Butterworth-Heinemann) p. 17 reads: "[t]he OAU definition does not, for example, suggest that victims of natural disasters or economic misfortune should become the responsibility of the international community as a shift away from concern about the adequacy of state protection in favour of a more generalized humanitarian commitment might have dictated".

131 Kälin, W. (2010) "Conceptualizing Climate-Induced Displacement" in J. McAdam (ed.) "Climate Change and Displacement: Multidisciplinary Perspectives" (Hart Publishing) p. 88.

132 Notably these people received *prima facie* refugee status in most of those countries. *See generally*, Kolmannskog & Afifi (2014) *Op. Cit.*

homes as climate refugees".[133] The regional consultation under the Nansen Initiative's Horn of Africa[134] also recognised the potential applicability of the ARC in particular, subsuming to "events seriously disturbing public order" disaster situations where the protection and assistance available to the affected populations is in part triggered by conflict.

4.3.2 Enhancing the protection of persons in events of "massive violations of human rights or other circumstances which have seriously disturbed public order"

Massive human rights violations and generalised violence, allied with the flux of substantial numbers of refugees in Latin America (particularly in Central America), led to the Cartagena Declaration on Refugees (CDR).[135] The CDR is based on the "commitments with regards to refugees" defined in the Contadora Act on Peace and Cooperation in Central America (which are, in turn, based on the CSRS).[136] Formulated in September 1984, the CDR includes detailed commitments to peace, democratisation, regional security, and economic cooperation, along with regional compliance mechanisms, thus paving the way for an enlarged protection scope. Its definition of refugee encompasses elements of both the CSRS's and ARC's definitions, but is also open and adaptable to:

> persons who have fled their country because their lives, safety or freedom have been threatened by generalized violence, foreign aggression, internal conflicts, massive violation of human rights or other circumstances which have seriously disturbed public order. [137]

The International Conference on Central American Refugees Legal Experts (Conferencia Internacional sobre Refugiados, Desplazados y Repatriados de Centro América – CIREFCA) 1989 report interpreted the CDR and affirmed

133 African Commission on Human and People's Rights (2009) "Final Communiqué of the 46th Ordinary Session of the African Commission on Human and People's Rights" (Banjul, Republic of the Gambia from 11 to 25 November) p. 3.

134 Nansen Initiative (2014) "Natural Hazards, Climate Change, and Cross-Border Displacement in the Greater Horn of Africa: Protecting People on the Move" Summary of Conclusion Nansen Initiative Greater Horn of Africa Regional Consultation (Nairobi, Kenya 21–23 May) p. 9 *available from:* www.nanseninitiative.org/greater-horn-africa-consultation-intergovernmental/ [accessed 17 August 2018].

135 The Cartagena Declaration on Refugees (1984) was adopted by "Colloquium on the International Protection of Refugees in Central America, Mexico" held at Cartagena, Colombia from 19–22 November 1984.

136 The Contadora Act on Peace and Cooperation in Central America developed on the Panamanian island of Contadora on January 8–9, 1983, and arose from efforts by the foreign ministers of Panama, Colombia, Venezuela, and Mexico to persuade the states of Central America to make peace with each other and with their guerrillas.

137 The Cartagena Declaration on Refugees (1984) III, Conclusion 3.

that events "seriously disturbing public order" do not include "environmental disasters" but do include human-made events, such as accidents.[138] Considering that environmental change has a human-made component, however, one must ask whether today the CIREFCA would make a more progressive interpretation. Indeed, scholars admit that:

> [i]t is perhaps this definition of a situation of seriously disturbed public order that comes closest to some form of official international recognition, which could potentially encompass those compelled to leave their country of origin due to environmental factors.[139]

Notably, CDR's refugee definition includes an additional element: the massive violation of human rights. The inclusion of this component obligates host states to extend protection and grant refugee status to those suffering "denial of civil, political, economic, social and cultural rights in a gross and consistent pattern".[140]

Accounts demonstrate that, in the aftermath of an environmental disaster, vulnerable groups are often at risk of human rights violations, especially in the absence of state protection. The operational guidelines and field manual on human rights protection in situations of natural disaster are revealing on this point:

> The tsunamis, hurricanes and earthquakes, which hit parts of Asia and the Americas in 2004/2005, highlighted the need to be attentive to the multiple human rights challenges victims of such disasters may face. All too often the human rights of disaster victims are not sufficiently taken into account. Unequal access to assistance, discrimination in aid provision, enforced relocation, sexual and gender-based violence, loss of documentation, recruitment of children into fighting forces, unsafe or involuntary return or resettlement, and issues of property restitution are just some of the problems that are often encountered by those affected by the consequences of natural disasters.[141]

In this context, human rights emerge as guiding tenets for the attribution of refugee status under the CDR, but they can also support enhanced obligations

138 Espiell, H. G., Picado, S. & Lanza, L. V. (1990) "Principles and Criteria for the Protection of and Assistance to Central American Refugees and Displaced Persons in Latin America" 2 International Journal of Refugee Law para. 34, pp. 83–117, pp. 96–97.

139 Renaud, F. *et al* (2007) "Control, Adapt or Flee: How to Face Environmental Migration?" Intersection Publications No. 5 (United Nations University Institute for Environment and Human Security) p. 12, pp. 1–47.

140 Espiell *et al. Op. Cit.* p. 94.

141 Brookings Bern Project on Internal Displacement (2008) "Human Rights and Natural Disasters, Operational Guidelines and Field Manual on Human Rights Protection in Situations of Natural Disaster", (Brookings Institution) p. 1.

of host states to protect EDPs. Though the CDR is soft law because of its limited enforceability and not legally binding, its principles have been widely accepted in the region and implemented into domestic legislation,[142] thereby codifying within the whole region what the IACHR considers to be the refugee definition.[143] Thus, they could be considered regional principles with customary character.[144] A more progressive interpretation, allied with state practice, would allow for manoeuvring host states' protection obligations towards EDPs. This evolutionary approach is feasible given that Latin American states tend to apply the extended definition in practice,[145] and only a few countries have explicitly limited the public order ground.[146]

4.3.3 Enhancing the protection of persons in "the occurrence of natural disasters or grave events"

While the OAU Convention and the CDR may provide some protection to EDPs who find themselves in situations analogous to conventional refugees, the 1994 Arab States Refugee Convention (ASRC)[147] goes a step further. The outcome of talks and recommendations by Arab experts on asylum and refugee issues,[148] the ASRC is the first official document that clearly offers protection to people affected by environmental disasters.

142 *See* UNHCR-Regional Legal Unit of the Americas (2005) "Memoir of the Twentieth Anniversary of the Cartagena Declaration on Refugees 1984–2004" (UNHCR) *available from:* www.acnur.org/fileadmin/Documentos/archivo/3868.pdf [accessed 17 August 2018]. Countries that included the broader CDR definition in their national legislation include: Argentina, Belize, Ecuador, Bolivia, El Salvador, Guatemala, Honduras, Mexico, Paraguay and Peru.

143 IACHR (1982) Annual Report 1981–82, OEA/Ser.L/V/II.57 doc.6 rev.1 (1982), Chapter IV, para.11(d).

144 Notably, in ICJ, *Colombia v Perú* (20 November 1950), commonly known as the asylum case, the court found that the custom of asylum was not uniformly or continuously executed sufficiently to demonstrate that the custom was of a generally applicable character at regional level. Nevertheless, the ICJ did recognise that the scope of Article 38 of the Statute of the International Court of Justice encompasses bilateral and regional international customary norms as well as general customary norms, in much the same way as it encompasses bilateral and multilateral treaties.

145 *See* Arboleda, E. (1991) "Refugee Definition in Africa and Latin America: The Lessons of Pragmatism" 3 International Journal of Refugee Law 2 pp. 185–207, p. 205.

146 *See* Article 2 of Bolivian High Decree N°19640 of 4 July 1983 which only includes events of a political nature threatening public order; *See* Brazilian Law N° 9474 of 22 July 1997 and Hondurian Decree N° 208 of 3 March 2003, which exclude public order grounds.

147 Arab Convention on Regulating Status of Refugees in the Arab Countries adopted 1994 by the League of Arab States, not in force.

148 The Arab Experts Group on Asylum and Refugee Issues had its first meeting in San Remo 16–17 January 1984. The subsequent meetings were held in Tunisia 15–18 May 1989, in Jordan 2–4 December 1991, and finally in Egypt 16–19 November 1992. For more details and on the suggested recommendations *see* UNHCR (2007) "Collection of

The ASRC was preceded by the Arab states' similarly broad 1992 Declaration on the Protection of Refugees and Displaced Persons in the Arab World, which provided that:

> [i]n situations which may not be covered by the 1951 Convention, the 1967 Protocol, or any other relevant instrument in force or United Nations General Assembly resolutions, refugees, asylum seekers and displaced persons *shall nevertheless be protected* by: (a) the humanitarian principles of asylum in Islamic law and Arab values, (b) the basic human rights rules, established by international and regional organisations, (c) other relevant principles or international law.[149]
>
> (emphasis added)

The ASRC recognises the essential objective of protection – the human person in all circumstances – using existing legal frameworks and principles of international human rights law to help those displaced. Unsurprisingly, in the subsequent development of the ASRC, "the occurrence of natural disasters or grave events" is a foundational element for refugee protection.[150] The treaty reveals a dynamic understanding of the concept of refugee protection, adapted to contemporary needs. This evolutionary approach results in part from the host states' collective understanding of their expanded obligations towards individuals or communities, including those displaced by environmental factors. Importantly, however, no states have yet ratified the ASRC, which narrows its authoritative character. Nevertheless, the ASRC paves the way for the expansion of host states' obligations beyond the CRSR and puts individuals' needs and human rights at the core of protection.

The interpretation of extended refugee definitions (*inter alia* host states' protection obligations), while feasible, would in practice mean the exclusion of most EDPs from the legal framework in any region. Furthermore, as previously noted, an extended understanding of the refugee notion in the regional context is usually applied ad hoc in situations of mass influx and outside any legal framework,[151] lending doubt that the issue would be treated systematically and coherently. Yet, one cannot disregard the evolution of circumstances and contexts

---

International Instruments and Legal Texts Concerning Refugees and Others of Concern of UNHCR" (UNHCR).

149 Declaration on the Protection of Refugees and Displaced Persons in the Arab World, 19 November 1992, Article 5.

150 The 1994 Arab Convention on Regulating the Status of Refugees in the Arab Countries states under Article 1 paragraph 2: "[a]ny person who unwillingly takes refuge in a country other than his country of origin or his habitual place of residence because of sustained aggression against, occupation and foreign domination of such country or because of *the occurrence of natural disasters or grave events* resulting in major disruption of public order in the whole country or any part thereof" (emphasis added).

151 Durieux, J. F. (1992) "Capturing the Central American Refugee Phenomenon" 4 International Journal of Refugee Law 3 pp. 301–325, p. 323; Edwards (2006) *Op. Cit.* p. 227.

that has made way for a normative evolution of the notion of protection underpinned by human rights principles to include environmental displacement.

4.4 The principle of *non-refoulement*: a common ground of protection

While EDPs may have limited protection under the CRSR and the aforementioned regional refugee instruments, those who are forcibly displaced from their residence to another state may find protection from other host state obligations deriving from human rights law. It is widely accepted that the prohibition of *non-refoulement* (i.e. returning anyone to an area where she/he would face persecution, torture, or other serious ill treatment) constitutes the cornerstone of the legal framework of international protection. As a fundamental principle of international law, it is one of the strongest limitations to states' sovereignty.

The principle's origin can be traced to refugee law[152] and international extradition regulations[153] and is enshrined in other human rights, instruments such as Article 3(1) of the Convention Against Torture (CAT). The *non-refoulement* principle is also a crucial implication from the prohibition of torture and other forms of ill treatment under Article 3 ECHR and ICCPR's Article 7 and is found in common humanitarian principles (principle to provide assistance to persons fleeing from generalised violence) and in international criminal law (on the grounds that there may be a real risk of exposure of the individual to acts forbidden under the Rome Statute: genocide, crimes against humanity, war crimes, and crimes of aggression).[154] *Non-refoulement* is now considered a principle of customary international law, beyond the application of treaties of refugee and human rights law.[155]

The principle is expressed in CRSR's Article 33, which prohibits state parties from returning a refugee to the frontiers of territories where his/her life or freedom would be threatened because of race, religion, nationality, membership

152 Article 33 CRSR; and Article II, African Refugee Convention.

153 *See* for example, Article 9 International Convention Against the Taking of Hostages, adopted on 17 December 1979 by the G.A. Res. 146 (XXXIV), U.N. GAOR, 34th Sess., Supp. No. 46, U.N. Doc. A/34/46; Article 3, European Convention on Extradition, adopted on 13 of July 1957; Article 5 of the European Convention on the Suppression of Terrorism, adopted on 27 January 1977; Article 4, Inter-American Convention on Extradition, adopted on 25 February 1981; and Article 3, U.N. Model Treaty on Extradition.

154 The Rome Statute of the International Criminal Court was adopted 17 July 1998, entered into force 1 July 2002; *See* McAdam (2007) *Op. Cit.* p. 9.

155 *See* International Institute of Humanitarian Law (2001) "San Remo Declaration on the Principle of Non-Refoulement" (2001) pp. 1–2 on the occasion of the fiftieth anniversary of the CRSR; Cançado Trindade (2010) *Op. Cit.* pp. 520–524.

in a particular social group, or political opinion.[156] While it first appears that Article 33 is limited to refugees, it is also applied to asylum seekers who have a "presumptive or prima facie claim for refugee status",[157] meaning that a formal refugee status determination is not required to claim protection against return. The provision nevertheless excludes those whose protection needs fall outside the CRSR, and this may include EDPs. Furthermore, under the CRSR, *non-refoulement* is not non-derogable.[158] Rather, it may be restricted on the grounds of danger and security to the host country, though the restrictions must be applied proportionately and must balance the interests of the state and the individual.[159]

The scope of the *non-refoulement* prohibition is broader in human rights law than in the CRSR, as the person in question is not required to prove fear of individual persecution related to a specific CSRS ground. What matters is the existence of the risk of ill treatment, not the reasons for it. It focuses on the needs of the individual (i.e. anyone exposed to a risk of torture or other forms of ill treatment through removal from the host state)[160] and constitutes a preventative method for protecting human rights.[161] Unlike the *non-refoulement*

156 *See generally*, on *non-refoulement* under the CRSR Goodwill-Gill, G. & McAdam, J. (2007) "The Refugee in International Law" (3rd edition Oxford University Press); Hathaway, J. (2005) "The Rights of Refugees under International Law" (Cambridge University Press) pp. 279–363.

157 Goodwill-Gill & McAdam (2007) *Op. Cit.* pp. 232–233; Lauterpacht, E. & Bethlehem, D. (2003) "The Scope and Content of the Principle of Non-Refoulement" in E. Feller, V. Türk & F. Nicholson (eds.) "Refugee Protection in International Law" (Cambridge University Press) p. 136.

158 *See* Article 33(2) of the CRSR ("The benefit of the present provision may not, however, be claimed by a refugee whom there are reasonable grounds for regarding as a danger to the security of the country in which he is, or who, having been convicted by a final judgement of a particular serious crime, constitutes a danger to the community of that country").

159 *See* Goodwin-Gill & McAdam (2007) *Op. Cit.* p. 240; Lauterpacht & Bethlehem (2001) *Op. Cit.* p. 169.

160 Human rights treaties other than the ACHPR do not contain the right of asylum seekers for *non-refoulement*. This concept is not defined in treaty-based rules of international human rights law. Instead, the case law of the various treaty bodies (whether judiciary or quasi-judiciary) have enunciated the criteria for *non-refoulement* (but not the definition) in relation to anti-torture provisions. While the person in question is not required to prove fear of individual persecution related to a specific CSRS ground, he/she still bears a burden of proof. It is incumbent on the applicant invoking the anti-torture provisions to show the substantive risk of persecution. The grounds developed by human rights monitoring bodies inevitably relate to torture or other maltreatment conditions, but the conceptual ambit of those grounds does not necessarily overlap with the ground of persecution, which may include treatment that falls short of torture or cruel/inhumane or degrading treatment. Some grounds of ill treatment that can be invoked by asylum seekers under anti-torture provisions may stem from non-human factors (including the environment) that are not included in the CRSR.

161 Suntinger, W. (1995) "The Principle of Non-Refoulement: Looking rather to Geneva than to Strasbourg" 49 Austrian Journal of Public International Law pp. 203–224.

protection under Article 33 of the CRSR, the protection under Article 3 of the ECHR, Article 3 of the CAT, and Article 7 of the ICCPR are not subject to derogations. These characteristics – broad personal scope and non-derogability – make the *non-refoulement* principle a potential tool for those who do not qualify as refugees but still, as EDPs, need protection. It reflects extension of the host state's "protection obligations beyond the 'refugee' category to include (at least) people at risk of arbitrary deprivation of life, torture, or cruel, inhuman or degrading treatment or punishment".[162]

A primary difference between the CSRS and the aforementioned legal instruments is that their implementation is monitored by judicial (e.g. the ECtHR) or quasi-judicial bodies (e.g. the ICCPR and the CAT).

Despite its potential, the provision of *non-refoulement* is hollow since it does not confer a right to residence or any specific legal status in a foreign country, thus allowing states considerable discretion in their treatment of foreigners in their territory. As Jane McAdam has observed,

> [t]hough a number of States have traditionally respected this additional non-refoulement obligation, they have been reluctant to grant beneficiaries a formal legal status analogous to that enjoyed by Convention Refugees. While such States have abided by their international duty not to deport people to certain conditions, they have tended to be less diligent in looking to international law to define what legal status those people should be given. Accordingly, protection has varied over time from identical rights to Conventional refugees, to a tolerated status with protection from refoulement but little more.[163]

Some acknowledge that the principle of non-return of EDPs seems unjustified because environmental change is not included in the international definition of torture.[164] Even if environmental change impacts or threatens human rights, it may be insufficient to justify a demand for protection.[165]

Nevertheless, the humanitarian character of the principle of *non-refoulement* obligates host states to not remove people from their territory if it would violate the principle. Essentially, as UNHRC has rightly stated, protection must be "available to all individuals, regardless of nationality or statelessness, such as asylum seekers, refugees, migrant workers and other persons, who may find

162 McAdam (2012) *Op. Cit.* p. 53.

163 McAdam, J. (2007) "Complementary Protection in International Law" (Oxford University Press) p. 5.

164 McAdam, J. & Saul, B. (2009) "An Insecure Climate for Human Security? Climate-Induced Displacement and International Law" University of Sydney, Faculty of Law, Working Paper No. 4, p. 12 *available from:* www.peacepalacelibrary.nl/ebooks/files/357399072.pdf [accessed 17 August 2018].

165 *Ibid.*

themselves in the territory or subject to the jurisdiction of the State Party".[166] The U.N. High Commissioner for Refugees has also acknowledged the *jus cogens*[167] nature of the principle of *non-refoulement* and its applicability to ensure the protection of those displaced by environmental factors.[168]

The principle may apply to cases not only where an environmental disaster leads to indiscriminate violence but also where life is no longer sustainable due to environmental changing conditions (e.g. disappearing island states due to sea level rise), impacting the right to life as well as a number of codified human rights. In Europe, Article 3 of the ECHR has gained particular relevance through ECtHR judgements, which have enlarged the scope of the principle of *non-refoulement* and served as a source of protection for displaced persons, arguably including EDPs.

If the principle of *non-refoulement* implies states' obligation not to return an individual whose life may be at risk, by analogy states bear the same responsibility to accept victims of environmental disasters, thereby offering them a minimum level of protection.[169] "In sum, it may be concluded that an obligation of non-denial of entry arises in all cases where return to the state of origin would jeopardise the achievement of human rights, including cases where the jeopardy stems from environmental degradation".[170] While, in theory, the scope of such obligation should not be underestimated, in practice, it should not be overestimated, as it does not entitle EDPs to stay in a foreign territory. As the Council of Europe has suggested, to overcome this limitation it is necessary that EDPs benefit from "subsidiary protection, for example granting them a status of temporary humanitarian resident or a permanent status in case of impossibility of return".[171] In reality, codified forms of subsidiary or complementary protection already exist and are found under the European Union's legal framework and form part of the holistic approach to protection for EDPs.

166 UNHRC (2004) "General Comment No. 31: The Nature of the General Legal Obligation Imposed on States Parties to the Covenant" (26 May) para. 10.

167 Goodwin-Gill & McAdam (2007) *Op. Cit.* p. 290.

168 UHCR (2009) "Forced Displacement in the Context of Climate Change: Challenges for States under International Law" 6th session Ad Hoc Working Group on Long-Term Cooperative Action under the Convention (AWG-LCA 6) 1–12 June Bonn p. 11; UNHCR (2005) "Providing International Protection Including through Complementary Forms of Protection" EC/55/SC/CRP (2 June) para. 22.

169 Magniny, V. (2008) "Des Victimes de l'Environnement aux Refugiès de l'Environnement" Revue Asylon(s) No. 6 p. 12 *available from*: www.reseau-terra.eu/article845.html [accessed 17 August 2018].

170 Epiney, A. (2011) "Environmental Refugees: Aspects of International State Responsibility" in E. Piguet, A. Pecoud & P. Guchteneire (eds.) "Migration and Climate Change" (Cambridge University Press) p. 400.

171 Council of Europe (2009) "Environmentally Induced Migration and Displacement: A 21st-Century Challenge" Parliamentary Assembly Resolution 1655 (30 January) (9th Sitting) para. 24, 5.

4.5 Conclusion

4.5.1 Residual protection afforded by CRSR

The CRSR, the primary international instrument focusing on the protection of displaced populations, materialises the collective responsibility of host states towards humankind. Its limitations show, however, in its interpretative approaches to how the polity of states can come together to offer protection for those in need. The main barrier is that the CRSR's definition of refugee does not formally include people displaced by environmental factors. While scholars moved by the global nature of the environmental change problem have paved the way for extended interpretative approaches to the concept of refugee to include EDPs, this solution is intrinsically weakened by financial, political, and social factors. Further, suggesting the amendment of the CRSR may undermine the protection of political refugees. The analysis therefore reinforces the protection needs of EDPs but also the limitations of the current international system of protection.

Even if EDPs are not characterised as refugees, they may be considered a social group subject to host state protection under CRSR obligations. Examples include when environmental degradation is carried out as a persecutory act by the country of origin ("environmental cleansing") or when a government intentionally fails to act, blocks aid to a certain group, or does not implement adequate adaptation programmes. Applicants generally must prove that no protection is available in their country of origin because it is unwilling or unable to protect them. However, a gap in protection would still remain for people in states that are not current signatories to the CRSR, like India and Bangladesh, which are considered vulnerable areas for environmental displacement and seen as important reception countries for EDPs.[172]

4.5.2 The stance on the principle of non-return

The limited protection under the CRSR may be surpassed by host states' other obligations deriving from human rights law. The fundamental international law principle of *non-refoulement* is of special relevance to EDPs, as it redefines sovereignty and curbs states' discretion to forcibly transfer individuals to their states of origin, where they would be persecuted or exposed to torture or cruel, inhumane, or degrading treatment or face a serious risk of violations of human rights. Though the principle does not confer legal status, it nonetheless highlights the needs of the individual (as he/she does not have to prove fear based on a specific ground) and acts preventatively to protect human rights.

172 *See, e.g.*, Burson (2008) *Op. Cit.* p. 9 (referring to India, which is not a signatory to the CRSR but is a key host country with regards to its neighbouring country Bangladesh).

4.5.3 Enhancing protection for EDPs: the regional outlook

International human rights law plays a key role, yet will not normally protect EDPs abroad. Host states may find that regional protection arrangements may be one way to close the protection gap: allowing the individuals, based on their own judgement, to cross the border to seek protection without first seeking protection within their countries of origin (needs approach); addressing regional and localised environmental degradation and changed realities, values, and cultures (contextual approach); and tailoring legal and policy solutions more likely to gain states' acceptance (tailored legal approach). Countries neighbouring the country of origin are where most refugees/displaced persons are hosted. Regional practices, most notably in Africa, though limited, demonstrate that some countries allow people who cross the border due to environmental disasters to remain temporarily. The extended interpretation of the refugee notion within the regional context is reinforced by the human rights paradigm and recognises that EDPs merit protection. Nonetheless, neither the CRSR nor the analysed regional regimes take a pre-emptive approach; they fail to see protection as a holistic enterprise. Therefore, to (re)conceptualise protection for EDPs, the additional regimes must be considered. Notably, the EU regional protection regime may offer tangible protection solutions and arguably serve as a model to consolidate home and host states' obligations towards EDPs to both prevent and address cross-border displacement.

5 Consolidating protection for environmental displacement

This chapter attempts to devise pragmatic – proactive and reactive – protection strategies for EDPs by looking at the European Union's regionally orientated complementary protection regime. The objective is not to discuss pros and cons of the EU immigration and asylum policy but rather to highlight protection – as a way of reflecting states' international human rights obligations – by consolidating existing proactive (*ex ante*) and reactive (*ex post*) protection measures. *Ex ante* protection emphasises the prevention of displacement by examining strategies to deal with the predicted effects of environmental change (e.g. circular labour migration through the Seasonal Workers Directive and/or Mobility Partnerships). *Ex post* protection addresses the effects of environmental change and the modes of available legal protection that can be adapted to protect EDPs once they cross an international border (e.g. temporary protection under the Temporary Protection Directive and subsidiary protection through the Qualification Directive). This regional protection framework, underpinned by the international human rights paradigm, can remedy the current protection gap within the international legal system. It offers effective and pragmatic solutions to consolidate protection for EDPs within the EU and beyond its borders and helps states view protection as a dynamic guiding concept.

5.1 Europe's normative power for protecting EDPs

A number of regional efforts have attempted to examine the impact of environmental change and human displacement.[1] Several international fora agree

1 Examples include: Niue Declaration on Climate Change 39th Pacific Islands Forum, Forum Communiqué, Annex B (19–20 August 2008); Anchorage Declaration of the Indigenous Peoples' Global Summit on Climate Change (24 April 2009); Ambo Declaration adopted at the Tarawa Climate Change Conference (10 November 2010). These non-binding agreements highlight the need to raise awareness of the impacts of environmental change, to prevent local populations from being forcibly displaced and to preserve their territorial and cultural integrity and existence, and to develop strategic frameworks to protect people affected by environmental events within and across international borders.

that regional approaches may be best for tailoring and implementing programmes to assist and protect those affected by environmental factors.[2] Further, some scholars are hopeful that regional normative arrangements could operate under a wider international umbrella framework given states' reluctance to commit to a formalised treaty potentially colliding with their socio-economic and political interests.[3] Not only can regional solutions be more personalised to local needs, but states can commit to different extents, depending on their human and financial resource capacity and timeframes. They also facilitate better-coordinated efforts and a forum for exchange of expertise and best practices. The elevation of regional solutions is also consistent with the current view favouring regional collaboration because of the perceived failure to deal with common challenges at the international and national levels.[4] Policy and institutional cooperation at the regional level can generate peer pressure and enhance countries' governance and capacity to act.

At a normative level, regional protection solutions have converged to protect people consistent with international human rights obligations to both prevent and address displacement.[5] The growth of complementary forms of protection – including those developed within the European Union – encourages exploration and may help states revisit and reorient the international protection regime for EDPs.

The EU is known to have "global clout" as the world's largest trading stage, biggest donor of humanitarian aid, and protector of the environment.[6] It has also become a key player in international affairs, acknowledging a responsibility

2 *See, e.g.*, UNHCR (2011) "Climate Change and Displacement: Identifying Gaps and Responses Expert Roundtable Concept Note" (Bellagio 22–26 February) p. 3 (referring to regional instruments such as the 1969 OAU Convention Governing the Specific Aspects of Refugee Problems in Africa and the 1984 Cartagena Declaration that would possibly offer wide protection and complementary protection arising from the application of the principle of *non-refoulement* enshrined in various international and regional human rights instruments where there is a latitude for progressive interpretation); African Union (2006) "The Migration Policy Framework for Africa" Executive Council, Ninth Ordinary Session EX.CL/276 (IX) (Banjul 25–29 June) recommends addressing displacement caused by disasters and other environmental factors through national and regional migration policies; Ferris, E. & Petz, D. (2013) "In the Neighborhood: The Growing Role of Regional Organisations in Disaster Risk Management" (The Brookings Institution, London School of Economics Project on Internal Displacement), (February 2013) highlighting the increasing role of regional organisations in disaster management to deal with the long-term effects of environmental change.

3 Williams, A. (2008) "Turning the Tide: Recognising Climate Change Refugees in International Law" 30 Law and Policy 4 p. 518.

4 Wetzel, J. (2012) "The EU as a 'Global Player' in Human Rights?" (Routledge) p. 16.

5 As noted, refugee crises have led regional organisations to revisit the international refugee protection regime and broaden their scope of protection on human rights grounds.

6 Wetzel (2012) *Op. Cit.* p. 1.

to defend and protect human rights.[7] What started as an economic integration of states has evolved into a broader structure of values[8] that are reflected in the two principal treaties on which the EU is based: the Treaty on European Union (TEU) and the Treaty on the Functioning of the European Union (TFEU).[9]

The Treaty of Lisbon[10] has both introduced and enhanced provisions that reinforce the protection of human rights. Article 2 TEU highlights the EU's foundational values: human dignity, freedom, democracy, equality, the rule of law, and respect for human rights (including the rights of minorities).[11] The EU's objectives include the protection of the environment and the promotion and protection of human rights and the well-being of its peoples (Article 3 TEU). The Lisbon Treaty's innovation is important for EDPs because it emphasises that internal action of the EU (such as protection of the environment) is oriented towards wider external objectives that directly impact EDPs.

Importantly, human rights within the EU have evolved from a tangential issue to a formalised, legally binding, black-letter standard.[12] Human rights also condition the exercise of the EU's wider competences. Since 1969,[13] the CJEU has highlighted that integration project should not prejudice fundamental

7 *See generally,* Besson, S. (2006) "The European Union and Human Rights: Towards a Post-National Human Rights Institution" 6 Human Rights Law Review 2 pp. 323–360.

8 *See generally,* Williams, A. (2010) "The Ethos of Europe: Values, Law and Justice in the EU" (Cambridge University Press) (arguing that by focusing on the realisation of human rights as a core institutional value, the EU can better define its moral limits so as to evolve as a more just project).

9 *See* the Treaty on European Union (TEU; Maastricht Treaty, effective since 1993); the Treaty on the Functioning of the European Union (TFEU; Treaty of Rome, effective since 1958). These treaties (plus their attached protocols and declarations) have been amended by subsequent treaties at least once a decade since their enactment, the latest being the Treaty of Lisbon in 2009.

10 The Treaty of Lisbon, amending the TEU and the Treaty Establishing the European Community, was signed in the Portuguese capital on 13 December 2007 by the representatives of the 27 member states. It entered into force on 1 December 2009, after ratification.

11 This provision is supported by a sanctions procedure in Article 7 TEU. The provision asserts that a member state's rights may be barred if it engages in a "serious and persistent breach (. . .) of values mentioned in Article 2". The provision has been triggered for the first time, against Poland.

12 Notably, governments started officially recognising human rights with the Treaty of Maastricht of 1992 provided that the EU would respect fundamental rights as listed in the ECHR and common to the constitutional traditions of the member states. In 1997, the Treaty of Amsterdam changed the focus to common values and principles underpinning the EU: the principles of liberty, democracy, respect for human rights and fundamental freedoms, and the rule of law. *See* Article 6 TEU that expressly recognises rights, freedoms, and principles set out in the Charter of Fundamental Rights of the European Union (CFREU).

13 [[Missing Footnote data]]

rights. The Court has also played a role in determining which values the EU should promote. The CJEU's view has evolved to recognise not only that human rights are part of the integration project but that they are independent values which constitute general principles of law and an integral part of the EU system.[14] Human rights have also driven institutional change. Enlargement obliges compliance with the normative and legal "Copenhagen Criteria",[15] which makes membership dependent on two important benchmarks: democracy and adequate protection of human rights. Notably, the EU's role as an external agent of human rights also significantly contributes to the protection of EDPs. Indeed, Article 3(5) of the TEU has been called the "missionary principle" of the EU in its global relations.[16] A "general clause" on human rights has been included in treaties between the EU and more than 120 states.[17] The EU also engages in political "Human Rights Dialogues" with countries or regions essential to the EU's overall strategy to promote sustainable development, peace, and stability.[18]

The EU's legal normative framework and competence vectors, cushioned by human rights, demonstrate that the EU can play a significant role in developing preventative or proactive protection measures and serve as a key partner in building long-term or reactive protection measures for EDPs. The TEU refers to values, part of the objectives of the EU, and principles, of paramount importance in international relations, and they must be seen as interchangeable rather than conflicting[19] because both reflect and embody normative standards that the EU encourages domestically and internationally.

14 CJEU, Case 5/88, *Wauchaf v Germany* (13 July 1989) ECR 2609; CJEU, Case C-438/05, *International Transport Workers' Federation and the Finnish Seamen's Union v Viking Line* (11 December 2007) ECR 10779; Case C-341/05, *Laval v Svenska Byggnadarbetareföbundet* (18 December 2007) ECR 11767; CJEU, Joined Cases C-402/05P and C-415/05P, *Kadi and Al Barakaat v Coucil and Commission* (3 September 2008) ECR I-6351.

15 More on the Copenhagen Criteria or the general conditions of Membership is *available from:* http://ec.europa.eu/enlargement/policy/conditions-membership/index_en.htm [accessed 17 August 2018].

16 Broberg, M. (2012) "Don't Mess with the Missionary Man! On the Principle of Coherence, the Missionary Principle and the European Union's Development Policy" in P. James Cardwell (ed.) "EU External Relations Law and Policy in the Post-Lisbon Era" (Springer) pp. 185–187, pp. 181–196.

17 European Parliament (2006) "Report on Human Rights and Democracy Clause in European Union Agreements" A6–0004/2006 Final (23 January) para. F *available from:* www.europarl.europa.eu/sides/getDoc.do?type=TA&reference=P6-TA-2006-0056&language=EN [accessed 17 August 2018].

18 EU Guidelines on Human Rights Dialogues with Third Countries where adopted in 2001, by the European Council were reviewed on 19 January 2009 *available from:* https://eur-lex.europa.eu/legal-content/EN/TXT/?uri=LEGISSUM%3Ar10115 [accessed 17 August 2018].

19 *See* Cremona, M. (2011) "Values in EU Foreign Policy" in M. Evans & P. Koutrakos (eds.) "Beyond the Established Legal Orders: Policy Interconnections between the EU

Proactive and *reactive* normative frameworks to protect EDPs figured prominently in a 2013 European Commission staff working document entitled "Climate Change, Environmental Degradation and Migration".[20] Though not legally binding, this document is, importantly, the first comprehensive EU text addressing the effects of environmental change and displacement. Although acknowledging the lack of a current legal framework providing EDPs adequate protection, it emphasises that there are "legally binding and soft-law" national and international legal instruments offering some form of status and/or protection in certain contexts.[21] The document is silent on how these standards can be legally operationalised, yet it is remarkable for its recognition of short- and medium-term solutions to safeguard EDPs. The text conveys an understanding that protection of EDPs is a holistic enterprise.

Importantly, scholars assert that the EU's normative platform has a "ripple effect" beyond the EU.[22] Its formalised regional protection regime is considered the world's most advanced because it blends asylum, refugee, and human rights principles geared towards greater uniformity in member states' laws and practices.[23] Furthermore, as the first supranational court to interpret and clarify provisions of the CRSR, the CJEU's rulings are enormously influential in promoting the standard interpretation in all EU states that are CRSR signatories.[24]

Legally, one can identify particular standards within the EU's asylum and immigration policy framework that may serve the purpose. While not directly targeting EDPs, they serve as a reference point for devising a normative proactive and reactive protection framework for EDPs.

5.2 Consolidating a proactive approach to protection for EDPs

As mentioned, a proactive approach to protecting EDPs emphasises pre-emptive human rights protection, which in turn emphasises preventative measures to avoid negative effects of environmental disruption and violation of human rights. To accomplish this, states must address the root causes of environmental displacement, i.e. "prevent the preventable". Anything that can prevent the root

and the Rest of the World" (Hart Publishing) p. 275 (discussing the values in EU foreign policy).

20 European Commission Staff Working Document (2013) "Climate Change, Environmental Degradation and Migration" SWD (2013) 138 Final (16 April).

21 *Ibid.* p. 16.

22 *See generally*, Lambert, H., McAdam, J. & Fullerton, M. (2013) "A Global Reach of European Refugee Law" (Cambridge University Press) p. 1. This is particularly visible with the evolution of international refugee law by means of altering customary law and UNHCR's practice.

23 *Ibid.*

24 *Ibid.* p. 19.

causes of displacement can be a preventative protection strategy, including environmental and human rights monitoring, disaster risk-based assessments, climate adaptation programmes, and development policies that avoid violating human rights. Arguably, states' obligation to prevent environmental displacement and ensure protection of human rights emerges as a customary legal norm. This development is due to the explicit and implicit recognition of this obligation in both hard and soft law instruments at the international, regional, and sub-regional levels and the *opinio juris* that construes such obligation.

5.2.1 Framing migration through labour mobility

The EU notes that "facilitating well-managed mobility and labour migration from degraded areas can represent an effective strategy to reduce environmentally induced displacement". Additionally, "when environmentally induced migration is undertaken voluntarily, it is far more likely to produce benefits for both receiving and sending communities".[25] Thus, labour mobility is asserted as an *ex ante* measure to prevent environmental displacement. As previously mentioned, migration is now seen not as a failure to adapt to environmental change but rather as a legitimate strategy that benefits countries of origin, host countries, and the individuals while also honouring states' emerging obligation to prohibit and prevent displacement of EDPs.[26] Access to work is a crucial component of any preventative protection strategy. Work will avoid displacement and allow diversification of income while also allowing individuals to send remittances to family, thereby building resilience and meeting EDPs' economic needs. A policy that builds on existing labour migration strategies is most likely to succeed in preventing displacement, lessening vulnerability, and achieving broader development goals.[27] It also avoids development of irregular migration channels.

(i) Circular and temporary migration

To some extent, cyclical non-regulated migratory movements have always existed. But, if regulated, cyclical migratory movements can be an effective tool.

25 European Commission Staff Working Document SWD (2013) *Op. Cit.* p. 26.

26 *See generally,* Davies, S. (1993) "Are Coping Strategies a Cop Out?" 24 Institute for Developing Studies Bulletin 4 pp. 60–72; Adger, W. N. *et al.* (2003) "Adaptation to Climate Change in the Developing World" 3 Progress in Development Studies pp. 179–195; McLeman, R. & Smit, B. (2006) "Migration as an Adaptation to Climate Change" 76 Climate Change pp. 31–53; Tacoli, C. (2009) "Crisis of Adaptation? Migration and Climate Change in a Context of High Mobility" 21 Environment and Urbanization pp. 513–525; Barnett, J. & O'Neil, S. J. (2012) "Islands, Resettlement and Adaptation" 2 Nature Climate Change pp. 8–10.

27 *See* Ober, K. (2014) "Migration as Adaptation: Exploring Mobility as a Coping Strategy for Climate Change" (UK Climate Change and Migration Coalition).

International organisations such as the United Nations,[28] the World Bank,[29] the International Organisation for Migration,[30] and the Global Commission on International Migration[31] advocate for circular migration.

Though circular migration, a labour rotation scheme, first appeared during the 1980s,[32] its origins may be in the "guest worker" programmes of the post-war period.[33]

In Europe, circular migration has regained popularity due to Europe's ageing population and economic necessities, but it also serves as a stimulus for developing countries as migrants return to and invest in their countries, thus avoiding "brain drain" in developing countries. In the so-called Fortress of Europe, temporary migration can be "politically easier to sell to electorates that have come to feel threatened by more immigration".[34] Despite internal disagreements

28 United Nations (2006) "International Migration and Development" Report of the Secretary General (New York) p. 18 (describing "a new era of mobility" characterised by more temporary movements and emphasising that temporary migration schemes are "beneficial synergies for migrants, countries of origin and countries of destination").

29 World Bank (2006) "International Labour Migration: Eastern Europe and the former Soviet Union" (World Bank, Europe and Central Asia Region) pp. 98, 109 (advocating that circular migration can not only encourage the transfer of knowledge and skills but also can reduce the negative economic effects of brain drain, allowing the matching of supply and demand for international labour and satisfying the preferences of migrants wishing to spend time abroad).

30 International Organization for Migration (IOM) (2005) "World Migration 2005: Costs and Benefits of international Migration" (IOM) p. 296 (encouraging circular movement by receiving countries and including measures (incentives and sanctions) to ensure that migration remains temporary (e.g. scholarships for students with attached conditions to return; reimbursement of social security contributions upon departure)).

31 Global Commission on International Migration (2005) "Migration in an Interconnected World: New Directions for Actions" (Geneva) p. 31. The Global Commission on International Migration was formed by Kofi Annan in 2003 to create a global response to international migration. In its 2005 report, the Commission encouraged states "to formulate policies and programmes that maximize the development impact of return and circular migration". The Commission opined that this new migration paradigm would progressively replace permanent migrant settlement.

32 *See generally,* Ozkul, D. (2010) "Circular Migration Schemes Renewed Interest of the Destination Countries" CARIM-VI Summer School on Euro-Mediterranean Migration and Development Essay Series (Robert Schuman Centre for Advanced Studies, European University Institute).

33 *See* Scheinder, H. & Wiesbrock, A. (2011) "Circular Migration: A Triple win Situation? Wishful Thinking or Serious Option for Sustainable Migration Policy?" in D. Schiek, U. Liebert & H. Schneider (eds.) "European Economic and Social Constitutionalism after the Treaty of Lisbon" (Cambridge University Press) p. 126, pp. 123–147. Both discuss the origin of circular migration in the guest worker programmes developed by Germany, the Netherlands, and Sweden after World War II.

34 Abella, M. (2006) "Policies and Best Practices for Management of Temporary Migration" International Symposium in International Migration and Development (United Nations Population Division Department of Economic and Social Affairs June) p. 1.

over the issue,[35] in 2007 the EU issued a Communication devoted to circular migration and mobility partnerships between the EU and third countries.[36] It defined circular migration "a form of migration that is managed in a way allowing some degree of legal mobility back and forth between two countries".[37] The 2007 Communication built on earlier Commission initiatives to fight illegal immigration, particularly barring illegal work and exploitation of migrants by employers, and gave operational substance to the EU's Global Approach to Migration.[38] The EU[39] and its member states[40] have introduced a number of legislative initiatives encouraging circular migration.

Though contexts differ, two current EU normative standards warrant examination, as their juridical value and potential replication make them models for the promotion of regional and international migration for people in environmentally vulnerable areas. The first, EU's Seasonal Workers Directive,[41] addresses circular migration in the context of seasonal work, the most common form of

35 *Ibid.* pp. 139–144. Member states still disagree regarding circular migration and how it should operate. Some see it as a way to manage migration and limit the entrance of third-country nationals to particular sectors (UK, France, Spain, Germany, the Netherlands), while others see it as a form of spontaneous migration broadly defined as temporary or more permanent.

36 European Commission Communication to the European Parliament, the Council, the European Economic and Social Committee and the Committee of the Regions (2007) "On Circular Migration and Mobility Partnerships between the European Union and Third Countries" COM (2007) 248 Final (16 May).

37 *Ibid.* p. 8.

38 The European Commission, Communication COM (2007) 248 Final *Op. Cit.* builds on earlier European Commission initiatives, in particular the European Commission "Communication on Migration and Development: Some Concrete Orientations" COM (2005) 390 (1 September), where the concept of circular migration appears for the first time, followed by European Commission Communication on "Policy Priorities in the Fight against Illegal Immigration of Third-Country Nationals" COM (2006) 402 (19 July) and "The Global Approach to Migration One Year on: Towards a Comprehensive European Migration Policy" COM (2006) 735 Final (30 November).

39 *See* The Council of the European Union Directive (2003) "Concerning the Status of Third-Country Nationals Who Are Long-Term Residents That Allows a Period of Absence" 2003/109/EC (25 November) Articles 9 (1)(c), 4 (3) (allowing periods of absence of less than 12 consecutive months without compromising attainment of long-term residence status); The Council of the European Union Directive (2009) "On the Conditions of Entry and Residence of Third-Country Nationals for the Purposes of Highly Qualified Employment" 2009/50/EC (25 May) Article 16 (3) (allowing periods of absence of up to 18 months without losing status).

40 *See, e.g.*, European Migration Network (2011) "Temporary and Circular Migration: Empirical Evidence, Current Policy Practice and Future Options in EU Member States" (September). Countries such as Portugal, Belgium, Spain, the United Kingdom, France, Italy, and the Netherlands have introduced circular migration by issuance of temporary work permits.

41 European Parliament and the Council of the European Union Directive (2014) "On the Conditions of Entry and Stay of Third-Country Nationals for the Purpose of Employment as Seasonal Workers" 2014/36/EU (26 February).

temporary migration.[42] The second, Mobility Partnerships,[43] derives from the EU's Global Approach to Migration.[44]

5.2.2 Seasonal Workers Directive

(i) Rationale

The European Commission has been open to establishing a common entry and residency for seasonal workers since the idea of a Directive appeared in the 2005 Policy Plan on Legal Migration.[45] The Directive aimed to set minimum conditions for an estimated 100,000 third-country national seasonal workers entering the EU annually, and some irregular migrants. In February 2014, the Council adopted the Directive, known as the Seasonal Workers Directive, "on the conditions of entry and stay of third-country nationals for the purpose of employment as seasonal workers".[46] Member states must transpose the Directive into their national legislation within 30 months of publication in the official journal.

(ii) Personal scope of application

The Directive takes a flexible approach to conditions of stay and entry of third-country nationals,[47] thus addressing the structural need for low-skilled seasonal workers while also preventing a temporary stay from becoming permanent. The Directive exclusively targets third-country nationals residing outside the EU, which is of particular relevance if one views seasonal labour migration as a preventative measure for EDPs. More importantly, the Directive emphasises the rights of seasonal workers during their stay, equal treatment, and their redress possibilities, providing – albeit with inherent limitations – a human rights

42 McLoughlin, S. *et al.* (2011) "Temporary and Circular Migration: Opportunities and Challenges" Working Paper No. 35 (European Policy Centre) p. 29.
43 European Commission, Staff Working Document (2009) "Mobility Partnerships as a Tool of the Global Approach to Migration" SEC (2009) 1240 Final (18 September).
44 European Commission (2006) COM (2006) 735 Final *Op. Cit.*
45 European Commission, Communication from the Commission (2005) "On a Policy Plan on Legal Migration" COM (2005) 669 Final (21 December).
46 Directive 2014/36/EU *Op. Cit.*
47 *Ibid.* paras. 6, 26. Paragraph 6 states: "[t]he Stockholm Programme, adopted by the European Council on 11 December 2009, recognises that labour immigration can contribute to increased competitiveness and economic validity and that, in the context of the important demographic challenges that will face the Union in the future with an increased demand for labour, *flexible immigration policies* will make an important contribution to the Union's economic development and performance in the long term" (emphasis added). Paragraph 26 states: "[p]rovision for a single procedure leading to *one combined permit, encompassing both stay and work*, should contribute to *simplifying the rules* currently applicable in Member States" (emphasis added).

dimension to seasonal work. The Directive's scope of application has three vectors: temporal, territorial, and substantive.

(iii) Temporal scope of application

The temporal conditions of stay and entrance for seasonal work are guided by flexibility. Admission for seasonal work requires a valid work contract or a binding job offer to work as a seasonal worker with an established employer in the member state. To avoid employers' exploitation of workers, the contract should specify the place and type of employment, duration, salary, number of working hours, and paid leave (Article 5). "The meaning of flexibility in this context is the availability and willingness of sufficient number of workers to work at prevailing wages".[48]

To limit overstays and enhance the potential of circular migration, the Directive allows stays of at least five months but not more than nine months in any twelve-month period (Article 14), but it allows for an extension of the contract or change of employer during that period (Article 15). This ensures that workers are not dependent on a given employer and that they do not lose their social and economic ties with their country of origin. It also enhances the flexibility of the labour market without permanent settlement by workers.

Prior to the Directive, European institutions hotly debated the length of permissible stay for seasonal workers. Many argued for a flexible approach because short timeframes would not answer the needs of employers, especially in particular sectors or in countries that only have two seasons.[49]

To safeguard mobility for the employee and the employer, Article 16 provides that member states shall facilitate the admission of non-EU workers who were admitted for seasonal employment at least once in the same member state in the last five years and who fully respected the relevant conditions in every stay. This allows issuance of a "several seasonal worker permit" in a single administrative act. Such flexibility opens mobility opportunities to people who are at risk of environmental stressors.

(iv) Territorial scope of application

Territorially, the Directive mainly targets third-country nationals living outside the EU. Some, particularly the British Member of the European Parliament,

48 Abella (2006) *Op. Cit.* p. 22.

49 *See, e.g.*, European Economic and Social Committee (2010) "Opinion Proposal for a Directive of the European Parliament and of the Council on the Conditions of Entry and Residence of Third-Country Nationals for the Purposes of Seasonal Employment" Rapporteur Christa Schweng COM (2010) 379 Final – 2010/0210 (COD) (27 July); Committee of the Regions (2011) "Opinion of the Committee of the Regions on Seasonal Workers and Intra-Corporate Transfer" Rapporteur Graziano Ernesto Milia CoR 2011/C166/10 (31 March–1 April).

Claude Moraes, who was in charge of the draft report, criticise its failure to cover immigrants already residing in the EU.[50] Yet, this territorial restriction opens possibilities for EDPs to work in Europe and send back remittances, which may help avoid displacement.

Conversely, the Directive only vaguely defines a seasonal worker. Seasonal work is defined as an "activity dependent on the passing of the seasons", meaning that it is tied to a certain time of the year or a pattern linked to seasonal conditions when labour is in greater demand. This definition does not provide much guidance as to when third-country nationals may expect to work, as work seasons may vary by country, and such uncertainty may demotivate potential workers from applying because they are unable to organise their family life prior to departure. Attempting to address this problem, the EU better defined the seasonally dependent sectors, such as agriculture, horticulture, and tourism, but the states still hold a great deal of discretion.[51]

(v) Substantive scope of application

Substantively, human rights underpin the Seasonal Workers Directive. The document is guided by the principle of equal treatment, i.e. guaranteeing migrant temporary seasonal workers the same rights as EU nationals (Chapter IV – Rights). The equality banner plays an important role in migration management and serves as an essential legal safety net for seasonal workers, especially those who face environmental stressors.

The concept of equality pervades the document and includes working conditions, the right to strike, back payments, access to social security and to public goods and services, access to advice services on seasonal work, recognition, and tax benefits (Article 23(1)). The rules also include education and training opportunities for seasonal workers, though the education or training must be linked to the specific employment activity (Article 23(2)(ii)). Seasonal workers are, however, not entitled to family and unemployment benefits (Article 23(2)(i)). The final version of the Directive has apparently taken into account at least some of the International Labour Organisation's recommendations with regards to equal treatment[52] (in particular some of those outlined in the revised inter-

50 European Parliament (2011) "Draft Report on the Conditions of Entry and Residence of Third-Country Nationals for the Purposes of Seasonal Employment" COM (2010)0379 – C7–0180/2010–2010/0210 (COD) (8 June) Committee on Civil Liberties, Justice and Home Affairs *available from:* www.europarl.europa.eu/meetdocs/2009_2014/documents/libe/pr/869/869849/869849en.pdf [accessed 17 August 2018].

51 Directive 2014/36/EU *Op. Cit.* para. 13.

52 *See* Council of the European Union (2011) "Note Received by the Council General Secretariat and Presidency Delegations from the ILO's Office for the European Union and the Benelux Countries" Doc 9564/11 (2 May) (analysing the Proposal for a Directive on seasonal employment in light of relevant international labour standards and, in

national labour standard on migration for employment, Convention No. 97 and Convention No. 143).[53] Article 25 urges member states to provide seasonal workers access to complaint mechanisms against employers as well as to measures protecting against an employer's retaliatory dismissal or adverse treatment due to a complaint.

Importantly, the Directive also protects seasonal workers' human right to adequate accommodations. Article 20, through its "right to adequate housing", urges member states to take the necessary steps to ensure that seasonal workers have accommodations that ensure an adequate standard of living under national law and/or practice. The member states extensively discussed the difficulties of including such a right during development of the draft Directive. Some considered it impractical,[54] while others considered it problematic[55] or going too far.[56] Nonetheless, the provision was ultimately included. NGOs provided useful guidance at the time of the discussions and insisted that the notion of adequate housing can be found under the U.N. Committee on Economic, Social, and Cultural Rights' General Comment No. 4, which expands on the provisions of Article 11 of the International Covenant on Economic, Social, and Cultural Rights.[57]

This provision aims to avoid exploitation by employers that arrange lodging by ensuring that accommodations meet a certain quality standard and that rents are not excessive and are not automatically deducted from the worker's wages. However, the rule provides no clear guidance as to what constitutes excessive

---

particular, the core ILO Conventions, as well specific conventions regarding migration and social security).

53 Convention concerning Migration for Employment N° 97 (*Revised*) adopted 01 July 1949, entered into force 22 January 1952 C97; Convention concerning Migrations in Abusive Conditions and the Promotion of Equality of Opportunity and Treatment of Migrant Workers N° 143 adopted 24 June 1975, entered into force 09 December 1978 C143. As of 15 of August 2015, Convention No. 97 had been ratified by 49 States Parties, including ten EU member states (Belgium, Cyprus, France, Germany, Italy, the Netherlands, Portugal, Slovenia, Spain, the United Kingdom), while Convention No. 143 had been ratified by 23 States Parties, including five EU member states (Cyprus, Italy, Portugal, Slovenia, Sweden).

54 *See generally,* European Economic Social Committee Opinion (2010) COM (2010) 379 Final – 2010/0210 (COD) *Op. Cit.* para. 4.12. The provision was deemed impractical if interpreted as an obligation for employers to provide accommodation for seasonal workers. If, however, an employer does provide accommodation, it should be inspected by the competent authorities.

55 *See* European Trade Union Confederation (ETUC) "Seasonal work and Intra-corporate transfer Executive meeting" (Brussels 13–14 October), available *from:* www.etuc.org/documents/seasonal-work-and-intra-corporate-transfer#.U1hs2_2-31o [accessed 17 August 2018].

56 *See generally,* Committee of the Regions Opinion on Seasonal Workers (2011) CoR 2011/C166/10 *Op. Cit.* para. 24.

57 Joint NGO Statement (2011) "EU Seasonal Migrant Workers' Directive: Full Respect of Equal Treatment Necessary" (20 April) *available from:* http://vps51229.ovh.net/aedh.dev/wp-content/uploads/2011/04/Version%20finale%20emplois%20saisonniers%2020_04_2011.pdf [accessed 17 August 2018].

rent, despite NGOs' recommendation that a specific salary to rent ratio should be included in the Directive.[58]

(vi) Cascading current state circular and temporary mobility practices to environmentally vulnerable communities: some illustrative examples

Given the EU's favourable legal framework for seasonal and circular migration for EDPs, it is worth examining current state practice. The European Commission has emphasised that promotion of migration as an adaptation measure is assisted by the experience gained through other relevant labour migration schemes implemented by the EU, its member states, and non-EU countries. Examined below are three temporary migration schemes resulting from bilateral agreements, as well as their potential value for EDPs.

Seasonal Agricultural Workers Program between Canada and the Caribbean: an international open and multileveled cooperative model

Canada's Seasonal Agricultural Workers Program (SAWP) started in the late 1960s when the Canadian government signed the first bilateral agreement with certain Caribbean countries.[59] In 1974, it signed with Mexico. The program consists of bilateral administrative arrangements between Canada and the countries of origin, which are formalised in Memoranda of Understanding (MOUs) and Employment Contracts between the agricultural sector and migrant workers and the government agents of the supply country. Notably, each agreement is defined as an "intergovernmental administrative arrangement" and not as a binding international agreement (though Canada's decisions may still be examined under the Canadian Charter of Rights and Freedoms and general principles of administrative law).[60] In Canada, the programme is implemented within the framework of the Immigration and Refugee *Protection Act* and *Regulations*. At the provincial level, statutes relating to employment standards, labour, and health govern program implementation.[61]

58 *Ibid.*

59 Parties to the agreement include Anguilla, Antigua and Barbuda, Barbados, Dominica, Grenada, Jamaica, Montserrat, St. Kitts-Nevis, St. Lucia, St. Vincent and the Grenadines, and Trinidad and Tobago. The first SAWP began as a pilot programme between Canada and Jamaica in 1966.

60 Verma, V. (2010) "The Mexican and Caribbean Seasonal Agricultural Workers Program: Regulatory and Policy Framework, Farm Industry Level Employment Practices and the Future of the Program under Unionization" Executive Summary Prepared for the North-South Institute *available from:* www.nsi-ins.ca/wp-content/uploads/2012/11/2002-The-Mexican-and-Caribbean-Seasonal-Agricultural-Workers-Program-Regulatory-and-Policy-Framework-Executive-Summary.pdf [accessed 17 august 2018].

61 *Ibid.*

Each year, more than 20,000 migrant workers from the designated countries, primarily those with low-level skills, travel to Canada mainly to work in the agricultural sector. They are allowed to stay for up to eight months, if required, and can return to the same employment the following year. Preference is given to workers with young families. The temporary nature of the programme appears to be successful, as the majority of workers return to their countries at the end of their contracts.[62]

Added value for environmentally displaced persons

Crucially, the programme is governed by both Canada and the countries of origin, so key stakeholders are involved in establishing their obligations and responsibilities, making it relevant in the context of environmentally vulnerable regions. The country of origin handles the recruitment process and establishes a pool of workers willing to work in Canada. National contact points are available to answer potential workers' questions regarding their rights and entitlements in Canada (e.g. adequate housing, working conditions, visa requirements, access to health services, and repatriation). This clears up workers' uncertainties prior to departure and eases the workers' integration into the host community. Canadian employers must guarantee the same pay to migrant workers as they would to Canadian workers and ensure that workers have medical coverage. Employers must also provide adequate accommodation and transportation costs to and from the country of origin. Importantly, the SAWP does not limit the number of workers who can benefit from it.[63]

Seasonal Employers Programme between New Zealand and insular states in the Pacific: a model with regional potential

New Zealand's Recognised Seasonal Employer programme (RSE), established in 2007, allows workers from the Pacific Islands to enter New Zealand to overcome the labour shortage, like the SAWP does for Canada's agricultural sector.[64] The programme stands out in its attempt to develop a "triple-win" framework benefiting the individual migrant and the sending and receiving countries.[65] It allows up to 8,000 Pacific Island citizens from Kiribati, Samoa, Tonga, Tuvalu, and Vanuatu to engage in seasonal work for a maximum of seven months per

62 McLoughlin, S. & Münz, R. (2011) "Temporary and Circular Migration: Opportunities and Challenges" Working Paper No. 3 (European Policy Centre March) p. 30.

63 *See generally,* Henneby, J. & Pribisch, K. (2010) "A Model for Managed Migration? Re-Examining Best Practices in Canada's Seasonal Agricultural Worker Program" (International Organization for Migration) (discussing the advantages and challenges of the SAWP).

64 *See* Ramasamy, S. *et al.* (2008) "The Recognised Seasonal Employer Policy: Seeking the Elusive Triple Wins for Development through International Migration" 23 Pacific Economic Bulletin 3 pp. 171–186; Lovelock, K. & Leopold, T. (2008) "Labour Force Shortages in Rural New Zealand: Temporary Migration and the Recognised Seasonal Employer Work (RSE) Policy" 33–34 New Zealand Population Review pp. 213–234 (discussing the origins and aims of the RSE programme).

65 Ramasamy *et al.* (2008) *Op. Cit.* p. 171.

eleven-month period, and employers can request that the same workers return for subsequent seasons.[66] Efforts are made to recruit people from more remote and poor areas of the Pacific to maximise the programme's impact in the local communities of origin. This enhanced circular migration scheme is relevant to and can be used as an *a priori* scheme for EDPs, particularly in regions like the Pacific, which are increasingly fustigated by environmental changing conditions.

Under the RSE, New Zealand employers must obtain approval and then apply for an Agreement to Recruit (AtR) island workers. Employers become accredited if they cover at least half the travel costs; provide housing, health insurance, and pastoral care (e.g. the ability to practice a religion); pay minimum wage; and guarantee a work minimum of 30 hours per week and 240 hours overall.[67] Governments supplying labour must prepare a list of available workers. An island worker with an offer from an employer with an AtR can apply for a work visa, but workers must undergo police and health checks and follow a pre-orientation departure programme.

Added value for environmentally displaced persons

The added value of this scheme is not only filling a labour shortage but, perhaps more importantly, impacting development in nearby home countries (particularly in way of remittances),[68] making it an especially valuable model in areas affected by environmentally changing conditions. McAdam opines that because the scheme was not developed with environmentally displaced people in mind, its impact may be limited.[69] The quota and the visa systems pose the main barriers. Fewer workers results in fewer remittances. Limited visa access means that visa renewal is permitted only after the worker is out of New Zealand's territory, thus discouraging workers. Furthermore, some allege that those who engage in temporary work abroad have difficulty reintegrating into their country and finding work between seasons.[70] Nevertheless, this regional circular migration scheme is important, as it can offer short- and medium-term solutions for communities vulnerable to environmental factors. The ease of reach of the scheme allows migrants to form regional cultural ties and thus feel less as outsiders.

66 *See* McLoughlin *et al.* (2011) *Op. Cit.* p. 31 (discussing quota established as of March 2009). *See also* Thorton, F. (2011) "Regional Labour Migration as Adaptation to Climate Change? Options in the Pacific" in M. Leighton, S. Xiaomeng & K. Warner (eds.) "Climate Change and Migration: Rethinking Policies for Adaptation and Disaster Risk Reduction" Source No. 15/2001 UNU-EHS (April) p. 85, pp. 82–91.

67 Thorton (2011) *Op. Cit.* p. 86.

68 *See generally,* World Bank (2011) "Migration and Remittances: Factbook 2011" (World Bank). The World Bank asserts that remittances from migrant workers to recipients in their home countries constitute one of the world's biggest financial flows. In 2010 alone, such remittances totalled around US $325. Evidence of the impact of remittances is conflicting, though, because different methodologies are used within a matrix of ongoing change.

69 McAdam, J. (2011) "Climate Change and International Law: Complementary Protection Standards" (UNHCR Legal and Protection Policy Series May) p. 45 *available from:* www.unhcr.org/4dff16e99.html

70 Lovelock & Leopold (2011) *Op. Cit.* p. 19.

Temporary and circular labour migration scheme between Spain and Colombia: a targeted model

In 2001, Spain and Colombia entered into a bilateral agreement that established a temporary circular migration programme (TLCM).[71] A federation of employers from the region of Catalonia (Unió de Pagesos and Fundació Pagesos Solidaris) created the programme to fill gaps in the agriculture sector.

The programme allows workers from vulnerable areas of Colombia to perform temporary and seasonal agriculture work for six to nine months in the Catalonia region. The scheme provides flexibility by allowing seasonal workers to work for different employers and encourages circular migration.[72] Colombian authorities organise pools of candidates but the Spanish authorities, sometimes together with the employer, make the selections.[73] The programme highlights human rights of migrant workers, guided by the principle of equal treatment (right to adequate working conditions, equal pay, and social protection).[74] To avoid worker exploitation, the seasonal worker contract must include the salary and accompanying working conditions.[75]

Like the RSE, the TLCM has a multilayered governance structure to accommodate all stakeholders (employers, country of origin, host country, and individuals). This is particularly reflected in the Spanish government's policy of "co-development", which "aims at identifying and promoting development opportunities for the countries of origin while incorporating co-development strategies in the process of integrating migrants".[76] Importantly, the TLCM emphasises workers as agents of development in their own countries, a spill-over effect of remittances (in the form of money and skills). To this end, prior to departure, the worker is invited to detail how he/she expects to spend the money.[77] This procedure also helps measure the success of the programme and facilitates the worker's reintegration into his/her home country's labour market.[78]

Added value for environmentally displaced persons

The European Commission has praised this scheme precisely because of its strong migration and development component, particularly targeting communities

71 Agreement between Spain and Colombia on the Regulation and Organisation of Migratory Flows for Employment 21 May 2001, Official State Bulletin No. 159, 4 July 2001 *available from:* www.migreurop.org/IMG/pdf/Accord_Espagne_-_Colombie.pdf [accessed 17 August 2018].

72 *Ibid.* Articles 10, 11.

73 *Ibid.* Article 4.

74 *Ibid.* Articles 6, 7, 8.

75 *Ibid.* Article 11.

76 Magri, N. (2009) "Temporary Circular Labour Migration between Colombia and Spain: A Model for Consolidation and Replication" Mpp Master's Thesis, Maastricht Graduate School of Governance, Maastricht University (2008–2009) pp. 72–73.

77 International Organization for Migration (2009) "Temporary and Circular Labour Migration: Experiences, Challenges and Opportunities" (IOM December) p. 19.

78 Agreement between Spain and Colombia, Official State Bulletin N° 159 (4 July 2001) *Op. Cit.* Article 12.

affected by recurring environmental disruptions (e.g. drought, floods, and volcanic eruptions).[79] In fact, when the Galeras volcano in southwest Colombia erupted in 2006, the TLCM provided migration opportunities to the thousands of people affected by the disaster. Colombians temporarily migrated to Spain and earned money to reconstruct their communities, thus becoming "an important source of post-disaster rehabilitation".[80] The programme was later expanded to rural populations whose livelihoods were particularly vulnerable to floods, droughts, and other environmental stressors.[81] This scheme is special because it can reduce the vulnerability of populations subject to environmental disruptions, thereby avoiding forced and/or permanent displacement.[82] The scheme has three obvious limitations, though. First, it is subject to the Spanish immigration rules that determine the recruitment and annual quotas of foreign workers, which can favour some migrants to the detriment of others in the same vulnerable situation. Second, it makes countries of origin dependent on the will of host countries and also regulates seasonal work, limiting the type of work foreign workers may perform. Third, Spain employs third-country nationals only if Spanish residents cannot or will not accept a particular job.

In 2007, IOM joined the TLCM project to strengthen its base and make it replicable. Under the EU-AENEAS[83] funding programme, IOM enlarged the initial project and its beneficiaries, including making a community's vulnerability to natural disasters one factor in the selection process.[84] This advancement makes the TLCM a great model to consolidate and replicate, as it has potential to work as a proactive protection measure for EDPs. IOM and the Spanish government judge that the programme is having a positive impact in the country of origin, together with its innovation component.[85] Migration is now included in the national development programmes of the country of origin, and innovative techniques have been implemented in the national agriculture sector.

79 European Commission, SWD (2013) 138 Final *Op. Cit.* p. 28.

80 IRIN Humanitarian News and Analysis (2010) "Fleeing Disaster Can be a Good Thing" (30 March). In particular Koko Warner statements ***available from:*** www.irinnews.org/report/88627/refugees-fleeing-disaster-can-be-a-good-thing [accessed 17 August 2018].

81 De Moor, N. (2011) "Temporary Labour Migration for Victims of Natural Disasters: The Case of Colombia" in M. Leighton, X. Shen & K. Warner (eds.) "Climate Change and Migration: Rethinking Policies for Adaptation and Disaster Risk Reduction" Source No. 15/2001 (United Nations University for Environment and Human Security April) p. 94, pp. 92–103.

82 Engleman, R. (2009) "The State of the World Population 2009: Facing a Changing World: World, Population and Climate Change" (United Nations Population Fund UNFA) ***available from:*** www.unfpa.org/webdav/site/global/shared/documents/publications/2009/state_of_world_population_2009.pdf [accessed 17 August 2018].

83 EU-AENEAS program – Program for financial and technical assistance to third countries in the area of migration and asylum, Project Name: "Temporary and Circular Labour Migration (TCLM) between Colombia and Spain: A Model for Consolidation and Replication" (MIGR/2006/120/237) ***available from:*** https://ec.europa.eu/europeaid/aeneas-programme-programme-financial-and-technical-assistance-third-countries-area-migration-and_en [accessed 17 August 2018].

84 European Commission, SWD (2013) 138 Final *Op. Cit.* p. 29.

85 IOM (2009) *Op. Cit.* p. 7.

(vii) Seeking the added protection value of the seasonal workers directive

THE POSITIVES

Seasonal migrant worker status is of key importance for EDPs because it is a fast-track procedure of common entry, residence conditions, and a set of rights embodied in a legal framework. Arguably, a formalised EU seasonal workers framework can be used as an expedited scheme for EDPs when no other targeted measures exist. Hence, seasonal circular migration can act as a preventative strategy to reduce environmentally induced displacement and increase resilience to environmental disruptions. The multi-seasonal permit ("several seasonal worker permit") in a single administrative act reduces bureaucracy, opens mobility opportunities, and facilitates re-entry. It presents an option for people at risk of environmental stressors. Circular migration does not reduce vulnerability to environmental change, but it reduces the pressure on natural resources and permits knowledge-building and income diversification that individuals and households can use to adapt to a changing environment.[86]

The Directive obligates states to afford migrant workers within their territories minimum standards of treatment. This human rights orientation prevents exploitation of seasonal workers. It can also ensure that EDPs' human rights are less compromised by environmental change.

THE NEGATIVES

The Directive suffers from a number of recognised *lacunae*. Unlike the Spanish and Canadian programmes, the Directive is silent with regards to transportation or visa costs. It does not cater to integration measures in the host country (e.g. language courses or training) or reintegration measures once the seasonal worker returns to his or her country. Family reunification is also neglected but is an equally pressing issue for seasonal workers. Here the lessons learned from the TLCM programme can be useful. The denial of these integration measures contradicts the objectives of the EU Integration Agenda and differentiated treatment regarding the right to family life. It also risks discriminating between third-country nationals on the grounds of the type of work and period employed.[87]

Furthermore, the multi-track approach to employment creates a system where states have the power to discriminate against third-country nationals in favour

86 Tacoli (2009) *Op. Cit.* p. 517.

87 Joint NGO Statement (2011) *Op. Cit. See, e.g.*, Proposal for a Directive of the European Parliament and of the Council (2010) "On the Conditions of Entry and Residence of Third-Country Nationals in the Framework of an Intra-Corporate Transfer" COM/2010/0378 Final – COD 2010/0209 (13 July), (guaranteeing intra-corporate transferees the right to family reunification even for postings of short duration).

of EU nationals as to unemployment and family benefits. Equal treatment is also limited in relation to tax benefits and education and vocational training. These inequities may discourage some from engaging in seasonal work, particularly those from environmentally vulnerable areas. In reality, it can increase rather than decrease vulnerability.

PRINCIPLE OF PREFERENCE: PREFERRING WHO?

The TFEU's principle of preference for EU citizens regarding access to member states' labour markets gives member states the right to determine the volumes of admission of third-country nationals into their territories. European law and policy appears to present a contradiction between a desire to make the European market competitive and erecting barriers to entrance of workers.

To devise a comprehensive preventative and proactive strategy for EDPs, these barriers must be overcome. A seasonal migration programme focusing on the needs of environmental migrants (in a true win-win-win) rather than the effective management of migration flows would help in the development of an adequate legal framework to avoid environmentally induced displacement.

Hope for EDPs lies with member states, who may establish more favourable standards for the entry and stay of seasonal workers as outlined in Article 4 of the Seasonal Workers Directive.[88] Blending the main advantages of each scheme, such as unlimited quotas, facilitation of family reunification, and overall targeted measures (in the country of origin and the host country, and for the migrant) could be valuable for people from areas prone to environmental stressors.

Member states could be encouraged to negotiate bilateral and multilateral agreements for seasonal work with third countries vulnerable to environmental changing conditions. As with the TLCM, the selection criteria could target and apply favourable treatment to nationals of specific third countries most vulnerable to environmental degradation (as allowed under national law and in accordance with the principle of non-discrimination in Article 10 TFEU).[89]

5.2.3 *Mobility partnerships*

(i) Rationale

The EU migration policy agenda has over the years been shaped by the need for mobility, grounded in dialogue and cooperation.[90] This EU externalisation

88 European Commission, SWD (2013) 138 Final *Op. Cit.* Article 4.

89 *Ibid.* para. 14.

90 In December 2006 the European Council called for member states to combine efforts against illegal migration with concrete proposals for incorporating legal migration opportunities into the EU's external policies in order to develop a balanced partnership with third countries adapted to EU member states' labour market needs. It subsequently launched a Communication "On Circular Migration and Mobility Partnerships between

agenda, based on partnership-building with third countries, results from the so-called Global Approach to Migration and Mobility (GAMM).[91] Mobility Partnerships (MPs), the first type of legal scheme utilising this cooperation mechanism,[92] flesh out the potentials of circular and temporary labour migration by offering visa facilitation and readmission agreements but incentivise third countries to help prevent illegal migration. MPs warrant analysis as potential preventative tools to adapt to environmental changing conditions and prevent displacement. In 2011, the European Commission noted that "[a]ddressing environmentally induced migration (. . .) should be considered part of the Global approach".[93] Arguably, seasonal labour mobility and other labour mobility patterns should be examined for potential application to EDPs.

(ii) Personal scope of application

An MP is a comprehensive policy tool that contributes to all aspects of migration. As Roderick Parkes acknowledges, it is by nature a composite instrument situated at the intersection between social, migration, economic, foreign, and development policy.[94] Because the EDP problem is horizontal by nature, also touching upon these different policies, migration based on an external component of "triple-win" (country of origin, host country, and individual migrant) can benefit those at risk of displacement. The programme encompasses a cohesive migration approach between receiving, sending, and transit countries within Europe, Africa, and along the Mediterranean, with *partnership* referring to the mutual commitments and shared responsibility, management, and ownership of the initiative by all parties, including mutual respect for human rights and

---

the European Union and Third Countries" European Commission 16 May 2007, COM (2007) 248 Final *Op. Cit.* But *see* Nellen-Stucky, R. (2010) "Partnering for Migration: The Ambiguous Case of Mobility Partnerships between the European Union and Selected Third Countries" Working Paper (Universität Luzern, Kultur-und Sozialwissenschaftliche Fakultät, Politikwissenschaftliches Seminar) p. 28, pp. 1–28 (asserting that the concept of MPs can be traced back to the beginning of communitarisation of migration and asylum policy under the Maastricht Treaty of 1991).

91 European Commission Communication from the Commission to the European Parliament, the Council, the European Economic and Social Committee (2011) "The Global Approach to Migration and Mobility" COM (2011) 743 Final (18 November). GAMM aspires to be Europe's overarching framework for external migration policy, complementary to foreign policy and development. It addresses the following thematic dimensions: promoting labour migration, addressing irregular migration, and enhancing the links between migration and development and those in need of international protection.

92 European Commission Staff Working Document (2009) "Mobility Partnerships as a Tool of the Global Approach to Migration" SEC (2009) 1240 Final (18 September).

93 European Commission COM (2011) 743 Final *Op. Cit.* p. 7.

94 Parkes, R. (2009) "EU Mobility Partnerships: A Model of Policy Coordination?" 11 European Journal of Migration and Law p. 328, pp. 321–345.

fundamental freedoms.[95] In 2008, pilots were launched with Cape Verde[96] and the Republic of Moldova.[97] A year later, another was launched with Georgia,[98] followed by Armenia[99] in 2011. Initial talks with Senegal stalled in 2009. More recently, the EU has MPs with Tunisia[100] and Morocco.[101]

(iii) Temporal scope of application

MPs are not international agreements; they are non-binding political declarations[102] and "little more than declarations of intent".[103] Authors criticise their relevance due to their lack of enforcement (or foreseen non-compliance sanctions), particularly when the EU can sign legally binding migration agreements.[104] But their value cannot be minimised. They are an innovative and pragmatic soft law tool, as they allow third states and EU member states to adhere to their

95 *See, e.g.*, Council of the European Union (2008) "Joint Declaration on a Mobility Partnership between the European Union and the Republic of Cape Verde" Doc 9460/08 ADD 2 (21 May) ("REAFFIRMING the strong commitment of the Signatories to conclude and effectively implement future agreements concerning the facilitation of the issuance of visas and the readmission of persons residing without authorisation; HAVE DECIDED to establish a Mobility Partnership ***based on reciprocity***. The Mobility Partnership will have the purpose of ***better managing legal and labour migration***, including circular and temporary migration, within the limits of the respective competences of the Signatories and taking into account their labour market and socio-economic situation, enhancing cooperation on migration and development and preventing and combating irregular migration and trafficking in and smuggling of human beings, as well as promoting an effective return and readmission policy, while respecting human rights and the relevant international instruments for the protection of refugees and taking into account the situation of individual migrants and the socioeconomic development of the Signatories") (emphasis added).

96 *Ibid.*

97 Council of the European Union (2008) "Joint Declaration on a Mobility Partnership between the European Union and the Republic of Moldova" Doc 9460/08 ADD1 (21 May).

98 Council of the European Union (2009) "Joint Declaration on a Mobility Partnership between the European Union and Georgia" Doc16396/09 ADD1 (20 November).

99 Council of the European Union (2011) "Joint Declaration on a Mobility Partnership between the European Union and Armenia" Doc 14963/11 ADD1 (6 October).

100 European Commission (2014) "Political Declaration Déclaration conjointe pour le Partenariat de Mobilité entre la Tunisie, l'Union Européenne et ses Etats membres participants" (3 March).

101 Council of the European Union (2011) "Joint Declaration on a Mobility Partnership between the European Union and the Kingdom of Morocco" Doc 6139/13 ADD1 Rev 3 (3 June).

102 Signed by the Community, the Presidency of the EU, interested member states, and the respective third-country partner.

103 Parkes (2009) *Op. Cit.* p. 331.

104 *See* TFEU Article 79(3). *See also, e.g.*, Parkes (2009) *Op. Cit.* p. 331. Hernández i Sagrera, R. & Carrera, S. (2009) "The Externalisation of the EU's Labour Immigration Policy Towards Mobility or Insecurity Partnerships" Centre for European Policy Studies Working Document No. 312 pp. 106, 138.

own set of policy objectives. MPs are cooperation agreements providing parties with great flexibility. They would, for example, allow states of origin to target labour mobility schemes to reduce or avoid environmentally induced displacement. Based on dialogue and cooperation with third states, the scheme is, however, biased towards the initiatives of the EU and member states.[105] But it outlines a list of projects (of general or more specific character) to operationalise the agreement, and its open-ended character guarantees added value for third countries because, once signed, other interested member states may still participate. Progress is monitored through a scoreboard (which contains information regarding all initiatives, partners involved, contact points, funding sources, applicable timeframes, and evaluation indicators) and facilitated by local structures together with EU institutions.[106] They reflect a new form of governance that could be used preventatively to benefit EDPs.[107]

(iv) Territorial scope of application

Under this framework, work opportunities within the EU should be more accessible to non-EU citizens. As mentioned, this externality has been influenced by the international agenda and the EU political landscape shift towards the migration-development nexus and mobility under the adage "more for more approach".[108]

Nonetheless, the EU also has internal motivations when choosing third-country parties, particularly those that include illegal migration corridors into the EU.[109] Not coincidentally, negotiations start at the European level by the Directorate General Internal Affairs, together with the EU's Presidency, after the Council's High-level Asylum and Migration group identifies partnering

105 *See,* e.g., Joint Mobility Partnerships *Op. Cit.* ("The EU intends to contribute to implementing the partnership through Community and member states' initiatives, ***within the limits of their respective competences***, in conformity with the applicable procedures and with due regard for the ***principle of Community preference***") (emphasis added).

106 *See* European Commission Staff Working Document SWD (2009) 1240 Final *Op. Cit.* p. 4 (explaining that actual implementation and progress is facilitated by pre-existing local structures in Cape Verde through "Groupe Local de Suivi" and in Moldova through a cooperation platform created for the effect, both comprised of national authorities, representatives of member state diplomatic missions, and an EC delegation).

107 *See generally,* Sgro, A. (2013) "Les Déplacés de L'Environnement à L'Épreuve de la Catégorisation en Droit de L'Union Européenne" Thèse pour le Doctorat en Droit Public Université de Nice Sophia Antipolis UFR Institut Du Droit de la Paix et du Dévelopment p. 379; Balzacq, T. (2009) "The Frontiers of Governance: Understanding the External Dimension of EU Justice and Home Affairs" in T. Balzacq (ed.) "The External Dimension of EU Justice and Home Affairs: Governance, Neighbours, Security" (Palgrave Macmillan) pp. 1–32 Both discuss governance within the EU's external dimension of Justice and Home Affairs.

108 *See* European Commission COM (2011) 743 *Op. Cit.* p. 11.

109 For example, Cape Verde and Moldova are both crucial transit points and/or sources for irregular migrants coming primarily from West Africa and Eastern Europe.

countries.[110] Plus, these long-term cooperation agreements are grounded in (and aim to add value to) existing bilateral frameworks with which the EU has already established ties.[111] Therefore, countries neighbouring the EU are identified as priority partners. The Arab Spring, for example, gave leeway to open negotiations with countries such as Morocco, Tunisia, and Egypt, given the "significant movements of people".[112] Nevertheless, these partnerships are interesting for EDPs coming from the south of the Mediterranean or that cross the territory, which is considered an EDP hotspot.[113]

(v) Substantive scope of application

MPs unquestionably have a human rights foundation because they have a migrant-centred focus. Thus, according to the European Commission, MPs should be based on "the principle that the migrant is at the core of the analysis and all action, and must be empowered to gain access to safe mobility".[114] This is pertinent for EDPs. All current MPs aim at operationalising the GAMM, which underscored the human rights of migrants as a cross-cutting issue.[115] The joint declarations with different partnering countries contain continuous references to the rights and protection of migrants, which should be "concrete and effective".[116] Importantly, they should facilitate labour mobility in the form of temporary and circular migration to third-country nationals.[117] Migrants have the right to be informed on the opportunities for legal migration, employment conditions, on-the-job opportunities, and the labour market situation, among

110 *See* Nellen-Stucky (2010) *Op. Cit.* p. 20. *See also* Council of the European Union (2010) "The Stockholm Programme: An Open and Secure Europe Serving and Protecting Citizens" 2010/C 115/01 para. 6.1.1 In 2010, with respect to the Stockholm Programme, the Council of the European Union noted that: "The principal focus should remain non cooperation with the most relevant countries in *Africa and Eastern and South-Eastern Europe*. Dialogue and cooperation should be further developed also with other countries and regions such as those in *Asia and Latin America* on the basis of the identification of *common interests* and *challenges*" (emphasis added).

111 Council of the European Union *Op. Cit.* 2010/C 115/01 para. 6.1.1 of the Stockholm Programme. Cooperative projects include Seahorse Networks funded by AENEAS, with Cape Verde and other West African countries, and the EU Border Assistance Mission to Moldova and Ukraine (EUBAM).

112 European Commission (2011) "Communication from the Commission to the European Parliament, the Council, the European Economic and Social Committee and the Committee of the Regions a Dialogue for Migration, Mobility and Security with the Southern Mediterranean Countries" COM (2011) 292 Final (24 May).

113 Sgro (2013) *Op. Cit.* p. 382.

114 European Commission COM (2011) 743 Final *Op. Cit.* p. 7.

115 *Ibid.*

116 Council of the European Union (2011) Doc 14963/11 ADD1 *Op. Cit.* Joint Mobility Partnership with Armenia p. 3 para.1.

117 *Ibid. See also* Council of the European Union (2009) Doc16396/09 *Op. Cit.* Joint Mobility Partnership with Georgia p. 9; Council of the European Union (2008) Doc 9460/08 ADD1 *Op. Cit.* Joint Mobility Partnership with Moldova p. 11 para.4.

other things.[118] Visa facilitation measures should be used for this purpose.[119] They particularly highlight the right to education in host states, including formal and/or vocational.[120] Though they do not require nationals of the originating countries to be treated equally to the member states' citizens, efforts must be made to safeguard the social rights of migrants and their families, including the portability of social security rights.[121]

In some cases, agreements provide for pre-departure training, including language education, to ensure migrants' integration into the host labour market.[122] Unlike the Seasonal Workers Directive, MPs particularly underscore reintegration measures upon migrants' return to their country (e.g. training and assistance in finding jobs, protection and assistance for vulnerable categories of returning migrants, or to develop entrepreneurship actions).[123] Unfortunately, though,

118 Council of the European Union (2011) Doc 14963/11 ADD1 *Op. Cit.* Joint Mobility Partnership with Armenia p. 4 para.3; Council of the European Union (2008) Doc 9460/08 ADD2 *Op. Cit.* Joint Mobility Partnership with Cape Verde p. 3 para.1.

119 *See, e.g.*, Council of the European Union (2011) Doc 14963/11 ADD1 *Op. Cit.* Joint Mobility Partnership with Armenia pp. 2, 4; Council of the European Union (2008) Doc 9460/08 ADD2 *Op. Cit.* Joint Mobility Partnership with Cape Verde p. 3 para. 5 p. 10; Council of the European Union (2009) Doc16396/09 *Op. Cit.* Joint Mobility Partner ship with Georgia pp. 2, 4; Council of the European Union (2008) Doc 9460/08 ADD1 *Op. Cit.* Joint Mobility Partnership with Moldova pp. 2, 3; Council of the European Union (2013) Doc 6139/13 ADD1 Rev 3 *Op. Cit.* Joint Mobility Partnership with the Kingdom of Morocco p. 5 paras.1,2,3.

120 *See, e.g.*, Council of the European Union (2011) Doc 14963/11 ADD1 *Op. Cit.* Joint Mobility Partnership with Armenia p. 11; Council of the European Union (2009) Doc16396/09 *Op. Cit.* Joint Mobility Partnership with Georgia p. 3 para. 4; Council of the European Union (2008) Doc 9460/08 ADD2 *Op. Cit.* Joint Mobility Partnership with Cape Verde p. 9; Council of the European Union (2008) Doc 9460/08 ADD1 *Op. Cit.* Joint Mobility Partnership with Moldova p. 14 para. 8 i; Council of the European Union (2013) (Doc 6139/13 ADD1 Rev 3) *Op. Cit.* Joint Mobility Partnership with the Kingdom of Morocco pp. 5, 9 para. 23.

121 *See, e.g.*, Council of the European Union (2011) Doc 14963/11 ADD1 *Op. Cit.* Joint Mobility Partnership with Armenia p. 4 para. 5 pp. 10, 11; Council of the European Union (2009) Doc16396/09 *Op. Cit.* Joint Mobility Partnership with Georgia p. 10; Council of the European Union (2008) Doc 9460/08 ADD1 *Op. Cit.* Joint Mobility Partnership with Moldova p. 4 para. 6 p. 13 para. 7 p. 14; Council of the European Union (2013) (Doc 6139/13 ADD1 Rev 3) *Op. Cit.* Joint Mobility Partnership with the Kingdom of Morocco p. 6 paras. 10, 11.

122 *See, e.g.*, Council of the European Union (2009) Doc16396/09 *Op. Cit.* Joint Mobility Partnership with Georgia p. 3 para. 4; Council of the European Union (2011) Doc 14963/11 ADD1 *Op. Cit.* Joint Mobility Partnership with Armenia p. 3 para. 4; Council of the European Union (2008) Doc 9460/08 ADD2 *Op. Cit.* Joint Mobility Partnership with Cape Verde p. 8 para. 2.

123 *See, e.g.*, Council of the European Union (2011) Doc 14963/11 ADD1 *Op. Cit.* Joint Mobility Partnership with Armenia p. 5 para. 8 pp. 11, 12; Council of the European Union (2008) Doc 9460/08 ADD2 *Op. Cit.* Joint Mobility Partnership with Cape Verde p. 4 para. 8; Council of the European Union (2009) Doc16396/09 *Op. Cit.* Joint Mobility Partnership with Georgia p. 4 para. 9 pp. 8, 9, 10; Council of the European Union (2008) Doc 9460/08 ADD1 *Op. Cit.* Joint Mobility Partnership with Moldova

MPs' declarations and the projects attached have a narrowed touch base. They are generally targeted at skilled and highly skilled migrants, thus reducing their potential impact for countries at risk of environmental degradation that could otherwise benefit from them.

(vi) Seeking the added protection value of Mobility Partnerships

THE POSITIVES

MPs offer a particular status and framework for the mobility of non-EU nationals and, by extension, EDPs, particularly when linked to a development approach. Their flexibility allows states to create tailor-made programmes according to their needs. The real challenge of MPs is when states' interests and motivations to take part are uncoordinated.

THE NEGATIVES

Contrary to their original purpose, MPs are not predominantly circular migration schemes. Rather, as noted by critics, they take a restrictive and coercive approach imposed by the EU.[124] They are selective and conditional and only entered into once certain conditions are met, such as cooperation on illegal migration and the existence of "effective mechanisms for readmission".[125] Realistically, they serve more as capacity-building mechanisms in migration management rather than labour mobility schemes. This mismatch of interests eventually stalled the negotiations between Senegal and the EU.[126] Instead of a dialogue, the EU tends to engage in a paternalistic monologue of security and control towards fragile third states with little power to influence the negotiations and the content of such undertakings.[127]

---

p. 4 para. 6 pp. 8, 10, 11, 12; Council of the European Union (2013) Doc 6139/13 ADD1 Rev 3 *Op. Cit.* Joint Mobility Partnership with the Kingdom of Morocco p. 8 paras. 18, 20 p. 9.

124 *See, e.g.*, Maroukis, T. & Triandafyllidou, A. (2013) "Mobility Partnerships: A Convincing Toll for the EU's Global Approach to Migration?" Policy Paper No.76 (Notre-Europe Jacque Delors Institute February 2013); Chou, M. H. (2009) "European Union Migration Strategy towards West-Africa: The Origin and Outlook of Mobility Partnerships with Cape Verde and Senegal" Paper for EUSA Biennial International Conference "Information and Ideas on the European Union" (Los Angeles 23–25 April).

125 European Commission *Op. Cit.* COM (2006) 735 Final.

126 *See* Chou, M-H. & Girbert, M. (2012) "The EU-Senegal Mobility Partnership from Launch to Suspension and Negotiation Failure" 8 Journal of Contemporary European Research 4 pp. 408–427 (providing a comprehensive account of the MP negotiation process between Senegal and the EU and their uncoordinated interests).

127 *See* Triandafyllidou, A. (2009) "Attempting the Impossible? The Prospects and Limits of Mobility Partnerships and Circular Migration" ELIAMEP Thesis 1 pp. 1–4.

The imbalance between labour migration arrangements and actions against irregular migration may be due to two factors: first, Europe's economic crisis, and second, the division of competences within the EU.[128] Member states still determine labour migration policies and have been reluctant to open legal entry channels to labour migrants. Without member states' commitment, the European Commission cannot offer attractive initiatives to third countries. Instead, it can offer only visas to certain categories of people. Readmissions and border control actions remain unattractive trade-offs for third countries. This begs the question of MPs' realistic potential for EDPs.

AN ARCHETYPAL COMPREHENSIVE TOOL?

Arguably, MPs represent an archetypal comprehensive tool with the potential to increase the leverage for both parties if they target local and regional needs by matching labour offers and demand through appropriate, migrant-centred schemes. As demonstrated, MPs aim to shift away from the hitherto restrictive approach of the EU by focusing on dialogue and the positive potential that properly managed migration may have on the development of both countries. In 2009, the European Commission recognised the need to take into account, more appropriately, the objectives of partnering third countries.[129] The human rights dimension of MPs, translated in effective and concrete mobility measures (e.g. circular migration for migrants of all skill levels, channelling remittances to investment plans, language courses or professional training), can reinforce their potential value for EDPs. Importantly, MPs should respond to migrant groups' vulnerabilities, employment aspirations, and family situations; increase skills; and provide equal treatment that respects, protects, and fulfils migrants' human rights. Circular migration is a potential source of transcultural capital to create and promote mutual business for both countries. Trading the EU's externalisation migration control agenda for one that is rights-based, targeted MPs may constitute a sustainable adaptation measure that prevents displacement with limited costs and great benefits.

5.2.4 Benefits and challenges of a proactive approach to protection

A proactive system of protection for EDPs embraces the idea of fostering labour mobility to promote migration as adaptation. Circular migration, for example, may allow communities to cope with changes in environmental conditions. It can facilitate livelihoods for those who move and economic value through

128 Council of the European Union (2014) "The Hague Programme: Strengthening Freedom, Security and Justice in the European Union" 16054/04 (13 December 2004) para. 1.4 (proclaiming that "the determination of volumes and of admission of labour migrants is a competence of the Member States").

129 European Commission SEC (2009) 1240 *Op. Cit.* p. 3.

remittances (at the household and at national level) for those who remain.[130] Moreover, migration as an adaptation strategy may ease demand on the third country's resources, thereby enabling some residents to remain longer, avoiding the loss of human capital or "brain drain" situations. Drawing upon state practices, bilateral pilot circular migration schemes can be replicated for EDPs.

The human rights orientation of both the Seasonal Workers Directive and the MPs, (inspired by the ECHR and other international human rights instruments), offers useful insights into practical and effective measures that could be used to protect those potentially affected by environmental factors. Member states' power to restrict immigration and asylum is not unlimited; it is shaped by international obligations and individual humanitarian traditions. The EU is founded on principles of liberty, democracy, respect for human rights and fundamental freedoms, and the rule of law, and any action taken under EU law must be based on these founding principles. Therefore, a fundamental change in how we see migration is needed at the international and regional levels: it should be viewed as an opportunity (rather than a burden) to accommodate changes resulting from environmental degradation.[131]

If labour migration is to work to prevent displacement under the Seasonal Workers Directive or the MPs, it cannot be a "managed" concept. Circular migration schemes under those instruments must seek the renewed interest and the context of destination countries. "Branded" measures to promote mobility for EDPs can be subsumed to ordinary migration schemes but must target the interests of EDPs. One-size-fits-all labour migration schemes may risk harm to both sending and receiving countries. Importantly, though, migration is not a silver bullet and can be maladaptive, thus resulting in a more instability.[132] Indeed, migration is "a complex process, involving not only the migrants themselves but also their relationship to their states of destination".[133]

Yet, labour migration, supported by hard and soft law mechanisms, can be seen as an extension of an *ex ante* and also complementary protection solution for EDPs. This will not erode but rather reinforce existing protection under the EU Qualification or Temporary Directives for those who may reach EU borders.

130 Julka, A. (2011) "Multidimensional Re-Creation of Vulnerabilities and Potential Resilience in International Migration" 49 International Migration pp. 30, 34, 41, pp. 30–49.

131 Tacoli (2009) *Op. Cit.* p. 513.

132 *See* Mc Leman, R. (2009) "Climate Change and Adaptive Human Migration: Lessons from Rural North America" in N. Adger, I. Lorenzoni & K. O'Brien (eds.) "Adapting to Climate Change" (Oxford University Press) pp. 296–310 (alerting that countries must be conscious of potential harms when utilising migration as an adaptation strategy).

133 U.N. Secretary General (2006) "International Migration and Development: Report of the Secretary General" U.N. Doc. 60/871 (18 May) para. 151.

5.3 Consolidating a reactive approach to protection for EDPs

Given that current international refugee law is of limited application for people who have crossed national borders due to environmental stressors, there is a need to explore complementary regional protection paths, such as allowing states to provide protection against return on human rights grounds. The EU's Qualification Directive (QD),[134] which provides subsidiary protection, exemplifies complementary protection. Individuals who are not refugees under the CRSR but nonetheless meet certain qualifications (particularly on *non-refoulement* grounds) may be entitled to subsidiary protection. This type of protection may be relevant for those forced to move on a permanent or quasi-permanent basis where the prospects of return may be slim and may include people affected by slow-onset environmental change patterns, such as desertification, sea level rise, or natural disasters.[135]

For people forced to cross an international border due to fast-onset environmental change, temporary protection measures are worth exploring. Though provisional protection measures vary worldwide, the EU Temporary Protection Directive grants protection in situations of mass influx. This legal mechanism ensures emergency protection from *refoulement* and great manoeuvring to protect EDPs.

5.3.1 Subsidiary protection under the European Qualification Directive

The QD is described as the first supranational codification of a complementary protection regime.[136] It obligates member states to grant subsidiary protection to persons who do not qualify for refugee status. Its development is rooted in the Tampere Summit in 1999,[137] during European Union discussions to establish a Common European Asylum System,[138] and was the result of the innovative evolution of the European asylum field built in the 1997 Amsterdam Treaty

134 Directive of European Parliament and of the Council (2004) "On Standards for the Qualification of Third-Country Nationals or Stateless Persons as Beneficiaries of International Protection, for a Uniform Status for Refugees or for Persons Eligible for Subsidiary Protection, and for the Content of the Protection Granted" 2004/83/EC (29 April) (Qualification Directive). This Directive has been recently recast by Directive of the European Parliament and of the Council. 2011/95/EU (13 December 2011).

135 European Commission, SWD (2013) 138 Final *Op. Cit.* p. 18.

136 *See* McAdam, J. (2005) "The European Qualification Directive: The Creation of a Subsidiary Protection Regime" 17 International Journal of Refugee Law 3 p. 462, pp. 461–516.

137 Council of the European Union (1999) "Tampere European Council 15 and 16 October 1999 Presidency Conclusions" *available from:* www.europarl.europa.eu/summits/tam_en.htm [accessed 17 august 2018].

138 Directive 2011/95/EU *Op. Cit.* Article 1.

(Article 63(2)(a)).[139] The QD regulates minimum eligibility standards of protection of third-country nationals or stateless persons, conferring upon them a status as refugees or persons otherwise needing international protection, i.e. subsidiary protection.

It intended to stop ad hoc and discretionary national practices of complementary protection, creating a harmonised system.[140] Subsidiary protection had not been fully developed in some countries,[141] while in others the concept was "geometrically variable".[142] Thus, establishing a common ground of subsidiary protection was deemed necessary to avoid fragmentation of the Common European Asylum System and prevent further protection gaps. Originally, the key premise was that "harmonisation would be based on the valid international human rights instruments relevant to subsidiary protection".[143] McAdam explains that human rights law played a complementary role, i.e. to enlarge beyond Article 1A(2) of the Refugee Convention the categories of persons to whom international protection is owed.[144] Yet, because EDPs were included and then excluded as a category of persons in need of protection, the role of human rights law in the development of the QD is questionable.

139 Consolidated version of the Treaty Establishing the European Community, signed 2 October 1997 Amsterdam Treaty Article 63 (2) (a) reads: "[t]he Council, acting in accordance with the procedure referred to in Article 67, shall, within a period of five years after the entry into force of the Treaty of Amsterdam, adopt: (2) measures on refugees and displaced persons within the following areas: (a) minimum standards for giving temporary protection to displaced persons from third countries who cannot return to their country of origin and for persons who otherwise need international protection".

140 *See generally,* McAdam (2005) *Op. Cit.* p. 463. The EU's initial development of the concept of subsidiary protection was launched in March 1997 by a Danish proposal to the Migration and Asylum working parties. An additional proposal on the same subject was tabled a month later by the Dutch Presidency. But it was only under the Austrian Presidency in 1998 that the concept was generally defined: "protection for persons from third states who do not fall within the scope of the Geneva Convention but who still have the need of some international protection".

141 *See* Presidency Note to Strategic Committee on Immigration, Frontiers and Asylum (2003) 5293/03 ASILE 3 (20 January) p. 4.

142 *See generally,* Bouteillet-Paquet, D. (2002) "Subsidiary Protection: Progress or Set-Back of Asylum Law in Europe? A Critical Analysis of the Legislation of the Member States of the European Union" in D. Bouteillet-Paquet (ed.) "Subsidiary Protection of Refugees in the European Union: Complementing the Geneva Convention?" (Bruylant) p. 226 sq. (detailing legislation in member states). Prior to the QD, only 12 EU member states offered complementary protection. Countries like Belgium, Ireland, and the UK had no definition of subsidiary protection and used discretionary measures to complement the 1951 Refugee Convention.

143 Council of the European Union (1999) "Note from the Presidency to Asylum Working Party Discussion Paper on Subsidiary Protection" 13167/99 ASILE 41 (19 November) p. 2 (mentioning ECHR and the Convention Against Torture and Other Cruel, Inhuman or Degrading Treatment).

144 McAdam (2005) *Op. Cit.* p. 465.

(i) Travaux preparatoires*: inclusion and exclusion of EDPs as a category of persons in need of protection*

The *travaux preparatoires* leading to the QD show that the European Commission, in a note to the European Council, supported broadening the categories of subsidiary protection[145] when it asked member states to articulate their positions on whether environmental disasters constituted a ground for subsidiary protection.

Interestingly, the European Commission's first version of the Directive, in October 2011, defined grounds for protection as follows:

> an applicant for international protection who is outside his or her country of origin, and cannot return there owing to a well-founded fear of being subjected to the following serious and unjustified harm:
>
> (a) torture or inhuman or degrading treatment or punishment; or
> (b) violation of a human right, sufficiently severe to engage the Member State's international obligations; or
> (c) a threat to his or her life, safety or freedom as a result of indiscriminate violence arising in situations of armed conflict, or as a result of systematic or generalised violations of their human rights.[146]

With human rights as leitmotif, the provision was wide-ranging and inclusive[147] and left room to extend subsidiary protection to human rights violations occurring without conflict, possibly including EDPs.[148] Vikram Kolmannskog and Finn Myrstad argue that point (c) could include EDPs when the government is unable or unwilling to provide protection. They refer to Cyclone Nargis in 2008, wherein many blamed the Burmese junta for human rights violations for

145 Council of the European Union (1999) "Reflection Documents on Subsidiary Protection" Note of the Presidency to the ASILE Group, Doc 13167/99 (19 November) p. 6.

146 European Commission (2001) "Proposal for a Council Directive on Minimum Standards for the Qualification and Status of Third Country Nationals and Stateless Persons as Refugees or as Persons Who Otherwise Need International Protection" COM (2001) 510 Final 2001/0207(CNS).

147 *Ibid.* Chapter IV states: "No specific EU acquis directly related to subsidiary or complementary protection exists but the ECHR and the case law of the European Court on Human Rights provides for a legally binding framework, which informed the choice of categories of beneficiaries in this Proposal. The categories and definitions of persons listed in this Chapter do not create new classes of persons that Member States are obliged to protect but represent a clarification and codification of existing practice. The three categories (. . .) are drawn much from the disparate Member State practices and are believed to encompass the best ones". The reference to ECHR and the ECtHR as legally binding frameworks informing elaboration of the proposal and the choice of categories demonstrates the intended inclusiveness of the initial proposal.

148 Piotrowicz, R. & Van Eck, C. (2004) "Subsidiary Protection and Primary Rights" 53 International and Comparative Law Quarterly p. 114, pp. 107–138.

rejecting international aid and being unable to provide adequate disaster relief to its population.[149]

However, a subsequent Asylum Working Party[150] analysis and consequent reservations by the delegations in June and July 2002 show states' reluctance to expand beneficiaries of subsidiary protection (and by extension EDPs).[151] Nevertheless, a compromise proposal presented in September 2002 added point (d) to Article 15:

> acts or treatment outside the scope of litra a-c in an applicant's country of origin or in the case of stateless persons, his or her country of formal habitual residence, when such acts or treatment are sufficiently severe to entitle the applicant to protection against refoulement in accordance with the international obligations of Member States.[152]

The addition would have provided subsidiary protection for human rights violations beyond those in Article 3 of the ECHR and Article 1 of the 6th Protocol to the ECHR and in line with the international obligations of member states, thus giving states the option to protect people in need of international protection, including EDPs. However, some governments were displeased with the provision's vagueness and its wide margin of interpretation,[153] leading the Council to peremptorily clarify "acts of treatment": "it is ensured that *only man-made situations*, and not for instance situations arising from natural disasters or situations of famine, will lead to the granting of subsidiary protection" (emphasis added).[154] While the Council affirmed the exclusion of natural disasters from the scope of the Directive, it also (perhaps naively) affirmed the inclusion of man-made situations. Given the overwhelming evidence that climate change is a man-made condition, people who are or will be affected by climate change could, arguably, benefit from subsidiary

149 Kolmannskog, V. & Myrstad, F. (2009) "Environmental Displacement in European Asylum Law" 11 European Journal of Migration and Law p. 320, pp. 313–326.

150 The Committee of Permanent Representatives of the Governments of the Member States to the European Union (known as "Coreper") prepares all work of the Council of the EU, with the exception of some agricultural matters. It is supported by more than 150 highly specialised working parties and committees, known as the "Council preparatory bodies", which examine legislative proposals and carry out studies and other work to prepare the ground for Council decisions. The Asylum Working Party deals with asylum issues under the Justice and Home Affairs banner.

151 *See* Council of the European Union (2002) Doc 9038/02 and Council of the European Union (2002) Doc 10596/02 for member states' reservations.

152 European Commission COM (2001) 510 *Op. Cit.*

153 Council of the European Union Doc 11356/02.

154 Council of the European Union (2002) "Presidency Note to the Strategic Committee on Immigration, Frontiers and Asylum" Doc 12148/02. Interinstitutional File: 2001/02017 (20 September) p. 7.

protection.[155] The intense nervousness around paragraph (d) caused the Council to eliminate it in October 2002.[156] The Council provided further reassurance on this point by adding recital 26 to the final version of the Directive, clarifying that "risks to which a population of a country or a section of the population is generally exposed to normally do not create in themselves an individual threat which would qualify as serious harm".[157] The Council unquestionably intended to delimit the protection regime in the final version of the QD, excluding EDPs.

The foregoing discussion demonstrates that the shrinking protection options for EDPs results from the EU's politicised and harmonised approach of concepts and methods of subsidiary protection (based on best national practices). In reality, the EU QD does not create per se a new system of protection but is, rather, a "regionally specific political manifestation of a broader legal concept"[158] undermining the very essence of the EU's harmonisation objective,[159] resulting in the creation and implicit recognition of persons not included but still in need of subsidiary protection under international law and current member state practice. During discussions of the QD proposal at the European Parliament, Jean Lambert highlighted precisely this point in the report:

> While current definitions of asylum seekers deal only with those suffering persecution, or the fear of it, at the hands of human agents, *we are ignoring the growing number of people who are forced to leave their homes due to poverty* and *environmental degradation*. These *people equally need protection* and there is an *urgent need to devise the appropriate instruments and policies of prevention*. Maybe that should provide step 2 of a Common European Asylum Policy.[160]
>
> (emphasis added)

155 U.N.'s International Strategy for Disaster Risk Reduction (2008) *Op. Cit.* p. 1 states that "[i]nformation on climate change is building *a new perception of disasters as of our own making*. The increase in storms, droughts and other hazards expected to arise from the accumulation of greenhouse gases in the atmosphere as a result of industrialisation and deforestation *is clearly not natural*" (emphasis added).

156 Council of the European Union (2002) Doc 12619/02.

157 *See* Directive 2004/83/EC *Op. Cit.* para. 26 and recast Council Directive 2011/95/EU *Op. Cit* para. 35.

158 McAdam (2005) *Op. Cit.* p. 465.

159 *See* Directive 2004/83/EC *Op. Cit.* para. 25 and recast Council Directive 2011/95/EU *Op. Cit.* para. 34. The Preamble of the recital reads: "[i]t is necessary to introduce criteria on the basis of which applicants for international protection are to be recognised as eligible for subsidiary protection".

160 European Parliament (2003) "On the Proposal for a Council Directive on Minimum Standards for the Qualification and Status of Third Country Nationals and Stateless Persons as Refugees or as Persons who Otherwise Need International Protection" COM (2001) 510 – C5-0573/2001-2001/0207(CNS) Committee on Citizens' Freedoms and Rights, Justice and Home Affairs Rapporteur: Jean Lambert (11 December) p. 25.

The final version of the QD shows a rather strict scope of application, as member states were hesitant to broaden the categories of persons entitled to subsidiary protection.[161]

Nevertheless, the QD's lack of latitude does not impede exploring its potential application to EDPs. First, the eligibility criteria for subsidiary protection are mostly based on human rights instruments (on the basis of which subsidiary protection developed),[162] as reflected in Article 19(2) of the EU Charter of Fundamental Rights,[163] which states that "no one may be removed, expelled or extradited to a State where there is a serious risk that he or she would be subjected to the death penalty, torture or other inhuman or degrading treatment or punishment". This leaves the door open to expansive (albeit pragmatically limited) options to broaden the category of persons eligible for subsidiary protection, including EDPs.

Second, the QD's (potential) exclusion of EDPs shows a protection gap that still needs to be bridged to comply with standards established under Article 78(1) TFEU, which refers to "offering an appropriate status to any third country national requiring international protection" as well as member states' practices.

(ii) Personal scope of subsidiary protection

As noted, the QD does not impose a new *ratione personae* protection obligation on member states but rather clarifies and codifies existing international and community obligations and member state practice. Article 2 makes third-country nationals and stateless persons eligible for subsidiary protection if they would face a real risk of suffering serious harm as a result of forced removal from EU territory. Article 15 defines "serious harm", thus limiting the scope of application of Article 2:

(a) the death penalty or execution,
(b) torture or inhuman or degrading treatment or punishment of an applicant in the country of origin, or
(c) serious and individual threat to a civilian's life of person by reason of indiscriminate violence in situations of international or internal armed conflict.

161 *See* Directive 2004/83/EC *Op. Cit.* and recast Council Directive 2011/95/EU *Op. Cit.* Article 15.

162 Article 3 ECHR; Article 3 CAT and Article 7 ICCPR. *See* Directive 2004/83/EC *Op. Cit.* para. 25 and recast Directive 2011/95/EU *Op. Cit.* para. 34. Preamble of recital reads: "[t]hose criteria should be drawn from international obligations under human rights instruments and practices existing in Member States".

163 European Union (2000) "Charter of Fundamental Rights of the European Union" 7 December 2000, Official Journal of the European Communities, OJ C364/01 (18 December).

Paragraphs (a) and (b) are based on obligations imposed by general human rights provisions under Articles 2 and 3 of the ECHR, Article 7 of the ICCPR, and Article 3 of the CAT, whereas paragraph (c) is linked to common humanitarian principles[164] (that are connected to international obligations of member states regarding *non-refoulement*).[165] These instruments prohibit states from transferring an individual (national or non-national, including migrants and refugees within a state's jurisdiction or at the state's border) by force to a state where he or she would be persecuted or exposed to torture or cruel, inhumane, or degrading treatment or would face serious risk of violation of human rights.

Within treaty law and customary law, non-return and non-rejection at the border "implies at least temporary admission to determine an individual's status".[166] Human rights law, however, includes an expanded prohibition of return such that "an individual is protected whenever there exists a real risk of violation of one of the individual's core fundamental rights in the country of destination",[167] thus constituting a preventative method to protect human rights. Notably, the QD is valuable because it specifically grants a status to non-returnable individuals, which potentially may include EDPs.

Despite criticisms, the rules on granting or revoking each form of status were not amended under a recent recast of the QD,[168] leaving the two last grounds as most relevant to environmental displacement. As mentioned, however, Article 15 is considered only when an applicant does not qualify for refugee status under the Refugee Convention or purposely applies for subsidiary protection.[169]

164 International Committee of the Red Cross (ICRC) (1949) "Geneva Convention Relative to the Protection of Civilian Persons in Time of War" (Fourth Geneva Convention), 75 UNTS 287 (12 August).

165 *See* Directive 2004/83/EC *Op. Cit.* paras. 25, 36; Directive 2011/95/EU (Recast) *Op. Cit.* para. 34. The Preamble of the recital reads: "[t]hose criteria should be drawn from international obligations under human rights instruments and practices existing in Member States". Para. 48 of the recital reads: "the implementation of the Directive should be evaluated at regular intervals, taking into consideration in particular the evolution of international obligations of Member States regarding *non-refoulement* ".

166 Goodwin-Gill, G. & McAdam, J. (2007) "The Refugee in International Law" (Oxford University Press) p. 215.

167 Vandova, V. (2010) "Protection of Non-Citizens against Removal under International Human Rights Law" in A. Edwards & C. Ferstman (eds.) "Human Security and Non Citizens: Law, Policy and International Affairs" (Cambridge University Press) p. 495.

168 *See generally,* European Council on Refugees and Exiles (ECRE) (2010) "Comments from ECRE on the European Commission's Proposal to Recast the Qualification Directive" (March) *available from:* www.ecre.org/component/downloads/downloads/128.html [accessed 15 May 2014]; "Comments from UNHCR the European Commission's Proposal to Recast the Qualification Directive" (July) *available from*: www.unhcr.org/4c5037f99.pdf [accessed 15 May 2014].

169 *See generally* McAdam (2005) *Op. Cit.* p. 474. Council Directive 2004/83/EC *Op. Cit.* Article 2(e) and recast Council Directive 2011/95/EU *Op. Cit.* Article 2(f) reads: "'[p]erson eligible for subsidiary protection' means a third-country national or stateless person *who does not qualify as a refugee.*" (emphasis added).

(iii) Seeking the added protection value of Article 15(b)

In analysing Article 15(b), one must remember that, unlike other human rights, the right to be free from torture and inhuman and degrading treatment, under Article 3 of the ECHR, is absolute. That right has also been the most effective basis for obtaining protection in individual cases, including cases of expulsion.[170] Article 15(b) also prohibits derogation from Article 2 of the ECHR (the right to life).

Chapter 3 outlined the risks that EDPs face, from loss of life, family, possessions, and livelihoods to the collateral effects of poverty, disease, poor health, and starvation, which simultaneously impact a number of codified rights.[171] Article 15(b) of the QD and Article 3 of the ECHR, read jointly, can provide protection for EDPs who cannot return to their countries because of conditions that would make their survival either very risky or impossible.[172] Both the right to life (Article 2) and the right guaranteed under Article 3 ECHR are non-derogable, even in time of war or other public emergencies.[173] Therefore, as previously mentioned, Article 3 provides more extensive protection than Articles 32 and 33 of the U.N. Refugee Convention, which allow exceptions to removal on the basis of national security and public order.[174]

The CJEU has highlighted the significance of the ECHR. In a 1996 opinion, the Court held that respect for human rights is a condition of the lawfulness of EU acts[175] (including the QD). The ECHR is widely regarded as a minimum standard for the protection of human rights within the EU, as exemplified by the CJEU's deference[176] to the ECtHR's case law.[177] This is advantageous because

170 *See, e.g.*, ECtHR, *Chahal v United Kingdom*, Application No. 22414/93 (15 November 1996); ECtHR, *Ahmed v Austria*, Application No. 25964/94 (17 December 1996).

171 *See* ECtHR, *Hilal v UK*, Application No. 45276/99 (6 March 2001).

172 *See generally*, McAdam, J. (2012) "Climate Change, Forced Migration and International Law" (Oxford University Press) p. 64 (advocating the pertinence of this scenario).

173 ECtHR, *Chahal v United Kingdom Op. Cit.* paras. 76, 79–81.

174 *See* Arai-Takahashi, Y. (2002) "Uneven, But in the Direction of Effectiveness: Anticipatory Ill Treatment under Article 3 ECHR" 20 Netherlands Quarterly of Human Rights p. 6, pp. 5–27 (referring to *Chahal v United Kingdom*, where the court refused the government's request for implied limitations on Article 3).

175 CJEU (1996) "Opinion 2/94 Pursuant to Article 228 of the EC Treaty-Accession by the Community to the European Convention for the Protection of Human Rights and Fundamental Freedoms" ECR I-1759 (28 March 1996) para. 34.

176 *See* Jacobs, F. (2007) "The Sovereignty of Law" (Cambridge) pp. 54–55 ("[t]he CJEU [. . .] has followed scrupulously the case-law of the European Court of Human Rights"); Callewaert, J. (2009) "The European Convention on Human Rights and European Union Law: A Long Way to Harmony" 6 European Human Rights Review pp. 768–783 (discussing the evolving relationship between the ECtHR and the CJEU).

177 *See, e.g.*, CJEU, Case 374/87, *Orkem v Commission* (18 October 1989) ECR 3283 para. 30; CJEU, Joined Cases 46/87 and 227/88, *Hoechst v Commission* (21 September 1989) ECR 2859 para. 13; CJEU, Case C-13/94, *P. v S. and Cornwall County Council* (30 April 1996) ECR I-2143 para. 16; CJEU, Case C-185/95, *P. Baustahlgewerbe v Commission* (17 December 1998) ECR I-8417 para. 29; CJEU, Case C-7/98, *Dieter Krombach*

it develops a more coherent approach to, and greater legal certainty of, the interpretation of fundamental rights and, ultimately, the protection of the human person. Notably, the CJEU has repeatedly emphasised that "in interpreting a provision of community law it is necessary to consider not only its wording but also the context in which it occurs and the objects of the rules of which is part",[178] thus justifying a progressive interpretation of Article 15 to protect EDPs.[179]

THE ACT OF ILL TREATMENT: THE SOERING THRESHOLD AND ITS PROGRESS

Since the *Soering* case,[180] the ECtHR has recognised the "inherent obligation" under Article 3 to not remove a person who is threatened or would face a real risk of torture, inhumane, or degrading treatment. The Court has eloquently affirmed that removal in the given situation would "plainly be contrary to the spirit and intendment of the Article" and would "hardly be compatible with the underlying values of the Convention".[181] While *Soering* did not concern an asylum seeker, the ECHR later applied the enunciated principle to its first refusal of asylum case, *Cruz Varas and Others v Sweden*,[182] which has had a great impact on the rights of asylum seekers in Europe.

The *degrading* threshold is reached if the act "was such as to arouse in its victims feelings of fear, anguish and inferiority capable of humiliating and

v André Bamberski (28 March 2000) ECR I-1935; CJEU, Case C-112/00, *Schmidberger v Austria* (12 June 2003) ECR I-5659 para. 79; CJEU, Joined Cases C-402/05 P and 415/05, *Kadi and Al Barakaat International Foundation v Council and Commission* (3 September 2008) ECR I-6351 paras. 256, 344, 360, 363, 368.

178 *See* CJEU, Case 292/82, *Merck v Hauptzollamt Hamburg-Jonas* (17 November 1983) ECR 3781 para.12; CJEU, Case 337/82, *St. Nikolaus Brennerei und Likörfabrik, Gustav Kniepf-Melde GmbH v Hauptzollamt Krefeld* (21 February 1984) ECR 1051 para. 10; CJEU, Case C-223/98, *Adidas-Salomon AG and Adidas Benelux BV v Fitnessworld Trading Ltd* (14 October 1999) ECR I-7081 para. 23; CJEU, Case C-17/03, *Vereniging voor Energie, Milieu en Water and Others v Directeur van de Dienst uitvoering en toezicht energie* (7 June 2005) ECR I-4983 para. 41; CJEU, Case T-576/08 *Federal Republic of Germany v European Commission* (13 April 2011) ECR 2011 para. 105.

179 Council of Europe Protocol 1 to the European Convention for the Protection of Human Rights and Fundamental Freedoms, 20 March 1952 ETS 9 (ECHR, as amended by Protocol 14). *See also* Article 59 (2). The ECHR now allows the EU to accede the Convention, where formerly only states could become parties. Nevertheless, it bears repeating that all member states are party to the ECHR.

180 ECtHR, *Soering v United Kingdom*, Application No. 14038/88 (7 July 1989) (*Soering*). German national Jens Soering was imprisoned in the UK and facing extradition to the U.S., where he would be tried for murder and face the death penalty. He alleged that, if sentenced to death, he would be exposed to the so-called death row phenomenon, arguably a breach of Article 3 ECHR.

181 ECtHR, *Soering Op. Cit.* paras. 88, 89, 91.

182 ECtHR, *Cruz Varas and Others v Sweden*, Application No.15576/89 (20 March 1991).

debasing them and possibly breaking their physical and moral resistance".[183] Recent scholarship acknowledges that degrading treatment may *inter alia* include a lack of basic services, such as health, social security, education, housing, and child protection, which are essential for a dignified life when a degree of severity is encountered.[184] In 1979, the Court candidly admitted that:

> [although] the [European] Convention [on Human Rights] sets forth what are essentially civil and political rights, *many of them have implications of social and economic nature*. The Court therefore considers, like the Commission, that the mere fact that an interpretation of the Convention may extend into the sphere of social and economic rights, should not be a decisive factor against such an interpretation; *there is no water-tight division* separating that sphere from the field covered by the Convention.[185]
>
> (emphasis added)

In *Soering*, the Court made clear that the severity assessment cannot be made in absolute terms, but all circumstances of the case need to be considered: "it depends on all circumstances of each case, such as the nature and context of the treatment or punishment, the manner and method of its execution, its duration, its physical or mental effects and, in some instances, the sex, age and state of health of the victim".[186] The provision prohibits removal where the individual fears ill treatment by the receiving state or by a non-state actor when the receiving state fails[187] or is unable to obviate the risk by providing adequate protection.[188] This situation, however, seems to eliminate liability of the receiving state's government.

Thus, the Court notes not only the implied principle of *non-refoulement* with respect to Articles 2 and 3 but also its expanding implications on other Convention rights.[189] It states:

183 ECtHR, *Soering Op. Cit.* para. 100; *accord* ECtHR, *Pretty v UK*, Application No. 2346/02 (29 April 2002) para. 52.

184 Blake, N. & Husain, R. (2003) "Immigration, Asylum and Human Rights" (Oxford University Press) p. 297; Schachter, O. (1983) "Human Dignity as a Normative Concept" 77 American Society of International Law 4 pp. 848, 851, pp. 848–854.

185 ECtHR, *Airey v Ireland*, Application No.6289/73 (9 October 1979) para. 26.

186 ECtHR, *Soering Op. Cit.* para. 100. *See also* ECtHR, *Ireland v UK*, Application No. 5310/71 (18 January 1978) para. 162; ECtHR, *N. v United Kingdom*, Application No. 26565/05 (27 May 2008) para. 29.

187 This principle is generally accepted by the ECtHR and the UK's supreme court (ex-House of Lords). *See, e.g.*, ECtHR, *Altun v Federal Republic of Germany* (1983); *Regina v Secretary of State for the Home Department*, ex parte Bagdanavicius (2005) para. 8 (Lord Brown).

188 ECtHR, *H.L.R. v France*, Application No. 24573/94 (29 April 1997) para. 40 (applicant challenged deportation to Colombia because of the threat of drug traffickers).

189 ECtHR, *Soering Op. Cit.* paras. 91, 113. *See also* ECtHR, *Cruz Varas v Sweden Op. Cit.* paras. 69–70; ECtHR, *Vilvarajah v United Kingdom*, Application No. 13163/87; 13164/87; 13165/87; 13447/87; 13448/87 (30 October 1991) para. 103.

The establishment of such responsibility inevitably involves an assessment of conditions in the requesting country against the standards of Article 3 (art. 3) of the Convention. Nonetheless, there is no question of adjudicating on or establishing the responsibility of the receiving country, whether under general international law, under the Convention or otherwise. In so far as any liability under the Convention is or may be incurred, it is liability incurred by the extraditing Contracting State by reason of its having taken action, which has as a direct consequence the exposure of an individual to proscribed ill-treatment.

THE ASSESSMENT OF "SPECULATIVE" ILL TREATMENT

The ECtHR's decisions have provided, as Arai-Takahashi rightly claims, "clear guidelines for the recognition of 'speculative ill-treatment'".[190] In other words, the Court does not require certitude of ill treatment and considers a "real risk" to be sufficient under Article 3. This is particularly relevant because the Court has acknowledged that the risk of the applicant being subject to ill treatment need not be of high probability or even probable for precluding an unsafe return.[191]

The risk of sending a person back to his/her country of origin when the country's conditions are so critical (drought, soil erosion, inexistent shelter or other basic services) as to put his/her life in peril can constitute ill or degrading treatment and merit protection under Article 15(b) of the QD. These risks are real, probable, and likely to impact protected human rights.

The Court held, however, that it requires "substantial grounds" for the applicant's belief that he/she could be a victim of a breach of Article 3 (facing a "real risk" of ill treatment). A finding of "substantial grounds" can be based on the overall country conditions, individual circumstances of the applicant, and a description of the human rights at risk.[192]

When assessing the degree of risk, the Court was apparently motivated, at least in part, by Article 3 of the CAT, which references "substantial grounds for believing that he would be in danger of being subjected to torture". In *Soering*, the Court stressed the similarity between the obligations under Article 3 of CAT and Article 3 of the ECHR:

> [t]he fact that a specialised treaty should spell out in detail a specific obligation attaching to the prohibition of torture does not mean an essentially

190 Arai-Takahashi (2002) *Op. Cit.* p. 8.

191 ECtHR *Soering Op. Cit.* para. 88.

192 To make a finding of substantial grounds, the ECtHR must take into account the past experience of the applicant, his profile, his credibility, the widespread and mass human rights violations in the country of origin, and the continuity of the risk. *See Ibid.* para. 91.

> similar obligation is not already inherent in the general terms of Article 3 of the European Convention.[193]

The Court adopted the phraseology "substantial grounds" rather than "danger" in its own risk assessment. This last term substituted with the expression *real risk*. According to Ralf Alleweldt, the Court likely made this distinction because it intended to accept not only "dangers" but also "very small risks", as long as they were real, in an attempt to make Article 3 practical and effective. The real risk is interpreted in such a way that even small risks are acknowledged, ensuring protection against return to all individuals threatened by ill treatment. The effectiveness principle justifies a broad interpretation of the expression *real risk*.[194]

Accordingly, the right to be protected against removal in the case of threat of ill treatment is evolving. The progressive, human rights approach[195] to interpreting ill treatment is key to substantiating EDPs' protection claim under the QD, and the ECtHR increasingly embraces this approach. The obligations of host states to provide protection cannot be dismissed. Risks are hardly "unreal", and every risk (even if small) is, in fact, a "real" one.[196]

The Court admits that

> [c]ertainly, "the Convention is a living instrument which . . . must be interpreted in the light of present-day conditions"; and, in assessing whether a given treatment or punishment is to be regarded as inhuman or degrading for the purposes of Article 3 (art. 3).[197]

For example, the restriction placed on states' freedom of action by Article 3 was extended in *D. v United Kingdom*[198] on the expulsion intention to St. Kitts of a drug courier dying of AIDS. The Court found that his removal would constitute "inhumane treatment" due to the unavailability of basic health services, social and family ties, or work prospects in his country of origin. Despite the judiciary's acknowledgement of the "exceptional circumstances", it applied a progressive interpretation on the grounds that the Court

> must reserve itself a sufficient level of flexibility to address the application of that Article (art. 3) in other contexts which might arise. (. . .) To limit

193 ECtHR, *Soering Op. Cit.* para. 88.
194 Alleweldt, R. (1993) "Protection against Expulsion under Article 3 of the European Convention on Human Rights" 4 European Journal of International Law pp. 366, pp. 360–376.
195 McAdam (2012) *Op. Cit.* p. 89.
196 Alleweldt (1993) *Op. Cit.*
197 ECtHR, *Soering Op. Cit.* para. 102.
198 ECtHR, *D. v United Kingdom*, Application No. 30240/96 (2 May 1997).

> the application of Article 3 in this manner would be to undermine the absolute character of its protection.[199]

Yet, in a later case, *Bensaid v United Kingdom*,[200] the Court made the opposite ruling, holding that the deportation to Algeria of a schizophrenic patient did not breach Articles 3 (prohibition of removal of a person who is threatened or would face a real risk of torture or inhumane or degrading treatment), 8 (right private and family life), or 13 (right to an effective remedy) of the ECHR, even though Algeria offered inadequate medical care. But, Judge Sir Nicolas Bratza, joined by judges Costa and Greve, dissented, finding

> powerful and compelling humanitarian considerations in the present case which would justify and merit reconsideration by the national authorities of the decision to move the applicant to Algeria.[201]

The joint reading of *D. v United Kingdom* and the dissenting opinions of *Bensaid v United Kingdom* suggest that an individual's only legal protection from removal against ill treatment is prevention.[202] Further, the Court takes a holistic view of what prevention entails: the (in)direct responsibility of protection from the expelling state (and not his dependence on services *per se*) "where even the indirect attribution of responsibility to a third state might not be necessary".[203] In other words, there is an increasing acceptance of responsibility of harm or risk by the host state to protect the individual against ill treatment due to circumstances in the state of origin.

In *N. v United Kingdom*,[204] the Court continued the development of the jurisprudence on socio-economic deprivation as a breach of Article 3 but as a retrograding chapter. In this case, the ECHR reasoned that forcible return of the HIV-positive applicant to Uganda, where she would not have access to the medical treatment she required, did not violate Articles 3 and 8 of the ECHR. The Court held that the delivery of medical treatment is not a state obligation under the ECHR since it falls within the scope of social economic rights and outside the sphere of Article 3. Scholars like Hemme Battjes have criticised the

199 *Ibid.* para. 49.

200 ECtHR, *Bensaid v United Kingdom*, Application No. 44599/98 (6 May 2001).

201 *Ibid.* p. 18 (Separate Opinion of Judge Sir Nicolas Bratza joined by Judges Costa and Greve).

202 *See generally,* Cassese, A. (1989) "International Law in a Divided World" (Clarendon Press) pp. 128–129.

203 *See* Arai-Takahashi (2002) *Op. Cit.* p. 12. Notably, in paragraph 91 of the ECtHR's *Soering* decision, the Court points out that "[i]n so far as any liability under the Convention is or may be incurred, it is liability incurred by the extraditing Contracting State by reason of its having taken action, which has a direct consequence the exposure of an individual to proscribed ill-treatment". The ECtHR's *Narsi v France* decision further emphasises this point. Application No. 19465/92 (13 July 1995).

204 ECtHR, *N. v United Kingdom*, Application No. 26565/05 (27 May 2008).

Court for focusing on the economic effects – a balancing exercise typical to the EHCR's qualified rights, which allow interference in accordance with the law – rather than applying the standard approach to Article 3.[205]

The progressive understanding of risk of ill treatment and its linkage with general living conditions was recently reinforced in *MSS v Belgium and Greece*.[206] In *MSS*, the applicant travelled from Afghanistan to Belgium via Greece, where his fingerprints were taken. In accordance with the Dublin Regulation[207] (which allocates state responsibility for the assessment of asylum applications according to a list of objective criteria and prevents applicants from "asylum shopping"), Belgium opted to return the applicant to Greece. His return, together with his subsequent treatment, formed the basis for his application.

The Court categorically condemned Belgium for returning the applicant to Greece thereby exposing him to "extreme material poverty" in a country "unable to cater for his most basic needs: food, hygiene and a place to live", especially "given the particular state of insecurity and vulnerability in which asylum seekers are known to live in Greece".[208] The Court held that Belgium violated Article 3 ECHR, but also noted that

> Article 3 cannot be interpreted as obliging the High Contracting Parties to provide everyone within their jurisdiction with a home (. . .) [n]or does Article 3 entail any general obligation to give refugees financial assistance to enable them to maintain a certain standard of living.[209]

However, members of the Court characterised the situation in Greece as "particularly serious"[210] and found that Belgium should not have returned the applicant to a country unable to provide decent material and human conditions to asylum seekers, which entered into positive law with the Greek legislation when they transposed the Reception Directive.[211] The Court held that Greece

205 *See* Battjes, H. (2009) "In Search of a Fair Balance: The Absolute Character of the Prohibition of Refoulement under Article 3 Reassessed" 22 Leiden Journal of International Law 3 pp. 583–621; Clayton, G. (2008) "Article 3 Jurisprudence: *N. v United Kingdom*: Not a Truly Exceptional Case?" 14 Immigration Law Digest 3 pp. 6–14.

206 ECtHR, *MSS v Belgium and Greece* (MSS), Application No. 30696/09 (21 January 2011).

207 Council of the European Union (2003) "Council Regulation (EC) No 343/2003 Establishing the Criteria and Mechanisms for Determining the Member State Responsible for Examining and Asylum Application Lodged in One of the Member States by a Thrid-Country National" (18 February).

208 *Ibid.* paras. 252, 254, 259.

209 *Ibid.* para. 249.

210 *Ibid.* para. 254.

211 Council of the European Union (2003) "Council Directive Laying Down Minimum Standards for the Reception of Asylum Seekers" 2003/9/EC (27 January). The Recital of Directives (5) and (6) states its respect for fundamental rights, particularly those recognised by the EU Charter of Fundamental Rights. It also states that, with respect to the treatment of persons within the scope of this Directive, member states are bound by

breached this Directive, which sets the minimum standards for receiving asylum seekers in the EU.[212] The case is a reminder of the importance of human rights protection in the EU supranational legal order.

Importantly, the judiciary emphasises the applicant's vulnerability as an asylum seeker:

> [t]he Court attaches considerable importance to the applicant's status as an asylum seeker and, as such, a member of a particularly underprivileged and vulnerable population group in need of special protection. (. . .) It notes the existence of a broad consensus at the international and European level concerning this need for special protection.[213]

Interestingly, the Court expresses a holistic understanding of the vulnerability of asylum seekers, in line with the recognised vulnerability of EDPs.[214]

The Court's justifications could arguably also apply to individuals with slim prospects of returning to their country of origin due to desertification, sea level rise, or disasters. Logically, returning them to their countries would expose them to extreme material poverty, thus violating Article 3 ECHR. Nevertheless, EDPs would need to show substantial grounds for believing they would be exposed to a "situation of serious deprivation or want incompatible with human dignity".[215]

The following elements can be gleaned from the case law and are relevant in considering whether a host state has breached Article 3[216] and its corresponding *non-refoulement* obligation for EDPs: 1) the state of origin is unable or unwilling to address desertification, sea level rise, or the outcome of a disaster and the applicant is dependent on the state for the resolution; 2) the applicant is faced with a situation of serious deprivation or want (such as food, hygiene, and shelter) that is incompatible with human dignity;[217] or 3) the applicant has

---

obligations under instruments of international law to which they are party and which prohibit discrimination.

212 ECtHR *MSS Op. Cit.* para. 263.

213 *Ibid.* para. 251.

214 *Ibid. See* Partly Concurring and Partly Dissenting Opinion of Judge Sajó pp. 104–105. "Asylum seekers are far from being homogeneous, if such group exists at all. (. . .) [But] [a]sylum-seekers are generally at least *somewhat* vulnerable because of their past experiences and the fact that they live in a new and different environment; more importantly, the uncertainty about their future can make them vulnerable" (emphasis added).

215 ECtHR, *MSS Op. Cit.* para. 253.

216 *See* Clayton, G. (2011) "Asylum Seekers in Europe: *M.S.S. v Belgium and Greece*" 11 Human Rights Law Review 4 p. 769, pp. 758–773.

217 *See* Schachter (1983) *Op. Cit.* pp. 851–852. Importantly, Schachter states: "human dignity involves a complex notion of the individual. It includes recognition of a distinct personal identity, reflecting individual autonomy and responsibility. It also embraces a recognition that the individual self is a part of larger collectivities and that they, too, must be considered in the meaning of the inherent dignity of the person".

pre-existing vulnerability. Individuals may have pre-existing vulnerability if they come from an identified vulnerable area; if they possess the unique characteristics of a person or group; or based on their circumstances, including the context and their capacity to resist and/or recover from environmental hazards.

In *Sufi and Elmi v United Kingdom*,[218] the Court applied the principles from *MSS* regarding "humanitarian crises", finding that if the applicants were returned to Somalian asylum camps they would be exposed to risky conditions (overcrowded shelters and limited water and sanitation facilities), contrary to Article 3.[219] Specifically, the Court noted that

> the conditions both in Afgooye Corridor and in Ddaab camps are sufficiently dire to amount to treatment reaching the threshold of Article 3 of the Convention. IDPs in the Afgooye Corridor have very limited access to food and water, and shelter appears to be an emerging problem as landlords seek to exploit their predicament for profit. Although humanitarian assistance is available in the Dadaab camps, due to extreme overcrowding access to shelter, water and sanitation facilities is extremely limited. The inhabitants of both camps are vulnerable to violent crime, exploitation abuse and forcible recruitment. Moreover, the refugees living in – or, indeed, trying to get to the Dadaab camps – are also at risk of *refoulement* by the Kenyan authorities. Finally, the Court notes that the inhabitants of both camps have very little prospect of their situation improving within a reasonable timeframe.

Furthermore, the Court highlighted that although the crisis (the conflict) is primarily due to the parties' own actions, drought has contributed to the humanitarian crises.[220] It also acknowledged that environmental factors contributed to displacement and instability within the region. For example, many assert the Darfur conflict resulted, at least partly, from climate change. In the mid-1980s, drought and famine killed more than one million people and laid waste to livestock herds, leading pastoralists and farmers to fight over land. Subsequently, "a string of conflicts broke out as both sides armed themselves, and

218 ECtHR *Sufi*, Applications Nos. 8319/07 and 11449/07 (28 June 2011).
219 *Ibid.* para. 291.
220 *Ibid.* paras. 194, 195 ("On 3 February 2011 the Guardian reported that Somalia was once again facing a malnutrition crisis. An estimated 2.4 million people – about a third of Somalia's population – required humanitarian aid after the failure of recent rains and *drought had overtaken insecurity as the leading cause of displacement.* In fact, *it was reported that as a consequence of the drought, the exodus from conflict-racked Mogadishu in recent years had been reversed, with thousands of people now leaving the countryside for the capital in search of food and water.* (. . .) [o]n 17 February 2011 the U.N. News Centre reported *that severe drought in Somalia was once again exacerbating the humanitarian crisis* with more people becoming internally displaced and others moving into refugee camps across the border in Kenya. Malnutrition rates among children, already above emergency levels in Somalia, had risen, and an estimated 2.4 million people – 32 per cent of the country's 7.2 million people – were in need of relief aid") (emphasis added).

those conflicts created the template for today's disaster".[221] The spread of the conflict in Darfur states, as well as in the neighbouring states of Chad and the Central African Republic, exemplifies how environmental degradation can increase conflict and that affected countries and their neighbours are sometimes unable to provide adequate protection for those environmentally displaced.[222]

Neither *Sufi* nor *MSS* clarifies "whether the claimant must be able to point to a risk of ill treatment on return, or whether return to circumstances where she is unable to cater for her basic needs and there is no prospect of her situation improving within a reasonable timeframe would suffice".[223] However, a more progressive understanding of protection from *refoulement* under Article 3 merits consideration of all three aforementioned elements in *MSS* if an individual faces a serious want and is unable to obtain food or shelter in situations of desertification, sea level rise, or disasters which are incompatible with his or her human dignity. Undoubtedly, host states may resist this interpretation and require substantial evidence of the likely fate of the applicant, but as the effects of environmental change become more visible, with some leading to conflict situations,[224] removal in these circumstances could likely constitute a violation of Article 3.

In summary, Colin Harvey states:

> The ECtHR understands the nature of the responsibilities of states, it acknowledges that they enjoy the collective right in international law to regulate migration, but underlines in the case law that this must all be undertaken within the constraints of legality. On this point, it is for the court to determine, in dialogue with others, the interpretative horizons of human rights.[225]

(iv) Seeking the added protection value of Article 15(c)

The possible protection of EDPs flowing from Article 15(c) of the QD is noteworthy because, in this case, the extension of protection is unconcerned with the cause of the armed conflict and therefore potentially applicable to environmental-related conflict[226] (where changes in the environment impact the lack of

221 Borger, J. (2007) "Scorched" The Guardian (28 April) *available from:* www.theguardian.com/environment/2007/apr/28/sudan.climatechange [accessed 17 August 2018].

222 Moberg, K. (2009) "Extending Refugee Definitions to Cover Environmentally Displaced Persons Displaces Necessary Protection" 94 Iowa Law Review p. 1134, pp. 1107–1136.

223 Scott (2014) *Op. Cit.* p. 416.

224 *See generally,* Nordås, R. & Gleditsh, P. (2014) "Chapter 3 Climate Change and Conflict" in S. Hartard & W. Liebert (eds.) "Competition and Conflicts on Resource Use" Natural Resource Management and Policy (Vol. 46) pp. 21–38.

225 Harvey, C. (2013) "Is Humanity Enough? Refugees, Asylum Seekers and the Rights Regime" in S. Juss & C. Harvey (eds.) "Contemporary Issues in Refugee Law" (Edward Elgar) p. 81.

226 *See* Edwards, A. (2012) "Climate Change and Refugee Law" in R. Rayfuse & S. Scott (eds.) "International Law in the Era of Climate Change" (Edward Elgar Publishing) pp. 72, pp. 58–83 (noting that although the provision would not normally cover sporadic

natural resources or means of subsistence, resulting in armed conflict). This has led, however, to divergences resulting from the application of subsidiary protection against a "serious and individual threat to a civilian's life or person by reason of indiscriminate violence in situations of international or internal armed conflict" since member states interpret circumstances differently.[227]

Hemme Battjes has advanced the idea that Article 15(c) has a wider scope than Article 15(b). In contrast to Article 15(b), which requires substantial grounds for believing that a person would face a real risk of ill treatment (inhuman or degrading ill treatment or punishment), Article 15(c) only requires that the individual face "a threat" of ill treatment.[228] Even if the "threat" prerequisite is less rigorous in this case, one must overcome another hurdle, as the "threat" under Article 15(c) must amount to a "serious and individual threat". Because of this, member states tend to narrow the scope of the provision, only accepting applicants who are personally targeted, in line with the restrictive approach of Recital 35 of the Recast QD.[229] UNHCR has criticised this, as it renders illusory the protection offered by the QD (and contradictory to Article 15(c) which provides protection from serious harm caused by "indiscriminate violence"). "However, that would appear to ignore that the proposition advanced by this recital [35] is qualified by the word 'normally:' to say that widely shared risks do not 'normally' create an individual threat must surely leave open the possibility that they 'abnormally' create such a threat".[230]

ELGAFAJI AND THE IMPORTANCE OF CONTEXT

In the first decision addressing subsidiary protection, *Elgafaji v Staatssecretaris van Justitie*,[231] the CJEU reasoned that Article 15(c) "covers a more general risk

armed conflict events, defining "armed conflict" with an overly strict link to humanitarian law would defeat the protection purpose of the provision.

227 *See* European Council on Refugees and Exiles (2010) "Comments on the European Commission Proposal to Recast the Qualification Directive" *Op. Cit.* p. 15. *See also* Garlic, M. (2007) "UNHCR and the Implementation of the EC Qualification Directive" in K. Zwan (ed.) "The Qualification Directive: Central Themes, Problem Issues, and Implementation in Selected Member States" (Wolf Legal Publishers 2007) p. 62.

228 Battjes, H. (2006) "European Asylum Law and International Law" (Martinus Nijhoff Publishers) pp. 239, 240.

229 Directive 2004/83/EC *Op. Cit.* para. 26 and recast Directive 2011/95/EU *Op. Cit.* para. 35 reads: "[r]isks to which a population is generally exposed to do normally not create in themselves an individual threat which would qualify as serious harm".

230 Storey, H. (2008) "EU Refugee Qualification Directive: A Brave New World?" 20 International Journal of Refugee Law 1 p. 34, pp. 1–49.

231 CJEU, Case C-465/07 Grand Chamber, *Elgafaji v Staatssecretaris van Justitie* (17 February 2009). Mr. and Mrs Elgafaji, Iraqi nationals, submitted applications for temporary residence permits in the Netherlands, together with evidence supporting the real risk to which they would be exposed if they were returned to Iraq. They stated, *inter alia*, that Mr Elgafaji, who is a Shiite Muslim, had worked for a British firm providing security for personnel transport between Baghdad airport and the "green" zone. Mr Elgafaji's uncle,

of harm" in comparison to Article 15(b). Thus, the threat need not be particular to the victim because of his personal circumstances (e.g. membership in a particular group), but the term *individual* denotes the likelihood of the risk/threat.

Article 15(c) refers to threat to life or person rather than to a particular act of violence, covering a broader risk of harm than paragraph (b) of the provision. It relates to risk in a particular context – that is, the situation of armed conflict or as a result of systematic or generalised violation of their human rights. Furthermore, the violence mentioned is an "indiscriminate one", "a term which implies that it may extend to people irrespective of their personal circumstances".[232] Therefore, the Court's decision sustains a link between the level of indiscriminate violence typifying the armed conflict and the existence of "substantial grounds for believing that a civilian's return to his country would face *solely on the account of his presence* a real risk of being subject to the serious threat mentioned by Article 15(c)".[233] The Court clarified, though, that this would represent an "exceptional situation".[234]

Interestingly, and relevant for EDPs, the applicant need not demonstrate that the threat to life is a targeted one due to factors specific to that applicant. Rather, he or she need only show that the *overall context* in the country of origin is so exceptionally severe as to qualify for subsidiary protection.[235] The Court also held that "the geographical scope of the situation of indiscriminate violence and the actual destination of the applicant in the event he is returned to the relevant country, (. . .) may be taken into account".[236] This interpretation is commendable, because it rejects individualisation and protects the applicant from serious risks that are situational, in full compliance with both international refugee law and

employed by the same firm, had been killed by militia. A short time later, a letter threatening "death to collaborators" was fixed to the door of the Elgafajis' residence. However, the Dutch authorities refused to grant them temporary residence permits, concluding they had not proved the circumstances on which they were relying and, therefore, had not established the real risk of serious and individual threat to which they claimed to be exposed in their country of origin. *See also* CJEU C-71/11 and C-99/11, *Germany v Y. and Z.* (5 September 2012); CJEU, Case C-277/11, *M.M. v Minister for Justice, Equality and Law Reform, Ireland, Attorney General* (22 November 2012); Case C-364/11, *Mostafa Abed El Karem El Kott, Chadi Amin A Radi, Hazem Kamel Ismail v Bevandorlasi es Allampolgarsagi Hivatal (BAH)* (19 December 2012).

232 CJEU, Case C-465/07, *Elgafaji Op. Cit.* para. 34.

233 *Ibid.* para. 35 (emphasis added). The CJEU also affirmed that "the more the applicant is able to show that he is specifically affected by reason of factors particular to his own circumstances the lower level of individual violence required for him to be eligible for subsidiary protection".

234 *Ibid.* para. 37.

235 *Ibid.* para. 43.

236 *Ibid.* paras. 40, 35.

human rights law[237] as well as the UNHCR's earlier recommendation to delete the term "individual" from Article 15(c) of the Directive.[238]

It is important to note that before the final grand chamber judgement, in an opinion given the previous year, Advocate General Poiares Maduro notably discussed the importance of ECHR in the community case law[239] and called the interpretation by the Strasbourg Court a "dynamic interpretation which is always changing".[240] He also emphasised the relevance of the Charter of Fundamental Rights[241] (Article 53(3)) and the leeway for "extensive protection" under EU law.[242]

The rationale of the judgement and the complementary interaction between both judicial orders (ECtHR and CJEU), emphasise a more dynamic interpretation of human rights, leading to the reasonable conclusion that subsidiary protection should not be limited to situations of international or internal armed conflict but could also cover situations of generalised violence and systematic human rights violations not qualifying as armed conflicts under international humanitarian law.[243] This can include, for example, situations of sexual violence towards women and children in a disaster's aftermath.[244]

Subsuming EDPs to the protection offered under Article 15(c) forces states to consider human rights, the context, and the geographical reach of the situation when evaluating an application for subsidiary protection. This collective consideration demonstrates that the international community cannot rely simply on states' discretion to meet the protection needs of individuals. Granting subsidiary protection goes beyond the threshold of mere solidarity into effective obligations of host states.

(v) "Internal flight alternative": narrowing the chances of rotection?

Upon examination, Article 8 of the QD seems to narrow subsidiary protection, noting that it is unavailable if a person is able to seek refuge in another part of

237 Notably, since the EctHR's judgement in *Salah Sheek v The Netherlands*, Application No. 1948/04 (11 January 2007), the ECtHR no longer requires an individual to be particularly targeted. *See also* ECtHR, *N. v United Kingdom*, Application No. 25904/07 (17 July 2008); ECtHR, *Sufi*, Application No. 8319/07 and 1149/07 (28 June 2011).

238 The UNHCR also recommended deleting the Recital 26 (now Recital 35 of the Recast QD).

239 CJEU, Case C-465/07, *Elgafaji Opinion of AG Poiares Maduro* (9 September 2008) ECR I-00921 para. 22.

240 *Ibid.* para. 20.

241 *Ibid.* para. 21.

242 *Ibid.* para. 23.

243 *See* ECRE (2010) "Comments on the Recast Qualification Directive" *Op. Cit.* p. 17.

244 *See* Alston, M. (2015) "Women and Climate Change" (Routledge) pp. 155–156; Azad, A., Hossain, K. & Nasreen, M. (2013) "Flood-Induced Vulnerabilities and Problems Encountered by Women in Northern Bangladesh" 4 International Journal of Disaster Risk Science 4 pp. 190–199; Sapir, D. G. (1993) "Natural and Man-Made Disasters: The Vulnerability of Women-Headed Households and Children without Families" 46 World Health Statistics Quarterly Rapport Trimestriel de Statistiques Sanitaires Mondiales 4 pp. 227–233.

his or her country (where there is no well-founded fear of being persecuted or no risk of suffering serious harm) and can reasonably be expected to stay in that region,[245] a concept known as "internal flight alternative". Rather than offering legal protection, the Directive acts more as a legal deterrent to keep an individual from seeking lawful protection in another country, obscuring the very essence of international protection. For EDPs who could avail themselves of protection in their own countries, their applications for subsidiary protection might be rejected. In practical terms, EDPs would be protected only if their country were entirely devastated by an environmental disaster or disappeared over time (in the case of small island states). Seemingly, people forced to leave by drought, despite the threat to their right to life, would not be protected if they could seek refuge in another part of the country.

This view would protect some while neglecting others equally at risk. The risk could be twofold: of an immediate nature and of a gradual nature. Risk of an immediate nature may include lack of sufficient basic services, such as shelter, food, education, or health. Risk of a gradual nature may include the predicted risk of climate or other environmental dangers and degradation and the potential resulting humanitarian crises or conflicts. In such a situation, a threat against the right to life (a right from which no derogation is allowed) is evidently imminent. Under such conditions, EDPs would arguably be unable to draw on protection from their country of origin.

Importantly, Article 8 of the QD directs member states to determine, as part of their assessment, whether the applicant can reasonably be expected to stay in that part of the country by considering circumstances prevailing in the region and the applicant's personal circumstances. This so-called reasonableness test, which has been adopted by the vast majority of jurisdictions, requires an assessment of the applicant's risk of future persecution and whether return would expose him or her to a real risk of serious harm.[246] However, the concept of reasonableness can be difficult to apply because of the typically disparate conditions of the country of origin and the host country. "These differences go to the core of global inequities resulting from instability and conflict, economic

245 Article 8 of the Qualification Directive *Op. Cit.* reads: "1. As part of the assessment of the application for international protection, Member States may determine that an applicant is not in need of international protection if in a part of the country of origin there is no well-founded fear of being persecuted or no real risk of suffering serious harm and the applicant can reasonably be expected to stay in that part of the country. 2. In examining whether a part of the country of origin is in accordance with paragraph 1, Member States shall at the time of taking the decision on the application have regard to the general circumstances prevailing in that part of the country and to the personal circumstances of the applicant. 3. Paragraph 1 may apply notwithstanding technical obstacles to return to the country of origin".

246 Including within EU member state countries.

inequalities, the imperfect realization of human rights norms, and varying cultural expectations in different parts of the world".[247]

The literature supports a "human rights approach to reasonableness"[248] of return: "whether meaningful protection is otherwise available in that area" and if it is practically sustainable economically and socially. Accordingly, the suitable benchmark should be "whether the claimant's basic civil, political and socio-economic human rights, as expressed in the Refugee Convention and other major human rights instruments would be protected there".[249] This theory is supported by the Austrian Federal Constitutional Court's Bundesverfassungsgericht (Österreich) decision. There, the Court overruled the asylum tribunal's ruling that a rejected asylum seeker could be sent back to his native Pakistan. The Court held that "the Tribunal had failed to examine under Article 3 ECHR whether the person concerned would have to go back to areas affected by the 2010 floods or would have been able to find a reasonable location alternative. Thus, while not determining the scope of Article 3 ECHR in cases of return to disaster-affected areas, the Constitutional court affirmed, albeit without further reasoning, the applicability, in principle, of the prohibition of inhumane treatment to such returns".[250] Thus, as previously highlighted, human rights norms are an important yardstick in any assessment of reasonableness, leaving room to consolidate the current protection regime to apply to EDPs.

(vi) The Recast Qualification Directive: a missed opportunity for the protection of EDPs

Despite inherent limitations, EDPs could arguably benefit from subsidiary protection under the QD if one utilises human rights law as a guide and a more dynamic interpretation methodology. An amendment to Article 15 of the Directive that adds environmental disasters as a basis for subsidiary protection would provide legal clarity. Interestingly, some countries, including Cyprus, Finland, and Sweden, already offer protection on the grounds of environmental disasters, thereby demonstrating the increasing trend to consolidate protection for EDPs. Others, including Denmark (even if not bound by the QD), have used their discretionary powers to grant humanitarian protection to people who could not return to their country due to extreme weather events.[251] See the table below.

247 Türk, V. & Nicholson, F. (2003) "Refugee Protection in International Law: An Overall Perspective" in E. Feller, V. Türk & F. Nicholson (eds.) "Refugee Protection in International Law an Overall Perspective" (Cambridge University Press) p. 27.

248 Kelley, N. (2002) "Internal Flight/Relocation/Protection Alternative: Is it Reasonable?" 14 International Journal of Refugee Law 1 p. 36, pp. 4–44.

249 *Ibid.*

250 Kälin, W. & Schrepfer, N. (2012) "Protecting People Crossing Borders in the Context of Climate Change: Normative Gaps and Possible Approaches" (UNHCR, Division of International Protection) PPLA/2012/01, (February 2012) p. 36. The authors refer to the Bundesverfassungsgericht (Österreich) decision U84/11 (19 September 2011).

251 *See* Kolmannskog & Myrstad (2009) *Op. Cit.* p. 324.

Legal national provisions addressing environmental displacement

Cyprus

Article 29(4) of the Refugee Law of 2000 states:[252]

> [n]o refugee or a person with subsidiary protection status shall be deported to any country where his life or freedom will be endangered or he will be in danger of being subjected to torture or inhuman or degrading treatment or punishment or persecution for reasons of sex, race, religion, nationality membership of a particular group or political opinion or because of armed conflict or ***environmental destruction***
>
> (emphasis added).

Finland

Chapter 6 Section 88a (1) of the Aliens Act 301/2004 grants humanitarian protection if:[253]

> [a]n alien residing in Finland is issued with a residence permit on the basis of humanitarian protection, if there are no grounds under section 87 or 88 for granting asylum or providing subsidiary protection, but he or she cannot return to his or her country of origin or country of formal habitual residence as a result of an ***environmental catastrophe*** or a bad security situation which may be due to an international or internal armed conflict or poor human rights situation
>
> (emphasis added).

Sweden

Chapter 4 Section 2 (3) of the Aliens Act 2005 provides:[254]

> [i]n this Act "a person otherwise in need of protection" is an alien who in cases other than those referred to in Section 1 [Refugee based grounds] is outside the country of the alien's nationality, as he or she is unable to return to the country of origin because of an ***environmental disaster***
>
> (emphasis added).

252 *See* Cyprus (2000) "The Refugee Law of 2000: a Law to Provide for the Recognition of Refugees and for the Better Implementation of the Convention relating to the Status of Refugees" Article 29 (4). However, Article 3(1) clarifies that this protection is only available to persons who have already been granted refugee status or humanitarian protection.

253 Finnish Aliens Act 301/2004 (amendments up to 458/2009 included) (30 April 2004).

254 Swedish Aliens Act 2005/716 (amendments up to and including Swedish Code of Statutes 2006:220) (29 September 2005).

These bottom-up examples show the potential to increase protection for EDPs, in line with the EU's consistency imperative and the harmonisation objectives of EU asylum policy in general and the QD in particular.

With the EU Treaty now authorising the EU to harmonise the asylum system (Article 78 TFEU), the recast QD presented a way to create a "uniform status" for beneficiaries of international protection that was "valid throughout the Union"[255] and served "the interest of clarity"[256] as it addressed the continuing "disparities" between member states "concerning the grant of protection and the forms that protection takes".[257] The recast Directive aimed not only to underline the principles of the previous Directive but to concomitantly achieve a "higher level of approximation of the rules on the recognition and content of international protection on the basis of higher standards".[258]

As to the content of international protection, the recast QD takes a positive step by providing an approximation of substantive rights of refugees and beneficiaries to subsidiary protection (including family unity,[259] access to employment,[260] access to accommodation,[261] better standards for vulnerable persons,[262] and healthcare).[263] Importantly, Article 7(2) requires protection to be "effective and of a non-temporary nature". Yet, the question still exists as to whether allowing member states to continue differentiating between these two protection statuses (e.g. with regards to residence permit[264] and access to social welfare[265] and integration facilities)[266] comports with the principles of equality and non-discrimination guaranteed under the Charter of Fundamental

255 Article 78 TFEU.
256 Qualification Directive *Op. Cit.* Recital 9.
257 *Ibid.* Recitals 1, 8.
258 *Ibid.* Recital 10.
259 *Ibid.* Article 23.
260 *Ibid.* Recitals 40, 42, Article 26.
261 *Ibid.* Article 32.
262 *Ibid.* Article 20(3) (referring to vulnerable groups, such as minors, unaccompanied minors, disabled people, elderly people, pregnant women, single parents with minor children, victims of human trafficking, persons with mental disorders and persons who have been subjected to torture, rape or other serious forms of psychological, physical, or sexual violence); Recitals 18, 19, 28, 38 and Articles 20(5), 31 (relating to the "best interests of the child"); Recital 20, Article 4(3) (c), Article 9(2) (f) and Article 10(1) (d) (containing gender-specific provisions).
263 *Ibid.* Recitals 40, 46, and Article 30.
264 Qualification Directive *Op. Cit.* Article 24 (1) (granting refugees a residence permit valid for at least three years and renewable); Article 24(2) (granting beneficiaries of subsidiary protection and their family members a renewable residence permit valid for at least one year and at least two years for renewal). Notably, beneficiaries of subsidiary protection can now obtain long-term residence permit status under Directive 2011/51 "amending Council Directive 2003/109/EC to extend its scope to beneficiaries of international protection" (11 May 2011), which cannot be lost due to cessation of the underlying protection status.
265 *Ibid.* Recital 45, Article 29.
266 *Ibid.* Recitals 40,41, 47, 48 and Article 34.

Rights[267] and overall international human rights commitments of the European Union and member states.[268]

The recast QD did not amend the rules on granting and revoking status categories despite criticisms of member states' continuous narrow interpretation of Article 15.[269] The recast QD was a missed opportunity to further enlarge the scope of subsidiary protection, which could have included EDPs and would have been consistent with the opinion of the European Economic and Social Committee finding "a need to agree on a way of expanding the range of people eligible for international protection: women suffering abuse, vulnerable people, environmental refugees, etc."[270] Importantly, it could have built on the European Parliament's earlier suggestion for a "step 2 of a Common European Asylum Policy".[271]

Discretion remains with member states to grant subsidiary protection based on humanitarian grounds (for human rights violations other than the right to life or to physical integrity) at the same level the Directive recognises for selective categories.[272] This discretion to introduce or retain more favourable human rights-based standards for a person eligible for subsidiary protection can undermine aspired-to harmonisation of the European Asylum Policy system and create wider protection gaps.

267 Articles 20 and 21 of the Charter of Fundamental Rights of the European Union (18 December 2000) OJ C364/1.

268 *Ibid.* But *see* Recital 39 ("While responding to the call of the Stockholm Programme for the establishment of a uniform status for refugees or for persons eligible for subsidiary protection, and with the *exception of derogations which are necessary and objectively justified*, beneficiaries of subsidiary protection status *should be granted the same rights and benefits* as those enjoyed by refugees under this Directive, and *should be subject to the same conditions of eligibility*") (emphasis added).

269 *See generally,* European Council on Refugees and Exiles (2010) "Comments on the European Commission's Proposal to recast the Qualification Directive" *Op. Cit.* and UNHCR (2010) "Comments on the European Commission's Proposal to Recast the Qualification Directive" *Op. Cit.* The European Commission initially intended to propose amendments to Article 15 due to wide divergences in interpretation between member states (*see* policy plan on asylum COM (2008) 360 17 June 2008) but ultimately did not, declaring that the *Elgafaji* judgement provided the necessary interpretation (*see* Recast Proposal, Explanatory Memorandum).

270 European Economic and Social Committee Opinion (2009) "On the Proposal for a Directive of the European Parliament and of the Council on Minimum Standards on Procedures in Member States for Granting and Withdrawing International Protection (Recast)" COM (2009) 554 Final – 2009/0165 (COD) SOC 369 Rapporteur: Antonello Pezzini (28 April).

271 European Parliament (2003) COM (2001) 510 – C5–0573/2001–2001/0207(CNS) Committee on Citizens' Freedoms and Rights, Justice and Home Affairs Rapporteur: Jean Lambert *Op. Cit.* p. 25.

272 *See* European Council on Refugees and Exiles (2008) "The Impact of the EU Qualification Directive on International Protection" (October) *available from:* www.ecre.org/wp-content/uploads/2016/07/ECRE-The-Impact-of-the-EU-Qualification-Directive-on-International-Protection_October-2008.pdf [accessed 17 august 2018].

Concomitantly, it can help identify other categories needing international protection, alerting states to take action. The eligibility criteria are especially important to beneficiaries because subsidiary protection is usually more permanent than the humanitarian protection status.[273]

However, hope still remains for EDPs since the recast QD requires evaluation of its implementation at regular intervals, with particular attention given to the evolution of member states' international obligations.[274]

5.3.2 *Prospective interpretation under the Qualification Directive to solidify protection of EDPs*

While reliance on human rights law as a means for protection of EDPs is promising, it is far from being widely accepted. The QD inherently limits its application to EDPs, particularly under Articles 8 and 15 and, pragmatically, a system of individual status determination may be unable to cope with potentially vast movements of persons resulting from environmental disasters. Nevertheless, plenty of room exists to expand interpretation and harmonisation to consolidate protection towards EDPs utilising human rights instruments and member states' legislative practices. Promoting a bottom-up consistency with existing legislative practices could open the door for wider consolidation of protection for EDPs.

While the recast QD was a missed opportunity to provide protection for EDPs, the EU legal political sphere notably continues to highlight the need to bridge the EDP protection gap. For example, the European Commission's staff working document on climate change, environmental degradation, and migration notes the QD's failure to include environmental degradation or climate change amongst the types of serious harm but also admits that some EU member states "have included in their legislation on refugee-type protection provisions concerning those who may be unable to return home owing to a natural disaster".[275]

While states tend to extend only the minimal protection obligations, jurisprudence is increasingly enlarging the scope of protection. The cross-fertilisation between the two legal orders within European human rights law – the ECHR and the European Union – presents opportunities to solidify protection for environmental displacement. Thus, nothing prevents one from purposively reading Article 15(b) and (c) of the QD to ensure wider conformity with case law

273 Nykänen, E. (2012) "On the Lines of Demarcation and their Significance: The Categories of Complementary Protection under the Finnish Aliens Act" 30 Nordic Journal of Human Rights 2 p. 173, pp. 148–173. Under Finnish legislation, those receiving subsidiary protection receive a first residence permit valid for four years, while beneficiaries of humanitarian protection receive a first residence permit valid for only one year.

274 Qualification Directive *Op. Cit.* Recital 48 and Article 38(2) (stating that the European Commission shall report to the European Parliament and the Council on the application of this Directive at least every five years).

275 European Commission SWD (2013) 138 Final *Op. Cit.* p. 18.

and protect EDPs. The developing jurisprudence on socio-economic deprivation and the increasing judicial recognition of the contribution of environmental factors (such as drought or floods) to the multicausality of a region's displacement and instability implies that states should apply a human rights approach to reasonableness of return to disaster-affected areas. The combined effects of the ECtHR and ECJ judgements should serve, therefore, as a "reference force" for the evolution and consolidation of EDP protection.

5.3.3 Temporary protection under the EU Temporary Protection Directive

(i) Rationale

In Europe, the Temporary Protection Directive (TPD) presented another response to the need for temporary protection (TP) of people displaced from a region by sudden disasters or crises.[276] "Temporary Protection must be understood as a complementary system to the 'European arrangements of asylum' devised to make it work correctly in emergency situations that demanded a singular regulatory treatment; a suitable regulation which could grasp the phenomenon completely".[277] This exceptional emergency protection mechanism was created in the aftermath of the Yugoslavian wars of the 1990s and especially designed for sudden mass influx situations from third countries (e.g. armed conflict, endemic violence, or generalised human rights violations)[278] TP is not meant to replace asylum but rather to offer immediate humanitarian protection to large groups of people forced to flee their homes.

TPD is the first piece of asylum legislation launched under the Amsterdam Treaty.[279] It aims at providing protection to those who cannot return to their

276 Council of the European Union (2001) "Council Directive on Minimum Standards for Giving Temporary Protection in the Event of a Mass Influx of Displaced Persons and on Measures Promoting a Balance of Efforts between Member States in Receiving Such Persons and Bearing the Consequences Thereof" 2001/55/EC (20 July). Member states had until 31 December 2002 to transpose it into their national legislation (with the exception of Denmark and Ireland, which have opted out).

277 Arenas, N. (2005) "The Concept of 'Mass Influx of Displaced Persons' in the European Directive Establishing the Temporary Protection System" 7 European Journal of Migration and Law p. 438, pp. 435–450.

278 *See generally*, Fitzpatrick, J. (2000) "Temporary Protection of Refugees: Elements of a Formalised Regime" 94 American Journal of International Law pp. 279–306.

279 Consolidated Version of the Treaty of the European Union (Treaty of Amsterdam) (2 October 1997) Article 63 ("The Council, acting in accordance with the procedure referred to in Article 67, shall, within a period of five years after the entry into force of the Treaty of Amsterdam, adopt measures on refugees and displaced persons within the following areas: 2. (a) minimum standards for giving temporary protection to displaced persons from third countries who cannot return to their country of origin and for persons who otherwise need international protection").

country of origin while at the same time promoting balanced burden-sharing between member states. TP is based on four foundational pillars: admission to safety, respect for human rights, protection against *refoulement*, and safe return to the country of origin when conditions permit.[280]

(ii) Travaux preparatoires*: inclusion and exclusion of EDPs as a category of persons in need of protection*

The aftermath of the Yugoslavia crisis created a sentiment of urgency in Europe to adopt legislation that could replace the flawed ad hoc protection policies of the time and adopt a coordinated solution based on member state solidarity.[281] The TPD did not totally exclude from its initial scope temporary protection for people suffering the consequences of environmental disasters. Summarising the process of determining whether to include EDPs will assist in understanding its relevance as a potential measure of consolidation of protection and *inter alia* host states' obligations.

The process for adoption of a common regime and concerted action of TP started in 1997 with the European Commission's first proposal.[282] It envisaged a wide scope of protection that included mixed categories of people which could have included EDPs.[283] A year later, however, to balance between member states the consequences of receiving refugees and displaced persons (under the adages of "solidarity" and "burden sharing"), a second proposal restricted the application of TP.[284] The European Commission included precise categories in the document to ensure the TP's effectiveness.[285] The mechanism would, however, remain flexible to include others not designated. The words *in par-*

280 Executive Committee of the High Commissioner's Programme Conclusion (EXCOM) (1981) No. 22 (XXXII). *See also* (EXCOM) (1994) Conclusion No. 74 (XLV) paras. r, t.

281 *See* European Commission (1997) "Proposal to the Council for a Joint Action Based on Article K3 (2) (b) of the Treaty on the European Union Concerning Temporary Protection of Displaced Persons" COM (1997) 93 Final 97/0081 (CNS) (4 April) paras. 2, 5, 6, 7. *See also* Joly, D. (1998) "Temporary Protection Regime within the Framework of a New European Asylum Regime" 2 International Journal of Human Rights 3 pp. 49–76 (describing the circumstances bringing about temporary protection in Europe).

282 *Ibid.*

283 *Ibid.* Article 1 of the joint action. People in need of temporary protection included: "persons who have fled from areas affected by armed conflict and persistent violence; persons who have been or are under a serious risk of exposure to systematic or widespread human rights abuses, including those belonging to groups compelled to leave their homes by campaigns of ethnic or religious persecution; and persons who for other reasons specific to their personal situation are presumed to be in need of international protection". The last paragraph is the most encompassing, as it could have included protection for EDPs. The joint action was perhaps inspired by the Executive Committee of the High Commissioner's Programme Conclusion. *See* (EXCOM) (1994) Conclusion No. 74 (XLV) *Op. Cit.* (discussing concept of temporary protection).

284 European Commission (1998) "Modified Proposal of a Joint Action Concerning Temporary Protection of Displaced Persons" COM (1998) 372 Final (24 June).

285 *Ibid.* para. 7.

ticular meant, according to the European Commission, that the list of categories was non-exhaustive.[286]

In 2000, after years of discussion, the European Commission presented to the Council the proposal of a Directive on TP,[287] an outcome with its base in Article 63(2)(a) of the Treaty of Amsterdam.[288] During Council discussions in December 2000, member states discussed protection of EDPs and the Finnish delegation suggested enlarging the scope of temporary protection to include them. But their Belgian and Spanish counterparts barred the idea, stating that no international refugee instrument clearly cited these types of situations.[289]

Member states possibly overlooked the historical developments of TP in Africa and the Americas, which were often generous,[290] but also wanted to avoid commitments in these situations. Though Joan Fitzpatrick considered that "persons fleeing severe natural disasters that deprive them of access to physical safety within their state of origin" could be part of a formalised policy on temporary protection, she admitted that this inclusion may be controversial because it strays from the refugee law paradigm.[291] Nevertheless, the European Economic and Social Committee further suggested guiding tenants on TP for persons displaced by natural disasters,[292] which were advocated by civil society organisations.[293] During the discussions,[294] the Council of Europe also proposed the inclusion of a category covering persons fleeing from natural or ecological

286 *Ibid.*

287 European Commission (2000) "Proposal for a Council Directive on Minimum Standards for Giving Temporary Protection in the Event of a Mass Influx of Displaced Persons and on Measures Promoting a Balance of Efforts between Member States in Receiving Such Persons and Bearing the Consequences Thereof" COM (2000) 303 2000/0127 (CNS) (24 May). *See generally,* Sgro (2013) *Op. Cit.* pp. 302, 303.

288 Council of Europe Committee of Ministers (2000) "Recommendation (2000) 9 on Temporary Protection (and Explanatory Memorandum)" (3 May).

289 Council of the European Union (2000) "Outcomes of Proceedings of Working Party on Asylum (ASILE)" Doc 13958/00 (7 December).

290 Fitzpatrick (2000) *Op. Cit.* pp. 283, 298.

291 *Ibid.* p. 294.

292 European Economic and Social Committee (2001) "Opinion on the Proposal for a Council Directive on Minimum Standards for Giving Temporary Protection in the Event of a Mass Influx of Displaced Persons and on Measures Promoting a Balance of Efforts between Member States in Receiving Such Persons and Bearing the Consequences Thereof" (COM (2000) 303 Final – 2000/0127 CNS) SOC/046 (28 March) para. 2.3 (asserting there might be a case for a ***directive providing temporary reception and protection mechanisms for persons displaced by natural disasters***, though acknowledging that proposal only applies to people fleeing from political situations) (emphasis added).

293 Justice (2000) "Comments on Proposal for a Council Directive on Minimum Standards for Temporary Protection" (November) p. 2 (noting that the European Commission's Proposal for a Directive on TP was too restrictive unless the scope of protection mentioned within the document was merely indicative where situations of environmental disasters could be included).

294 Standing Committee Report (1997) "Temporary Protection of Persons Forced to Flee Their Countries" Rapporteur: Mrs. Elisabeth Arnold, Denmark, Liberal, Democratic and Reformers' Group, Doc 7889 (18 July).

disasters.[295] This climate of inclusion was, ultimately, not entirely abandoned but (perhaps) postponed until the final version of a flexible TP Directive.

(iii) Personal scope of temporary protection

UNSELECTIVE CHARACTER OF THE INFLUX

In contrast to the QD, the TPD allows more flexibility in granting temporary protection, which is particularly noticeable in its wording. Article 2(c) of the TPD states that "displaced persons"

> means third country nationals or stateless persons who have had to leave their country or region of origin, or have been evacuated, in particular in response to an appeal by an international organisation, and are unable to return in safe and durable conditions because of the situation prevailing in that country, who may fall within the scope of Article 1A of the Geneva Convention or other international or national instruments giving international protection in particular:
>
> (i) persons who have fled areas of armed conflict or endemic violence
> (ii) persons at serious risk of, or who have been the victims of, systematic or generalised violations of their human rights.

Arguably, the combined reading of Article 2(c) and Article 7(1)[296] demonstrates that the TP regime was designed to prioritise TP to "certain persons displaced in mass" while also not disregarding "additional categories of protected persons". Article 2(c) states that when an applicant's situation does not fall under the Refugee Convention, he or she may be protected under "other international or national instruments giving protection".[297] The TPD uses the wording *in particular* to reinforce this point, thus not totally excluding EDPs from its scope, whether or not so intended by member states in the *travaux preparatoires.* As Nuria Arenas notes, "temporary protection becomes the route to *expand* the categories of protected persons; therefore, it incorporates a new qualified immigration status 'the status of the temporary protection person', which is one of the most important consequences of the system". Plus, "the Directive does not expose a formula of

295 *See* Council of Europe Committee of Ministers (2000), "Recommendation (2000) 9 on Temporary Protection (and Explanatory Memorandum)" *Op. Cit.*

296 Council of the European Union Directive 2001/55/EC *Op. Cit.* Article 7 (1) reads: "[m]ember States may extend temporary protection as provided for in this Directive to additional categories of displaced persons over and above those to whom the Council Decision provided for in Article 5 applies, where they are displaced for the same reasons and from the same country or region of origin. They shall notify the Council and the Commission immediately".

297 In particular, the international obligations derived from Article 3 of ECHR, Article 7 of the ICCPR, and Article 3 of the CAT.

assessed causes. This means that *it is not exhaustive*; therefore, according to the evolution of consensus in the EU, the Council would be able to include other cases ."[298]

(iv) Seeking the added protection value of the Temporary Protection Directive

(IN)FLEXIBILITY OF TP FOR EDPS

The definition of *mass influx* is the chief concept that differentiates the TPD from the regular asylum system. Under the TPD, "mass influx" is generally defined as the arrival in the community of a large number of displaced persons (spontaneously or aided) who come from a specific country or geographical area and who cannot return to their country of origin (Article 2(d)). Though rather vague, the concept is original and relevant. The UNHCR's Executive Committee stated that, though the term is not defined, it can entail "some or all or the following characteristics: (i) considerable numbers of people arriving over an international border; (ii) rapid rate of arrival; (iii) inadequate absorption or response capacity in host States, particularly during the emergency; (iv) individual asylum procedures, where they exist, which are unable to deal with the assessment in large numbers".[299] According to the European Council of Refugees and Exiles (ECRE), the definition of an emergency requiring the activation of TP should relate to both the large scale of the outflow and the consequences of a sudden large-scale arrival of persons who cannot return. The ECRE adds that it is "not only a question of absolute numbers, but is relative to past experience of arrivals and the capacity of a local area to provide assistance and secure protection".[300]

Under the TPD, the concept of mass influx gains even more weight, as protection is only initiated when there is institutional cooperation in determining the existence of mass influx (Article 5(1)). The term excludes individuals who do not arrive under such conditions, even if in need of protection. Therefore, the system of TP does not create a new right to temporary asylum because it is not initiated by the individual applicant but rather is dependent on a qualified decision of the Council upon an initial proposal of the European Commission. The Council's discretionary power and the undetermined nature of the TPD's terms could put at risk the effectiveness of the TPD,[301] particularly side line protection for EDPs.

Using elliptical language still has merit, however, as TP expands protection to non-Convention refugees, entitling them to an immediate provisional status.

298 Arenas (2005) *Op. Cit.* pp. 445, 446.

299 Executive Committee UNHCR EXCOM (2004) "Conclusion on International Cooperation and Burden and Responsibility Sharing in Mass Influx Situations" para. a) Conclusions No. 100 (LV) – 2004 (8 October).

300 European Council on Refugees and Exiles (1997) "Position of the European Council on Refugees and Exiles on Temporary Protection" (March) para. 12, 13.

301 *Ibid.* p. 438.

Applying a *prima facie* determination to EDPs eschews complex causation issues and masks identity differences, saving states administrative costs while meeting short-protection needs. Importantly, the EU TP mechanism provides a three-year maximum stay (Articles 4(1)(2) and 6(1)(a)),[302] which may, as Gibney explains, balance the interests of state control and humanitarian objectives.[303] Some point out, though, that protection will only be "temporary" in situations where international efforts are deployed to resolve the crisis and people can return to their country of origin in a short period of time.[304] The Council must end TP only after analysing the situation in the country of origin and ensuring that any returns will be safe and durable with due respect for human rights, fundamental freedoms, and member states' obligations regarding *non-refoulement* (Article 6(2)). The Council shall consider any compelling humanitarian motives that make return impossible or unreasonable, including, for example, the degrading state of environmentally vulnerable regions or health factors that will make travel and return difficult (Articles 22(2) and 23(1)). The TPD seemingly applies the reasoning of the ECtHR in *D v United Kingdom* (from an "exceptional circumstance" to a codified, mainstreamed one).[305]

The states will be challenged to mobilise and agree on such a TP format for EDPs. TP may offer an important protection response for sudden environmental disasters that need cross-border movement but may, however, be limited to cases where the people's movement may not be so evident, arising from gradual land degradation or resource curtailment (because the impact on host states would not be so obvious). It may be a short-term solution for situations leading to statelessness or other permanent situations, calling for a combination of alternative long-term solutions.

(v) The Temporary Protection Directive: a contemporary missed opportunity for the protection of EDPs?

The TPD mechanism has never been triggered, so its practical potential for EDPs is unknown. Application of the TPD could provide practical information from which good practices could be derived and perhaps replicated to other urgent mass influx situations.

Malta and Italy failed in their attempt to activate the provision to ensure equal distribution of asylum seekers among member states as a result of mass

302 The first European Council decision grants temporary protection for one year. Article 4(1) para. (1). If not terminated by a Council decision it is automatically extended for six months and up to a year. Article 6 para.1 (b); Article 4 para. 1. After the second year it may be extended by a Council decision by a qualified majority on a proposal from the European Commission for another year. Article 4 para.2.

303 Gibney, M. (2000) "Between Control and Humanitarianism: Temporary Protection in Contemporary Europe" 14 Georgetown Immigration Law Journal pp. 689–707.

304 Koser, K., Walsh, M. & Black, R. (1998) "Temporary Protection and the Assisted Return of Refugees from the European Union" 10 International Journal of Refugee Law 3 p. 444, pp. 444–461.

305 *See* Section 3.1.2.1.

influx from Libya and Tunisia. Instead, the European Commission provided financial and operational support through the Directorate General ECHO in response to the humanitarian needs triggered by the "Arab Spring" crisis.[306] Recent calls by civil society organisations to activate TP regarding the Syrian crisis were also unsuccessful.[307] Authors like Elspeth Guild affirmed that the TPD is openly politicised because it introduced a selective mechanism enabling the Council to choose which groups to protect, thereby risking frustration by political inertia. This is why, she adds, the mechanism has also not been operationalised for the Afghanistan and Iraqi crises, proving that the EU favours financial aid over protecting people within its territory.[308] In addition, the interinstitutional approach requiring cooperation to activate the TP procedure, while laudable, is complex, implicating that three institutions work rapidly in a transparent way.[309] Despite criticisms, it holds great potential and adaptability to exceptional situations of mass influx urgency for EDPs.

As Nuria Arenas explains, the EU TP regime is important for two reasons. For the first time, a legal framework establishes a "binding legal obligation of temporary asylum" through an exceptional scheme initiated by the EU institutions based on solidarity. Second, "it confirms the general obligation of any State to allow entry or, at least, the temporary protection, provided that the principle of *non-refoulement* is applicable in cases of large-scale displacement".[310]

It is a balancing mechanism emphasising financial (Article 24 measures of temporary protection benefit from the previous European Refugee Fund (ERF) and current Asylum, Migration and Integration Fund (AMIF))[311] and physical

306 Abass, A. Kingah, S. & Nita, S. (2011) "Regional Responses to the Libyan Crisis" United Nations University Institute on Comparative Regional Integration Studies UNU-CRIS Policy Brief No. 1 pp. 5, 6 (September).

307 Human Rights Watch (2013) "EU Provide Protection to Syrian Refugees" *available from:* www.hrw.org/news/2012/12/23/eu-provide-protection-syrian-refugees [accessed 17 August 2018] ("As the number of Syrians seeking protection in the EU grows, EU member states should consider invoking an EU-wide temporary protection regime, similar to the approach already taken by Syria's neighbours, Human Rights Watch said. If the EU were to invoke the Temporary Protection Directive in relation to Syria, all Syrians would be granted a residence permit for the entire duration of the protection period, giving them work authorization, access to accommodation, and medical treatment. The mechanism would also encourage EU member states to resettle beneficiaries from other member states where reception capacity is overwhelmed").

308 Guild, E. (2004) "Seeking Asylum: Storm Clouds between International Commitments and EU Legislative Measures" 29 European Law Review 2 pp. 198–218.

309 *See generally,* Roots, L. (2009) "The Impact of the Lisbon Treaty on the Development of EU Immigration Legislation" 5 Croatian Yearbook of Legal Studies pp. 261–281.

310 Arenas (2005) *Op. Cit.* p. 437.

311 The ERF (€ 630 million over the period 2008–2013) supported EU countries' efforts in receiving refugees and displaced persons and in guaranteeing access to consistent, fair, and effective asylum procedures. The fund also supported resettlement programmes and actions related to the integration of persons whose stay is of a lasting and stable nature. It also provided for emergency measures to address sudden arrivals of large numbers of persons in need of international protection *available from:* http://ec.europa.eu/dgs/home-affairs/financing/fundings/migration-asylum-borders/refugee-fund/index_en.htm

(Articles 25 and 26, based on the principle of "double voluntariness" on the host state and the person seeking protection) burden-sharing between member states and further reinforcing the principles of solidarity and fair sharing of responsibility, guiding tenants under the Common European Asylum System (Article 80 TFEU).

The TPD sets member states' "minimum" protection obligations[312] towards persons enjoying temporary protection. States' treatment of such persons must meet the standards set out in Articles 9 to 16, though states retain a large margin of appreciation concerning certain human rights. The European Parliament and UNHCR unsuccessfully suggested[313] a special right of freedom of movement within the EU, which was criticised as imprecise and unclear.[314] The ECRE also highlighted limitations, including, for example, access to urgent healthcare or employment that prioritises EU nationals.[315] The original European Commission proposal contained a non-discrimination obligation, but it was dropped in the course of the debates. Notably, the member states are still bound by the non-discrimination obligations in the Charter of Fundamental Rights, the ECHR, or other international instruments, allowing only reasonable restrictions on the rights of persons benefiting from TP (Recital 16).

Despite inherent limitations, the flexibility of TP, coupled with the general harmonisation goal of the asylum system under the EU Treaty, might favour expansion and consolidation of current protection options of EDPs. The TFEU does not use, however, the term *uniform status*, which is typically employed regarding asylum and subsidiary protection, instead highlighting a "common

[accessed 17 August 2018]. For the period 2014–2020, the AMIF was funded with € 3.137 billion. It promotes the efficient management of migration flows and the implementation, strengthening, and development of a common EU approach to asylum and immigration. The AMIF also contributes to the achievement of four specific objectives: asylum, legal migration and integration, return, and solidarity *available from:* http://ec.europa.eu/dgs/home-affairs/financing/fundings/migration-asylum-borders/asylum-migration-integration-fund/index_en.htm [accessed 17 August 2018].

312 Council of the European Union Directive 2001/55/EC *Op. Cit.* Recital 8; Article 1.

313 *See* European Parliament (2001) C 343/86 "On the Proposal for a Council Directive on Minimum Standards for Giving Temporary Protection in the Event of a Mass Influx of Displaced Persons and on Measures Promoting a Balance of Efforts between Member States in Receiving Such Persons and Bearing the Consequences Thereof" (13 March); UNHCR (2000) "UNHCR Summary Observations on the Commission Proposal for a Council Directive on Minimum Standards for Giving Temporary Protection in the Event of a Mass Influx (COM (2000) 303, 24 May 2000)" (15 September).

314 Directive 2001/55/EC *Op. Cit.* Article 8(3) reads: "[t]he Member States shall, *if necessary*, provide persons to be admitted to their territory for the purposes of temporary protection with every facility for obtaining the necessary visas, including transit visas. Formalities must be reduced to a minimum because of the urgency of the situation. Visas should be free of charge or their cost reduced to a minimum" (emphasis added). *See also* Sgro (2013) *Op. Cit.* p. 312 and Boutruche, S. (2010) "La protection temporaire des personnes déplacées en droit de l'Union européenne: un nouveau modèle en cas d'afflux massifs?" Thèse de doctorat Université Aix-Marseille for discussions on the content of Article 8(3).

315 European Council on Refugees and Exiles (2001) "Information Note on the Council Directive 2001/55/EC of 20 July 2001" (1 September).

system of temporary protection".[316] This wording may suggest that temporary protection is secondary to asylum and subsidiary protection, particularly because *common system* may be read as less than a uniform system. Actually, it may reinforce the importance of the TPD as a complementary system of shared competence (which coexists with national temporary protection regimes). EU measures, however, must comply with the general EU harmonisation objectives of "offering appropriate status to any third-country national requiring international protection and ensuring compliance with the principle of *non-refoulement*" under Article 78(1) TFEU. A reading of *common system*, therefore, cannot be detached from the EU's general principle of cooperation, which defines all international common policies and actions in order to assist populations, countries, and regions confronting natural or man-made disasters while also consolidating human rights (Article 21 TFEU).[317]

The TPD leaves room to include EDPs within its scope. The lack of activation of the TPD has not prevented states from developing legislation offering temporary protection to people in the event of environmental disasters. Article 3(5) and Recital 12 of the TPD allows member states "to introduce or maintain more favourable conditions for persons enjoying temporary protection in the event of a mass influx of displaced persons". National actions on temporary protection at the EU level and at large (in the US and other states ad hoc measures) may provide guidance in bridging the EU temporary protection gap to include EDPs within the wider scope of the Directive. They may also offer insight for EU member states to activate TP when necessary.

5.3.4 *Temporary protection efforts in the EU addressing environmental displacement*

A number of non-harmonised protection mechanisms and terminologies continue to arise around the world, including *complementary forms of protection*, *categorical protection*, or simply *humanitarian statuses*. This results from the cross-fertilisation between national and European courts, based on national human rights law and ECHR obligations, as states try to fill protection gaps exposed as the world and people's protection needs become more complex.[318] A 2010

316 Article 78(2)(c) of the TFEU states that "the European Parliament and the Council, acting in accordance with the ordinary legislative procedure, *shall* adopt measures for a common European asylum system comprising: c) a *common system of temporary protection* for displaced persons in the event of a massive inflow" (emphasis added).

317 *See* Sgro (2013) *Op. Cit.* p. 323 (arguing that the emergency clause under Article 78(3) of TFEU, allowing the Council to take provisional measures when one or more member states is confronted with an emergency situation characterised by a sudden inflow of nationals of third countries, could also justify the activation of TP for environmentally displaced persons within or outside the EU). The clause does not concern the protection of third-country nationals per se, but rather the protection of member states within the asylum regime.

318 *See* Kraler, A. (2011) "Fixing, Adjusting, Regulating, Protecting Human Rights: The Shifting Uses of Regularisations in the European Union" 13 European Journal of Migration and Law 3 pp. 297–316.

report by the European Migration Network identified a minimum of 60 varied non-harmonised protection statuses within EU member states alone.[319]

Member states seemingly grant TP on humanitarian grounds and as a result of sudden environmental disasters, leaving a narrow scope of protection for victims of slow-onset environmental degradation conditions. But protection for these victims cannot be overlooked. Only Finland provides a formalised model that provides TP status for a maximum of three years and that may include EDPs.[320] Others, including Italy, provide for exceptional temporary protection measures to be adopted in case of natural disaster situations.

Legal national provisions addressing environmental displacement

Finland

Chapter 6 Section 109 (1) of the Aliens Act 301/2004 provides:[321]

> *Temporary protection* may be given to aliens who need international protection and who cannot return safely to their home country or country of permanent residence, because there has been a massive displacement of people in the country of its neighbouring areas as a result of an armed conflict, some other violent situation or an *environmental disaster* (emphasis added).

Italy

Article 20(1) Legislative Decree nr 286 of 25 July 1998:[322]

> By decree of the Prime Ministers (. . .) the *temporary protection measures* should be adopted, as an exception to the provisions of this single text, in case of major humanitarian needs, on the occasion of conflicts, *natural disasters* or other particularly serious events *in countries outside the EU* (emphasis added).

Until now, EDPs have not benefited from any of these TP national regimes, which are more theoretical than a practical good practice model subject to replication elsewhere. There is also interpretation potential to include EDPs in

319 European Migration Network (2010) "The Different National Practices Concerning Granting Non-EU Harmonised Protection Statuses" (European Migration Network) p. 105.
320 *See generally,* Sgro (2013) *Op. Cit.* pp. 326–329.
321 Finnish Aliens Act 301/2004 (amendments up to 458/2009 included) (30 April 2004).
322 Italian Legislative Decree No. 286 (1998) "Consolidated Act of Provisions Concerning Immigration and the Condition of Third Country Nationals" (25 July).

other EU member states' legislation.[323] But even here, with room to make the "environmental argument" on humanitarian grounds, there are no specifics about protection and its content. Interpretative efforts of Swiss law on temporary stay and subsidiary protection may also meet the needs of EDPs displaced by sudden-onset disasters rather than those endangered by slow-onset changes.[324]

The mechanism put in place by the British government after the 1995 volcano eruptions on the island of Montserrat merits discussion. Studies cite to it as an example of a practical model in the EU for environmental displacement management.[325] The ad hoc "Voluntary Evacuation Scheme" included financial relocation assistance for those affected by disasters ("Assistance Passages Programme") and a two-year residence permit to live in the UK.[326] The Montserrat example, though, is unusual because Montserrat is a British Overseas Territory and under the jurisdiction and sovereignty of the UK, so the British government was explicitly obligated to operationalise TP measures.[327] The scheme, however, highlights some important aspects that governments must consider when structuring and activating these schemes for EDPs. First, states must have in place evacuation measures for sudden disasters and ensure inter-departmental cooperation.[328] Second, while environmental scenarios may be predictable, government authorities must accept and manage a certain level of risk.[329] Third, states

323 *See* Kraler, Cernei & Noack (2011) *Op. Cit.* pp. 57–60 (providing an overview of temporary protection mechanisms, mostly based on humanitarian grounds, offered in Belgium, Ireland, Lithuania, Latvia, Malta, and Slovakia, which may be interpreted to cover environmental displacement).

324 Kälin, W. (2010) "Conceptualising Climate Induced-Displacement" in J. McAdam (ed.) "Climate Change and Displacement: Multidisciplinary Perspectives" (Hart Publishing) p. 100, pp. 81–104.

325 *See, e.g.*, Kolmannskog & Myrstad (2009) *Op. Cit.* p. 318; Sgro (2013) *Op. Cit.* p. 336.

326 *See, e.g.*, Foreign and Commonwealth Office (1998) "Memorandum from the Parliamentary Under-Secretary of State Baroness Symons" (9 February); Clay, E. *et al.* (1999) "An Evaluation of the HMG's Response to Montserrat Volcanic Emergency" Report EV635 (Overseas Development Institute Department for International Development Evaluation December).

327 Citizens of Montserrat are British nationals but not British citizens. An account of the different types of British nationality is *available from:* www.gov.uk/types-of-british-nationality [accessed 17 August 2018].

328 *See generally,* Patullo, P. (2000) "Fire from the Mountain: The Tragedy of Montserrat and the Betrayal of Its People" (Constable) (providing an overview of the challenges of the Montserrat case, particularly the UK government's unpreparedness for disaster situations).

329 *See generally,* Aspinall, W. *et al.* (2002) "The Montserrat Volcano Observatory: Its Evolution, Organisation, Role and Activities" in T. Druit & B. Kokelaar (eds.) "The eruption of Soufrière Hills Volcano, Montserrat, from 1995 to 1999" Geological Society (Vol. 21) pp. 71–91. *See also* Haynes, K. (2000) "Volcanic Island in Crisis: Investigating Environmental Uncertainty and the Complexities It Brings" 21 Australian Journal of Emergency Management 4 pp. 21–28.

need to make any TP scheme part of a wider sustainable protection solution upon return, resettlement, and reintegration.[330]

5.3.5 *Temporary protection status in the United States*

Prior to 1980, the United States offered temporary protection through the Immigration and Nationality Act (INA). Section 203(a)(7) "provided a quota for persons fleeing persecution in certain countries or from natural calamities".[331] Today, the INA[332] awards Temporary Protection Status (TPS) only to individuals already in the United States and temporarily unable to return to their country of origin because of instability due to an ongoing armed conflict, environmental disaster, epidemic, or any other unusual temporary condition.[333]

Protection under this framework is discretionary and not automatic. The Attorney General must "designate" a country of concern[334] by evaluating the individual's incapacity of return as a result of serious environmental destruction as well as the affected country's capacity to accommodate incoming flows of nationals. Plus, the affected country must make a formal request to the US government.[335] As a result, it makes temporary protection dependent on a number of conditions and realistically only protects those individuals who are already in the United States. It is primarily a form of relief that focuses on the general needs of the country of origin (objective/outwards conditions) rather than the specific needs of the individual (subjective/inwards conditions). It generally grants the applicant a six to eighteen month period to reside and work without fear of deportation.[336] The status is renewable upon the unchangeable conditions of the country of origin. The word *temporary* denotes the weakness of the provision and the legal limbo that a person may face, as it may be years before individuals can return safely to their country of origin.

There are currently 11 countries designated under the US TPS procedures: El Salvador, Guinea, Haiti, Honduras, Liberia, Nicaragua, Sierra Leone, Somalia, Sudan, South Sudan, and Syria. Some are designated due to natural disasters

330 *Ibid. See also* Clay, E. *et al.* (1999) *Op. Cit.* p. 53 sq. Sgro (2013) *Op. Cit.* p. 336. Today, there are approximately 4,500 inhabitants in Montserrat compared to 10,400 before. More than 8,000 people left after the volcanic eruption.

331 Parker, J. (1982) "Victims of Natural Disasters in U.S. Refugee Law and Policy: Transnational Legal Problems of Refugees" Michigan Year Book of International Legal Studies pp. 137–139.

332 The INA was enacted in 1952 and has been amended many times over the years, but it is still the foundation of US immigration law. It is codified at 8 U.S.C. §1101 et. seq. (1952).

333 Section 244 paras. (b)(1)(A-C) of the INA sets forth circumstances under which the US Attorney General may designate a foreign country one whose citizens are eligible for temporary protection.

334 *Ibid.*

335 *Ibid.*

336 INA Section 244 para (b)(2)(B).

(e.g. El Salvador, Haiti, Honduras, and Nicaragua), while others are due to conflict situations (e.g. Sudan, South Sudan, and Syria),[337] and some are due to both. Recently, because of natural disasters, some suggested the administration should designate countries such as Peru, Pakistan, Sri Lanka, India, Indonesia, Thailand, Myanmar, Malaysia, the Maldives, Tanzania, the Seychelles, Bangladesh, and Kenya. This resulted in a proposition to enact a "Tsunamis Temporary Protection Act" offering temporary protection to people from tsunami-affected areas.[338] However, there has been little support from the government to enact those measures.[339] The Philippines is yet another example. As the country became devastated by Typhoon Haiyan (Yolanda), which claimed the lives of 6,000 people and displaced more than 3.43 million, the Filipino government formally requested that the US government designate TPS for Filipinos, but the US Congress took no action on a proposed bill that would have provided such protection.[340]

Yet, the US government decided to prolong the TPS for those countries already designated due to natural disasters (e.g. Nicaragua and El Salvador as the result of Hurricane Mitch in 1998 and/or a series of earthquakes in 2001), as those areas remain "unable, temporarily, to handle adequately the return of its nationals".[341]

While nothing prevents EDPs from acquiring TPS in the United States, it is mostly a politically vested form of protection consistent with the US government's discretionary power. Furthermore, it is useless for people from disappearing Small Island States,[342] as individuals would have no place to return.

337 *See* US TPS *available from:* www.uscis.gov/humanitarian/temporary-protected-status-deferred-enforced-departure/temporary-protected-status#Countries%20Currently%20Designated%20for%20TPS [accessed 17 August 2018].

338 House of Representatives (2005) "Tsunamis Temporary Protection Status Act of 2005" House of Representatives, 60, 109th Congress (1st Session) (4 January). This bill was introduced by Sheila Jackson-Lee.

339 Wasem, R. & Ester, R. (2010) "Temporary Protection Status: Current Immigration Policy and Issues" (RS20844) (Washington, DC: Congressional Research Service) p. 6 *available from:* http://digitalcommons.ilr.cornell.edu/cgi/viewcontent.cgi?article=1562&context=key_workplace [accessed 17 August 2018].

340 *See* Seghetti, L., Wasem, R. & Ester, R. (2015) "Temporary Protection Status: Current Immigration Policy and Issues" (RS20844) (Washington, DC: Congressional Research Service) pp. 4, 7 *available from:* http://fas.org/sgp/crs/homesec/RS20844.pdf [accessed 20 March 2015].

341 *Ibid.* p. 7.

342 Mortom, A. (2009) "Climate Refugees Start Move to New Island" The Age National (29 July) *available from:* www.theage.com.au/national/first-climate-refugees-start-move-to-new-island-home-20090728-e06x.html [accessed 17 august 2018]. As mentioned, in 2009 more than 2,700 residents of the Carteret Islands in the South Pacific were evacuated to Papua New Guinea.

5.3.5 Other international temporary protection ad hoc schemes

In the absence of specific legislation, states have created ad hoc schemes based on humanitarian principles: humanity, cooperation, and solidarity to protect victims of disasters. Typically, these schemes are activated in exceptional situations, on a case-by-case basis. By relying on such exceptional protection measures, states can avoid the consolidation of a particular status upon initial expectation of the arrival of migratory flows. Rather than *ex ante* mechanisms, they constitute *ex post* instruments of protection, typically for emergency situations. Sometimes they arise from geopolitical considerations.

For example, African states offered protection to Haiti after the 2010 earthquake as a "sense of duty and memory and solidarity".[343] Senegal not only offered assistance to victims but also proposed helping relocate Haitians by offering them available land.[344] Liberia took the same approach.[345] The February 2014 free movement agreement between the governments of Kenya, Uganda, and Rwanda, a more formalised arrangement, could be used to admit EDPs under a temporary protection regime.[346]

Canada[347] and Australia[348] adapted their immigration regimes to provide temporary visas and permanent residency permits to the 2004 tsunami victims, based on family reunification (i.e. where a member of the family already resided on a permanent basis in the country). Many other governments also considered

343 *See* Baldauf, S. (2010) "Haitians to Africa? Senegal Resettlement Plans Gain Steam" Christian Science Monitor (2 February) *available from:* www.csmonitor.com/World/Africa/2010/0202/Haitians-to-Africa-Senegal-resettlement-plans-gain-steam [accessed 17 August 2017]; Aljazerra (2010) "Africa Mulls Resettling Haitians" (31 January) *available from:* www.aljazeera.com/news/americas/2010/01/2010131155417123157.html [accessed 17 August 2018]. The African Union considered a proposal from the Senegalese President to resettle thousands of Haitians affected by the 2010 earthquake. Among the proposals were the naturalisation of Haitians who sought new nationality after the disaster and an adoption programme for orphaned children across Africa, including creating a new country within Africa for Haitians. In the words of the African Union President at the time: "[i]t is out of *a sense of duty and memory and solidarity* that we can further the proposal to create in Africa the conditions for the return of Haitians who wish to return after the effect of the disaster that ravaged Haiti" (emphasis added).

344 BBC News (2010) "Senegal Offers Land to Haitians" (17 January) *available from:* http://news.bbc.co.uk/2/hi/africa/8463921.stm [accessed 17 August 2018].

345 Africa Resource (2010) "World Response to Haitian Earthquake" (3 March) *available from:* www.africaresource.com/arts-a-culture/newsworthy/711-world-response-to-haitian-earthquake [accessed 17 August 2018].

346 Tamara, W. (2015) "Developing Temporary Protection in Africa" 49 Forced Migration Review p. 25, pp. 23–25.

347 Laczko F. & Collett E. (2005) "Assessing the Tsunami's Effects on Migration" The Online Journal of the Migration Policy Institute (1 April) *available from:* www.migrationpolicy.org/article/assessing-tsunamis-effects-migration [accessed 17 August 2018].

348 Stephen, S. (2005) "Responding to the Tsunami Refugee Crisis" Green Left Weekly (19 January) *available from:* www.greenleft.org.au/node/33360 [accessed 17 August 2018].

the UNHCR's appeal to postpone the victims' return to ravaged areas.[349] Switzerland and the UK postponed the expulsion of rejected asylum seekers from affected areas.[350] Botswana and Tanzania opened their borders to people displaced by natural disasters from neighbouring regions on temporary, ad hoc, or humanitarian grounds.[351] Latin American countries, including Brazil, faced an influx of Haitians after the 2010 earthquake. Conscious of the limitations of its laws to address such a situation, it is developing a draft legislation to offer an extended form of protection for those persons facing crisis, calamities, or serious and generalised human rights violations.[352]

5.3.6 Prospective interpretation under the EU Temporary Protection Directive to solidify protection of EDPs

The TPD offers insight for the protection of EDPs and member states' obligations towards persons enjoying TP in mass influx situations. The flexibility of the language coupled with the solidarity of the mechanism outlined in the Directive render a potential TP status *prima facie* for EDPs. TP closes "protection gaps" and is a pragmatic solution between the binding principle of *non-refoulement* and – to some extent – the discretionary character of the EU's asylum regime.

Because it does not involve individual applications, the TPD treats TP as an exceptional response that must overcome high political thresholds to be activated. The mechanism has never been used in practice, which may render it less effective in dealing with EDPs.

Nevertheless, other outlined forms of TP demonstrate the willingness of countries to adjust their immigration policies in the wake of environmental disasters. Those adjustments, however, are mostly reactive humanitarian measures to assist disaster victims, not formalised ones. A facilitated immigration procedure or temporary visa is only the first step, though. The analysis reveals a space for a mainstreamed system of TP for EDPs. TP may provide a blueprint for events to come and can be used based on the implementation already made. A more harmonised system of TP could be achieved, drawing from EU National Provisions Addressing Environmental Displacement. Ensuring bottom-up consistency with EU national legislative practices, together with the panoply of TP measures applied in the wake of environmental disasters around the world, even if framed

349 Executive Committee of the High Commissioner's Program (2006) "Providing International Protection Including through Complementary Forms of Protection" 25 Refugee Survey Quarterly 1 para. 22 p. 148, pp. 143–152.

350 Laczko, F. & Collett, E. (2005) "Assessing the Tsunami's Effects on Migration" *available from:* www.migrationpolicy.org/article/assessing-tsunamis-effects-migration [accessed 17 August 2018].

351 Kälin & Schrepfer (2012) *Op. Cit.* p. 37.

352 Piacentini de Andrade, I. (2015) "Brazil's Draft Migration Law" 49 Forced Migration Review (May) pp. 36–37.

differently, can only reinforce the evolving inclusion of EDPs, not only within the scope of the Directive but also towards an emerging formalised regime of TP, without prejudicing states' obligations under international law.[353]

5.4 (Re)Conceptualising protection of EDPs: protection as a dynamic guiding concept

After this analysis of potential solutions to consolidating protection for EDPs within the EU and beyond its borders, one question arises: are we moving towards a new protection paradigm in the environmental displacement context?

The answer is positive to the extent there is a need to rethink protection as a legal dynamic guiding concept of both *proactive* and *reactive* measures. In other words, states need to prevent and deal with displacement holistically, viewing it as an enterprise underpinned by the human rights paradigm and their concomitant international law obligations. Particularly, states must see protection as a dynamic guiding concept to which people are entitled when their state of origin is unable or unwilling to offer human rights protection or "the widest possible exercise of fundamental rights and freedoms [which all] human beings [should] enjoy without discrimination".[354] Importantly, the notion of protection must necessarily evolve over time to accommodate the human rights and needs of people facing complex realities (in the pre- and post-displacement phases), such as the changing environment. Accordingly, the normative force of this expansive protection paradigm for environmental-induced displacement can be "understood as a dynamic of creation, of orientation and of application of the law exerted from the outer limits of the legal thought up to the most daily application of the legal standard (. . .) [thus] it is important to understand the different present forces [proactive and reactive] which givethe paradigm life and consistency".[355]

The answer is also negative to the extent this book does not advocate an abandonment of the current legal protection paradigm. On the contrary, in the short term one must look at existing regional normative protection frameworks – such

353 This path is particularly grounded in the UNHCR Guidelines on Temporary Protection or Stay Arrangements that aim to assist governments' response to humanitarian crises as well as complex or mixed population movements where current responses are inappropriate or lacking. (February 2014) *available from:* www.refworld.org/docid/52fba2404.html [accessed 17 august 2018]. The Guidelines encourage predictability in states' responses to crises or situations (to circumvent discretionary and ad hoc protection practices) through "standing arrangements" on temporary protection seen as "a pragmatic tool" to be concluded on a multilateral or regional basis.

354 Convention Relating to the Status of Refugees, adopted on 28 July 1951, 189 UNTS 137, Preamble.

355 Gaillard-Sebileau, E. (2009) "La Force Normative du Paradigme Juridique" in C. Thibierge *et al.* (eds.) "La Force Normative – Naissance d'un Concept" (Lextenso Éditions 2009) p. 171, pp. 171–182 (author's own free translation).

as the EU's – which complement and enlarge the scope of protection in general and constitute stepping-stones to consolidating protection for EDPs in particular. There is much scope not to prevent migration per se but rather to consider labour migration a preventative and complementary protection measure to adapt and avoid displacement, matching the interests of the receiving state and EDPs. Any cooperation to develop third-countries' protection capacities should be based on responsibility sharing.

There is also much scope to furthering the current EU complementary protection regime if specific serious human rights deprivations occur. At a minimum, host states are internationally obligated to provide temporary or longer-term sanctuary when someone's life is seriously threatened and there is a failure or absence of state protection.[356] Indeed, some assert that states' obligations towards environmental-induced displacement require not only *ex post* relief to disaster victims but also active protection that moves beyond mere ad hoc response measures to construct a whole system of protection targeting both pre- and post-displacement. The laws of European states are increasingly recognising protection on the grounds of environmental disasters, an approach that should be envisaged at a collective level.

The EU regional protection framework offers legal statuses that, while not directly aimed at environmental displacement, could be used, adapted, and reinforced within the EU and arguably replicated elsewhere. The identified "normative gap" affecting the protection of EDPs can be narrowed and solidified by existing regional protection solutions. Departing from a theory of inclusion (an evolutionary and contextual interpretation of the existing EU regional legal framework, in accordance with international human rights and principles established in the contemporary, ever-evolving global and regional legal orders) before exclusion is one path and is particularly important at a time when powerful states have little appetite for developing new treaties.

Above all, as Harvey neatly says:

> The defence of "humanity" that emerges is often a reminder of what is now embedded in legality, through the advance of human rights law. In each of these instances, and in others like them, the invitation is to "see the person" within the layers of bureaucracy and administration and to give this moral aspiration a definite legal meaning. The work that human rights will do is test, probe and nudge the strategies of states, as well as sharpen the progressive development of refugee law. Even the eventual adoption of new categorizations will not terminate this interplay because states will

356 *See* Edwards (2012) *Op. Cit.* p. 82 (advancing the notion that Hathaway's formula for determining "persecution" under the 1951 Convention may gain renewed relevance under this analysis – "persecution = harm + failure of state protection" – and that it could be adapted to apply to climate displaced (and others) as: "need for IP [International Protection] = serious threat to life or freedom + failure of state protection").

> generally not open themselves unconditionally to suffering others. What makes these modern debates so intriguing is that states have bound themselves to the standards within which the contest takes place. Even if view in sceptical terms, this will continue to offer normative footholds for imagining alternative configurations and, significantly, give practical hope to suffering others in need.[357]

In reality, there are many sources of protection for people who are or will be displaced by environmental factors. This research demonstrates that the EDPs' protection paradigm is a driving force for states to balance existing patchwork and interconnected protection standards and, in the long term, build a comprehensive framework (*ex ante* and *ex post*) for protecting EDPs. The international legal system contains the necessary elements for construction of a protection framework able to respond to this new problematic, at least in part. A new or renewed model of protection must utilise existing rules and principles from different branches of law. Though this book endorses a rather compartmentalised outlook, the protection regimes for environmental displacement and *inter alia* states' obligations must be seen as conflating rather than conflicting, as they reflect the *cumulative effects* of normative and operational frameworks and (quasi) judicial decisions towards the protection of the human person. These complementary effects are conducive to the construction of a more effective multidisciplinary and holistic protection regime.

As Cançado Trindade explains:

> The approximations or convergence between complementary regimes of protection (. . .), dictated by the *necessities* themselves of protection and manifested at normative, hermeneutic and operative levels, contribute to the search for effective solutions to current problems in this domain, and to the improvement and strengthening of the human person in any situations or circumstances. It is necessary to keep on advancing decidedly in this direction.[358]

EU states are obligated by treaty to protect against environmental-induced displacement by connecting internal and external policy objectives.[359] Member states' power to restrict immigration and asylum is not unlimited but is shaped by international obligations and individual humanitarian traditions. The legitimacy

357 Harvey (2013) *Op. Cit.* p. 87.

358 Cançado Trindade, A. (2010) "International Law of Humankind, towards a New *Jus Gentium*" (Martinus Nijhoff Publishers) p. 525.

359 As noted, Article 208(1) TEU stipulates that the EU and member states' policies shall "complement and reinforce each other" and "the Union shall take account of the objectives of development cooperation in the policies that it implements which are likely to affect developing countries" (Article 208 (2)). With this goal, the TEU imposes duties of consultation and cooperation (Article 201 (1) TEU).

of actions taken under EU law (even within the context of environmentally induced displacement) is based on the founding principle of protection of human rights. The EU's scheme, notably its legal and political position, multilevel framework, double judicial check (ECtHR and CJEU), and *sui generis* status at the intersection of EU and international law, serves as a useful example,[360] and the protection of EDPs should be (re)conceptualised against this background.[361]

5.5 Conclusion

The protection of people displaced by environmental factors warrants the development of a legal framework of proactive and reactive protection measures. The EU legal framework offers effective and pragmatic solutions to consolidate protection for EDPs. On the one hand, the chapter shows that circular labour migration through the Seasonal Workers Directive and/or Mobility Partnerships could help states to deal with the predicted effects of environmental change. On the other hand, both the Temporary Protection Directive and Qualification Directive could help states to protect EDPs once they cross an international border. This chapter reflects the much-needed development of a holistic protection framework for EDPs. It shows states and policymakers the fulcrum upon which existing human rights standards can remedy the current protection gap within the international legal system. Protection is a dynamic guiding concept to which people are entitled in the wake of new displacement challenges, such as those posed by a changing environment.

360 Carozza, P. (2003) "Subsidiarity as a Structural Principle of International Human Rights Law" 97 American Journal of International Law 1 p. 57, pp. 38–79 ("As a result of that *sui generis* status, the European Union has developed unparalleled relationships between national and supranational norms, actors, and institutions, and is constantly pulled taut between the commonality of integration and the particularity of separate national units. The same tension also characterizes many of the most persistent challenges of international human rights law (. . .). Thus, the very singularity of the Union, (. . .) gives it the possibility of contributing to the larger question before us").

361 Within the EU, the European Commission currently leads development on the issue of environmental displacement through the Directorate General for Development and Cooperation – EuropeAid. The EC examines the integration of migration into development strategies and into the post-2015 development agenda by focusing on selected priority areas, namely employment and decent work, inclusive growth, environment and climate change, and access to basic social services (notably health and education). Though governments increasingly recognise migration's potential to positively contribute to adaptation in countries vulnerable to the effects of climate change, many still fail to view protection as a holistic and formalised matter for environmental displacement through a "lens of combined forces". Consequently, it is being sidelined by other Directorate Generals, in particular, the DG for Migration and Home Affairs.

6 Conclusion

This book explored the increasing concern over the extent to which those suffering from forced (or potential) cross-border displacement as a result of environmental change are protected under international law, in particular human rights law. Centred around a holistic understanding of protection – before-during-after displacement (but concentrating only on the first and last phases of environmental displacement) – the intervening chapters seek to provide adequate answers to two basic questions: 1) whether and to what extent existing international law protects cross-border environmental displacement and 2) whether and how existing formalised regional complementary protection standards can interpretively solidify and (re)conceptualise protection for cross-border environmental displacement.

In dealing with these queries, the book underscores the plight of such individuals, the obligations of states within the international legal human rights protection regime, and related instruments informed by the interpretative dynamic of (quasi) judicial decisions. In this context, the book suggests pragmatically how the identified international "legal protection gap" might be remediated by means of consolidating existing (proactive and reactive) regional complementary protection standards, both to prevent and deal with environmental displacement.

6.1 The increasing legal recognition of environmentally displaced persons

The first part conceptualises and examines who are EDPs. This was not just another futile attempt to impose rigid labelling but rather a necessary exercise to understand the complex reality of those in need of international protection. By exploring the meaning of environmental change, as well as its human impact, the book investigates the factors that influence displacement and exposes a number of different environmental displacement scenarios. While the study recognises the multicausality of human mobility (stemming from economic, social, political, demographic, and environmental factors), it asserts that it is important to consider the environment as an autonomous factor that leads to displacement for two reasons: first, because the environmental stressors over a period of time will be more exacerbated for the environmental driver, and second, those people will be forcibly displaced across the border (where moving is not an option; to stay or to go is a "no choice option"). Since the concept of vulnerability is intimately related to protection in human rights law, the study uses the concept of "vulnerability layers" in order to expose those vulnerable areas (geographical "hotspots") affected by environmental change where people's human rights are at risk and in need of legal protection contemplation.

Contextualising the study also helps understand the *protection paradox* between the "guesstimates" and realities of people displaced by environmental factors. It is important to assert that some of the dangers of environmental change, while intangible, and their impacts on cross-border displacement are to some extent currently (in)visible. There is a need to act (to use academic research channels and rely on existing protection standards as remedies) and not to wait for the problem of forced displacement of populations to become more visible and acute. The fear of people becoming displaced by environmental factors has become a reality and so is their recognition academically, institutionally, and within the overarching international protection agenda. Article 14(f) of the Cancun Agreement on long-term cooperative action under the UNFCC recognises the need for protection of cross-border displacement through a triangulation of efforts at the international, regional, and national levels and the introduction of planned relocation as part of assistance and protection measures. Both the Council of Europe and the European Union have elevated the protection debate of environmental displacement. The gradual consensus-building that took place under the Nansen Initiative leading to the Platform on Disasters Displacement is developing a more coherent and consistent view at the international level for cross-border environmental displacement and helps to develop a more effective normative and institutional approach in this regard.

6.2 Protection obligations from cross-border environmental displacement arise from legal cumulative effects

The theoretical legal analysis carried out in Chapter 3 generally concludes that environmental change violates human rights and national governments, both individually and as members of the international community, incur specific obligations under international and regional human rights treaties. Under these treaties, international human rights courts and intertwined interpretative guidance offered by quasi-judicial organs proclaim that states have the obligation to take preventative action to respect, avoid the violation of, and take positive steps to fulfil human rights – including those of EDPs. The obligations to respect, protect, and fulfil warrants states adopting laws at the national and regional levels to prevent displacement and take coordinate action regarding slow- and fast-onset environmental changing conditions. The obligations to respect, protect, and fulfil conflate with the needs and rights of EDPs: the obligation to protect the right to life, health, and property; provide adequate food and housing; supply water; and respect vulnerable groups (older people, disabled people, children, minorities, and indigenous peoples). Furthermore, states have the obligation to ensure procedural rights (right to information, right to public participation and consultation, right to access to justice) in particular to collect information about environmental-induced displacement and disseminate it to all relevant stakeholders who should be consulted on a regular basis to ensure that adequate solutions to the challenges of EDPs are sought. The international community has a duty to cooperate and ensure that that financial, technical, and logistical assistance is in place for countries that are affected by environmental factors, thereby fulfilling their human rights obligations towards EDPs.

The human rights paradigm ensures that the legitimate rights of people affected by environmental factors are duly respected. Importantly, it identifies the "minimum standards of treatment" that should be afforded to EDPs: i.e. identifying the rights violated or at risk, noting how states need to deal with environmental risks (including displacement risks), and taking measures to deal with them. The study underlines that the minimum scope of protection warranted by states towards all individuals, regardless of nationality or statelessness, is not totally dependent on financial resources. In the *Örnerlydiz* decision, the ECtHR emphasised the fact that the protective function of the state can often be reflected in existing laws and constitutional provisions to ensure and to promote the effective protection of individuals whose lives might be endangered by immediate and known risks – and these may include those from a changing environment – and not necessarily taken to account in existing financial resources. A specific example derives from the right to information, which is established in the case law of the convention institutions regarding classical environmental matters.

Following from this, the book concludes that there is an increasing manifestation of a preventative dimension in the domain of the protection of the human person, that is seen gaining ground amidst international and (quasi) judicial decisions. This is further evident in a number of interconnected normative (hard and soft law) and operational frameworks that – explicitly or implicitly – place obligations on states to prevent environmental displacement and the violation of peoples' human rights.

An explicit recognition of the duty of states to protect from displacement in cases of natural and human-made disasters has been progressively recognised at the international, regional, and subregional levels. A good example at the international level is found in Principles 5, 6, and 9 of the GPID and the Peninsula Principles on climate displacement. At the regional level, this is exemplified in Article 4 of the Kampala Convention. At the subregional level the IDP Protocol to the Great Lakes Pact makes recognition of this by extension, as it imposes obligations on state parties to adopt and implement the GPID. The majority of the instruments analysed are particular to the internal displacement context, yet they have an exponential influence also outlining the general obligations of states to avoid environmental cross-border displacement. States must not only refrain from carrying out arbitrary displacement but at the same time prevent and, where possible, mitigate displacement caused by natural or human-made risks or other third parties. While the innovative impact of these instruments, such as GPID, may be limited (because they do not formally bind states), they gain a certain degree of recognition because they have been progressively incorporated into states' national legislation and policies. The Kampala Convention, for example, despite its regional outreach, is the most powerful mechanism due to its binding character. First, it solidifies a general preventative approach to protection found in international instruments. Second, it elevates the recognition of a vulnerable population group in need of protection due to natural and human-made disasters. It offers conceptual clarity and the legal definition of what constitutes displacement, both within and across international borders. Therefore, at the regional level it fills a previous international legal protection gap and may serve as a model for other regions when developing a holistic approach to protection.

At the same time, the extensive elaboration on preventing disasters and/or adapting to environmental change in operational frameworks on disaster risk reduction and adaptation to climate change at the international and regional levels – while not dealing with displacement *per se* – highlight the obligations of states to take preventative action to reduce vulnerabilities and protect the human rights of those (potentially) affected. The Hyogo Framework on Disaster Risk Reduction followed by the Sendai Framework of Disaster Risk Reduction, as non-binding international instruments, are complemented by binding human rights obligations which include the duty of states to reduce natural and man-made environmental risks by introducing legislation, programmes, and policies to protect vulnerable populations. These obligations have been made explicit on constitutional provisions or through the adoption of specific national provisions in different countries.

The book highlights that the protection of the human person is not only an *ex post facto* obligation of states but must increasingly be seen as an *ex ante* one. It requires a transformational change in government practices towards working in a proactive rather a reactive matter. Here labour migration – as a new status of protection – has a legitimate role to play for vulnerable communities in particular when adapting to environmental change. As the fields of human rights and the environment expand and intertwine, so do the *legal cumulative effects* of these frameworks, which highlight the prevention of, or protection from, cross-border environmental displacement as an important protection dimension of emerging customary nature. This path is increasingly confirmed by the work carried out by the ILC Draft Articles on the Protection of Persons in the Event of Disasters, giving precision to prevention as a principle of international law. The development of a normatively grounded preventative dimension to protection for EDPs does not imply, however, the curtailment of the right to seek asylum abroad.

6.3 Protection obligations after cross-border environmental displacement arise contextually

In Chapter 4 the book explores the extent to which host states' duties, which materialised under the Refugee Convention, are transferrable to protecting

EDPs. The study shows the need to rethink a legal regime that has traditionally been geared towards the narrow class of those people fleeing political persecution. This present legal structure is relevant as a point of comparison, and offers protection and status to those who cross the border due to environmental factors in certain circumstances (where environmental impacts may amount to persecution based on qualified grounds). Yet it is still largely inadequate. The Refugee Convention was created for a different purpose and, therefore, has limited application to engage host states in particular obligations. Whereas the discussion highlights the legal academic discourses that support enhancing the meaning of refugeehood to include EDPs, this path is currently barred by institutional scepticism towards reopening negotiations concerning the refugee treaty. The worry is that it could lower the current protection standards for refugees under the existing definition; there also is a general dislike and stigmatisation of the term *refugee*. States such as New Zealand have recently made useful contributions towards our jurisdictional understanding of how the terms of the Refugee Convention are too strict to apply in this embryonic area. In two emblematic cases, *Teitiota v The Chief Executive of the Ministry of Business and Employment* and *AD (Tuvalu) v New Zealand Immigration and Protection Tribunal*, the applicants were considered not to be in need of international protection due to environmental factors.

These exposed barriers have not been an impediment to the evolution of the law of protection of the human person for cross-border displacement at the regional level that came into existence in order to fill existing regional gaps in the international protection regime. The enhanced interpretative human rights dimension of regional protection standards reveals that states have *contextually developed the protection of environmental displacement*. Both the African Refugee Convention and Cartagena Declaration on Refugees may provide some sort of protection for EDPs if they find themselves in analogous situations of conventional refugees, and the Arab States Convention clearly offers protection to those people affected by environmental disasters.

State practice, primarily in the African context, has demonstrated that countries have allowed people who cross the border due to environmental factors to remain temporarily. It is true however, that environmental displacement could remain excluded from the legal framework of these regions due to a lack of ratification (like the Arab States Convention) or the non-binding character (like the Cartagena Declaration on Refugees) of some of these regional instruments, which narrow their authoritative character. This is coupled with the general state practice to grant protection status solely in situations of mass influx or on an ad hoc basis. It is therefore doubtful that the issue will be dealt with in a systematic and coherent matter. Nonetheless, extended protection obligations may be derived from a common ground of protection – the principle of *non-refoulement* – echoed in the case law of various treaty bodies (judiciary or quasi-judiciary in particular, Article 3 of ECHR which gains relevance through the judgements of the ECtHR) and embodied in complementary protection standards at the European Union level.

6.4 Towards a new human rights-based protection paradigm for environmental displacement

Chapter 5 of this book highlights the protection of environmental displacement as a way of both reflecting states' human rights obligations and narrowing the identified legal protection gaps. The analysis of the European Union's regionally orientated protection regime can help states to consolidate an evolving *protection paradigm of proactive and reactive measures* being erected at the international level for environmental cross-border displacement. In other words, it helps states to (re)conceptualise protection as a holistic and dynamic enterprise. The positioning of the EU in the international sphere, underpinned by the paradigm for the protection of human rights, can remedy the current protection gap that exists within the international legal system. It offers effective and pragmatic solutions that can be consolidated within the European Union and beyond its borders, even if it did not have environmental displacees in mind.

Fostering labour migration through the EU Seasonal Workers Directive and/or Mobility Partnerships is suggested as an *ex ante* displacement protection measure that may enable populations to adapt to environmental change. Building on the experience gained within a number of relevant labour migration schemes implemented at the European level and beyond, it could promote amongst states the use of migration as form of adaptation. The Seasonal Workers Directive offers a fast-track procedure of common entry, residence conditions, and a set of rights for migrant seasonal workers and could be used as a preventative strategy to reduce displacement by targeting communities of origin who are most vulnerable to environmental change and to increase their resilience to environmental disruptions. The multi-seasonal permit in a single act reduces bureaucracy, offers a legal status, opens mobility opportunities, and facilitates re-entry, but to function, states cannot be reluctant to open legal entry channels to labour migrants. The same can be said with regards to Mobility Partnerships. This cooperation agreement, which reflects a new form of governance on mutual commitments and shared responsibility between third states and EU member states, can make a contribution into all aspects of migration (migration and development, legal migration, and illegal migration) but can work only if it has the potential to increase the leverage on both sides.

Other existing complementary standards may allow states to provide *ex post* protection against return on human rights grounds to those who have crossed a border due to environmental factors. For example, it is argued that subsidiary protection under the EU Qualification Directive may be extended to those who are forced to move on a permanent or quasi-permanent basis where the prospects of return may be slim. This can include people affected by slow-onset environmental change patterns such as desertification, sea level rise, or certain situations of natural disasters. Despite the inherent limitations of the QD, the scope of protection may be confirmed by an enhanced interpretative and contextual dynamic of the Directive, together with Article 2 (right to life) and Article 3 (freedom from torture and inhuman and degrading treatment) of the ECHR and the jurisprudential glow of two legal orders with European human rights law (ECHR and EU) which provide protection in individual cases, including expulsion. The development of the jurisprudence on socio-economic deprivation (in *D. v United Kingdom*, for example), the increasing judicial recognition of how environmental factors such as drought or floods contribute to the multi-causality of displacement and instability in a region (as highlighted in *Sufi and Elmi v United Kingdom* and further elaborated in *MSS v Belgium and Greece*) and/or the exceptionally severe context in the country of origin (found in *Elgafagi v Staatssecretaris van Justitie*), imply that a human rights approach to reasonableness of return to disaster-affected areas should evidently apply. In cases of forced movement due to fast-onset disasters, it is argued that the EU Temporary Protection Directive may provide temporary protection status *prima facie* for situations of mass influx even if it would have to overcome a number of political thresholds. Existing national legislative practices, both on subsidiary and temporary protection within (and beyond) the EU addressing environmental displacement, may confirm an emerging *ex post* formalised regime of normative consistency that shows the consolidation of protection for people displaced by environmental factors.

The analysis shows that the legal sources of protection for people who are, or will be, displaced by environmental factors are not insufficient. Policymakers must, however, have their attention drawn to the issue. The possibilities of existing law should be made clear to them and they must be encouraged to embrace its expansive interpretative dimension, underpinned by the human rights legal order to (re)conceptualise and remedy protection for environmental displacement. The increased recognition of environmental displacement reveals the existence of a unanimous sentiment to put into action effective protection. Scholarship, civil society at large, and international organisations as a whole have a role to play in this regard. While international law has developed considerably in the past 20 years in addressing displacement and the protection of the human person, "the time for complacency has certainly yet to arrive".[1] Perhaps the question at this point should no longer be how much law exists and how much it protects but what the transformative capacity is of human rights law in the wake of new challenges, i.e. to enhance the protection regime for a newly-concerned legal category based on their needs.

> This means that, despite the new challenges and some worrisome steps backwards in our days (e.g. forced migrations and uprootedness, restrictive and abusive migration policies, the closing of the frontiers and xenophobia), human conscience keeps on moving Law ahead, as its ultimate material source. Thus, despite the incongruities of the practice of States in our times, the *opinio juris communis* keeps on enlightening the path to follow, which

1 Leckie, S. (1995) "When Push Comes to Shove: Forced Evictions and Human Rights" (Habitat International Coalition) p. 98.

> cannot be other than that of the prevalence of the fundamental rights of the human person in all and any circumstances and of the consolidation of the obligations *erga omnes* of protection. This implies, ultimately, the primacy of the *raison d'humanité* over the old *raison d'État*.[2]

The new protection paradigm for environmental displacement currently being erected by the interplay of international and regional normative forces and legal and policy developments is not clearly dictated but rather progressively being constructed. The end of this book, however, is just the beginning of a theme around which more discussion is still needed in order to protect the human person in the wake of new challenges.

* * *

2 Cançado Trindade, A. (2010) "International Law of Humankind, towards a New *Jus Gentium*" (Martinus Nijhoff Publishers) p. 528.

Bibliography

Books/chapters of books/articles

Abass, A., Kingah, S. & Nita, S. (2011) "Regional Responses to the Libyan Crisis" United Nations University Institute on Comparative Regional Integration Studies Policy Brief No.1 (United Nations University Institute for the Environment and Human Security September).

Abella, M. (2006) "Policies and Best Practices for Management of Temporary Migration" International Symposium in International Migration and Development (United Nations Population Division Department of Economic and Social Affairs June).

Adger, W. N. (2006) "Vulnerability" 16 Global Environmental Change pp. 268–281.

Adger, W. N. *et al.* (2003) "Adaptation to Climate Change in the Developing World" 3 Progress in Development Studies pp. 179–195.

Ahmed, K. (2009) "Environmental Refugees a New Wave" 76 New Times (October).

Aleinikoff, A. (1991) "The Meaning of 'Persecution' in U.S. Asylum Law" in H. Adelman (ed.) "Refugee Policy: Canada and the United States" (Centre for Refugee Studies & Centre for Migration Studies York University).

Aleinikoff, A. (2003) "Protected Characteristics and Social Perceptions: An Analysis of the Meaning of 'Membership of a Particular Social Group'" in E. Feller, V. Türk & F. Nicholson (eds.) "Refugee Protection in International Law" (Cambridge University Press).

Alemanno, A. (2007) "The Shaping of the Precautionary Principle by European Courts from Scientific Uncertainty to Legal Certainty" in L. Cuocolo & L. Luparia (eds.) "Valori Costituzionale e Nuove Politihe del Diritto, Scritti raccolti in occasione del decennale della rivista" (Cahiers Europèens).

Alexander, M. (1999) "Refugee Status Determination by UNHCR" 11 International Journal of Refugee Law 2 pp. 251–289.

Alleweldt, R. (1993) "Protection against Expulsion under Article 3 of the European Convention on Human Rights" 4 European Journal of International Law pp. 360–376.

Alston, M. (2015) "Women and Climate Change" (Routledge).

American Society International Law (1999) "Symposium on Method in International Law" 93 American Journal of International Law pp. 291–423.

Ammer, M. (2009) "Climate Change and Human Rights: The Status of Climate Refugees in Europe" (Ludwig Boltzmann Institute of Human Rights).

Andenæs, M. (2015) "Reassertion and Transformation: From Fragmentation to Convergence in International Law" 46 Georgetown Journal of International Law 3 pp. 685–734.

Arai-Takahashi, Y. (2002) "Uneven, But in the Direction of Effectiveness: Anticipatory Ill-Treatment under Article 3 ECHR" 20 Netherlands Quarterly of Human Rights pp. 5–27.

Arenas, N. (2005) "The Concept of 'Mass Influx of Displaced Persons' in the European Directive Establishing the Temporary Protection System" 7 European Journal of Migration and Law pp. 435–450.

Arnaud, A.-J. (2009) "La Force Normative Pierre Angulaire d'Une Intelligence Juridique" in C. Thibierge *et al.* (eds.) "La Force Normative – Naissance d'un Concept" (Lextenso Éditions).

Aspinall, W. *et al.* (2002) "The Montserrat Volcano Observatory: Its Evolution, Organisation, Role and Activities" in T. Druit & B. Kokelaar (eds.) "The Eruption of Soufrière Hills Volcano, Montserrat, from 1995 to 1999" 21 Geological Society pp. 71–91.

Atapattu, S. (2006) "Emerging Principles of International Environmental Law" (Transnational Publishers).

Aufenvenne, P. & Felgentreff, C. (2013) "Umweltmigranten und Klimaflüchtlinge – Zweifelhafte Kategorien in der Aktuellen Debatte" IMIS-Beiträge pp. 9–44.

Azad, A., Hossain, K. & Nasreen, M. (2013) "Flood-Induced Vulnerabilities and Problems Encountered by Women in Northern Bangladesh" 4 International Journal Disaster Risk Science 4 pp. 190–199.

Baberjee, S., Black, R. & Kniveton, R. (2012) "Migration as an Effective Model of Adaptation to Climate Change: Policy Paper for the European Commission" (Sussex Centre for Migration Research).

Balabanova, E. (2015) "The Media and Human Rights. The Cosmopolitan Promise" (Routledge).

Baldwin, D. (1997) "The Concept of Security" 23 Review of International Studies pp. 5–26.

Bals, C. *et al.* (2008) "Climate Change, Food Security and the Right to Adequate Food" (Diakonisches Werk derEKD & German Watch e.V.).

Balzacq, T. (2009) "The Frontiers of Governance: Understanding the External Dimension of EU Justice and Home Affairs" in T. Balzacq (ed.) "The External Dimension of EU Justice and Home Affairs: Governance, Neighbours, Security" (Palgrave).

Barnett, J. (2001) "Security and Climate Change" Research Working Paper No. 7 (Tydall Centre for Climate Change).

Barnett, J. & O'Neil, S. J. (2012) "Islands, Resettlement and Adaptation" 2 Nature Climate Change pp. 8–10.

Barnett, J. & Webber, M. (2009) "Accommodating Migration to Promote Adaptation to Climate Change" (Commission on Climate Change and Development).

Bates, D. (2002) "Environmental Refugees? Classifying Human Migrations Caused by Environmental Change" 23 Population and Environment 5 pp. 465–477.

Battjes, H. (2006) "European Asylum and International Law" (Martinus Nijhoff Publishers).

Battjes, H. (2009) "In Search of a Fair Balance: The Absolute Character of the Prohibition of Refoulement under Article 3 Reassessed" 22 Leiden Journal of International Law, 3 pp. 583–621.

Baxter, R. (1966) "Multilateral Treaties as Evidence of Customary International Law" British Yearbook of International Law pp. 275–300.
Beck, U. (1992) "Risk Society" (Sage).
Belo, C. (1998) "The Dignity of the Individual" in B. Van Der Heijden & B. Tahzib-Lie (eds.) "Reflection on the Universal Declaration of Human Rights" (Kluwer Law International).
Bennet, J. (1998) "Forced Migration Within National Borders: The IDP Agenda" 1 Forced Migration Review pp. 4–7.
Bergoffen, D. (2011) "Contesting the Politics of Genocidal Rape: Affirming the Dignity of the Vulnerable Body" (Routledge).
Besson, S. (2006) "The European Union and Human Rights: Towards a Post-National Human Rights Institution" 6 Human Rights Law Review 2 pp. 323–360.
Betts, A. (ed.) (2011) "Global Migration Governance" (Oxford University Press).
Black, R. (2001) "Environmental Refugees: Myth or Reality?" UNHCR New Issues in Refugee Research Working Paper No. 34 pp. 2–3.
Black, R. *et al.* (2011) "The Effect of Environmental Change on Human Migration" 21 Global Environmental Change pp. S3–S11.
Blake, N. & Husain, R. (2003) "Immigration, Asylum and Human Rights" (Oxford University Press).
Boano, C., Zetter, R. & Morris, T. (2007) "Environmentally Displaced People: Understanding the Linkages between Environmental Change, Livelihoods and Forced Migration" Refugee Studies Centre (Oxford University).
Boesen, J. & Martin, T. (2007) "Applying a Rights-Based Approach: An Inspirational Guide for Civil Society" (Danish Institute for Human Rights).
Bogardi, J. *et al.* (2007) "Control, Adapt of Flee: How to Face Environmental Degradation?" UN Intersections No. 5 (United Nations University).
Bouteillet-Paquet, D. (2002) "Subsidiary Protection: Progress or Set-Back of Asylum Law in Europe? A Critical Analysis of the Legislation of the Member States of the European Union" in D. Bouteillet-Paquet (ed.) "Subsidiary Protection of Refugees in the European Union: Complementing the Geneva Convention?" (Bruylant).
Boyd, D. (2012) "The Environmental Rights Revolution: A Global Study of Constitutions, Human Rights and the Environment" (UBC Press).
Brandtner, B. & Rosas, A. (1998) "Human Rights and the External Relations of the European Community: An Analysis of Doctrine and Practice" 9 European Journal of International Law pp. 468–490.
Bretherton, C. & Vogler, J. (2006) "The European Union as a Global Actor" (Routledge).
Brinkmann, G. (2004) "The Immigration and Asylum Agenda" 10 European Law Journal 3 pp. 182–199.
Broberg, M. (2012) "Don't Mess with the Missionary Man! On the Principle of Coherence, the Missionary Principle and the European Union's Development Policy" in P. James Cardwell (ed.), "EU External Relations Law and Policy in the Post-Lisbon Era" (Springer).
Brookings Institution & University of Bern (2005) "Protecting Internally Displaced Persons: Manual for Law and Policy Makers" (Brookings Institution October 2008).
Brown, L. R. (2009) "Plan B 2.0: Rescuing a Planet under Stress and a Civilization in Trouble" Earth Policy Institute (W.W. Norton & Company).

Brown, O. (2008) "Migration and Climate Change" 31 Migration Research Studies (International Organisation for Migration).

Bryson, R. & Murray, T. J. (1977) "Climates of Hunger: Mankind and the World's Changing Weather" (University of Wisconsin Press).

Burson, B. (2010) "Environmentally Induced Displacement and the 1951 Refugee Convention: Pathways to Recognition" in T. Afifi & J. Jäger (eds.)" Environment, Forced Migration and Social Vulnerability" (Springer-Verlag).

Callewaert, J. (2009) "The European Convention on Human Rights and European Union Law: A Long Way to Harmony" 6 European Human Rights Review pp. 768–783.

Calum, N. (2012) "The Place of Epistemological Due Diligence in Relation to the Social and Political Science of Climate Change: The Case of Environmental Migration" Paper presentation ClimMig Conference on 'Human Rights, Environmental Change, Migration and Displacement' Ludwig Boltzmann Institute Human Rights; IDDRI, SciencesPo. (Vienna 20–21 September) pp. 1–20.

Cameron-Glickenhaus, J. P. (2008) "Coral Reef Protections" 31 Forced Migration Review Climate Change and Displacement pp. 52–53.

Cançado Trindade, A. (2010) "International Law of Humankind, towards a New *Jus Gentium*" (Martinus Nijhoff Publishers).

Carozza, P. (2003) "Subsidiarity as a Structural Principle of International Human Rights Law" 97 American Journal of International Law 1 pp. 38–79.

Cassese, A. (1989) "International Law in a Divided World" (Clarendon Press).

Cassese, A. (2005) "International Law" (2nd edition Oxford University Press).

Castberg, F. (1968) "Natural Law and Human Rights" 1 Revue des Droits de l'Homme/Human Rights Journal pp. 14–40.

Castles, S. (2002) "Environmental Change and Forced Migration: Making Sense of the Debate" New Issues in Refugee Research Working Paper No. 70 (United Nations High Commissioner for Refugees October).

Centre for Housing Rights and Evictions (2007) "Fair Play for Housing Rights: Mega Events, Olympic Games and Housing Rights" (Centre for Housing Rights and Evictions).

Centre for Housing Rights and Evictions & The National Law Centre on Homelessness and Poverty (2007) "Housing Rights for All: Promoting and Defending Housing Rights in the United States" (The National Law Centre on Homelessness and Poverty).

Cernea, M. (1999) "La Dimension Humaine dans Les Projets du Développement: les Variables Sociologiques et Culturelles" (Éditions Karthala).

Chandrappa, R. *et al.* (2011) "Coping with Climate Change" (Springer).

Chapman, A. R. & Carbonetti, B. (2011) "Human Rights Protections for Vulnerable and Disadvantages Groups: The Contributions of the U.N. Committee on Economic, Social and Cultural Rights" 33 Human Rights Quarterly pp. 682–732.

Chou, M.-H. (2009) "European Union Migration Strategy towards West-Africa: The Origin and Outlook of Mobility Partnerships with Cape Verde and Senegal" Paper for EUSA Biennial International Conference 'Information and Ideas on the European Union' (Los Angeles 23–25 April).

Chou, M.-H. & Girbert, M. (2012) "The EU-Senegal Mobility Partnership from Launch to Suspension and Negotiation Failure" 8 Journal of Contemporary European Research 4 pp. 408–427.

Christiansen, S. M. (2010) "Environmental Refugees, a Legal Perspective" (Wolf Legal Publishers).

Clay, E. *et al.* (1999) "An Evaluation of the HMG's Response to Montserrat Volcanic Emergency" Report EV635 (Overseas Development Institute Department for International Development Evaluation).

Clayton, G. (2008) "Article 3 Jurisprudence – *N. v UK*: Not a Truly Exceptional Case?" 14 Immigration Law Digest 3 pp. 6–14.

Clayton, G. (2011) "Asylum Seekers in Europe: *M.S.S. v Belgium and Greece*" 11 Human Rights Law Review 4 pp. 758–773.

Cohen, H., Giorgetti, C. & Payne, C. (2012) "An Introduction: Confronting Complexity" 106 American Society of International Law pp. 1–3.

Cohen, R. (2009) "The Burma Cyclone and the Responsibility to Protect" 1 Global Responsibility to Protect 2 pp. 253–257.

Coinsbee, M. & Simms, A. (2003) "Environmental Refugees: The Case for Recognition" (New Economics Foundation).

Coomans, F., Grunfeld, F. & Kamminga, M. (2009) "Methods of Human Rights Research" (Intersentia).

Cooper, J. (1998) "Environmental Refugees: Meeting the Requirements of the Refugee Definition" 6 New York University Environmental Law Journal pp. 480–488.

Cournil, C. (2006) "Les Réfugiés Écologiques: Quelle(s) protection(s), Quell(s) Status?" 4 Revue du Droit Public pp. 1035–1066.

Cournil, C. & Mazzega, P. (2007) "Refléctions Prospectives sur une Protection Juridique des Refugiés Écologiques" 23 Revue des Migrations Internationales pp. 7–34.

Cremona, M. (2011) "Values in EU Foreign Policy" in M. Evans & P. Koutrakos (eds.) "Beyond the Established Legal Orders: Policy Interconnections between the EU and the Rest of the World" (Hart Publishing).

Crisp, J. (2006) "Environmental Refugees: A UNHCR Perspective" (United Nations High Commissioner for Refugees).

Cryer, R. *et al.* (2011) "Research Methodologies in EU and International Law" (Hart Publishing).

Davies, S. (1993) "Are Coping Estrategies a Cop Out?" 24 Institute for Developing Studies Bulletin 4 pp. 60–72.

De Feyter, K. (2009) "Treaty Interpretation and Social Sciences" in F. Coomans, F. Grünfeld & M. Kamminga (eds.) "Methods of Human Rights Research" (Intersentia).

De Moor, N. (2011) "Temporary Labour Migration for Victims of Natural Disasters: The Case of Colombia" in M. Leighton, X. Shen & K. Warner (eds.) "Climate Change and Migration: Rethinking Policies for Adaptation and Disaster Risk Reduction" Source No. 15/2001 (United Nations University for Environment and Human Security).

De Sadeleer, N. (2002) "Environmental Principles from Slogans to Legal Rules" (Oxford University Press).

Dilley, M. *et al.* (2015) "Natural Disaster Hotspots, a Global Risk Analysis" in "Disasters Management Series" (Vol. 5 World Bank).

Docherty, B. & Giannini, T. (2009) "Confronting a Rising Tide: A Proposal for a Convention on Climate Change Refugees" 33 Harvard Environmental Law Review pp. 349–403.

Donders, Y. (2015) "International Covenant on Economic, Social and Cultural Rights: Accessibility and the Right to Information" in T. MacGonagle & Y. Donders (eds.) "The United Nations and Freedom of Expression and Information Critical Perspectives" (Oxford University Press).

Drumbl, M. A. (2005) "Symposium: The International Responses to Environmental Impacts of War" 17 Georgetown International Environmental Law pp. 565–643.

Duquette, E. (2001) "Human Rights in the European Union: Internal versus External Objectives" 34 Cornell International Law Journal pp. 364–395.

Durieux, J. F. (1992) "Capturing the Central American Refugee Phenomenon" 4 International Journal of Refugee Law 3 pp. 301–325.

Ebel, R. (1994) "Chernobyl and Its Aftermath" (The Centre for Strategic and International Studies).

Edwards, A. (2006) "Refugee Status Determination in Africa" 14 African Journal of International & Comparative Law pp. 204–233.

Edwards, A. (2012) "Climate Change and Refugee Law" in R. Rayfuse & S. Scott (eds.) "International Law in the Era of Climate Change" (Edward Elgar Publishing).

Eeckhout, P. (2011) "EU External Relations Law" (2nd edition Oxford University Press).

Eleftheriadis, P. (2011) "The Moral Distinctiveness of the European Union" 9 International Journal of Constitutional Law 3–4 pp. 695–713.

El-Hinnawi, E. (1985) "Environmental Refugees" (United Nations Environment Programme).

Environmental Justice Foundation (2009) "No Place Like Home: Where Next for Climate Refugees" (Environmental Justice Foundation).

Environmental Justice Foundation (2014) "Falling through the Cracks: A Briefing on Climate Change and International Governance Frameworks" (Environmental Justice Foundation).

Epiney, A. (2011) "Environmental Refugees: Aspects of International State Responsibility" in E. Piguet, A. Pecoud & P. Guchteneire (eds.) "Migration and Climate Change" (Cambridge University Press).

Espiell, H. G., Picado, S. & Lanza, L. V. (1990) "Principles and Criteria for the Protection of and Assistance to Central American Refugees and Displaced Persons in Latin America" 2 International Journal Refugee Law pp. 83–117.

European Council on Refugees and Exiles (1997) "Position of the European Council on Refugees and Exiles on Temporary Protection" (European Council on Refugees and Exiles).

European Council on Refugees and Exiles (2001) "Information Note on the Council Directive 2001/55/EC of 20 July 2001" (European Council on Refugees and Exiles).

European Migration Network (2010) "The Different National Practices Concerning Granting Non-EU Harmonised Protection Statuses" (European Migration Network).

European Migration Network (2011) "Temporary and Circular Migration: Empirical Evidence, Current Policy Practice and Future Options in EU Member States" (European Migration Network).

Executive Committee of the High Commissioner's Program (2006) "Providing International Protection Including through Complementary Forms of Protection" 25 Refugee Survey Quarterly 1 pp. 143–152.

Falstrom, D. Z. (2001) "Stemming the Flow of Environmental Displacement: Creating a Convention to Protect Persons and Preserve the Environment" 1 Colorado Journal of Environmental Law & Policy pp. 5–21.
Fatima, R., Wadud, A. & Coelho, S. (2014) "Human Rights, Climate Change, Environmental Degradation and Migration: A New Paradigm" Issue No. 8 (International Organisation for Migration & Migration Policy Institute) pp. 1–11.
Ferris, E. & Petz, D. (2011) "A Year of Living Dangerously: A Review of Natural Disasters in 2010" (The Brookings Institution & London School of Economics).
Ferris, E. & Petz, D. (2013) "In the Neighborhood: The Growing Role of Regional Organisations in Disaster Risk Management" (The Brookings Institution & London School of Economics Project on Internal Displacement).
Fineman, M. (2008) "The Vulnerable Subject: Anchoring Equality in the Human Condition" 20 Yale Journal of Law and Feminism pp. 1–23.
Fineman, M. (2012) "Elderly as Vulnerable: Rethinking the Nature of Individual and Societal Responsibility" 20 The Elder Law Journal 1 pp. 71–112, p. 101.
Fisher, D. (2010) "Legal Implementation of Human Rights Obligations to Prevent Displacement Due to Natural Disasters" in K. Koser & A. Solomon (eds.) "Incorporating the Guiding Principles on Internal Displacement into Domestic Law: Issues and Challenges" pp. 551–590.
Fitzpatrick, J. (2000) "Temporary Protection of Refugees: Elements of a Formalised Regime" 94 American Journal of International Law pp. 279–306.
Foster, M. (2007) "International Refugee Law and Socio-Economic Rights Refuge from Deprivation" (Cambridge Studies in International and Comparative Law).
Friedmann, W. (1962) "The Changing Dimensions of International Law" 62 Columbia Law Review 7 pp. 1147–1165.
Frigo, M. (2011) "Migration and International Human Rights Law" Practitioners Guide No. 6 (International Commission of Jurists).
Gagnon-Lebrun, F. & Agrawala, S. (2006) "Progress to Adaptation to Climate Change in Developed Countries" (Organization for Economic Co-Operation and Development).
Gaillard-Sebileau, E. (2009) "La Force Normative du Paradigme Juridique" in C. Thibierge *et al.* (eds.) "La Force Normative – Naissance d'un Concept" (Lextenso Éditions).
Garlic, M. (2007) "UNHCR and the Implementation of the EC Qualification Directive" in K. Zwan (ed.) "The Qualification Directive: Central Themes, Problem Issues, and Implementation in Selected Member States" (Wolf Legal Publishers).
Geddes, A. (2008) "Immigration and European Integration: Beyond Fortress Europe?" (2nd edition Manchester University Press).
Gemenne, F. (2011) "Migrations et Déplacements de Populations dans un Monde à + 4°C" 414 Etudes pp. 723–738.
Gibney, M. (2000) "Between Control and Humanitarianism: Temporary Protection in Contemporary Europe" 14 Georgetown Immigration Law Journal pp. 689–707.
Giddens, A. (1999) "Risk and Responsibility" 62 Modern Law Review 1 pp. 1–10.
Gillepsie, A. (2004) "Small Islands in the Face of Climatic Change: The End of the Line in International Environmental Responsibility" 22 UCLA Journal of Environmental Law & Policy pp. 175–218.
Glantz, M. H. (1994a) "Creeping Environmental: Are Societies Equipped to Deal with Them?" Workshop Creeping Environmental Phenomena and Societal

Responses to Them National Centre for Atmospheric Research Boulder (Colorado 7–8 February).
Glantz, M. H. (1994b) “Creeping Environmental Problems Natural Science Essay” The World and I pp. 218–225.
Gomilova, M. & Jagers, N. (2013) “Climate Change Induced Displacement and International Law” in J. Verscguuren (ed.) “Research Handbook on Climate Change and Adaptation Law” (Edward Elgar Publishing).
Goodwin-Gill, G. (1986) “Non-Refoulement and the New Asylum Seekers” 26 Virginia Journal of International Law pp. 897–918.
Goodwin-Gill, G. (1989) “The Language of Protection” 1 International Journal of Refugee Law 1 pp. 6–19.
Goodwill-Gill, G. & McAdam, J. (2007) “The Refugee in International Law” (3rd edition Oxford University Press).
Grahl-Madsen, A. (1966) “The Status of Refugees in International Law” (Vol. 1 Sijthoff).
Grahl-Madsen, A. (1983) “Identifying the World’s Refugees” in “Annals of the American Academy of Political and Social Science: The Global Refugee Problem: U. S. and World Response” (Vol. 467) pp. 11–23 (Sage Publications).
Grear, A. (2010) “Redirecting Human Rights: Facing the Challenge of Corporate Legal Humanity” (Palgrave Macmillan).
Guild, E. (2004) “Seeking Asylum: Storm Clouds between International Commitments and EU Legislative Measures” 29 European Law Review 2 p. 198–218.
Haddad, E. (2004) “Who Is (Not) a Refugee?” Working Paper No. 2004/6 (European University Institute) pp. 1–28.
Harrell-Bond, B. & Voutira, E. (1992) “Anthropology and the Study of Refugees” 8 Anthropology Today 4 pp. 6–10.
Harris, P. (2008) “Climate Change and Global Citizenship” 30 Law Policy 4 pp. 481–501.
Hartmann, B. (1998) “Population, Environment and Security: A New Trinity” 10 Environment and Urbanization 2 pp. 113–127.
Harvey, C. (2013) “Is Humanity Enough? Refugees, Asylum Seekers and the Rights Regime” in S. Juss & C. Harvey (eds.) “Contemporary Issues in Refugee Law” (Edward Elgar Publishing).
Hathaway, J. (1991) “The Law of Refugee Status” (Butterworth’s).
Hathaway, J. (2005) “The Rights of Refugees under International Law” (Cambridge University Press).
Haynes, K. (2000) “Volcanic Island in Crisis: Investigating Environmental Uncertainty and the Complexities it Brings” 21 Australian Journal of Emergency Management 4 pp. 21–28.
Henneby, J. & Pribisch, K. (2010) “A Model for Managed Migration? Re-Examining Best Practices in Canada’s Seasonal Agricultural Worker Program” (International Organisation for Migration).
Herlin-Karnell, E. (2013) “EU Values and the Shaping of the International Legal Context” in D. Kochenov & F. Amtenbrink (eds.) “European Union’s Shaping of International Legal Order” (Cambridge University Press).
Hernández i Sagrera, R. & Carrera, S. (2009) “The Externalisation of the EU’s Labour Immigration Policy: Towards Mobility or Insecurity Partnerships” Centre for European Policy Studies Working Document No. 312.

Hesselink, M. (2009) "A European Legal Method? On European Private Law and Scientific Method" 15 European Law Journal pp. 20–45.

Higgins, R. (1968) "Policy Considerations and the International Judicial Process" 17 International and Comparative Law Quarterly pp. 58–84.

Higgins, R. (1994) "Problems and Process: International Law and How We Use It" (Oxford University Press).

Ho, C. & Loucky, J. (2012) "Humane Migration, Establishing Legitimacy and Rights for Displaced People" (Kumarian Press).

Hong, J. (2001) "Refugees of the 21st Century: Environmental Injustice" 10 Cornell Journal of Law & Public Policy pp. 323–348.

Hugo, G. (1996) "Environmental Concerns and International Migration" 30 International Migration Review 1, Special Issue: Ethics, Migration, and Global Stewardship pp. 105–131.

Hugo, G. (2008) "Migration, Development and Environment" Migration Research Series 35 (International Organization for Migration).

Humphreys, S. (2010) "Introduction: Human Rights and Climate Change" in S. Humphreys (ed.) "Human Rights and Climate Change" (Cambridge University Press).

Islam, R. (2013) "Climate Refugees and International Refugee Law" in R. Islam & J. Bhuiyan (eds.) "An Introduction to Refugee Law" (Martinus Nijhoff Publishers).

Jacobs, F. (2007) "The Sovereignty of Law" (Cambridge University Press).

Jacobson, J. (1988) "Environmental Refugees: A Yardstick of Habitability" World Watch Paper No. 86 (World Watch Institute).

Jakuleviciene, L. (2010) "Is There a Need for an Extension of Subsidiary Protection in the European Union Qualification Directive?" 2 Jurisprudence 120 pp. 215–232.

Johnston, J. S. (2008) "A Looming Policy Disaster" 31 Regulation 3 pp. 38–44.

Joly, D. (1998) "Temporary Protection Regime within the Framework of a New European Asylum Regime" 2 International Journal of Human Rights 3 pp. 49–76.

Julka, A. (2011) "Multidimensional Re-Creation of Vulnerabilities and Potential Resilience in International Migration" 49 International Migration pp. 30–49.

Juss, S. (2007) "International Migration and Global Justice" (Ashgate Publishing).

Justice (2000) "Comments on Proposal for a Council Directive on Minimum Standards for Temporary Protection" (Justice).

Kälin, W. (2000) "Guiding Principles on Internal Displacement: Annotations" Studies in Transnational Legal Policy No. 38 (American Society of International Law & The Brookings Institution).

Kälin, W. (2010) "Conceptualizing Climate-Induced Displacement" in J. McAdam (ed.), "Climate Change and Displacement: Multidisciplinary Perspectives" (Hart Publishing).

Kälin, W. & Kunzli, J. (2010) "The Law of International Human Rights Protection" (Oxford University Press).

Kälin, W. & Schrepfer, N. (2012) "Protecting People Crossing Borders in the Context of Climate Change Normative Gaps and Possible Approaches" (United Nations High Commissioner for Refugees Division of International Protection).

Keane, D. (2004) "The Environmental Causes and Consequences of Migration: A Search for the Meaning of 'Environmental Refugees'" 16 Georgetown International Law Review pp. 209–223.

Kelley, N. (2002) "Internal Flight/Relocation/Protection Alternative: Is it Reasonable?" 14 International Journal of Refugee Law 1 pp. 4–44.

Khondker, H. (2010) "Globalisation, Disasters and Disaster Purpose" in B. Turner (ed.) "The Routledge International Handbook of Globalisation Studies" (Routledge).

Kibreab, G. (1997) "Environmental Causes and Impact of Refugee Movements: A Critique of the Current Debate" 21 Disasters 1 pp. 20–38.

Kiss, A. (1989) "Definition et Nature Juridique d'un Droit de l'Homme a l'Environment" in P. Kromarek (ed.) "Environnement et Droits de l'Homme" (United Nations Educational, Scientific and Cultural Organisation) pp. 13–28.

Kiss, A. (2003) "The Right to the Conservation of the Environment" in R. Picolotti & J. D. Taillant (eds.) "Linking Human Rights and the Environment" (The University of Arizona Press).

Kolmannskog, V. (2013) "'We Are in between': Securing Effective Rights for Persons Displaced in the Context of Climate Change and Natural Hazard-Related Disasters" Doctoral Dissertation, Department of Criminology and Sociology of Law (University of Oslo).

Kolmannskog, V. & Myrstad, F. (2009) "Environmental Displacement in European Asylum Law" 11 European Journal of Migration and Law pp. 313–326.

Koser, K., Walsh, M. & Black, R. (1998) "Temporary Protection and the Assisted Return of Refugees from the European Union" 10 International Journal of Refugee Law 3 pp. 444–461.

Koskenniemi, M. (1999) "Letter to the Editors of the Symposium" 93 American Journal of International Law pp. 351–379.

Kozoll C. (2004) "Poisoning the Well: persecution, the environment, and refugee status" 15 Journal of International Environmental Law and Policy 2 pp. 271–272, pp. 271–307.

Kraler, A. (2011) "Fixing, Adjusting, Regulating, Protecting Human Rights: The Shifting Uses of Regularisations in the European Union" 13 European Journal of Migration and Law 3 pp. 297–316.

Kraler, A., Cernei, T. & Noack, M. (2011) "Climate Refugees: Legal and Policy Responses to Environmentally Induced Migration" DG for Internal Policies Policy Department C: Citizen's Rights and Constitutional Affairs Study (European Parliament).

Laczko, F. & Aghazarm, C. (2009) "Migration, Environment and Climate Change Assessing the Evidence" (International Organization for Migration).

Lambert, H., McAdam, J. & Fullerton, M. (2013) "A Global Reach of European Refugee Law" (Cambridge University Press).

Lauterpacht, E. & Bethlehem, D. (2003) "The Scope and Content of the Principle of Non-Refoulement" in E. Feller, V. Türk & F. Nicholson (eds.), "Refugee Protection in International Law" (Cambridge University Press).

Lazarus, D. S. (1990) "Environmental Refugees: New Strangers at the Doors" 2 Our Planet 3 pp. 12–13.

Leckie, S. (1995) "When Push Comes to Shove: Forced Evictions and Human Rights" (Habitat International Coalition).

Legum, C. (1998) "Africa Contemporary Record" Annual Survey and Documents (Vol. 17 Africana Publishing).

Leib, H. L. (2011) "Human Rights and the Environment Philosophical, Theoretical and Legal Perspectives" (Brill).

Leiderman, S. & Hall, J. (1995) "Environmental Refugees and Ecological Restoration" (Fourth World Project).

Leighton, M. (2010) "Climate Change and Migration: Key Issues for Legal Protection of Migrants and Displaced Persons" in "Syllabus, Protecting Environmental Migrants: Creating New Policy and Institutional Frameworks" (United Nations University Institute for Environment and Human Security).
Leighton, M. (2012) "Population Displacement, Relocation, and Migration" in M. B. Gerrard & K. F. Kuh (eds.) "The Law of Adaptation to Climate Change: U.S. and International Aspects" (American Bar Association).
Leroy, S. F. (2006) "Can Human Rights Bodies be Used to Produce Interim Measures to Protect Environment-Related Human Rights?" 15 Review of European Comparative & International Environmental Law 1 pp. 66–81.
Letsas, G. (2007) "A Theory of Interpretation of the European Convention on Human Rights" (Oxford University Press).
Letsas, G. (2010) "Strasbourg's Interpretative Ethic: Lessons for the International Lawyer" 21 European Journal of International Law 3 pp. 509–541.
Limon, M. (2010) "Human Rights and Climate Change: Constructing a Case for Political Action" 33 Harvard Environmental Law Review pp. 439–576.
Loescher, G., Betts, A. & Milner, J. (2008) "The Politics and Practice of Refugee Protection in the Twenty-First Century" (Routledge).
Lonergan, S. (1998) "The Role of Environmental Degradation in Population Displacement" 4 Environmental Change Security Project pp. 5–15.
Long, K. (2009) "Extending Protection? Labour Migration and Durable Solutions for Refugees" New Issues in Refugee Research No. 176 (United Nation High Commissioner for Refugees).
Lopez, A. (2007) "The Protection of Environmentally-Displaced Persons in International Law" 37 Environmental Law pp. 365–409.
Loughry, M. & McAdam, J. (2008) "Kiribati-Relocation or Adaptation" 31 Forced Migration Review: Climate Change and Displacement pp. 38–39.
Lovelock, K. & Leopold, T. (2008) "Labour Force Shortages in Rural New Zealand: Temporary Migration and the Recognised Seasonal Employer Work Policy" 33–34 New Zealand Population Review pp. 213–234.
Lucarelli, S. & Fioramonti, L. (eds.) (2010) "External Perception of the European Union as a Global Actor" (Routledge).
Luna, F. (2009) "Elucidating the Concept of Vulnerability: Layers Not Labels" 2 The International Journal of Feminist Approaches to Bioethics 1 pp. 121–139.
Magniny, V. (1999) "Les Réfugiés de L'Environnement Hypothèse Juridique à Propos d'une Menace Écologique" Doctoral Dissertation, Department of Law (University Paris I Panthéon-Sorbonne).
Magri, N. (2009) "Temporary Circular Labour Migration between Colombia and Spain: A Model for Consolidation and Replication" Mpp Masters Thesis, Maastricht Graduate School of Governance (Maastricht University) (2008–2009).
Manner, I. (2002) "Normative Power Europe: A Contradiction in Terms?" 40 Journal of Common Market Studies pp. 235–258.
Marcs, C. (2008) "Spoiling Movi's River: Towards Recognition of Persecutory Environmental Harm within the Meaning of the Refugee Convention" 24 American University International Law Review pp. 31–71.
Maroukis, T. & Triandafyllidou, A. (2013) "Mobility Partnerships: A Convincing Toll for the EU's Global Approach to Migration?" Policy Paper No. 76 (Notre-Europe Jacque Delors Institute).

Martin, D. (1991) "The Refugee Concept: On Definitions, Politics, and Careful Use of Scarce Resource" in H. Aldelman (ed.) "Refugee Policy: Canada and the United States" (York Lanes Press).
Maru, M. T. (2011) "The Kampala Convention and Its Contribution in Filling the Protection Gap in International Law" 1 Journal of Internal Displacement 1 pp. 91–130.
Mayer, B. (2013) "Climate Change and International Law on the Grim Days" 24 The European Journal of International Law 3 pp. 947–970.
McAdam, J. (2005) "The European Qualification Directive: The Creation of a Subsidiary Protection Regime" 17 International Journal of Refugee Law 3 pp. 461–516.
McAdam, J. (2007) "Complementary Protection in International Law" (Oxford University Press).
McAdam, J. (2011) "Environmental Migration" in A. Betts (ed.) "Global Migration Governance" (Oxford University Press).
McAdam, J. (2012) "Climate Change, Forced Migration, and International Law" (Oxford University Press).
McCue, G. (1993) "Environmental Refugees: Applying International Environmental Law to Involuntary Migration" 6 Georgetown Environmental Law Review pp. 151–190.
McDonald, G. (1998) "The Universal Declaration of Human Rights: The International and the American Dream" in B. Van Der Heijden & B. Tahzib-Lie (eds.) "Reflection on the Universal Declaration of Human Rights" (Kluwer Law International) pp. 179–186.
McInerney-Lankford, S., Darrow, M. & Rajamani, L. (2011) "Human Rights and Climate Change: A Review of the International Legal Dimensions" (World Bank).
McLeman, R. (2009) "Climate Change and Adaptive Human Migration: Lessons from Rural North America" in N. Adger, I. Lorenzoni & K. O'Brien (eds.) "Adapting to Climate Change" (Oxford University Press).
McLeman, R. & Smit, B. (2006) "Migration as an Adaptation to Climate Change" 76 Climate Change pp. 31–53.
McLoughlin, S. & Münz, R. (2011) "Temporary and Circular Migration: Opportunities and Challenges" Working Paper No. 3 (European Policy Centre).
Mercure, P. F. (2006) "A la Recherche d'un Statut Juridique pour les Migrants Environnementaux Transfrontaliers: la Problématique de la Notion de Réfugié" 37 Revue de Droit de L'Université de Sherbrooke pp. 1–39.
Meyer, J. *et al.* (eds.) (1997) "The Structuring of a World Environment Regime, 1870–1990" 51 International Organisation pp. 623–651.
Meyers, N. & Kent, J. (1995) "Environmental Exodus: An Emergent Crisis in the Global Arena" (Climate Institute).
Michelot-Draft, A. (2006) "Enjeux de la Reconnaissance du Statut de Réfugié Ecologique pour la Construction d'une Nouvelle Responsabilité International" 4 Revue Européenne du Droit de l'Environnement pp. 428–445.
Moberg, K. (2009) "Extending Refugee Definitions to Cover Environmentally Displaced Persons Displaces Necessary Protection" 94 Iowa Law Review pp. 1107–1136.
Morel, M. (2014) "The Right Not to Be Displaced in International Law" (Intersentia).
Myers, N. (1993a) "Tropical Forests: The Main Deforestation Fronts" 20 Environmental Conservation 1 pp. 9–16.
Myers, N. (1993b) "How Many Migrants for Europe?" 2 People and the Planet 3.

Myers, N. (1993c) "Environmental Refugees in a Globally Warmed World" 43 Bioscience pp. 752–761.

Myers, N. (1993d) "Ultimate Security: The Environmental Basis of Political Stability" (W.W. Norton & Company).

Myers, N. (1996) "Environmentally-Induced Displacements: The State of the Art" in International Organization for Migration, United Nations High Commissioner for Refugees & Refugee Policy Group (ed.) "Environmentally-Induced Population Displacements and Environmental Impacts Resulting from Mass Migration" (International Organization for Migration).

Myers, N. (1997) "Environmental Refugees" 19 Population and Environment: A Journal of Interdisciplinary Studies 2 pp. 167–182.

Myers, N. (2005) "Environmental Refugees an Emergent Security Issue" 13th Economic Forum (23–27 May).

Myers, N. & Kent, J. (1995) "Environmental Exodus: An Emergent Crisis in the Global Arena" (The Climate Institute).

Neal, M. (2012) "Not Gods But Animals: Human Dignity and Vulnerable Subjecthood" 33 Liverpool Law Review pp. 177–200.

Nellen-Stucky, R. (2010) "Partnering for Migration: The Ambiguous Case of Mobility Partnerships between the European Union and Selected Third Countries" Working Paper (Universität Luzern, Kultur-und Sozialwissenschaftliche Fakultät, Politikwissenschaftliches Seminar) pp. 1–28.

Newman, F. & Vasak, K. (1982) "Civil and Political Rights" in K. Vasak (ed.) "The International Dimensions of Human Rights" (Vol. 2 United Nations Educational, Scientific and Cultural Organisation).

Nordås, R. & Gleditsh, P. (2014) "Chapter 3 Climate Change and Conflict" in S. Hartard & W. Liebert (eds.) "Competition and Conflicts on Resource Use" Natural Resource Management and Policy (Vol. 46) pp. 21–38 (Springer).

Nykänen, E. (2012) "On the Lines of Demarcation and Their Significance: The Categories of Complementary Protection Under the Finish Aliens Act" 30 Nordic Journal of Human Rights 2 pp. 148–173.

Ober, K. (2014) "Migration as Adaptation: Exploring Mobility as a Coping Strategy for Climate Change" (UK Climate Change & Migration Coalition).

O'Brien, K. *et al.* (2008) "Disaster Risk Reduction, Climate Change Adaptation and Human Security: A Commissioned Report for the Norwegian Ministry of Foreign Affairs" (University of Oslo).

O'Connell, M. (1999) "New International Legal Process" 93 American Journal of International Law pp. 334–351.

Ozkul, D. (2010) "Circular Migration Schemes Renewed Interest of the Destination Countries" CARIM-VI Summer School on Euro-Mediterranean Migration and Development European University Institute Essay Series (Robert Schuman Centre for Advanced Studies).

Pardel, O. (2012) "Desplazados Medioambientales Una Nova Realidade" Cuadermos Deusto de Derechos Humanos (Vol. 66 Deusto Publicaciones).

Parker, J. (1982) "Victims of Natural Disasters in U.S. Refugee Law and Policy, Transnational Legal Problems of Refugees" Michigan Year Book of International Legal Studies pp. 137–139.

Parkes, R. (2009) "EU Mobility Partnerships: A Model of Policy Coordination?" 11 European Journal of Migration and Law pp. 321–345.

Patullo, P. (2000) "Fire from the Mountain: The Tragedy of Montserrat and the Betrayal of Its People" (Constable).
Pearce, F. (2000) "Turning Back the Tide" 165 New Scientist 2225 pp. 44–47.
Peers, S. (2012) "Legislative Update 2011, EU Immigration and Asylum Law: The Recast Qualification Directive" 14 European Journal of Migration and Law pp. 199–221.
Penz, P. (2010) "International Ethical Responsibilities to 'Climate Change Refugees'" in J. McAdam (ed.) "Climate Change and Displacement: Multidisciplinary Perspectives" (Oxford University Press).
Peroni, L. & Timmer, A. (2013) "Vulnerable Groups: The Promise of an Emerging Concept in European Human Rights Convention Law" 11 International Journal of Constitutional Law 4 pp. 1056–1085.
Pfaff, W. (1998) "Everyone Has a Responsibility" in B. Van Der Heijden & B. Tahzib-Lie (eds.) "Reflection on the Universal Declaration of Human Rights" (Kluwer Law International).
Phuong, V. (2004) "International Protection of Internally Displaced Persons" (Cambridge University Press).
Piacentini de Andrade, I. (2015) "Brazil's Draft Migration Law" 49 Forced Migration Review pp. 36–37.
Piguet, E. (2008) "Climate Change and Forced Migration" New Issues in Refugee Research Paper No. 153 (United Nations High Commissioner for Refugees).
Piotrowicz, R. & Van Eck, C. (2004) "Subsidiary Protection and Primary Rights" 53 International and Comparative Law Quarterly pp. 107–138.
Popovic, N. (1995) "Humanitarian Law, Protection of the Environment and Human Rights" 8 Georgetown International Environmental Law Review pp. 67–89.
Popovic, N. (1996) "In Pursuit of Environmental Human Rights: Commentary on the Draft Declaration of Principles on Human Rights and the Environment" 27 Columbia Human Rights Law Review pp. 487–603.
Posner, E. A. (2014) "The Twilight of Human Rights Law" (Oxford University Press).
Posner, R. A. (2002) "Legal Scholarship Today" 115 Harvard Law Review 5 pp. 1314–1326.
Prieur, M. *et al.* (2008) "Projet de Convention Relative au Statut International des Déplacés Environnementaux" University of Limoges (CRIDEAU-CRDP-OMIJ-CIDCE) 4 Revue Européenne de Droit de l'environnement pp. 391–406.
Rajan, S. (2008) "Climate Migrants in South Asia: Estimates and Solutions" (Greenpeace India Society).
Ramasamy, S. *et al.* (2008) "The Recognised Seasonal Employer Policy: Seeking the Elusive Triple Wins for Development Through International Migration" 23 Pacific Economic Bulletin 3 pp. 171–186.
Ratner, S. & Slaughter, A.-M. (1999) "Symposium on Method in International Law: Appraising the Methods of International Law: A Prospectus for Readers" 93 The American Journal of International Law pp. 291–302.
Renaud, F., Bogardi, J. & Warner, K. (2008) "Environmental Degradation and Migration" (Berlin Institute für Bevölkerung und Entwicklung).
Renaud, F. *et al.* (2007) "Control Adapt or Flee, How to Face Environmental Migration?" Interdisciplinary Security Connection No. 5 (United Nations University Institute for Environment and Human Security).

Renaud, F. *et al.* (2011) "A Decision Framework for Environmentally Induced Migration" 49 International Migration S1 pp. 5–29.
Roots, L. (2009) "The Impact of the Lisbon Treaty on the Development of EU Immigration Legislation" 5 Croatian Yearbook of Legal Studies pp. 261–281.
Ruof, M. C. (2004) "Vulnerability, Vulnerable Populations, and Policy" 14 Kennedy Institute of Ethics Journal pp. 411–425.
Saario, V. & Cass, R. H. (1977) "United Nations and the International Protection of Human Rights: A Legal Analysis and Interpretation" 7 California Western International Law Journal pp. 591–614.
Sand, I.-J. (2001) "The Legal Regulation of the Environment and New Technologies in View of Changing Relations between Law, Politics and Science" 22 Zeitschrift für Rechtssoziologies pp. 1–38.
Sands, P. (2003) "Principles of International Environmental Law" (Cambridge University Press).
Sané, P. (1998) "The Unfinished Revolution" in B. Van Der Heijden & B. Tahzib-Lie (eds.) "Reflection on the Universal Declaration of Human Rights" (Kluwer Law International).
Sapir, D. G. (1993) "Natural and Man-Made Disasters: The Vulnerability of Women-Headed Households and Children without Families" 46 World Health Statistics Quarterly Rapport Trimestriel de Statistiques Sanitaires Mondiales 4 pp. 227–233.
Sartor, G. (2007) "A Teleological Approach to Legal Dialogue" in G. Pavlakos (ed.) "Law, Rights and Discourse: The Legal Theory of Robert Alexy" (Hart Publishing).
Schachter, O. (1983) "Human Dignity as a Normative Concept" 77 American Society of International Law 4 pp. 848–854.
Schacknove, E. A. (1985) "Who Is a Refugee?" 95 Ethics 2 pp. 274–284.
Scheinder, H. & Wiesbrock, A. (2011) "A. Circular Migration: A Triple Win Situation? Wishful Thinking or Serious Option for Sustainable Migration Policy" in D. Schiek, U. Liebert & H. Schneider (eds.) "European Economic and Social Constitutionalism after the Treaty of Lisbon" (Cambridge University Press).
Schwartz, M. (1993) "International Legal Protection for Victims of Environmental Abuse" 18 Yale Journal of International Law pp. 355–365.
Scott, C. (1989) "Interdependence and Permeability of Human Rights Norms: Towards a Partial Fusion of the International Covenants on Human Rights" 27 Osgoode Hall Law Journal 3 pp. 769–878.
Scott, M. (2014) "Natural Disasters, Climate Change and Non-Refoulement: What Scope for Resisting Expulsion under Articles 3 and 8 of the European Convention on Human Rights?" 26 International Journal of Refugee Law 3 pp. 404–432.
Sevensson, E.-M. (2007) "Boundary-Work in Legal Scholarship" in A. Gunnarsson, E.-M. Svensson & M. Davies (eds.) "Exploiting the Limits of the Law, Swedish Feminism and the Challenge to Pessimism" (Ashgate Publishing).
Sgro, A. (2013) "Les Déplacés de L'Environnement à L'Épreuve de la Catégorisation en Droit de L'Union Européenne" Doctoral Dissertation (Université de Nice Sophia Antipolis UFR Institut Du Droit de la Paix et du Dévelopment).
Shaw, M. (2003) "International Law" (5th edition Cambridge University Press).
Shelton, D. (1991) "Human Rights, Environmental Rights and the Right to Environment" 28 Stanford Journal of International Law pp. 103–138.
Shelton, D. (2000) "Commentary and Conclusions" in D. Shelton (ed.) "Commitment and Compliance" (Oxford University Press).

Simma, B. & Paulus, A. (1999) "The Responsibility of Individuals for Human Rights Abuses in Internal Conflicts: A Positivist View" 93 American Journal of International Law 2 pp. 302–316.

Simons, M. (2002) "The Emergence of a Norm against Arbitrary Forced Relocation" 34 Columbia Human Rights Law Review pp. 95–156.

Sitaropoulos, N. (1999) "Refugee: A Legal Definition in Search of a Principled Interpretation by Domestic Fora" 52 Revue Hellénique de Droit International pp. 151–190.

Smit, B. & Wandel, J. (2006) "Adaptation, Adaptive Capacity and Vulnerability" 16 Global Environmental Change pp. 282–292.

Smits, J. M. (2009) "Redefining Normative Legal Science: Towards an Argumentative Discipline" in F. Coomans, F. Grunfeld & M. Kamminga (eds.) "Methods of Human Rights Research" (Intersentia).

Söderbaum, F. & Van Langehove, L. (eds.) (2008) "The EU as a Global Player: The Politics of Interregionalism" (Routledge).

Solbakk, J. H. (2011) "Vulnerability: A Futile or Useful Principle in Healthcare Ethics?" in R. Chadwick, H. ten Have & E. M. Meslin (eds.) The Sage Handbook of Health Care Ethics: core and emerging issues (Sage Publications).

Söllner, S. (2007) "The Breakthrough of the Right to Food" 11 Max Planck Yearbook of UN Law pp. 391–415.

Stavropoulou, M. (1994) "The Right Not to Be Displaced" 9 The American University Journal of International Law and Policy" 3 pp. 689–749.

Stavropoulou, M. (1998) "Displacement and Human Rights: Reflections on UN Practice" 20 Human Rights Quarterly 3 pp. 515–554.

Stavropoulou, M. (2010) "The Kampala Convention and Protection from Arbitrary Displacement" 36 Forced Migration Review pp. 62–63.

Stern, N. (2005) "The Economics of Climate Change: The Stern Review" (Cambridge University Press).

Storey, H. (2008) "EU Refugee Qualification Directive: A Brave New World?" 20 International Journal of Refugee Law pp. 1–49.

Stringer, C. & Mckie, R. (1996) "African Exodus: The Origins of Modern Humanity" (Henry Holt and Company).

Sudre, F. (2005) "Droit Européen et International des Droits de l'Homme" (7th edition Presses Universitaires de France).

Suhrke, A. (1983) "Global Refugee Movements and Strategies of Response" in M. Kritz (ed.) "U.S. Immigration Policy: Global and Domestic Issues" (Lexington Books).

Suhrke, A. (1994) "Environmental Degradation and Population Flows" 47 Journal of International Affairs 2 pp. 473–496.

Suhrke, A. & Visentin, A. (1991) "The Environmental Refugee: A New Approach" 2 Ecodecision pp. 73–74.

Tacoli, C. (2009) "Crisis of Adaptation? Migration and Climate Change in a Context of High Mobility" 21 Environment and Urbanization pp. 513–525.

Tamara, W. (2015) "Developing Temporary Protection in Africa" 49 Forced Migration Review pp. 23–25.

Teubner, G. (1998) "Legal Irritants: Good Faith in British Law or How Unifying Law Ends Up in New Divergences" 61 Modern Law Review pp. 11–32.

Thibierge, C. *et al.* (2009) "La Force Normative: Naissance d'un Concept" (Lextenso Éditions).

Thieleman, E. & El-Enany, N. (2010) "Refugee Protection as a Collective Action Problem: Is the EU Shrinking Its Responsibilities" 19 European Security pp. 209–229.
Thirlway, H. (2006) "The Sources of International Law" in D. Evans (ed.) "International Law" (2nd edition Oxford University Press).
Thomalla, F. *et al.* (2006) "Reducing Hazard Vulnerability: Towards a Common Approach between Disaster Risk Reduction and Climate Adaptation" Disasters pp. 39–48.
Thorme, M. (1991) "Establishing Environment as a Human Right" 19 Denver Journal of International Law and Policy pp. 301–342.
Thorton, F. (2011) "Regional Labour Migration as Adaptation to Climate Change? Options in the Pacific" in M. Leighton, S. Xiaomeng & K. Warner (eds.) "Climate Change and Migration: Rethinking Policies for Adaptation and Disaster Risk Reduction" Source No. 15/2001 (United Nations University Institute for the Environment and Human Security).
Tkachenko, A. (2002) "The Economy of the Iraq Marshes in the 1990s" in E. Nicholson & P. Clark (eds.) "The Iraqui Marshlands" (Politco's).
Tompkins, E. *et al.* (2005) "Surviving Climate Change in Small Islands: A Guidebook" (Tyndall Centre for Climate Change Research).
Triandafyllidou, A. (2009) "Attempting the Impossible? The Prospects and Limits of Mobility Partnerships and Circular Migration" ELIAMEP Thesis 1 pp. 1–4.
Tubiana, L. Gemenne, F. & Magnan, A. (2010) "Anticiper pour s'Adapter. Le nouvel Enjeu du Changement Climatique" (Pearson).
Tuori, K. (2009) "Critical Legal Positivism" (Ashgate Publishing).
Türk, V. & Nicholson, F. (2003) "Refugee Protection in International Law: An Overall Perspective" in E. Feller, V. Türk & F. Nicholson (eds.) "Refugee Protection in International Law an Overall Perspective" (Cambridge University Press).
Turner, B. S. (2006) "Vulnerability and Human Rights" (Essays on Human Rights).
Turton, D. (2003) "Conceptualising Forced Migration" 12 Refugee Studies Centre Working Paper (University of Oxford).
Twining, W. (2000) "Globalisation and Legal Theory" (Cambridge University Press).
Twining, W. (2004) "Diffusion of Law a Global Perspective" 49 Journal of Legal Pluralism pp. 1–45.
Twining, W. (2005) "Social Science and Difussion of the Law" 32 Journal of Law and Society pp. 203–240.
Twining, W. (2010) "Normative and Legal Pluralism: A Global Perspective" 20 Duke Journal of Comparative and International Law pp. 473–517.
United Nations High Commissioner for Refugees (1992) "Handbook on Procedures and Criteria for Determining Refugee Status under the 1951 Convention and the 1967 Protocol" (Geneva 1979, re-edited 1992) (United Nations High Commissioner for Refugees).
United Nations High Commissioner for Refugees (2000) "UNHCR Summary Observations on the Commission Proposal for a Council Directive on Minimum Standards for Giving Temporary Protection in the Event of a Mass Influx (COM(2000) 303, 24 May 2000)" (United Nations High Commissioner Refugees).
University of Adelaide, Flinders University, The University of Waikato (2009) "Climate Change and Migration in Asia and the Pacific" (Asian Development Bank) pp. 25–27.
Van Alstine, M. (1998) "Dynamic Treaty Interpretation" 146 University of Pennsylvania Law Review pp. 687–793.

Vandova, V. (2010) "Protection of Non-Citizens against Removal under International Human Rights Law" in A. Edwards & C. Ferstman (eds.) "Human Security and Non Citizens: Law, Policy and International Affairs" (Cambridge University Press).

Van Gestel, R., Micklitz, H.-W. & Poiares Maduro, M. (2013) "Methodology in the New Legal World" EUI Working Papers Department of Law pp. 1–23.

Van Hoof, G. J. H. (1984) "The Legal Nature of Economic, Social and Cultural Rights: A Rebuttal of Some Traditional Views" in P. Alston & K. Tomasevski (eds.) "The Right to Food" (Martinus Nijhoff).

Varju, M. (2012) "European Human Rights Law as a Multi-Layered Human Rights Regime" in J. Wetzel (ed.) "The EU as a 'Global Player' in Human Rights" (Routledge).

Vevstad, V. (1997) "Refugee Protection A European Challenge" (Tano Aschehoug).

Voght, W. (1948) "Road to Survival" (William Sloan Associates).

Von Doussa, J., Corkery, A. & Chartres, R. (2008) "Human Rights and Climate Change" Background Paper (Australian Human Rights and Equal Opportunity Commission).

Warner, K. (2010) "Assessing Institutional and Governance Needs Related to Environmental Change and Human Migration" Study Team on Climate-Induced Displacement (German Marshall Fund of the United States).

Warner, K. *et al.* (2014) "Integrating Human Mobility Issues within National Adaptation Plans" Policy Brief No. 9 (United Nations University Institute for the Environment and Human Security).

Watson, J., Michelle, G. & Connolly, M. (2007) "Epidemics after Natural Disasters" 13 Emerging 1 pp. 1–5.

Weinstein, A. H. (2005) "Pioneer on the Environmental Impact of War" (Springer).

Weinstein, T. (2005) "Prosecuting Attacks That Destroy the Environment: Environmental Crimes or Humanitarian Atrocities?" 17 Georgetown Immigration Law Journal pp. 697–722.

Wellens, K. (2005) "Solidarity as a Constitutional Principle: Its Expanding Role and Inherent Limitations" in R. St. J. Macdonald & D. M. Johnston (eds.) "Towards World Constitutionalism: Issues in the Legal Ordering of the World Community" (Martinus Nijhoff).

Wellens, K. (2010) "Revisiting Solidarity as a (Re-)Emerging Constitutional Principle: Some Further Reflections" in R. Wolfrum & C. Kojima (eds.) "Solidarity: A Structural Principle of International Law" (Springer).

Wetzel, J. (2012) "The EU as a 'Global Player' in Human Rights?" (Routledge).

Wiessner, S. & Willard, A. (1999) "Policy-Oriented Jurisprudence and Human Rights Abuses in Internal Conflict: Toward a World Public Order of Human Dignity" 93 American Journal of International Law 2 pp. 316–334.

Williams, A. (2008) "Turning the Tide: Recognising Climate Change Refugees in International Law" 30 Law and Policy 4 pp. 502–529.

Williams, A. (2010) "The Ethos of Europe: Values, Law and Justice in the EU" (Cambridge University Press).

Woehiche, M. (1993) "Environmental Refugees" Aussenpolitik 3 pp. 115–143.

Woodcock, A. (2006) "Jacques Maritain, Natural Law and the Universal Declaration of Human Rights" 8 Journal of History of International Law pp. 245–266.

Zolberg, R. A., Suhrke, A. & Aguayo, S. (1989) "Escape from Violence: Conflict and the Refugee Crisis in the Developing World" (Oxford University Press).

Reports

Asian Development Bank (2012) "Addressing Climate Change and Migration in Asia and the Pacific" (Asian Development Bank).

Global Commission on International Migration (2005) "Migration in an Interconnected World: New Directions for Actions" (Global Commission on International Migration).

Inter-Agency Standing Committee (1999) "Protection of Internally Displaced Persons" Inter-Agency Standing Committee Policy Paper (December).

Internal Displacement Monitoring Centre (2011) "Briefing Paper on Flood-Displaced Women in Sindh Province, Pakistan" (Norwegian Refugee Council).

Internal Displacement Monitoring Centre & UN Office for the Coordination of Humanitarian Affairs (2009) "Monitoring Disaster Displacement in the Context of Climate Change: Finding of a Study by the United Nations Office for the Coordination of Humanitarian Affairs and Internal Displacement Monitoring Centre" (Norwegian Refugee Council).

International Council on Human Rights Policy (2008) "Climate Change and Human Rights: A Rough Guide" (International Council on Human Rights Policy).

International Federation of the Red Cross and Red Crescent Societies (2009) "Tsunami Five-Year Progress Report 2004–2009" (International Federation of the Red Cross and Red Crescent Societies).

International Federation of the Red Cross and Red Crescent Societies (2007) "World Disasters Report: Focus on Discrimination" (International Federation of Red Cross and Red Crescent Societies).

International Federation of the Red Cross and Red Crescent Societies (2012) "World Disasters Report: Focus on Forced Migration and Displacement" (International Federation of Red Cross and Red Crescent Societies).

International Federation Red Cross and Red Crescent Societies (2007) "Guidelines for the Domestic Facilitation and Regulation of International Disaster Relief and Initial Recovery Assistance" (International Federation Red Cross and Red Crescent Societies).

International Organization for Migration (2005) "World Migration 2005: Costs and Benefits of International Migration" (International Organization for Migration).

International Organization for Migration (2009) "Temporary and Circular Labour Migration: Experiences, Challenges and Opportunities" (International Organization for Migration).

International Strategy for Disaster Reduction (2008) "Climate Change and Disaster Risk Reduction" Briefing Note 1.

Millennium Ecosystem Assessment (2005) "Ecosystems and Human Well-Being: Current State and Trends" (Vol. 1 Island Press).

Pachauri, R. & Reisinger, A. (eds.) (2007) "IPCC Climate Change 2007: Synthesis Report, Summary for Policymakers, Contribution of Working Groups I, II, and II to the Fourth Assessment Report" (Intergovernmental Panel on Climate Change).

United Nations (2006) "International Migration and Development" Report of the Secretary General (United Nations).

United Nations Development Programme (2006) "Human Development Report 2006 Beyond Scarcity: Power, Poverty and the Global Water Crisis" (Palgrave Macmillan).

United Nations Development Programme (2007) "Human Development Report 2007/2008 Fighting Climate Change: Human Solidarity in a Divided World" (United Nations Development Programme).

Watson, R. *et al.* (eds.) (1997) "IPCC Special Report: The Regional Impacts of Climate Change: An Assessment of Vulnerability: Summary for Policymakers" (Intergovernmental Panel on Climate Change).

World Bank (2006) "International Labour Migration: Eastern Europe and the Former Soviet Union" (The World Bank Europe & Central Asia Region).

World Bank (2011) "Migration and Remittances: Factbook 2011" (World Bank).

World Bank (2014) "Migration and Remittances: Recent Developments and Outlook Special Topic: Forced Migration" 23 Migration and Development Brief.

World Bank *et al.* (2003) "Poverty and Climate Change: Reducing the Vulnerability of the Poor through Adaptation" (World Bank).

Index

For Product Safety Concerns and Information please contact our EU
representative GPSR@taylorandfrancis.com
Taylor & Francis Verlag GmbH, Kaufingerstraße 24, 80331 München, Germany

www.ingramcontent.com/pod-product-compliance
Ingram Content Group UK Ltd.
Pitfield, Milton Keynes, MK11 3LW, UK
UKHW020013200926
475702UK00014B/1865

* 9 7 8 0 3 6 7 5 3 4 1 5 8 *